מסורה

The ArtScroll Series®

Rabbi Nosson Scherman / Rabbi Meir Zlotowitz
General Editors

LIVING

Published by

Mesorah Publications, ltd

EACH DAY

by

Rabbi Abraham J. Twerski, M.D.

FIRST EDITION
First Impression . . . August 1988
Second Impression . . . May 1989
SECOND EDITION
First Impression . . . April 1990
Second Impression . . . October 1990

Published and Distributed by
MESORAH PUBLICATIONS, Ltd.
Brooklyn, New York 11232

Distributed in Israel by
MESORAH MAFITZIM / J. GROSSMAN
Rechov Harav Uziel 117
Jerusalem, Israel

Distributed in Australia & New Zealand by
GOLD'S BOOK & GIFT CO.
36 William Street
Balaclava 3183, Vic., Australia

Distributed in Europe by
J. LEHMANN HEBREW BOOKSELLERS
20 Cambridge Terrace
Gateshead, Tyne and Wear
England NE8 1RP

Distributed in South Africa by
KOLLEL BOOKSHOP
22 Muller Street
Yeoville 2198, Johannesburg
South Africa

THE ARTSCROLL SERIES ®
LIVING EACH DAY
© Copyright 1988, 1990 by MESORAH PUBLICATIONS, Ltd.
4401 Second Avenue / Brooklyn, N.Y. 11232 / (718) 921-9000

ISBN:
0-89906-560-0 (hard cover)
0-89906-561-9 (paperback)

Printed in the United States of America by Noble Book Press Corp.
Bound by Sefercraft Quality Bookbinders, Ltd., Brooklyn, N.Y.

✑ Publisher's Foreword

I t is commonplace in our world to speak of living one day at a time, fighting one battle at a time, tackling one project at a time. A great scholar once counseled his students that if they set themselves the task of mastering the entire Talmud with its thousands of pages and infinite commentaries, they would probably stare at the shelves of their library and conclude, quite logically, that the task was impossible. But if they undertook the goal of mastering *one* page, they would succeed, and then go on to another page, and another and another. As the pages turned, the task would become less oppressive and less impossible.

Life is hard, and the world is crowded with people who find it harder than they can bear, because they are overwhelmed by tasks and responsibilities and challenges and problems and goals and handicaps and . . . and . . . and . . . That accounts for the proliferation of "self help" and "how to" books that attempt to deal with the mounting frustrations and demands of everyday life. But they don't seem to work. Perhaps solutions forged in the crucible of the present are not enough; perhaps the past has more to teach us than the champions of modernity like to acknowledge.

In addition, there are countless people who are very satisfied with themselves, and with good reason. Though their student days are behind them, they maintain a Torah schedule, often juggling many other obligations to do so. But, imperceptibly, the old sense of challenge and aspiration weakens and falters. Lacking is the incentive to meet each day head on and utilize it as if it were the only day available.

Chiddushei HaRim put it masterfully: "If not now — when?" *(Avos 1:14).* Every moment is a new "now" with its own potential, and it will never come back. The next moment has its own mission. If we waste a "now" — when can we ever make up the loss? There is nothing more tragic than a backward look at wasted days, months, years, or at time that was expended without having purchased sixty minutes on the hour. Fortunes have been spent on tinsel; time, too, is a fortune.

❧　　❧　　❧

Rabbi Abraham J. Twerski is one of those rare people who has learned how to help others master life. He grew up in a home where people could come for warmth, comfort, and guidance whenever they needed it; where no one screened calls and where there were no office hours or answering machines. His father was a Talmudic scholar and Chassidic leader who succeeded uniquely in nurturing the learning and values of his Torah heritage in Middle America. To his children he bequeathed the fertile soil of eternity, and it was in that soil that their subsequent learning, training, and experience took root and flourished.

A major component of that heritage is its perspective on life. The Torah's message and the philosophy of its great exponents speak to us all. In a stressful, often chaotic age, we need their wise counsel and mellowing experience. If we can deal intelligently with the present, then we will manage to repent what we must of the past and lay the groundwork for the future.

In this book, Rabbi Twerski shines the searchlight of the past on the present, on today — to help us survive today, because if we can grow and be productive today, we will be better able to welcome and conquer tomorrow. The author mines rich lodes of wisdom and slices them into daily portions. For each day of the year, he selects a brief prayer and a pithy saying from the Jewish classics. And he flavors these little treasures with thoughtful, incisive comments that enlighten and inspire. This book succeeds on many levels. It is good reading. It gives strength and insight. It relieves anxiety and broadens horizons. It provides a Torah perspective. And it accomplishes all this without demanding special training or scholarship from the reader. The book is accessible to everyone, and it will be a rare reader indeed who will not benefit from it, day by day.

Living each day is no easy matter nowadays, but *Living Each Day* will make it much more enjoyable, pleasant and worthwhile.

❧   ❧   ❧

Rabbi Twerski began his rabbinical career by assisting his father who was the founder and spiritual leader of Congregation Beth Yehudah in Milwaukee. Today he is president, and gives daily *shiurim*, at the Lubavitcher Center in Pittsburgh.

In 1954, Rabbi Twerski entered the medical profession. From 1965 to 1985 he served as Clinical Director of Psychiatry at St. Francis Hospital in Pittsburgh.

Currently, he is Medical Director of Gateway Rehabilitation Center, an institution he founded in 1972 for the treatment of alcoholism and other substance-abuse addictions; Associate Clinical Professor of Psychiatry at the University of Pittsburgh School of Medicine; and often is a guest lecturer in various schools and hospitals.

Rabbi Twerski has also authored many books and articles on Torah topics, as well as works on various facets of psychology and psychiatry.

⁌ Introduction

E very age and every era has had its unique characteristics. For reasons known and unknown, whether social, political, ecologic, or economic, people throughout history have varied in their ideas, behavior, goals, and emotional needs.

In Judaism, the ultimate and comprehensive goal — the total and absolute acceptance of and adherence to Torah — has never changed. Yet, even within this framework there are differences in emphasis, as the commentaries remark on the *Mishnah (Ethics of the Fathers 1:2)*: "There are three pillars that support the world: Torah, worship, and acts of loving-kindness." Although at no time can any of the pillars be dispensed with, there are variations in emphasis.

According to the above formula, we submit that in our era Torah and *avodah* (worship) should manifest themselves in *gemilas chasadim* (acts of loving-kindness).

One might think that acts of kindness are self-evident, and are not contingent upon a knowledge of Torah. Cannot a person be charitable without a knowledge of Torah? Can we not be kind to and considerate of others independent of *avodah*?

The answer is a firm and unequivocal negative. Man's unaided intellect and logic can lead him to absurd concepts of morality and propriety. Human logic is so vulnerable to distortion that the grossest injustices have been committed under misguided concepts of kindness and consideration.

לֹא נִתְּנָה תוֹרָה אֶלָּא לְצָרֵף בָּה אֶת הַבְּרִיוֹת, Torah was not given to mankind for any purpose other than to refine people *(Bereishis Rabbah 44:1)*. This is a very penetrating statement. It does not assert that *one* of the purposes of Torah is to refine people, but that the *sole* purpose of Torah is refinement of character.

This principle is stated in another context by Ramban (Nachmanides), in his comment on the verse, "You shall be holy unto G-d" *(Leviticus 19:2)*. Ramban states that going through the motions of complying with the *mitzvos* of the Torah is inadequate. One can be נָבָל בִּרְשׁוּת הַתּוֹרָה, vulgar and indulgent while not technically violating any Torah commandment. For observance of Torah to be that which G-d desired, it must result in a refinement of personality, in the attainment of spirituality and קְדוּשָׁה (sanctity).

During this era of acts of loving-kindness, we are fortunate to have masters of morals and ethics to enlighten us on the refinement of character according to Torah principles. The great work of Rabbi Moshe Chaim Luzzato, *Mesillas Yeshorim (Path of the Just)*, is a basic text in character development. The many

Chassidic and *mussar* texts are indispensable for personality development and refinement.

A most important rule in character development was stated by Rabbenu Bachya in *Chovos Halevavos (Duties of the Heart;* Gate of Abstention, chapter 5), wherein he states that for character development to occur at all, it must be comprehensive. There is no character trait in which one can be remiss. Just as the tiniest of punctures in a large container will allow all the contents to flow out, so even a minor defect in any character trait will eventually result in total degeneracy.

This does not mean that a person must achieve perfection all at once. Clearly that is beyond human capability. Rather, it is essential that we strive for overall perfection, and we can be assured that as long as we are sincerely engaged in such striving, G-d will protect us from errors in those personality traits which we have not as yet adequately cultivated.

The following pages are an effort to facilitate access to the concepts of spirituality and character development, by excerpting from our vast treasury of *tefillah* — liturgy and prayer — that forms our *avodah,* and from Torah — both the Scriptures and the works of the Sages — with some commentary on each. Torah tells us what we are to do, and *tefillah* (prayer) is an appeal for Divine guidance in achieving our goals. The arrangement according to the daily calendar should facilitate gradual absorption and integration of Torah concepts into our lives, so that we may achieve that refinement of character which is the ultimate purpose of Torah. Sources are given for the excerpts, and it is certainly hoped that the reader will not be satisfied with the excerpts, but make every effort to pursue the wealth of knowledge and guidance in the originals.

Organizing a daily guide book around the Jewish calendar presents some problems. Firstly, many Jews are unfamiliar with the Jewish calendar, and secondly, it can be a rather confusing instrument.

The Jewish calendar is based on the lunar month, which consists of approximately 29 1/2 days. Twelve lunar months are thus 354 days. There is an 11-day discrepancy between this and the 365-day solar calendar, and unless an adjustment is made, Passover — which the Torah ordains for the spring — would occur variably in the summer, fall, or winter.

Bringing the two calendars into alignment is accomplished by having a leap year, with an additional *month,* occur seven times in a nineteen-year cycle. Thus, every few years the month of Adar is followed by Adar Sheni.

This system also causes variability in the weekly portion of the Torah. Obviously, in each leap year there will be an additional four Sabbaths. In addition, when one of the festivals falls on the Sabbath, the regular portion of the Torah is deferred to the following week. There is thus some irregularity in the weekly schedule of Torah readings from year to year.

All this notwithstanding, I feel it is nevertheless essential to follow the Jewish calendar in this book. Many of the prayers do relate to specific days or to significant events in Jewish life, so that although following the Jewish calendar may be a bit confusing, this relevance would be lost if the book were structured on the secular calendar.

The prayers selected for this book are for special reflection for the day, over and above the prayers prescribed by Jewish law and tradition for the weekdays, Sabbath, Festivals, and special days. At the end of the book, there is a brief discourse on each of the weekly portions.

Whereas some of the Torah material is particularly relevant to specific days, it can be equally helpful on any day of the week or year. In this sense, as in its eternal sense, Torah is truly timeless.

LIVING EACH DAY

TISHREI

1

תשרי

**First Day of
Rosh Hashanah**

Sept. 20, 1990

Sept. 9, 1991

Sept. 28, 1992

Sept. 16, 1993

Sept. 6, 1994

Sept. 25, 1995

From our Prayers

זֶה הַיּוֹם תְּחִלַּת מַעֲשֶׂיךָ . . .

This day is the beginning of Your creation . . . the day on which the universe was conceived . . . the day on which all beings stand before You in judgment . . . May all mankind join together as one, to do Your will with their entire hearts . . . Inscribe us in the book of life, blessing, and peace . . . (*Rosh Hashanah liturgy*).

These excerpts from the Rosh Hashanah liturgy may appear to be disjointed, but if we look more closely at them, we will see that they do follow a theme.

A created universe, as opposed to one that just "happens" to be there, connotes an intent and a purpose by its Creator. In a universe that is purposeful all life can have meaning, and in a meaningful life there is both responsibility and an obligation to achieve one's purpose in creation.

In a purposeful world there is also a concept of being judged on our efforts in working toward that purpose. We believe that purpose is to discover the Divine will and to strive to fulfill that will. The ideal for all mankind is therefore to unite to do the will of G-d. For the individual person as well as for the multitudes, this achievement is the blessing that can enrich life, not with passive contentment, but with positive and constructive peace.

From the Sages

Envy, craving, and the drive for acclaim take a person out of the world (*Ethics of the Fathers 4:28*).

Sometimes I may think that if I rid myself of my character defects I am doing a noble and selfless act of piety. The fact is, however, that if I pursue the kinds of selfish drives that can impinge on the happiness of others, this can be as destructive to my own life and health as the most potent poisons. If I overcome these traits, it is really in the interest of my own survival and welfare as much as in consideration of others.

Superficially, it might seem that the opposite is true, and that gratifying my desires is in my self-interest, whereas denying gratification is an act of sacrifice. The Sages of the Talmud teach us otherwise. The drive for personal acquisitions and glory are often ruinous. If one focuses only on the short term, one might think that one can gain by selfishness. Just a bit of thinking beyond the moment of immediate gratification reveals the truth, that the durable gain for oneself is in the consideration of others.

NOTES

9/14/96

9/19/2009

וּתְשׁוּבָה וּתְפִלָּה וּצְדָקָה מַעֲבִירִין אֶת רֹעַ הַגְּזֵרָה *From*
M aking amends, prayer and acts of kind- *our*
ness revoke harsh judgments ... Man *Prayers*
is of earth and shall return to earth. His
existence is so fleeting, yet he can rise to
serve You, O G-d, the eternal Sovereign
(*Rosh Hashanah liturgy*).

Second Day of
Rosh Hashanah
Sept. 21, 1990
Sept. 10, 1991
Sept. 29, 1992
Sept. 17, 1993
Sept. 7, 1994
Sept. 26, 1995

Humility and greatness, far from being mutually exclusive, are actually complementary.

The beauty of life is that a being of such humble origins as man can achieve the dazzling heights to which some humans have risen, and which are actually within every person's reach.

Yes, on Rosh Hashanah we are judged by G-d, but this is a judgment by a compassionate G-d. The harshest judgments we experience are not those by G-d, but those we pronounce upon ouselves, the self-condemnation which occurs when we fail to transcend our earthy origin. If we fail to actualize our potential, we are actually punishing ourselves.

If we overcome our personal frailties and reach out to G-d in prayer and to our fellow humans in kindness, then we approach eternal and Divine values. Thus, to be ideally human is to strive toward Divinity, and such striving is well within our means.

Make someone into your teacher, acquire a friend, and judge all people favorably (*Ethics of the Fathers 1:6*).

From the Sages

These three seemingly disjointed statements are in fact closely related.

Sometimes I may feel that I know all that there is to know about living, and that there is no one wise enough to give me guidance and counsel, nor that there is any gain in sharing my thoughts and feelings with another person.

Not so, say the Rabbis. If you do not have a teacher, *make* someone into your teacher. Also, sharing yourself with another person is so important that you must try to *acquire* a friend if you have none.

If I find myself having difficulty in finding a teacher or getting a friend, perhaps I would be more successful in both if I began having a more kindly attitude toward *all* people. It might just be possible that if I felt more kindly toward others, I would more easily find people who would be glad to teach me and be my friends.

Fast of Gedaliah
*[When 3 Tishrei
falls on the Sabbath
the fast is observed
on Sunday.]*

Sept. 22, 1990

Sept. 11, 1991

Sept. 30, 1992

Sept. 18, 1993

Sept. 8, 1994

Sept. 27, 1995

*From
our
Prayers*

כִּי גָדוֹל אַתָּה וְעוֹשֵׂה נִפְלָאוֹת . . .
אֲשֶׁר בְּיָדוֹ נֶפֶשׁ כָּל חָי . . .

You are great and do wonders, You alone,
O G-d . . . In Your hands are the depths
of the land and the loftiest mountains
too . . . In His hands are the souls of all
living things, and the spirits of all men
(Selichos).

We recite the adoration of G-d not to tell G-d how great
He is, but rather to remind us to recognize and accept His
absolute sovereignty.

As humans, we have the freedom of choice to do good or
evil, but we should recognize that except for this choice,
there is little else that we really control. Rather than worry
and expend endless amounts of energy to manipulate those
things that are beyond our control, we would do better to
turn them over to G-d and direct our energies to those
things that we can change. This can provide us with
serenity, as was so aptly stated by one man who had
sleepless nights due to worrying and who finally decided,
''G-d is going to stay awake all night anyway. There is no
point in both of us being up.''

*From
the Sages*

**Wherever you find the word "now" in the Torah, it
refers to repentance** *(Bereishis Rabbah 21).*

This cryptic statement simply means that the key to
repentance is *prompt* recognition and admission that I have
done something wrong. I must admit *now*, rather than
later. Too often I may tend to rationalize and explain away
my behavior, insisting that I was right in what I did. Only
after all my rationalizations are exhausted do I reluctantly
concede that I was wrong.

The Rabbis teach us that it is unwise to defend a mistake.
If I promptly admit a mistake, it is so much easier to correct
it. After all, correcting mistakes is really what repentance is
all about, and a major portion of spiritual growth is just that
— correcting mistakes.

Because we are human, we are vulnerable to doing
wrong. Because we are spiritual beings, we are capable of
learning from our mistakes and thereby refining our
characters. We should not delay this opportunity for
character growth.

NOTES

9/15/96

4/21/09

מ"ד

From our Prayers . . . בְּסֵפֶר חַיִּים בְּרָכָה וְשָׁלוֹם . . .

May we be inscribed in the book of life, blessing, peace, good sustenance, favorable decrees, salvation, and consolation . . . (*addendum to the daily Amidah for the Ten Days of Repentance*).

Sept. 23, 1990
Sept. 12, 1991
Oct. 1, 1992
Sept. 19, 1993
Sept. 9, 1994
Sept. 28, 1995

Although repentance is effective and desirable at all times, the Talmud says that the days between Rosh Hashanah and Yom Kippur are especially propitious for repentance.

At the end of the year, a person is more apt to make an accounting of the bygone year, and see whether he is indeed where he had hoped to be at this time. If he sees that he has not utilized the year well, he may be more determined in his resolve to improve in the year to come. In addition, during these special days one is joined by many others in repentance, and the collective virtue is of great merit.

By virtue of our joining together with others in greater unity of purpose, and by dedicating ourselves sincerely toward improving ourselves, we will merit the many wonderful Divine blessings.

I am He who removes your sins for My sake, and your transgressions I will not recall (*Isaiah 43:25*).

From the Scriptures

Rabbi Levi Yitzchok of Berdichev, who always pleaded Israel's cause before G-d, once said, "Master of the Universe, You are acclaimed for Your infinite mercy and forgiveness. If there were no sin, what use could You make of these Divine attributes?"

Similarly, the Maggid of Dubno explained Moses' plea, "Please, G-d, stay among us, for we are a defiant people" (*Exodus 34:9*): A peddler of cheap tableware complained that he had not sold any of his wares. When he related that he had hawked in the wealthiest section of the city, his friends laughed at him. "You fool! Wealthy people will not buy your merchandise. They use the finest silver and gold utensils. Go peddle your wares among the poor!"

Thus Moses pleaded to G-d, "What can You do with Your attributes of infinite mercy and forgiveness among the heavenly angels? They have no need for them, because they are obedient. They do not sin. Dwell among us on earth, among a stubborn and defiant people. Here is where Your mercy and forgiveness are needed and will be appreciated."

NOTES

9/19/96

9/22/09

Sept. 24, 1990
Sept. 13, 1991
Oct. 2, 1992
Sept. 20, 1993
Sept. 10, 1994
Sept. 29, 1995

From our Prayers

אִם עֲוֹנוֹת תִּשְׁמָר . . . כִּי עִמְּךָ הַסְּלִיחָה

If You, O G-d, will mark the iniquities of man, then who can stand before You? For with You there is forgiveness, so that You may be feared** (*morning service, Monday and Thursday; Psalms 130:3,4*).

What is meant by fear of G-d?

While it is true that G-d knows our frailties and that we cannot be perfect, and is abundant in forgiveness, this does not permit us to be frivolous. The Talmud states that if one says, "I will sin and then I will repent," he is not granted the opportunity to repent.

The true meaning of fear of G-d is that we should be aware that when we deviate from His will, we are injuring ourselves just as if we were to ingest a poisonous substance. Sin is destructive, and we should therefore fear it as we would fear anything that is very dangerous.

But although we may not be able to undo the physical harm that we do to ourselves, G-d assures us that if we repent, He will undo the spiritual harm that we have done to ourselves. We dare not abuse this grace, this wonderful gift of forgiveness.

From the Scriptures

Give thanks to G-d for He is good; His kindness endures forever (*Psalms 118:1*).

Rabbi Boruch of Medziboz recited the Friday evening prayer before *Kiddush,* and when he came to the words, "I offer thanks to You, O G-d, for all the grace You have done unto me and for what You will do for me in the future," he paused and reflected, "Why should I give thanks now for future grace? I can offer thanks when the grace is done to me."

Then Rabbi Boruch continued, "But perhaps when I receive that Divine grace, I may not recognize it as such, and may not realize that I must offer thanks. That is why I must offer thanks in advance."

Rabbi Boruch burst into tears. "How tragic that I can be so blind, that I might not to be able to recognize G-d's grace for what it is, and might not appreciate the good that He will be doing for me."

So often we understand G-d's kindness only in retrospect. We should believe at all times that G-d is compassionate, even when we are unable to understand the mysteries of His ways.

NOTES

9/19/96

9/23/09

... הוֹרֵיתָ לָנוּ לוֹמַר שְׁלֹשׁ עֶשְׂרֵה ... *From*

O G-d, You have instructed us to repeat *our*
the thirteen Divine attributes ... *Prayers*
which You revealed to Moses ... G-d is
merciful, compassionate, slow to anger,
abundant in loving-kindness and truth, He
preserves kindness for thousands of generations, forgives sins and transgressions,
and cleanses us *(Selichos)*.

Sept. 25, 1990
Sept. 14, 1991
Oct. 3, 1992
Sept. 21, 1993
Sept. 11, 1994
Sept. 30, 1995

The Talmud says that if we emulate the Divine attributes, and we become merciful, compassionate, slow to
anger, etc., then we merit complete forgiveness.

Sins are symptoms of character defects. If we grow
spiritually and overcome our character defects, we will
remove the cause of sin. This is repentance at its very best.

We must be "abundant in truth." Truth must accompany all the other attributes, because if they are insincere,
they do not improve our character, and they do not
remove sin.

And G-d said to Adam, "Where are you?" *(Genesis
3:9).*

*From the
Scriptures*

When Rabbi Shneur Zalman was in prison in Russia
awaiting trial for the charge that his teaching chassidic
philosophy constituted treason, the chief of the gendarmes
entered into a discussion with him and questioned him
about portions of the Scriptures which he did not
understand.

"Why did G-d ask Adam, 'Where are you?' Did G-d not
know where Adam was?" he asked.

Rabbi Shneur Zalman answered, "The Torah is not
merely a history book, but rather a teaching for all men at
all times.

"In every era," Rabbi Shneur Zalman said, "G-d calls
out to man, 'Where are you? Where are you in your world?
What have you accomplished with the days allotted to
you?' And to you He says, 'What have you, Igor, achieved
in the forty-six and one-half years of your life?' "

The chief of the gendarmes, who was exactly forty-six
and one-half years old, responded, "Bravo!" But in his
heart he trembled.

Every day G-d calls out to man, "Where are you?" Every
day man should be ready to give an account for himself.

NOTES
9/19/96
9/24/09

Sept. 26, 1990
Sept. 15, 1991
Oct. 4, 1992
Sept. 22, 1993
Sept. 12, 1994
Oct. 1, 1995

*From
our
Prayers*

אַל תַּשְׁלִיכֵנוּ מִלְּפָנֶיךָ וְרוּחַ
קָדְשְׁךָ אַל תִּקַּח מִמֶּנּוּ . . .

Do not cast us away from Your presence, and may Your holy spirit never leave us. Do not forsake us in our old age; when our strength fails us, do not abandon us *(Selichos; Psalms 51:13, 71:9).*

We pray for long life although we are fully aware that in advanced age we may be quite feeble.

How well we will tolerate our later years may depend greatly on how we lived our earlier years. If we live a life that is abundant in fulfilling the Divine will, we will be spared the agony of remorse that plagues old age when one realizes that his life has been relatively unproductive. Also, study of Torah and contemplation of G-dliness can be continued even when physical limitations of advanced age restrict many other activities, and in this way our vintage years can continue to be productive.

If we stand with G-d when we are young, we can be assured that He will stand with us when we are old. People who are well versed in economics know that they must make wise investments that will benefit them in the future. We should accord our spiritual welfare at least as much consideration as we do our economic well-being.

*From the
Scriptures*

Return, O Israel, unto the Lord your G-d, for you have blundered in your sinfulness *(Hoshea 14:2).*

The Rabbis comment that "blunder" connotes accidental behavior, whereas committing sin is often intentional. Why does the prophet confuse the two?

However, the Rabbis also say that if a person were truly aware of how destructive sin is to his welfare, he would certainly refrain from intentional sin. It is therefore his lack of awareness, whether due to ignorance or to being blinded by passion, that he sins. All sins, even intentional ones, can thus be understood as "blunders" to some extent.

NOTES

9/20/96
9/25/09

If we resolve to learn more about what G-d demands of us so that we overcome our ignorance, and if we resolve not to let our judgment be distorted by temptation but rather to seek guidance for our behavior, then we may justly ask G-d to forgive us and we can be assured that He will bring us close to Him.

It is within our means to come to G-d. We must make every effort to eliminate our "blunders".

הַנְּשָׁמָה לָךְ וְהַגּוּף פָּעֳלָךְ *From*
חוּסָה עַל עֲמָלָךְ . . . *our*

[M]y] soul is Yours and [my] body is Your *Prayers*
work, so have mercy on Your own
handiwork. Yes, the soul is Yours and the
body is Yours, O G-d, act for the sake of
Your great name (*Selichos*).

Sept. 27, 1990
Sept. 16, 1991
Oct. 5, 1992
Sept. 23, 1993
Sept. 13, 1994
Oct. 2, 1995

How can we merit forgiveness from G-d? By sincerely
regretting the wrongs we have done, and making a
determination that we will not repeat them.

But since such promises are often soon forgotten,
we must do more than just make resolutions. We must
do something to deter ourselves from transgressing the
Divine will.

If we can recognize ourselves to be the beautiful
handiwork of G-d that we all are, this awareness can
prevent us from doing things that are beneath our dignity.
So we pray that we may come to know who we are and
what we are, for this knowledge can guide our behavior,
and it is then that we can merit forgiveness.

Privileged is man, for he was created in the image
of G-d. But it was an act of special favor that it was
made known to him that he was created in His image
(*Ethics of the Fathers 3:18*).

From
the Sages

Knowing who we are and what we are, how much beauty
resides within us, and how carefully we must protect
ourselves — the wonderful beings that we are — from
anything harmful, should not at all result in vanity or
conceit. We should be able to recognize our greatness as a
Divine blessing.

Indeed, if we were only truly aware of our greatness, this
would inspire us to great performance. At the same time
this would make us humble because we would realize that
we have not fulfilled our potential. Rather than being vain
and expecting honor and acclaim for what we have done,
we would understand that given our enormous capabilities
for spiritual growth, we are still far short of what we can
and should be. We should at all times realize that regardless of how much we have accomplished, there is still
much more that we must do.

Greatness and humility are perfectly compatible.

NOTES
9/21/96
9/26/09

Erev Yom Kippur
[Eve of Yom Kippur]
Sept. 28, 1990
Sept. 17, 1991
Oct. 6, 1992
Sept. 24, 1993
Sept. 14, 1994
Oct. 3, 1995

From
our
Prayers

יֵרָצֶה צוֹם עַמְּךָ . . .

Accept the fast of Your people, and perceive their prayers . . . for their tears are their drink and their sighs are their bread *(Selichos)*.

The Talmud states that partaking of food on the day before Yom Kippur (in preparation for the next day's fast) is reckoned as the equivalent of denying ourselves nourishment on Yom Kippur.

Denying our needs is not always the greatest virtue, and withdrawing from all pleasures of life is not necessarily saintliness. What is important is that when we do partake of the good things of life, we do so with the sanctity and the spirituality that befits a human being. All of life can be sacred. There need not be any distinction between the secular and the holy.

All the good of life can be enjoyed with gratitude toward G-d. By utilizing this good in the service of G-d, we have elevated it to the status of holiness.

From
the Sages

Rabbi Nachman of Breslov interpreted the verse in Psalms 38:19, "I admit my sin; I worry about my transgression," as meaning that ruminating about old mistakes and about the past can in itself be sinful.

I realize that as a human, I can hardly escape ever doing wrong. The purpose of the painful sensation of guilt is to deter me from doing the kinds of things that would make me feel guilty, and to stimulate me to make the proper amends for the wrongs I have done.

However, once I have indeed made the proper amends, I should be able to put the past behind me. Persistent rumination about my past mistakes is destructive, since it will so depress me and drain my energies that I will not be able to go on with the necessary business of life, and to do whatever is G-d's will for me. To allow that to happen is the greatest sin of all.

To have true faith in G-d's forgiveness is to realize that G-d completely removes our sins when our repentance is sincere. We should then be able to move forward with joy and vigor to fulfill our mission in life.

NOTES

9/22/9
9/27/09

From אַתָּה הִבְדַּלְתָּ אֱנוֹשׁ מֵרֹאשׁ ...
our
Prayers

From the beginning You have distin-
guished man and acknowledged him
to stand before You ... and in Your
love for us You have given us this Day of
Atonement, a finality of forgiveness (Yom
Kippur liturgy).

To stand before G-d, to come into close relationship with
Him is the ultimate goal of man. When our behavior is
contrary to the Divine will, we set up barriers and put
distances between ourselves and G-d.

With prayer and proper atonement we can achieve a
complete forgiveness which wipes the slate clean and
allows us to stand in the immediate presence of G-d.

Yom Kippur
[Yizkor]
Sept. 29, 1990
Sept. 18, 1991
Oct. 7, 1992
Sept. 25, 1993
Sept. 15, 1994
Oct. 4, 1995

From
the Sages

There are three types of exile and they are of
increasing severity. The first is when Jews are in
exile among other nations, the second is when Jews
are in exile among fellow Jews, and the third and
most severe is when a Jew is alien to himself, for
then he is both captor and captive, in exile within
himself (Rabbi Sholom Rokeach of Belz).

Yom Kippur is G-d's gift to mankind, a day of grace
which enables man to cleanse himself and begin life anew.
But even when Divine forgiveness is attained, man sometimes refuses to forgive *himself,* and he thus becomes a
prisoner to himself within his own dungeon.

We are taught that we must try to emulate G-d. Just as
He forgives us when we have merited forgiveness, so we
must learn to forgive ourselves.

☙ ☙ ☙

Just suppose that Yom Kippur occurred only once in a
century, that only once in a hundred years was there a
special day of grace on which G-d removed all our sins and
enabled us to begin life anew.

Those who were fortunate to have this unique day occur
during their lifetime would consider themselves blessed
with good fortune. Those who did not would consider
themselves deprived of this special gift.

But in His infinite kindness, G-d gave us this day of Yom
Kippur each year, and we thus have many opportunities to
begin life anew, unencumbered by the mistakes of the past.

How privileged we should feel! How joyous we should
be on this special day!

NOTES
9/28/09
_____
_____
_____
_____
_____
_____
_____

Sept. 30, 1990
Sept. 19, 1991
Oct. 8, 1992
Sept. 26, 1993
Sept. 16, 1994
Oct. 5, 1995

From our Prayers

יְהִי רָצוֹן מִלְּפָנֶיךָ . . .
שֶׁלֹּא תַעֲלֶה קִנְאַת אָדָם עָלַי . . .

May it be Your will . . . that I do not incur the envy of others, that I should not envy them, and that I should not do anything today that would displease You. Protect me from evil impulses and fill my heart with humility *(the daily Amidah, nusach Sefard).*

Although we have complete freedom of choice between moral right and wrong, it is nevertheless appropriate to pray for Divine assistance to do that which is right. In fact, the Talmud says that the force of temptation is so powerful that without Divine assistance we could not resist it.

It takes a Power greater than ourselves to save us from the folly of sin. We can merit the assistance of that Power if we seek it with utmost sincerity.

Freedom of choice thus means that we have the ability to wish to do what is right, and to ask G-d for His help to enable us to overcome temptation.

From the Sages

The Baal Shem Tov said, "Would that I could have as great a love for the most righteous person as G-d has for the worst sinner."

We can learn to love others by seeing the good in them. Rabbi Levi Yitzchok of Berdichev once encountered a man eating on the fast day of Tishah B'Av. "Surely you have forgotten that this is a fast day," he said.

"No," answered the man. "I know today is Tishah B'Av." "Aha! You are not well and your doctor has instructed you not to fast," said the Rabbi.

"No, I am perfectly healthy," the man replied.

Rabbi Levi Yitzchok lifted his eyes toward heaven. "Look how precious Your children are, dear G-d. I have provided this man with ample excuses to explain away his behavior, but he refuses to deviate from the truth, even when it incriminates him."

Goodness can be found in all people. You just have to want to see it.

NOTES

9/29/09
_____
_____
_____
_____
_____
_____
_____
_____

מוֹדֶה אֲנִי לְפָנֶיךָ מֶלֶךְ חַי וְקַיָּם . . . *From our Prayers*

I thank You, eternal King, for restoring my soul to me with Your great compassion. My trust in You abounds *(prayer upon arising).*

Oct. 1, 1990
Sept. 20, 1991
Oct. 9, 1992
Sept. 27, 1993
Sept. 17, 1994
Oct. 6, 1995

There can be times when the stresses and distresses of life are so great that life itself seems burdensome. At such times all reasoning and all philosophical arguments may be of no avail, and only complete faith in the absolute benevolence of G-d can help us accept that life itself, even when painful, is a precious gift.

Similarly, the intensity of our distress may make us question Divine benevolence. At such moments, an unfaltering trust in G-d and the conviction that G-d is compassionate — even though we do not understand how and why He allows such things to happen — can enable us to be grateful for life itself.

From the Sages

Spiritual growth is rarely continuous, but is rather marked by pauses and plateaus. It is like going uphill in a wagon, where there is upward progress as long as there is active movement. But if the wagon comes to a stop, it will slip and roll back down unless one puts blocks under the wheels to prevent it from rolling back *(Rabbi Michel of Zlotchow)*

Although making mistakes is unfortunate, few of us can get through life without making any number of them.

A mistake should constitute only temporary pause in our growth and upward progress. In order to prevent us from slipping back, we need protective "blocks". If we can avoid slipping back, we can almost always learn from our mistakes, and we are then actually stimulated to further growth.

NOTES
9/30/09

We can have these protective "blocks" if we have a support system of friends and teachers who can relate to us in honesty and frankness, and who can help us prevent regression and share in our growth. We cannot do this alone. Without teachers to guide us and friends to support us when we falter, we are at a great risk of slipping.

Oct. 2, 1990
Sept. 21, 1991
Oct. 10, 1992
Sept. 28, 1993
Sept. 18, 1994
Oct. 7, 1995

From our Prayers

אֱלֹקַי, נְשָׁמָה שֶׁנָּתַתָּ בִּי טְהוֹרָה הִיא . . .

O G-d, the soul that You have placed within me is pure. You have created it, You have fashioned it, You have breathed it into me, and You protect it within me *(daily morning service)*.

Our souls are of Divine origin, and we are their custodians. We should at all times remember that within us there is an element of G-dliness. This is a matter of fact, and not a matter of choice. We are what we are because that is how we were fashioned.

Improper behavior should be avoided not because of fear of punishment, but because we should consider it beneath our dignity, as keepers of Divine souls, to do improper things. We must know that we are just too good to lower ourselves to indecent behavior.

When one wears an expensive silk garment, one takes great caution to avoid soiling it. Awareness of the beauty and nobility of the soul should stimulate us to guard it zealously.

False pride is destructive. But there is a true pride that comes from an awareness of the greatness within us. We should be too proud to behave in a way that does not befit us.

From the Scriptures

Do not detest your brother in your heart . . . Do not seek revenge . . . and have reverence for your G-d *(Leviticus 19:17-18).*

NOTES

10/1/09

We generally think that we must rid ourselves of hatred and vengeance out of consideration for others. This is not the complete story. Hatred and vengeance are destructive poisons. They bring ruin to those who harbor them, and they become barriers between man and G-d.

We must learn to rid ourselves of resentments for our own sakes as well as out of consideration for others. The harm that we may do to others is apt to be transient. The deterioration of our own characters when we act out of vengeance and hatred can be long lasting.

Ridding ourselves of character defects benefits us more than it does others.

אַשְׁרֵינוּ מַה טוֹב חֶלְקֵנוּ . . . *From our Prayers*

How fortunate we are, how good is our portion and how beautiful our heritage. How fortunate we are that upon arising and upon retiring we declare with love . . . "Hear O Israel, the L-rd our G-d, the L-rd is one"** *(daily morning service)*.

Imagine a person in severe distress being notified that he was granted an audience with the king. The honor and thrill of being in the presence of the king may well overshadow and at least temporarily mitigate his misery.

Even when things happen that cause us great pain, we can find joy and pride in having the privilege to be welcomed in the court of the Great King.

We are told, "You are children unto G-d. Do not mutilate yourself when in grief" *(Deuteronomy 14:1)*. Even when in grief, remember who you are and maintain your majesty.

Erev Succos
[Eve of Succos]
Oct. 3, 1990
Sept. 22, 1991
Oct. 11, 1992
Sept. 29, 1993
Sept. 19, 1994
Oct. 8, 1995

And from there (from the midst of exile) you will seek G-d and you will find Him *(Deuteronomy 4:29)*. **"From 'there,' " said the Baal Shem Tov, "means from wherever you may happen to be."**

From the Sages

Sometimes I may feel that I have lost contact with G-d. Perhaps I feel that I am not deserving and that I do not merit His attention, and that my actions have driven Him away from me.

Not so, says the Baal Shem Tov. G-d is everywhere, and can be found at every level. At whatever point you may be, you will find Him, if only you look for Him.

A child who feels that he has caused his parents great distress may feel very uneasy in their presence. It is only when that child grows up and has children of his own that he can appreciate how parents crave their children's closeness to them, and how anxious they are to overlook a child's past errant ways when the child realizes his mistakes.

G-d's love for us surpasses the love of a father for a child. He has promised us that He will never abandon us. We are always close to Him, and He is always accessible to us.

NOTES

10/2/09

*First Day
of Succos*

Oct. 4, 1990

Sept. 23, 1991

Oct. 12, 1992

Sept. 30, 1993

Sept. 20, 1994

Oct. 9, 1995

*From
our
Prayers*

. . . אַתָּה בְחַרְתָּנוּ מִכָּל הָעַמִּים

You have chosen us from among all peoples; You have loved us and taken pleasure in us. You have exalted us above all tongues and have sanctified us by Your commandments. You have drawn us near to Your service, and have called Your great and holy name upon us *(Festival Amidah).*

To be the chosen people of G-d is both a privilege and responsibility. Some people think they can enjoy privileges without assuming commensurate responsibilities. There is a law of living which must be accepted: There are no privileges without attendant responsibilities.

"You have sanctified us with Your commandments and have drawn us near to Your service." The obligation to diligently observe the Divine will is the responsibility that accompanies the election as G-d's chosen people.

We are proud to be the chosen, but we must realize that our behavior reflects not only on us as individuals, not only on us as a nation, but also on us as the chosen people of G-d. We must fulfill the obligation that this station demands.

*From
the Sages*

Rabbi Akiva says, "The succah commemorates the thatched huts wherein the Israelites dwelt during their wanderings in the desert following the exodus from Egypt" *(Succah 11b).*

What is so wonderful about living in thatched huts that warrants commemoration by an eight-day festival?

We celebrate Passover in commemoration of the wondrous miracles that G-d performed in our deliverance from the enslavement in Egypt. We celebrate Shavuos in observance of the great revelation at Sinai and the receiving of the Torah. Compared to these epochal events, of what significance are thatched huts?

That is precisely the point. We must learn to be grateful for the small things in life as well as the great gifts we receive.

It was not beyond G-d to create luxurious palaces in the desert. However, He wanted us to learn that we must be appreciative of everything given to us, regardless of how little it may be.

Succos is referred to as the "festival of harvest" and the "time of our rejoicing." Our harvest may be abundant or it may be meager. In either case, we must be appreciative of and grateful for what we are given.

NOTES

TISHREI

תשרי

*Second Day
of Succos*

*[In the Land of Israel
this is the first day of
Chol Hamoed, the
Intermediate Days.]*

Oct. 5, 1990
Sept. 24, 1991
Oct. 13, 1992
Oct. 1, 1993
Sept. 21, 1994
Oct. 10, 1995

*From
our
Prayers*

. . . לֹא אָמוּת כִּי אֶחְיֶה . . .

I shall not die, but I shall rather live, and tell of the deeds of G-d. G-d has indeed chastised me, but has not surrendered me to death. Open the gates of justice for me; I will enter and praise G-d . . . This is the day that G-d has made; let us be glad and rejoice therein *(Hallel, Psalms 118:17-24).*

We can more fully appreciate the comfort provided by the Psalms if we know the biography of the composer.

King David's life, from infancy to death, was replete with tragedy and suffering. The Talmud states that David did not have a single good day in his entire life. Yet David could sing the praises of G-d, even sing them with joy.

The acceptance of Divine justice as supreme, even when it conflicts with our personal sense of justice, even when it causes us great distress, is the key to a life of joy.

*From
the Sages*

On the first day of Succos we begin reckoning sins *(Midrash).*

Rabbi Levi Yitzchok of Berdichev explains by citing the Talmudic teaching that repentance done out of awe, as on Yom Kippur, mitigates sins. However, repentance done out of love for G-d converts sins to virtues. Thus, the joy of Succos can bring us to a state of intense love for G-d, which can result in the transformation of our sins to virtues. This is then the time to make a reckoning of our sins, to determine the number of our virtues.

How is it possible that sins can be converted into virtues?

If I recognize that something I did was wrong, and out of sincere love for G-d and desire not to displease Him I resolve never to repeat that act again, then I have learned something valuable. Anything that is a positive learning experience is a virtue.

If I take inventory of what I have done in my life, I may at first be saddened by the many mistakes I have made. But if I can learn from these mistakes not to repeat them, then I can take pleasure in my growth and rejoice in the knowledge that G-d now considers these valuable learning experiences to be virtues.

Rabbi Levi Yitzchok once remarked to a very profligate person, "How I envy you. One day you will change your ways, and then all your sins will be transformed into merits. Your sum of *mitzvos* will then far surpass those I have accumulated."

NOTES

10/4/09

**Chol Hamoed
Succos**
*Oct. 6, 1990
Sept. 25, 1991
Oct. 14, 1992
Oct. 2, 1993
Sept. 22, 1994
Oct. 11, 1995*

*From
our
Prayers*

. . . וְצִוָּנוּ לֵישֵׁב בַּסֻּכָּה

Blessed is G-d, Sovereign of the universe, Who has sanctified us with His commandments and has commanded us to dwell in the succah *(Blessing upon entering the succah).*

In contrast to our sturdy, permanent homes, the *succah* is a fragile hut, suited only for temporary dwelling.

The *succah* can be seen as a symbol of our sojourn in the physical world. If we realize that our earthly existence is transitory, and that we are to live our lives in preparation for the eternal world, then we can indeed be sanctified and achieve the holiness that eludes those who have no goals other than to satisfy their physical desires.

Succos is a joyous festival. Luxurious mansions are often inhabited by people who are unhappy. The message of the *succah* is that regardless of our earthly possessions, there is an ultimate joy that awaits us.

*From
the Sages*

Of the four species used in the Succos ritual, the esrog (citron) has both taste and fragrance, the hadas (myrtle) has fragrance but no taste, the lulav (date palm) bears fruit which has taste but no fragrance, and the aravah (willow branch) has neither taste nor fragrance. All four species must be taken together, and absence of any one makes the mitzvah incomplete *(Midrash).*

We often place values on people whether by virtue of their character, knowledge, wealth, or social status.

It is well to remember that before G-d we are all equal. The *mitzvah* of the four species is as incomplete when the insipid willow branch is lacking as when the succulent citron is absent.

When we are unified, bound together with bonds of compassion and affection, then we are complete, and as with the *mitzvah,* we have *kedushah* (sanctity). If we reject a person because we do not consider him worthy enough, we thereby diminish our own value as well.

If we are all united together, we are everything. If we reject one another, we are nothing.

NOTES

... וְיִהְיוּ דְבָרַי אֵלֶּה אֲשֶׁר הִתְחַנַּנְתִּי *From*
May the words of my prayer ... be near *our*
to G-d. May He do justice to His *Prayers*
servant and to His people, day by day
(Succos liturgy).

Chol Hamoed
Succos
Oct. 7, 1990
Sept. 26, 1991
Oct. 15, 1992
Oct. 3, 1993
Sept. 23, 1994
Oct. 12, 1995

If we think that our lives as a whole may not merit
Divine reward, we may nevertheless pray that G-d judge
us day by day, overlooking the wrongs of our past, and
considering only our actions of today.

To deserve this grace, we too must relate to others
with a "day by day" attitude, and be willing to overlook
what others may have done to us in the past. We cannot
expect to be judged by any other standards than those
we use to judge others.

**The Baal Shem Tov interpreted the verse in
Psalms 121:5, "G-d is your shadow, at your right
hand," to mean that G-d will relate to man as man
relates to others, just as the shadow follows one's
movements.**

*From
the Sages*

Rabbi Zusia had a follower who used to help support
him. One time this follower learned that Rabbi Zusia was
a disciple of the great Maggid (preacher) of Mezeritch,
and therefore decided that rather than support Rabbi
Zusia, he would now go to the great Maggid. Strangely,
his fortune began to suffer.

"Why did this happen to me?" the man asked Rabbi
Zusia. "Surely your rabbi must be greater than you. Why
did my fortune turn downward when I became a sup-
porter of your rabbi?"

"It is quite simple," Rabbi Zusia answered. "When you
did not discriminate and you helped even someone like
myself, then G-d did not discriminate, and blessed you
whether you deserved it or not. But when you began to
look for special people to whom you would give, then
G-d acted similarly toward you, and He, too, saved His
gifts for special people."

It is much to our own advantage to be indiscriminate in
acts of kindness towards others.

Chol Hamoed
Succos
Oct. 8, 1990
Sept. 27, 1991
Oct. 16, 1992
Oct. 4, 1993
Sept. 24, 1994
Oct. 13, 1995

From our Prayers

אֶת יוֹם חַג הַסֻּכּוֹת הַזֶּה . . .

. . . זְמַן שִׂמְחָתֵנוּ

You have given us the joyous festivals, this day of Succos, a time of joy, to commemorate our liberation from Egypt *(Amidah of Succos).*

This *succah* commemorates the tents wherein the Israelites dwelt during their forty-year sojourn in the desert.

One of the miracles whereby the Israelites survived in the desert was the *manna* bread, which fell from heaven and was collected each day, but would not keep until the next day.

It is common knowledge that even affluent people have anxiety and tension because they are in fear of financial reversals. Having wealth is obviously no guarantee for peace of mind, let alone joy.

Our ancestors learned to live one day at a time, and to trust in G-d to provide for tomorrow. The festivals commemorating their wandering in the desert can be a source of joy to us, if we, too, learn to live one day at a time.

From the Scriptures

It is better to have less if it is with peace of mind, than to have abundant wealth but with a tormented spirit *(Ecclesiastes 4:6).*

This passage confirms the interpretation of the above prayer. The drive to acquire wealth in the hope that it will enable us to feel secure and give us peace of mind is a universal mistake. We tend to forget that the struggle to acquire wealth can in itself be very tormenting, and that rather than bringing the coveted security, wealth often brings the anxiety that it may be lost.

We often observe people who have amassed great wealth, yet strive to acquire even more, although they could not possibly consume what they already have even if they lived a thousand years. To these people money has lost its value as a means of acquiring something else, and has become an end in itself. These people can never have a sense of satisfaction.

The peace of mind of being content with less by far surpasses the fantasized security of wealth.

NOTES

_____
_____
_____
_____
_____
_____
_____
_____
_____

From our Prayers

מִן הַמֵּצַר קָרָאתִי קָּה . . .

I have called out to G-d in my oppression, and He has answered me with comfort. When G-d is with me, I have no fear of what any mortal may do to me (*Hallel, Psalms 118:5-6*).

Chol Hamoed
Succos
Oct. 9, 1990
Sept. 28, 1991
Oct. 17, 1992
Oct. 5, 1993
Sept. 25, 1994
Oct. 14, 1995

Nothing is as frightening as loneliness. When we are alone, the world may appear awesome, and even harmless shadows may take on an ominous character.

"Even when I walk through the valley of the shadow of death, I will fear no evil because You are with me" (*Psalms 23:4*). When we know G-d is with us, we can feel as secure as an infant cradled in its parent's protective arms. But to have G-d's presence, we must call upon Him, as the Psalmist says *(91:15)*, "He shall call upon Me, and I shall answer him." Sincere prayer brings us closer to G-d.

From the Scriptures

Every place where I would have My name remembered, I will come to you and bless you (*Exodus 20:21*).

Rabbi Mendel of Kotzk was a young man when he first met his teacher, Rabbi Bunim of Pshis'cha.

"Young man," said Rabbi Bunim, "where can G-d be found?"

"Why, G-d is everywhere!" Rabbi Mendel answered.

"Young man, did you not hear me?" asked Rabbi Bunim. "Where can G-d be found?"

"The fullness of the universe is His glory!" Rabbi Mendel answered.

"Young man, I ask you again, where can G-d be found?" Rabbi Bunim said.

"Well, if none of my answers satisfy you, then you tell me," said Rabbi Mendel.

"Listen to me, young man," Rabbi Bunim said. "G-d can be found where He is invited, only where He is invited."

Yes, G-d can be with us, but we must act in such a manner that we invite His presence.

NOTES
_____
_____
_____
_____
_____
_____
_____
_____

Hoshana Rabbah

Oct. 10, 1990
Sept. 29, 1991
Oct. 18, 1992
Oct. 6, 1993
Sept. 26, 1994
Oct. 15, 1995

From our Prayers

אֲדוֹן הַמּוֹשִׁיעַ, בִּלְתְּךָ אֵין לְהוֹשִׁיעַ . . .

You are the Master of salvation, and but for You, there is no salvation. You are mighty, and Your salvation is abundant. I am so impoverished, and in need of Your salvation *(Succos liturgy)*.

If we humble ourselves, and realize that our own resources are so meager and our wisdom so limited, then we can acknowledge the sovereignty of G-d. But if we are arrogant and believe that we control our own destiny, then we are apt to deny Divine providence.

If we sincerely turn our lives over to the care of G-d, then we merit Divine salvation, as the Psalmist says *(31:6)*, "Into Your hands I commit my spirit, for You have redeemed me, O G-d of truth."

An absolute trust in G-d may not be easy to achieve, but such trust is the very essence of faith. But an arrogant, inflated ego can preclude developing trust in G-d.

From the Scriptures

You shall celebrate the festival of Succos . . . when you gather your harvest from your barn and your wine-press. You shall rejoice in your festival, along with your sons and daughters . . . and with the stranger, and the orphan, and the widow among you *(Deuteronomy 16:13-14)*.

Gathering the bountiful produce of the land is indeed a happy occasion.

The Torah reminds us that true joy can be attained only when we share our blessings with others, and especially when we make certain that those who are less fortunate are provided for in such a manner that they, too, can rejoice. The physical pleasures we enjoy are very fleeting and are soon forgotten. The knowledge that we have helped others enjoy life can be of long duration.

Think of some pleasurable experience that you had last week. What gratification does it provide you today? Now think of something that you did years ago to help another person. The good feeling still persists.

Selfish joy is really no joy at all.

NOTES

_____
_____
_____
_____
_____
_____
_____
_____
_____
_____

זְכוֹר ... *From our Prayers*

לָכֵן הַבְטַחְתּוֹ הֱיוֹת עִמּוֹ בָּאֵשׁ וּבַמָּיִם

Remember for us the virtue of our ancestor, the patriarch Jacob, who ... **survived his struggle with a fiery angel, and to whom You vowed that You would be with his descendants in the travails of fire and water** *(Succos liturgy)*.

When we dedicate our lives to the service of G-d, nothing should deter us from our goal.

At times of severe hardship it may seem to us that supernatural forces have been unleashed against us. Even then we must have faith and stand our ground in the struggle for truth and righteousness.

Our forefather Jacob taught us that with trust in G-d we can triumph even over fiery angels. Our history as a people has amply demonstrated our ability to survive enormous adversity. Our capacity to overcome difficulties in our own lives is no less.

Shemini Atzeres
[Yizkor —
in the Land of Israel
this day is also
celebrated as
Simchas Torah]

Oct. 11, 1990
Sept. 30, 1991
Oct. 19, 1992
Oct. 7, 1993
Sept. 27, 1994
Oct. 16, 1995

From the Sages

All seven days of Succos, special services were offered in the Sanctuary for the welfare of all nations of the earth. On the eighth day G-d says to Israel, "Tarry with me one more day, so that we may rejoice together" *(Midrash)*.

Many are the gifts that Israel has given to the world.

In their prophetic foresight, the Sages knew that — in relating to the peoples of the earth — we may risk losing our own identity. They therefore instructed us, "Pray for all, be kind to all, and do for all, but do not forget who *you* are. Keep together, and your togetherness will keep you."

In unity there is not only strength, but also a sense of identity. Throughout history, Jews have wandered in exile from one country to another. They have been subjected to severe oppressive as well as assimilative forces, but they have survived nevertheless.

To survive and to retain our identity we must stay together with each other, and together with G-d.

NOTES
_____
_____
_____
_____
_____
_____
_____
_____
_____

Simchas Torah
Oct. 12, 1990
Oct. 1, 1991
Oct. 20, 1992
Oct. 8, 1993
Sept. 28, 1994
Oct. 17, 1995

From our Prayers

אֱלֹקֵי הָרוּחוֹת הוֹשִׁיעָה נָּא . . .

G-d of all spirits, be our salvation. Searcher of all hearts, bless us with success. **Mighty Redeemer, answer us when we call out to You** *(prayer of procession with the Torah, Simchas Torah liturgy).*

We carry the Torah in procession around the *bimah*, and rejoice in song that we have completed another cycle of reading the Torah, and are bringing the festivals of the month to completion.

But joy and celebration may not be with frivolity. There can be joy and glee with soberness. While we are light on our feet as we dance, our minds dare not shed the weight of responsible living.

In Jewishness there is a concept of "rejoicing while trembling" *(Psalms 2:11),* which means that the awesome reverence one has in standing in the presence of the Almighty and feelings of joy are not incompatible.

While we dance with the Torah to lively melodies, we recite solemn prayers. Joy and solemnity can coexist.

From the Sages

From amongst your brethren you shall take upon yourself a sovereign *(Deuteronomy 17:15).* **Rabbi Moshe of Kobrin said that this could also be read as, "Only out of brotherhood can you accept upon yourself the sovereignty of G-d." The key to being dutiful to G-d is unity with one another.**

NOTES

_____
_____
_____
_____
_____
_____
_____
_____
_____

One of the lively celebrants on Simchas Torah was a man of very meager learning.

"Why are you celebrating?" he was asked. "Do you know any of the Torah that you are so happy with it?"

"Not really," the man answered. "But if my brother was marrying off his child, I would certainly rejoice and celebrate along with him. So I now rejoice along with my brethren who do study the Torah, and their *simchah* is my *simchah*, too."

When we share with others, their joy becomes ours.

וּזְכָר לָנוּ . . . אֶת הַבְּרִית וְאֶת הַחֶסֶד . . . *From our Prayers*

Remember for us . . . the covenant, the kindness and the promise that You swore to the patriarch Abraham when he bound his son Isaac to the altar to do Your will with faith (*daily morning service*).

Oct. 13, 1990
Oct. 2, 1991
Oct. 21, 1992
Oct. 9, 1993
Sept. 29, 1994
Oct. 18, 1995

Abraham's absolute devotion to G-d and his willingness to sacrifice Isaac are cited many times in our prayers.

Jewish history is replete with heroic martyrs. Why does Abraham stand out so uniquely?

G-d had promised Abraham that Isaac would be the father of the Jewish nation. The commandment to sacrifice Isaac would have annulled this promise, hence Abraham could justifiably have questioned this new commandment, since it conflicted with the earlier promise.

The greatness of Abraham was that he did not stop to analyze the Divine decree. He did not even consider the non-existence of the Jewish nation as a deterrent to fulfilling the Divine wish. He did not allow his reasoning, regardless of how sound it was, to interfere with prompt obedience to G-d's command. G-d spoke and Abraham obeyed with unfaltering faith, and in this he was indeed unique.

Rabbi Zusia said, "If I could arrange that I be Abraham and that Abraham be Zusia, I would not do so. For what would G-d gain thereby? There would still be only one Abraham and one Zusia." *From the Sages*

Man was created for the glory of G-d, not for his own personal glory.

What would our lives be like if everything we did was sincerely motivated only by the wish to bring greater glory to G-d, rather than by the quest for personal gain?

Many of the stresses and pressures that so heavily tax us both emotionally and physically would be greatly diminished, since our sensitive egos would not be at stake. We would then be healthier as well as happier. Ironically, by diverting our attention *from* our personal gain, we would actually *achieve* the ultimate in personal gain: health and happiness.

Oct. 14, 1990
Oct. 3, 1991
Oct. 22, 1992
Oct. 10, 1993
Sept. 30, 1994
Oct. 19, 1995

From our Prayers

וְאָהַבְתָּ אֵת ה' אֱלֹקֶיךָ
בְּכָל לְבָבְךָ וּבְכָל נַפְשְׁךָ וּבְכָל מְאֹדֶךָ

You shall love the L-rd your G-d with all your heart and with all your soul and with all your might *(the Shema)*.

Since love is an emotion, how can we be commanded to feel something? A feeling is either present or absent, but can hardly be generated at will or upon demand.

The answer to this is that there is a natural affection of the human soul for G-d. Inasmuch as the soul is of Divine origin, it is naturally attracted to its source, much as iron filings are attracted to a magnet. If one does not feel love for G-d, it is because there are barriers to this natural love which interfere with the attractive force. These barriers are those acts which are in defiance of the Divine will.

To feel our love for G-d, all we must do is eliminate the obstructive barriers, and the natural emotion will then prevail.

From the Scriptures

Do not be quick to anger, for rage tends to linger in the bosom of a fool *(Ecclesiastes 7:9)*.

Some things we acquire we can easily dispose of at our will.

Not so with anger. Like a stubborn virus, once we have it, it has us in its grip. The Talmud states that anger is very destructive. If a person is wise, anger ruins his wisdom, and even if he is a prophet, it robs him of his prophetic powers.

NOTES

_____
_____
_____
_____
_____
_____
_____
_____
_____
_____

If we defend and rationalize our anger, we only reinforce it. Perhaps if we were truly wise, we could discover ways to rid ourselves of anger. But then, if we were truly wise, perhaps we would not have become angry in the first place. If we had our priorities in order, and had a proper perception of which things in life are truly important and which are not, we might realize that some things we thought of as being of great moment are actually insignificant, things which are not worthy of causing us aggravation.

**From
our
Prayers**

... שֶׁיִּבָּנֶה בֵּית הַמִּקְדָּשׁ ... יְהִי רָצוֹן מִלְפָנֶיךָ ...

May it be Your will, our G-d and G-d of
our fathers, that the Sanctuary be soon
rebuilt in our days, and give us our share in
Your Torah (daily service).

Oct. 15, 1990
Oct. 4, 1991
Oct. 23, 1992
Oct. 11, 1993
Oct. 1, 1994
Oct. 20, 1995

Jewishness stresses the importance of the hope for the Redemption, at which time all evil will be eradicated and all mankind will join in acknowledging the sovereignty of G-d.

While we await the hoped-for Divine redemption, we must work for our personal redemption, to overcome our personality defects, and to come into a closer relationship with G-d. We can achieve this by studying the Divine teachings of Torah, and applying them in our everyday lives.

If we cultivate our share in the Torah, we can refine our character, and thereby build a sanctuary for the Divine presence within ourselves.

*From
the Sages*

No human being leaves this world having achieved even half of his material aspirations. If one has one hundred dinars, he craves two hundred. If he has two hundred dinars, he craves four hundred (Koheles Rabbah 13).

''Whence comes man's insatiability?'' asked the Maggid of Dubno. ''Why is it that when animals satiate their physical drives, they stop, and only man appears to indulge in excesses?''

The Maggid explains that man is unique in that he is indeed created with an insatiable drive — his quest for spirituality. Inasmuch as spirituality involves coming closer to G-d and achieving a more profound understanding of G-dliness, this drive is indeed insatiable, because G-d is infinite.

NOTES

However, man may not correctly identify the true nature of this craving. When he feels unsatisfied, he may attempt to quell this craving with other gratifications, whether they be food, drink, or acquisition of riches. These, of course, do nothing to satisfy the quest for spirituality, and his indulgence in these excesses can lead to very self-destructive consequences.

Recognition of our need for spiritual growth and our pursuit of spirituality can save us from such self-destructive behavior.

Oct. 16, 1990
Oct. 5, 1991
Oct. 24, 1992
Oct. 12, 1993
Oct. 2, 1994
Oct. 21, 1995

From our Prayers

הַשָּׁמַיִם מְסַפְּרִים כְּבוֹד קֵל . . .

The heavens recount the glory of G-d, and the firmament tells the work of His hands. Day to day utters speech, and night to night speaks knowledge (*Shabbos morning service, Psalms 19:2-3*).

If my eyes are open, my ears unclogged, and my mind receptive, then the universe itself attests to the existence of its Designer. If I fail to perceive the hand of G-d in the wondrous design of the universe, it is only because some forces within me operate in a manner to cause denial of the obvious.

When people who are addicted to alcohol or drugs deny their addiction, it is often because realization of the truth would necessitate a change; namely, to give up the use of their chemical, and this would cause them discomfort. Similarly, when people refuse to acknowledge the truth of the sovereignty of G-d, it is because such realization would call for changes in their lives, and it is usually more comfortable not to change.

If I pray to be shown the truth, I must be prepared to sacrifice some comfort in order to live the truth.

From the Sages

The greater a person is, the greater is the force of his temptation (*Succah 52a*).

One might think that great people are not subject to the lure of physical desires.

Not so, say the Sages. The greatness of man lies precisely in his struggle to overcome his drives. Inasmuch as G-d does not subject a person to stresses that are beyond his coping capacities, it follows that the intensity of a temptation is actually an indicator of the capacities one possesses to master it.

If I can understand that temptation reveals to me how powerful my coping capacities actually are, then I have even greater reason to overcome it. For how can someone as capable as I do something so base, something which is beneath my status and an affront to my dignity?

The wise person can turn the forces of temptation back upon themselves to vanquish them.

NOTES

_____
_____
_____
_____
_____
_____
_____
_____
_____

חָנֵּנִי אֱלֹקִים חָנֵּנִי כִּי בְךָ חָסָיָה נַפְשִׁי . . . *From our Prayers*

Be gracious to me, O G-d, because it is in You that my spirit trusts, and I will conceal myself in the shadow of Your wings until the evil has passed. I will call unto G-d, the Most High, to the Almighty One, who will bring things to a conclusion for me *(Psalms 57:2-3)*.

Oct. 17, 1990
Oct. 6, 1991
Oct. 25, 1992
Oct. 13, 1993
Oct. 3, 1994
Oct. 22, 1995

We can hear the anguish of the Psalmist who asks for salvation as an act of Divine grace and mercy, even though he feels he may not be deserving of it. He is saying, "My spirit, my soul does indeed trust in You, and if the whole of my being is lacking in faith, it is because the flesh, when under torment, is subject to doubt. Bear with me through this ordeal, G-d, and the faith of my spirit will prevail."

At times when we feel ourselves to be distant from G-d, these words of the Psalmist are comforting. We can be strengthened by the knowledge that G-d will be patient with us while we do our utmost in the struggle to resist the lures of temptation and to do His will.

Do not deceive your fellow man *(Leviticus 25:17).* **The Rabbi of Kotzk commented, "Not to deceive another person is mandated by law. The pious person also refrains from deceiving himself."** *From the Sages*

The only problem I have with the Rabbi of Kotzk's remark is that avoiding self-deception appears to me to be a matter of good sense in the interest of survival rather than a trait of piety.

If I deceive another person, then I may gain a temporary advantage through unjust means. Unfortunately, avarice can mislead some people to profit by unjust means and to gain by victimizing another person. This is forbidden as a criminal act.

But if I deceive *myself,* what possible gain can there be? I then become the victim of my own deviousness! Any victory in self-deception is therefore a loss. Yet we may be misled by our own impulses and desires, and we then rationalize and deceive ourselves that we acted justly.

To victimize another person is criminal. To victimize oneself is simply stupid.

NOTES

*Erev
Rosh Chodesh
[Eve of the
New Month]*

Oct. 18, 1990
Oct. 7, 1991
Oct. 26, 1992
Oct. 14, 1993
Oct. 4, 1994
Oct. 23, 1995

*From
our
Prayers*

אֱלֹקֵינוּ אָבִינוּ רְעֵנוּ זוּנֵנוּ פַּרְנְסֵנוּ וְכַלְכְּלֵנוּ . . .

Our G-d, our Father, tend us, feed us, sustain us, nourish us, and let us not be in need of the gifts of human hands or of their loans, but only of Your hand, which is full, open, holy, and ample, so that we need never be ashamed or embarrassed

(Blessing following the meal).

If the food on my table is truly mine, and the clothes on my person are of my own honest earning, then they are truly a blessing.

Sometimes my needs and aspirations may lead me to extend myself beyond my means, and to become burdened with debt, or to impose myself on others. The gratification attained by such methods is far outweighed by the distress of indebtedness or the embarrassment of being beholden to others.

I ask G-d to provide me with my needs, and to help me realize that I really do not need anything more than He provides.

*From
the Sages*

Among the fowl that are forbidden as food is the *chasidah.* **[whose exact identification is not known]**
(Leviticus 11:19.)

Rashi comments that the name *chasidah* **is derived from the word** *chesed* **(kindness). The** *chasida* **is a bird that acts kindly toward its own kin.**

"Why, then, is this bird trefah (not kosher)?" asked the Rabbi of Kotzk. "Because," he answered, "to be kosher you must behave kindly toward everyone, and not only toward your own."

Spiritual growth calls for overcoming resistances. Simply following our emotional tendencies is not true virtue, even when the actions are laudable.

It is human nature to behave kindly toward one's own, because they are extensions of ourselves. When we are kind to our own, we are actually being kind to ourselves.

Virtue requires being kind to everyone. This requires overcoming the resistance to give to others whom we do not consider to be extensions of ourselves, or better yet, to overcome the resistance toward recognizing all people as extensions of ourselves.

NOTES

_____
_____
_____
_____
_____
_____
_____
_____
_____

From

But as for me, my prayer to You, O G-d, *our*
is for but one instant of favor. O G-d, *Prayers*
Who even while judging remains in abundance of loving-kindness, answer me with
the truth of Your salvation *(Shabbos afternoon service, Psalms 69:14).*

וַאֲנִי תְפִלָּתִי לְךָ ה' עֵת רָצוֹן . . .

Hardly anyone excapes suffering, and since the reasons
for this suffering generally elude us, it seems unjust, and
may arouse resentment toward G-d.

While we pray for visible good in life, for blessings that
are not disguised, we also pray for one instant of Divine
favor: to be blessed with the faith that all of G-d's
judgments are in loving-kindness, even those that appear
harsh, for they are then easier to bear. We pray for the
serenity to accept things we cannot change, even those
things that cause us distress.

Just a glimpse of the Divine truth can be our salvation.

*First Day of
Rosh Chodesh
Cheshvan*

Oct. 19, 1990
Oct. 8, 1991
Oct. 27, 1992
Oct.15, 1993
Oct. 5, 1994
Oct. 24, 1995

**[When you redeem the tithes of your produce,
then] you shall bind the money in your hand [and
carry it to Jerusalem]** *(Deuteronomy 14:25).*

**Rabbi Meir of Premishlan remarked, "The Torah
tells you that you should bind the money in your
hand, to indicate that you should be in possession of
your money, rather than allowing your money to be
in possession of you."**

*From
the Sages*

How timeless are the teachings of Torah!

To the wise person, money is a means toward an end. He
uses money to obtain the necessities of life. Money is but a
tool, and its owner is its master.

There are people who lack this wisdom, and who
accumulate riches for the sake of accumulation. They are
unable to partake of it themselves.

Thus the Torah exhorts, "Your wealth, like any other
tool, should be in your hands, and you must be its master.
If your wealth possesses you, then you are not its master,
but rather its slave."

NOTES

_____
_____
_____
_____
_____
_____
_____
_____
_____

Second Day of
Rosh Chodesh
Cheshvan
Oct. 20, 1990
Oct. 9, 1991
Oct. 28, 1992
Oct. 16, 1993
Oct. 6, 1994
Oct. 25, 1995

From . . .
our
Prayers

הַשָּׁמַיִם שָׁמַיִם לַה' וְהָאָרֶץ נָתַן לִבְנֵי אָדָם

As for the heavens, the heavens are to G-d, but the earth He gave to the children of man. It is not the dead who can proclaim the glory of G-d, or those who descend into silence. But we can praise G-d, from now and unto eternity *(Hallel, Psalms 115:16-18).*

The Rabbi of Kotzk commented, "The heavens are spiritual because G-d fashioned them so. The earthly world was given to man that he should convert it so that it too should be spiritual."

Eating is a physical act, but if we take food because nourishment is essential to sustain life so that we may be able to do the will of G-d, then that food is transformed into a vehicle of spirituality. A coin is a physical object, but when it is given in charity to provide for the needy, it is transformed into a spiritual object.

With our thoughts, prayers, and deeds we can do the will of G-d and proclaim His sovereignty. This is the reason we were given the gift of life. It is both our privilege and responsibility to bring spirituality into the physical world.

From the
Scriptures

It is obligatory that we commemorate our deliverance from bondage each day, as the Torah says, "So that you may remember the day of deliverance from Egypt every day of your life" *(Deuteronomy 16:3).*

The dignity of man is his freedom. Slavery is abhorrent not only because it is cruel but also because it deprives man of freedom, which is the essence of humanity.

Just as a person can be a slave to another person, he can also be a slave to himself, if he becomes the prisoner of his own passions, and if his impulses are master over him rather than he over them. He can be enslaved by various habits and addictions. Whatever form the enslavement may take, it diminishes the quality of humanity because it detracts from freedom.

Just as deliverance from the enslavement of Egypt was possible with Divine help, so is emergence from all other types of enslavement which prevent us from being truly free humans.

Each day we recite a prayer of gratitude to G-d that we are not slaves. We should cherish our freedom, and not allow ourselves to become enslaved, even to ourselves.

NOTES

_____
_____
_____
_____
_____
_____
_____
_____
_____
_____

הַשְׁכִּיבֵנוּ ה' אֱלֹקֵינוּ לְשָׁלוֹם **From**
וְהַעֲמִידֵנוּ מַלְכֵּנוּ לְחַיִּים . . . **our**

Cause us, L-rd our G-d, to lie down in **Prayers**
peace, and cause us to arise again, our
King, to good life ... and peace (daily
evening service).

How we arise to greet the new day may depend on how
we retired the previous night.

If we retire with our hearts burdened with worry,
grudges, and resentments, we are apt to awaken exhausted and depressed. If we unburden ourselves of these
negative feelings before retiring, discard our resentments,
and return our souls to G-d with trust in His providence,
we can awaken to a constructive day of peace and
goodness.

Along with prayer for peace and happiness, we must
divest ourselves of those traits that preclude peace and
happiness. If we wish our prayer to be effective, we must
do our share.

Oct. 21, 1990
Oct. 10, 1991
Oct. 29, 1992
Oct. 17, 1993
Oct. 7, 1994
Oct. 26, 1995

**The Rabbi of Karlin was asked, "Why is it that
chassidim dance so frequently?"**

**"Because," answered the Rabbi, "in dancing you
lift your feet and you thus elevate yourself a few
centimeters from the earth and become a few
centimeters closer to heaven."**

*From
the Sages*

A person who is totally preoccupied with gratifying his
earthly desires can never achieve joy. It is a law of nature
that the more one satisfies a physical drive, the more it is
stimulated to cause even greater craving, with the inevitable result being chronic dissatisfaction.

NOTES

Although the distance from earth to heaven may appear
to be infinite, all that man has to do is to make the effort, to
try and get just a few centimeters closer to G-d, to make
just the slightest beginning in detaching himself from
earthly pursuits, and he will then receive Divine help to
achieve greater heights.

True joy is lifting oneself above the surface of the
earth and reaching up to the heavens in quest of
spirituality.

Oct. 22, 1990
Oct. 11, 1991
Oct. 30, 1992
Oct. 18, 1993
Oct. 8, 1994
Oct. 27, 1995

*From
our
Prayers*

. . . זוֹרֵעַ צְדָקוֹת מַצְמִיחַ יְשׁוּעוֹת
בּוֹרֵא רְפוּאוֹת . . .

G-d sows justice, brings forth salvation, and creates healing. He is the Master of the universe, and constantly renews each day the work of creation (*daily morning service*).

We should learn to face each day as though it were the first day of creation. The world is fresh, and we are new beings. We can start each day unencumbered by the past.

But how can we do so when the stark reality is that so often the burdens of the past rest heavily upon us?

This is possible only in the Divine realm of justice. G-d has provided for the healing of our ills and wounds, and this can indeed be our salvation. He can not only forgive us our past, but thoroughly erase it as though it had never occurred. He can renew us with the freshness of a new life.

G-d is truly the Master of the universe, and He allows us to live our lives so that, in His eyes, every day is the first day of our lives.

*From the
Scriptures*

You shall be holy, for I, your G-d, am holy (*Leviticus 19:2*).

Some Torah commentaries interpret the term "shall" in the above passage not in its imperative sense, but as a statement of fact. It does not mean "you *must* be holy", but rather "you *will* be holy."

Inasmuch as the soul of man is identified with G-d himself, it is a matter of fact that man must ultimately achieve holiness. Since this is inevitable, why delay it by indulgence in behavior that detracts from holiness?

If we find ourselves in despair of achieving holiness, and believe that we have strayed too far to be close to G-d, then we must remember that such despair is delusional. If we are not yet one with G-d, we eventually will be so.

NOTES

———————
———————
———————
———————
———————
———————
———————
———————
———————
———————

Happy is the man who reveres G-d, who **. . . אַשְׁרֵי אִישׁ יָרֵא אֶת ה' . . .** *From our Prayers* desires to do His commandments . . . He will never falter, the memory of the righteous will endure. He will not fear evil things, for his heart is secure in G-d. In his heart he depends on G-d, hence he has no fear *(Shabbos afternoon service, nusach Sefard; Psalms 112:1,6-8).*

Oct. 23, 1990
Oct. 12, 1991
Oct. 31, 1992
Oct. 19, 1993
Oct. 9, 1994
Oct. 28, 1995

There is nothing as destructive to man as anxiety, the persistent sensation of impending harm, which prevents man from enjoying the present and makes him dread the future.

A tiny infant may feel overwhelmed by the gigantic world about him, but when he is held securely in his parent's arms, he feels safe.

The person who places his trust in G-d, and knows that, even if he is put to the test of suffering, no evil can befall him because G-d is there to protect him, can enjoy what he has, and does not anticipate that harm will befall him.

Hasten to do even the slightest mitzvah, and flee from all sin. Because one mitzvah will lead to another, and one sin will lead to another *(Ethics of the Fathers 4:2).*

From the Sages

People who have recovered from addiction to alcohol or drugs can teach us a great deal. They know that even after long abstinence, just one drink or one drug use is likely to precipitate a disastrous relapse.

The Talmud teaches that this is true of all behavior. One *mitzvah*, one positive act, will encourage additional positive acts, whereas one negative action may initiate a destructive chain reaction. It is essential that we be particularly cautious about even "slight" slips in behavior, for even apparent trivial misdeeds can eventually lead to grave consequences.

It is told that a pious man once accidentally bumped into his table on *Shabbos,* causing a candle to fall and become extinguished. When his family saw how upset he was, they reminded him that this was but an accident, a pure mishap for which he should feel no guilt.

"I am not worried about this particular incident," he said, "but it is a law of nature that one transgression brings another in its wake. What upsets me is the consequences of this accidental misdeed, and to what greater transgressions it may lead."

NOTES
_____
_____
_____
_____
_____
_____
_____
_____
_____

Oct. 24, 1990
Oct. 13, 1991
Nov. 1, 1992
Oct. 20, 1993
Oct. 10, 1994
Oct. 29, 1995

From our Prayers

בָּרוּךְ הוּא אֱלֹקֵינוּ שֶׁבְּרָאָנוּ לִכְבוֹדוֹ . . .

Blessed is G-d, Who has created us for His glory and has set us apart from those who go astray, and Who gave us the Torah . . . May He put the love and fear of Him in our hearts, so that we may do His will and serve Him with a whole heart *(daily morning service).*

What is life without a goal beyond self-gratification, without an awareness that there is an ultimate purpose to existence which makes everything we do meaningful?

Man's limited intelligence might not always lead him to the truth of his existence. We are grateful to G-d for revealing Himself to us and giving us His laws of life.

The phrase "those who go astray" often refers to idolaters. Idolatry is essentially the reverse of the proposition that G-d created man, because in idolatry man creates gods to suit his own desires. Idolatry is thus worship of oneself rather than a Supreme Being. A goal of self-gratification, even if couched in religious terms, is nothing but idolatry.

From the Sages

Let the honor of your fellow man be as dear to you as your own, and do not be easily moved to anger *(Ethics of the Fathers 2:15).*

NOTES

_____
_____
_____
_____
_____
_____
_____
_____
_____
_____

The Torah requires the utmost reverence for every human being. A person who has forfeited his life by commitment of a heinous crime must be treated with dignity even as he is put to death.

When someone wrongs us, we must be able to separate the deed from the person. A particular deed may be despicable, and the person who commits an offense may need to be punished to deter him and others from repeating the act, but the person himself never loses his sanctity.

To degrade another person is to degrade oneself. We maintain self-esteem by according others the respect due to a being created in the likeness of G-d.

שֶׁאֵין אָנוּ עַזֵּי פָנִים וּקְשֵׁי עֹרֶף . . . *From*
. . . לוֹמַר לְפָנֶיךָ *our*

Our G-d and G-d of our fathers . . . we *Prayers*
are not impudent to say before You . . .
"We are righteous and have not sinned,"
for truly we have sinned . . . but You are
merciful and have taught us the way of
repentance (*Selichos, daily morning service*).

Oct. 25, 1990
Oct. 14, 1991
Nov. 2, 1992
Oct. 21, 1993
Oct. 11, 1994
Oct. 30, 1995

It is foolish as well as false to delude ourselves that we are saints. We cannot deceive ourselves any more than we can deceive the all-knowing G-d. But the frailties of being human need not deter us from striving for perfection.

G-d has provided us with a way of repentance, whereby we confess our misdeeds and sincerely resolve not to repeat them. We may then be secure in the knowledge that G-d has erased our iniquities. We should then be free to employ the enormous forces at our disposal in the fulfillment of the Divine will.

The status achieved by penitents is greater than that achieved by the completely righteous (*Berachos 34b*).

From the Sages

The Talmud refers to a concept of "descent in the interest of ascent". The person who achieves a devotion to G-d so that he is able to overcome even deeply engrained habits and a life style of self-gratification may be held in higher esteem than one who was always pious and never had to struggle to reverse his pattern of life.

Because of this, once we have truly repented our misdeeds and corrected them, there is no longer any need to ruminate about them. By the acts of true repentance these very misdeeds have become valuable experiences and steps to personality growth.

The popular aphorism, "Experience is a harsh teacher, but fools will learn no other way," is clearly wrong. Fools are those who do *not* learn from experiences. It is the wise that do.

We grow in spirituality by learning from our mistakes.

NOTES
_____
_____
_____
_____
_____
_____
_____
_____
_____
_____

Oct. 26, 1990
Oct. 15, 1991
Nov. 3, 1992
Oct. 22, 1993
Oct. 12, 1994
Oct. 31, 1995

From our Prayers

יְבָרֶכְךָ ה' וְיִשְׁמְרֶךָ . . . וְיָשֵׂם לְךָ שָׁלוֹם

May G-d bless and protect you. May G-d cause His countenance to shine upon you and be gracious to you. May G-d lift His countenance to you and bless you with peace (*Priestly blessing, daily morning service*).

The Talmud states that the above blessings are given to those who are appreciative of G-d's bounty, and who are grateful to G-d for what He has given them.

Some human appetites can be insatiable. Those whose desires are like bottomless pits cannot be true beneficiaries of blessings, because whatever they receive only stimulates more desire. This results in persistent feelings of frustration and deprivation rather than gratitude.

The ultimate blessing, that of peace, can be ours only if we are at peace with ourselves, satisfied with what we have, and grateful to G-d for what He has given us.

From the Sages

Be exceedingly humble in spirit (*Ethics of the Fathers 4:4*).

At every level of Torah, from the Scriptures down to the most recent ethical works, humility is given prime importance.

Says Rabbi Pinchas of Koritz, "Almost every other transgression is contingent upon having some object external to oneself. You cannot steal unless there is something to steal, you cannot eat forbidden food unless you have it, and you cannot violate the Sabbath without some physical object wherewith to do the proscribed act. The sin of vanity, however, requires no object outside of oneself. One can lie in bed in complete seclusion and think, "I am the greatest," and be guilty of vanity.

Extreme efforts are therefore necessary to avoid a sin which is so readily transgressed.

NOTES
_____
_____
_____
_____
_____
_____
_____
_____
_____

יְהֵא רַעֲוָא קֳדָמָךְ *From*
דְּתוֹרִיךְ לָן חַיִּין בְּטִיבוּתָא ... *our*

May it be Your will to prolong our lives in *Prayers*
happiness, and that I may be counted
among the righteous (*prayer upon taking out
the Torah*).

Since humility requires that we not take credit for what
we have done, and indeed, rather think of ourselves as
remiss for not having done enough, how then can we
consider ourselves deserving of Divine reward?

One method is that we not ask for ourselves as
individuals, but as members of a group. It does not
detract from personal humility to appreciate others as
righteous and deserving, and if we are unified with
others, supportive of them in their times of need, and
share ourselves with them, then we can ask for our share
in the communal blessing.

Oct. 27, 1990
Oct. 16, 1991
Nov. 4, 1992
Oct. 23, 1993
Oct. 13, 1994
Nov. 1, 1995

The Divine revelation at the crossing of the Red *From*
Sea was so great that the lowliest person achieved a *the Sages*
greater prophetic vision than did the great prophet
Ezekiel (*Mechilta*).

Yet, remark the Sages, Ezekiel was a prophet whose
words were preserved for posterity, whereas those who
perceived the intense Divine revelation at the Red Sea
contributed nothing and remain unknown.

The reason for this is that Ezekiel struggled and
agonized to achieve a level of spirituality that enabled
him to merit prophetic vision. The person who happened
to perceive a Divine revelation but who had done nothing
to merit it did not grow with it. The vision does not
elevate the person; rather, it is the person who elevates
and expands the vision.

Spirituality is durable and productive only if I work to
achieve it, or if I utilize precious moments of grace and
build upon them. Without my own efforts, even the
greatest insights can remain but barren visions.

NOTES
_____
_____
_____
_____
_____
_____
_____
_____
_____
_____

Oct. 28, 1990
Oct. 17, 1991
Nov. 5, 1992
Oct. 24, 1993
Oct. 14, 1994
Nov. 2, 1995

From . . . שֶׁתַּצִּילֵנִי הַיּוֹם וּבְכָל יוֹם מֵעַזֵּי פָנִים *. . .*

our **M**ay it be Your will, my G-d and G-d of
Prayers my fathers, to deliver me this day and
every day from impudent people, from
insolence, from evil people, and from bad
companions (*daily morning prayer*).

Our Sages tell us that prayer achieves only part of a
person's aspirations. The rest one must do for himself.

In the above prayer we ask G-d to protect us from
various types of evil. For some deliverances we are totally
dependent upon G-d, and for others we must contribute
our share of effort.

G-d can protect man from others who are impudent, but
to overcome our own insolence it is necessary that we take
action. G-d can protect us from encounters with evil
people, but who we have as companions is our own
choice.

Only when man walks together with G-d and participates
in his own character development does he achieve his goal.

From   **The reward for a virtuous deed is the deed itself,**
the Sages   **and the recompense for a sin is the sin itself** (*Ethics of
the Fathers 4:2*).

We tend to think of reward and punishment as being
only external to the things we do, given to us or imposed
upon us from without.

When one is working for others, he expects to be paid,
and if one injures someone else, he understands that he
must pay for his actions. This is not true when one works
for or does to oneself, when he benefits from his profits
and suffers from his losses. He is the beneficiary or the
victim of his own actions.

We should do that which is right because it is in our own
interest to do so, and we should avoid doing wrong
because it is to our own detriment. A true understanding of
right and wrong will help us see that living a virtuous life is
to our own advantage.

NOTES

_____
_____
_____
_____
_____
_____
_____
_____
_____
_____

CHESHVAN

10

חשון

From our Prayers . . . רִבּוֹן כָּל הָעוֹלָמִים לֹא עַל צִדְקוֹתֵינוּ

Master of the universe, it is not on the basis of our merits that we pour out our supplications before You, but rather because of our trust in Your boundless compassion (*daily morning service*).

Some people may actually hesitate to enjoy anything they have, for fear that they do not deserve it, and hence if they were to allow themselves to enjoy it, it might be taken from them.

One way to quell this anxiety is to realize that G-d gives to us because of His infinite goodness and His desire to give, and not necessarily because it is earned. Even more than parents enjoy giving to their children, G-d enjoys being bountiful to His children.

As long as we do not misuse G-d's gifts in a destructive manner, we need not fear losing them.

Oct. 29, 1990
Oct. 18, 1991
Nov. 6, 1992
Oct. 25, 1993
Oct. 15, 1994
Nov. 3, 1995

If a person's heart is heavy with worry, let him unburden himself to other people (*Yoma 75a*).

From the Sages

The great chassidic master, Rabbi Tzvi Elimelech, said that in addition to the psychological value of unburdening oneself to another, there is yet an additional advantage to doing so.

Assume, he said, that person A was adjudged by G-d to bear suffering. If A relates his plight to person B, and B so empathizes and identifies with A that he shares A's suffering, then B now suffers as well. However, since the Divine judgment was not for B to suffer, justice requires that B be relieved of his suffering. But B's relief is contingent upon A's relief, and the Divine justice therefore requires that A be relieved of his distress to spare B from unjust suffering.

The essential ingredient of this method, said Rabbi Tzvi Elimelech, is that when one listens to a person's distress, he should sincerely empathize and feel the other's suffering as much as though it were his own.

NOTES
_____
_____
_____
_____
_____
_____
_____
_____
_____
_____

Oct. 30, 1990
Oct. 19, 1991
Nov. 7, 1992
Oct. 26, 1993
Oct. 16, 1994
Nov. 4, 1995

From our Prayers

אֲבָל אֲנַחְנוּ עַמְּךָ בְּנֵי בְרִיתֶךָ . . .

We are Your people, the children of Abraham who so loved You and to whom You made a promise on Mt. Moriah; the descendants of Isaac, his only son, who was tied to the altar as a sacrifice; the community of Jacob, whom You named Israel and Jeshurun because of Your love for him (*daily morning service*).

One more reason why we may enjoy the good things of life without the fear that because we are undeserving of them we may lose them, is the fact that just as children inherit the fortune which their parents accumulated even though they did not work to earn the wealth, so we as descendants of ancestors who did merit great rewards are the legitimate heirs of these rewards.

Abraham, Isaac, Jacob, and our ancestors earned many rewards by their piety, and we may justly enjoy their bequests.

From the Sages

One of the chassidic masters interpreted Psalms 16:8, "I perceive G-d opposite to me," as meaning that G-d and I are indeed opposites. He is everything, I am nothing.

Humility need not cause feelings of worthlessness. Although a zero may be nothing when it stands by itself, adding zeros to another digit can result in a number of astronomical magnitude.

If we stand alone, we are nothing. But when we stand together with G-d and with one another, we constitute a value of infinite proportion. When we bring ourselves close to G-d and unite with our fellow men, we can be both humble and great. If, in true humility, we think of ourselves as "zeros", we then stand close to G-d, who abides with the humble, and we are then infinitely great.

NOTES

_____
_____
_____
_____
_____
_____
_____
_____
_____

From our Prayers

CHESHVAN

12

חשון

Oct. 31, 1990
Oct. 20, 1991
Nov. 8, 1992
Oct. 27, 1993
Oct. 17, 1994
Nov. 5, 1995

Blessed be G-d day by day. He gives us a burden to bear, but G-d is our salvation **בָּרוּךְ ה' יוֹם יוֹם ...** *(daily morning service, Psalms 68:20).*

Every person has his particular burden in life, and we pray to G-d for the strength to bear this burden.

We may be secure in the fact that G-d will indeed give us the strength to bear the burden that *He* has given us. However, a person may take on unnecessary burdens which G-d did not intend for him to carry.

G-d intends for us to carry only today's burdens today, and in that task He will surely help us. If we insist on taking on the burdens of the future today, and worry today about things which we cannot do anything about today, that burden is of our own doing, and then we are on our own.

From the Sages

Things may turn out successfully or otherwise, happily or otherwise. Since there is at least as much chance of a favorable as an unfavorable outcome, why worry about the negative when you can enjoy anticipating the positive? *(Maimonides, Guide to Good Health).*

On Tishah B'Av (the 9th day of Av, commemorating the destruction of the Sanctuary and the fall of Jerusalem), after the conclusion of the morning service, the Rabbi of Tchechanov would take the pamphlet of lamentations and hymns of mourning and put it with the worn-out sacred items which would be given a respectful burial.

"No need to save these for next year Tishah B'Av," he would say. "By then there will surely have been the Redemption, and there will be no need to mourn."

The Rabbi was upset with those who saved the lamentation booklets for the following year. "Why anticipate grief when you can just as easily anticipate joy?"

NOTES

_____
_____
_____
_____
_____
_____
_____
_____
_____

Nov. 1, 1990
Oct. 21, 1991
Nov. 9, 1992
Oct. 28, 1993
Oct. 18, 1994
Nov. 6, 1995

From our Prayers

בָּרֵךְ עָלֵינוּ ה' אֱלֹקֵינוּ אֶת הַשָּׁנָה הַזֹּאת . . .

Bless for us, our G-d, this year and all the varieties of its produce. Bestow a blessing upon the land and satisfy us with Your bounty (*daily Amidah*).

The Talmud tell us that we will acquire only that quantity of wealth that has been Divinely decreed to be ours and not one bit more, regardless of our efforts. Our spiritual achievements, on the other hand, are not Divinely decreed, for these are in the realm of moral choice, which G-d leaves totally in the hands of man.

Good sense dictates, therefore, that we should exercise greatest concern and effort in accumulating spiritual wealth, and entrust our economic well-being to G-d. How unwise of us to often do just the reverse!

From the Sages

A person's provisions are decreed for him from the start of the year (*Beitzah 16a*).

One of the chassidic masters saw a man running in the street. "Why are you hurrying so?" he asked.

"I'm running after my *parnassah* (livelihood)," the man answered.

"How do you know that your *parnassah* is in the direction toward which you are running? Perhaps it is in the opposite direction, and you are actually running away from it?"

Time and again we have seen that what we thought would bring us profit did not do so at all, and that some income came from totally unexpected sources.

Man must indeed work to earn his living. But it would be well to remember that extra exertion will not bring us more than was decreed for us to have. If the extra effort were directed toward improving our spiritual lives through the study of Torah and good deeds, our finances would not suffer and our spiritual lives would be richer.

NOTES

_____
_____
_____
_____
_____
_____
_____
_____
_____

... יְשִׂמְךָ אֱלֹקִים כְּאֶפְרַיִם וְכִמְנַשֶּׁה
כְּשָׂרָה רִבְקָה רָחֵל וְלֵאָה

May G-d grant that you be as Ephraim and Menashe *(Blessing to sons)*.

May G-d grant that you be as Sarah, Rebecca, Rachel, and Leah *(Blessing to daughters)*.

Nov. 2, 1990
Oct. 22, 1991
Nov. 10, 1992
Oct. 29, 1993
Oct. 19, 1994
Nov. 7, 1995

The above is the traditional blessing bestowed by the father upon his children on Friday evening.

The secular world sees humanity as progressive, as attested to by the technological and scientific achievements unknown to the ancients. It often loses sight that on the whole, humanity has actually regressed morally while advancing technologically.

The spirit of *Shabbos* is inaugurated by blessing our children that they aspire to the spiritual achievements of their forebears. We look back with profound humility as we realize that we have not attained the spirituality of our ancestors.

The conversation of the servants of the patriarchs is dearer than the Torah study of their descendants *(Bereishis Rabbah 60)*.

_ There is no question that Torah study is of the highest priority. However, the Talmud states that the importance of Torah study is that it leads to proper behavior.

The servants of the patriarchs observed the manner in which their masters lived, and they related the purity and holiness of their lives.

Throughout Jewish history great men and women have taught Torah principles by the exemplary lives they led. To this very day there are models of Torah living whom we can emulate.

The Torah is a repository of principles for living in a manner that befits a human being. Simple knowledge of Torah does not suffice. We must absorb and apply Torah principles in every aspect of our lives. We must live Torah as well as study Torah.

Nov. 3, 1990
Oct. 23, 1991
Nov. 11, 1992
Oct. 30, 1993
Oct. 20, 1994
Nov. 8, 1995

From our Prayers מִמִּצְרַיִם גְּאַלְתָּנוּ . . . וּמִבֵּית עֲבָדִים פְּדִיתָנוּ

You have redeemed us from Egypt, our G-d, and freed us from the house of bondage. You have fed us in famine, and satisfied us in plenty. You have delivered us from the sword, and freed us from pestilence. Until now Your compassion has helped us, and Your kindness has not forsaken us. So L-rd our G-d, never do forsake us (*Shabbos morning service*).

This beautiful prayer did not fully impact upon me until I heard a man who had survived many severe ordeals describe his attitude toward the problems he was currently facing.

"G-d did not bring me all this way only to abandon me now," he said.

Regardless of the difficulties we may be experiencing, a reflection on the past will reveal that only with Divine help could we have survived. G-d certainly did not bring us this far to let us down now.

From the Sages

They (the Israelites) could not drink from the waters of Marah because they were bitter (*Exodus 15:23*). **The Baal Shem Tov said that the pronoun "they" does not refer to the waters, but to the Israelites themselves.**

Sensory experiences are often completely subjective and relative.

I may feel anger and resentment toward the external world, and I often consider the world unjust. Yet because I experience the external world only through my sensory perceptions, the injustices that I perceive may sometimes exist only in my mind, rather than in reality. To the embittered Israelites, even sweet water tasted bitter.

Before we pass harsh judgment on others, we would do well to reflect whether these judgments are indeed warranted in reality, or whether they might perhaps be distortions or projections of our own attitudes. Thinking back on previous experiences may help. How often did we think badly about other people, only to subsequently discover that we were mistaken?

We would be wise to check some of our impressions with others who are more objective, to help us with the validity of our perceptions.

NOTES

_____
_____
_____
_____
_____
_____
_____
_____
_____

... נְקַדֵּשׁ אֶת שִׁמְךָ בָּעוֹלָם *From*

We will sanctify Your name in this world, *our* even as they sanctify it in the heavens *Prayers* above, as it is written by Your prophet, "And one angel calls to another and says, 'Holy, holy, holy is G-d. The fullness of earth is His glory' " *(Kedushah, from the daily Amidah)*.

Nov. 4, 1990
Oct. 24, 1991
Nov. 12, 1992
Oct. 31, 1993
Oct. 21, 1994
Nov. 9, 1995

How can a person sanctify the Divine name?

Angels do so by calling, "Holy, holy, holy". For humans that does not suffice. We must sanctify G-d by demonstrating that His glory fills the entire world.

When a person lives according to the Divine commandments and manifests in his life the Divine attributes of love, mercy, tolerance, justice, forgiveness, and kindness, he thereby brings the glory of G-d into the world.

And Pharaoh awoke, and slept again *(Genesis 41:4-5).* **But of Jacob it is written: And Jacob awoke from his sleep and said, "Verily, the presence of G-d is in this place"** *(Genesis 28:16).*

From the Sages

The spiritual person thinks of G-d the moment he awakens. The hedonist thinks only of self-indulgence, and turns over to sleep again *(Rabbi Meir of Premishlan).*

Sleep, like food and water, is a necessity of life. To the spiritual person, the necessities of life are a means to an end. The goal of life remains uppermost in his mind, and upon awakening he is aware that sleep has restored his energies, enabling him to pursue his spiritual growth. The one who is devoid of spirituality, and who aims only at achieving the maximum in earthly pleasures, will indulge in as much pleasant sleep as he can get.

Cows in the pasture are content with eating and sleeping. Is it any wonder that Pharaoh dreamt of cows? Should human aspiration not be qualitatively different from bovine contentment?

We can awaken from sleep and turn over to sleep again, arising only when the demands of reality force us out of bed. Or we can awaken with the inspiration to arise and get about our mission to fulfill the Divine will.

The choice is ours.

NOTES

_____
_____
_____
_____
_____
_____
_____
_____
_____

Nov. 5, 1990
Oct. 25, 1991
Nov. 13, 1992
Nov. 1, 1993
Oct. 22, 1994
Nov. 10, 1995

From our Prayers

אִמְרֵי הַאֲזִינָה ה' בִּינָה הֲגִיגִי . . .

Hear my words, O G-d, and penetrate my thoughtful meditations. Hearken unto the voice of my cry, my King and my G-d, for it is to You that I strive to pray (*Selichos, Psalms 5:2-3*).

At a weekend retreat for people recovering from alcoholism and addiction, one woman expressed her frustration upon seeing people at *Shabbos* services. "I am so distraught when I see others pray," she said. "I would like to pray too, but I can't seem to do it."

I pointed out to her how mistaken she was. "Let's look at this from what might be G-d's perspective. Those of us who pray regularly often implore G-d for health, happiness, and various needs of life. Perhaps the Divine reaction may be, 'Here they come again, asking for more handouts.'

"But when you are tormented by your inability to pray, you *are* actually praying. You are praying for the ability to pray! And this time the Divine reaction may be, 'Look how My dear child is struggling to find a way to reach Me.'

"Now, tell me," I said, "whose prayer is more genuine, mine or yours?"

From the Sages

You shall be holy persons unto Me (*Exodus 22:30*). The Rabbi of Kotzk said, "Holiness as persons, as normal people, is what G-d demands of us, not holiness as angels."

Throughout the ages there have been individuals or groups who have withdrawn from society to a life of seclusion as celibates and contemplatives.

The Rabbi of Kotzk says that this is not the Divine will. People are to achieve holiness *in* life, and not outside of it.

Everything that a person does can be either sacred or profane. Any act which is performed with the purpose of spiritual growth, of achieving a closeness to G-d, and of fulfilling His will, is sacred. Those acts devoid of such intent are profane.

Holiness can be achieved in the midst of the most turbulent metropolis as well as in a desert retreat.

NOTES

_____
_____
_____
_____
_____
_____
_____
_____
_____
_____

רְאֵה נָא בְעָנְיֵנוּ וְרִיבָה רִיבֵנוּ . . . *From our Prayers*

Look, please, upon our affliction, and fight our battles. Redeem us speedily with a full redemption for the sake of Your name, for You are a mighty Redeemer (*daily Amidah*).

Nov. 6, 1990
Oct. 26, 1991
Nov. 14, 1992
Nov. 2, 1993
Oct. 23, 1994
Nov. 11, 1995

With what right do we ask G-d to fight our battles for us?

If our desire to be relieved of distress is solely for our own comfort, then it is most presumptuous of us to ask G-d to do battle for us. If, however, we dedicate our lives to doing His will, and we find ourselves unable to do so because of various obstacles and impediments, then we may pray for Divine intervention so that we may be able to accomplish that which He wishes us to do.

We thus pray for Divine intervention in order that we may bring greater glory to His name.

From the Sages

Love your neighbor as you do your self (*Leviticus 19:18*). **Rabbi Yaakov Yitzchok of Pshis'cha said that just as with your own person you may value one part of your body more than another — such as your heart more than your hand, or your eye more than your foot — nevertheless you take great caution not to allow any part of yourself to be injured; so it should be with your fellow man. Even the person whom you esteem the least warrants great respect.**

Some people espouse an unrealistic concept of equality. The simple fact is that people are not all equally endowed, and hence there are people whom we may value above others for a variety of reasons.

NOTES

Yet, said the Rabbi of Pshis'cha, such distinctions do not permit us to slight someone whom we consider to be of lesser stature.

Although our hearts and eyes have far greater value than our toes and finger, we are nevertheless very protective of the latter. To love your neighbor as your *self* means to accord the least of men the same respect that you do to the least of your *self*.

CHESHVAN

19

חשון

Nov. 7, 1990
Oct. 27, 1991
Nov. 15, 1992
Nov. 3, 1993
Oct. 24, 1994
Nov. 12, 1995

From our Prayers

מַה נִּתְאוֹנֵן מַה נֹּאמַר
מַה נְּדַבֵּר וּמַה נִּצְטַדָּק . . .

What complaint can we make, what can we say, what can we speak, or how can we justify ourselves? We will search into our ways and examine them and return to You, for Your right hand is extended to receive all those who return** (*morning service for Monday and Thursday*).

True forgiveness is achieved when we recognize our mistakes and when we do an honest moral inventory to seek them out so that we may correct them.

People sometimes try to justify their misdeeds by disavowing their true intentions or by blaming their actions on others. As long as one tries to justify his behavior, he is unable to see it as wrong, and unless we recognize our wrong actions as such, there is no way we can make amends, ask forgiveness, or change our ways.

We may try to rationalize and explain away our behavior, but G-d cannot be deceived. An honest soul-searching brings one closer to G-d.

From the Sages

NOTES

_____
_____
_____
_____
_____
_____
_____
_____
_____

And you shall choose life, so that you may live (*Deuteronomy 30:19*).

The Rabbi of Gur cites this verse as proof that choosing to live is a mitzvah.

A *mitzvah* requires great diligence for proper fulfillment.

How can I choose life? One way is to avoid anything and everything that can in any way curtail life. Proper health habits that are conducive to life are thus a *mitzvah*. Anything we do to maximize life is a *mitzvah*.

Some may think that a *mitzvah* is limited to a ritual performance. Not so. Avoiding smoking is a *mitzvah*. Healthy eating habits are a *mitzvah*. Avoiding alcohol excess or drugs is a *mitzvah*. One can accumulate countless *mitzvos* just by keeping oneself in good health.

From our Prayers נוֹדֶה לְּךָ וּנְסַפֵּר תְּהִלָּתֶךָ . . .

We avow our thanks to You and recount Your praises, for our lives which are committed to Your hand and for our souls which are in Your care, and for Your miracles which are with us each day *(daily Amidah).*

Nov. 8, 1990
Oct. 28, 1991
Nov. 16, 1992
Nov. 4, 1993
Oct. 25, 1994
Nov. 13, 1995

We may think that miracles are only very unusual and extraordinary events wherein the laws of nature are abrogated. Not so. As one person said so aptly, "Coincidences are really miracles where G-d preferred to remain anonymous."

The Talmud states that most often the beneficiary of a miracle does not even recognize that he was saved or what it was that saved him. Divine providence is often cloaked in natural phenomena, and the direct hand of G-d is concealed.

The fact is that G-d looks after us in His own special way, and for this we must always be grateful.

Who is strong? He who subdues his passions *(Ethics of the Fathers 4:1).*

From the Sages

The popular concept is that a powerful person is a ruler or chief, someone who has subordinates under his command.

The fact is, however, that the quest for power is often an effort to overcome an inherent feeling of insecurity or inferiority. The person who feels inadequate may lust for power to compensate for the tormenting sensation of inadequacy. The truly great world leaders throughout history did not pursue power, but rather had it thrust upon them.

The Torah attitude is that strength is mastery over *oneself* rather than over others. It is this type of strength to which we should aspire.

NOTES

_____
_____
_____
_____
_____
_____
_____
_____

Nov. 9, 1990
Oct. 29, 1991
Nov. 17, 1992
Nov. 5, 1993
Oct. 26, 1994
Nov. 14, 1995

From . . .

our
Prayers

שָׁלוֹם עֲלֵיכֶם מַלְאֲכֵי הַשָּׁרֵת מַלְאֲכֵי עֶלְיוֹן

Peace unto you, O ministering angels, angels of the Most High, from the King of Kings, the Holy One, Blessed is He (*Zemiros, festive songs, of the Friday night meal*).

Shabbos should not be thought of merely as a day of rest whereby we recharge our batteries for the work week that is to follow. That would make *Shabbos* subordinate to the weekdays, and would make work a goal rather than a means.

Shabbos is the goal of creation. By abstaining from all weekday activities we have greater opportunity to study, to meditate, to contemplate, and hopefully arrive at the conclusion that we must dedicate our lives to do the will of G-d. We then unite with the heavenly host, who exist to glorify G-d.

On *Shabbos* we welcome the heavenly angels into our home, for *Shabbos* enables us to identify with them.

From the Sages

Other peoples of the world hearken to soothsayers and necromancers. But you, not so has G-d given to you (*Deuteronomy 18:14*).

Rabbi Bunim of Pshis'cha said, "G-d has given you the capacity to resist, and to say 'Not so.' "

It is not an easy task to steer a course for oneself that is at odds with the accepted norm. Yet in matters of morality we must be fiercely independent. Moral right and wrong are not issues to be decided by majority vote.

Although there may be great pressure to conform, and conformity is clearly the path of least resistance, we are not absolved of doing wrong if we fail to follow the dictates of our conscience, based upon the Divinely revealed principles of morality.

We cannot rationalize that we do not have the capacity to resist conformity. Rabbi Bunim assures us that G-d gives us the strength to say, "Not so."

NOTES

_____
_____
_____
_____
_____
_____
_____
_____
_____

From our Prayers

... יָדַעְנוּ כִּי אֵין בָּנוּ מַעֲשִׂים

We know that we have no merits; deal kindly with us for Your name's sake. Even as a father has compassion on his children, so do You have compassion upon us, O G-d *(morning service for Monday and Thursday).*

Nov. 10, 1990
Oct. 30, 1991
Nov. 18, 1992
Nov. 6, 1993
Oct. 27, 1994
Nov. 15, 1995

The Talmud states that even Moses, who certainly had served G-d with absolute devotion, did not ask for rewards for his good deeds, but threw himself on the mercy of G-d.

In this way, the greatest and the most humble are equal. We all pray for Divine mercy rather than reward for what we believe we have earned.

No one should therefore hesitate to pray for his needs. Nor need prayer be reserved for only major requests. It is as appropriate for a child to ask his father for something trivial as it is for something of great importance.

From the Sages

Keep a distance from falsehood (Exodus 23:7).

Rabbi Zusia notes that whereas all other prohibitions are in the form of "do not do thus", only in regard to falsehood does the Torah command us to keep a distance from it.

Truth is the foundation of Torah living. Without truth all else is meaningless. In the kaballah writings, Satan is the embodiment of falsehood.

It is not enough not to lie. We must take great caution to avoid anything that could in any way contribute to falsehood. If I behave in a way that I might later have to deny, then I am contributing to falsehood, because I am setting myself up to lie.

A simple and good guide to proper human behavior is to ask yourself, "Would there ever be a reason why I would have to deny having done what I am about to do?" If the answer is "Yes," don't do it.

NOTES

_____
_____
_____
_____
_____
_____
_____
_____

Nov. 11, 1990
Oct. 31, 1991
Nov. 19, 1992
Nov. 7, 1993
Oct. 28, 1994
Nov. 16, 1995

From our Prayers ... רְפָאֵנוּ ה' וְנֵרָפֵא הוֹשִׁיעֵנוּ וְנִוָּשֵׁעָה

Heal us, O G-d, and we shall be healed. Save us, and we shall be saved, for You are our praise. Bring complete healing to all our afflictions, for You are the great and merciful Healer (*daily Amidah*).

The rabbis state that if the adversary argues before G-d that a person is not deserving of Divine healing, and that impartial justice does not permit granting special favors, G-d silences the adversary by saying, "This person is not praying for his own sake. He is praising Me as the true Healer, and he pleads for healing so that he may sing My praise. Such a prayer cannot be refused."

Sometimes we may be our own adversaries, and may despair of Divine help because we feel undeserving of it. We should then remember that we may always pray for help to bring greater glory to G-d, and such prayers are never turned away.

From the Sages

NOTES

_____
_____
_____
_____
_____
_____
_____
_____
_____
_____
_____

Judge every man favorably (*Ethics of the Fathers 1:6*).

"We all pass judgment on ourselves," said the Baal Shem Tov.

When the prophet chastised David for the Bathsheba incident (*II Samuel 12*), he told him of a wealthy man who stole the only lamb of his poor neighbor. David was outraged and exclaimed that this man was a villain who deserved to be put to death, whereupon the prophet said, "You are that man."

"Be careful," said the Baal Shem Tov, "when you pass judgment on another person. It is really yourself whom you may be judging."

When I show tolerance and consideration towards others, I merit tolerance and consideration for myself.

From our Prayers

אַתָּה עָשִׂיתָ אֶת הַשָּׁמַיִם וְאֶת הָאָרֶץ . . . **You fashioned the heavens and the earth, the sea and all that is therein. Who amongst all Your creations, above or below, can tell You what You must do and what You must achieve** (daily morning service).

Nov. 12, 1990
Nov. 1, 1991
Nov. 20, 1992
Nov. 8, 1993
Oct. 29, 1994
Nov. 17, 1995

Some people think that when we pray to G-d for something and He does not give us what we sought, it is because G-d did not hear our prayer.

This is a misunderstanding of the nature of prayer, and such thinking is indicative of infantile thought. For just as small infants think that they can control their parents with their wishes, so some grownups think that they can control G-d with their prayers. This represents a sharp turnabout, in that we wish G-d to do *our* will rather than we doing *His* will.

G-d hears everyone's prayers. If He denies us what we ask, it is because in His infinite wisdom He knows that, contrary to our thinking, it is not in our best interest.

"Am I not a happy man?" asked the Rabbi of Rimanov. **"I was never in need of anything until I already had it."**

From the Sages

It is easy to have many needs. In fact, we are tempted to have anything which we think we have even a remote chance of acquiring. Relatively few things seem superfluous and totally useless to us.

The Rabbi of Rimanov is telling us that if we have absolute faith and trust in G-d, then we never lack for anything, because we realize that if it were truly to our advantage, then G-d would have provided us with it. If I do not have something, I should understand that it is not to my advantage to have it.

Why, then, should I expend my efforts to attain something which is not good for me?

NOTES
_____
_____
_____
_____
_____
_____
_____
_____
_____

Nov. 13, 1990
Nov. 2, 1991
Nov. 21, 1992
Nov. 9, 1993
Oct. 30, 1994
Nov. 18, 1995

From our Prayers

ה' הוֹשִׁיעָה הַמֶּלֶךְ יַעֲנֵנוּ בְיוֹם קָרְאֵנוּ . . .

O G-d, help us; the King will indeed answer us on the day we call upon Him. For He knows our temptation, He remembers that we are but of earth *(daily morning service)*.

Why is it that some people carry burdens of guilt and do not feel that G-d has forgiven them?

Perhaps it is because they have been unable to forgive themselves, and they project this attitude onto G-d.

But G-d knows of what He made us. He fully understands our emotions and our frailties. If we do err, but then recognize our mistakes and sincerely seek to correct our ways, then He forgives us. We should be accepting of His forgiveness.

Some people think of G-d as stern. The fact is, we are much harsher to ourselves than He is to us.

From the Sages

Neither sourdough nor honey should be brought on the Altar as an offering to G-d *(Leviticus 2:11).*

"Apparently," said the Rabbi of Kotzk, "G-d does not like anything too sour or too sweet."

Maimonides teaches that virtuous traits are characterized by moderation. For example, cowardice and recklessness are both unacceptable extremes, between which lies the virtue of judicious courage. Miserliness and dissipation are extremes, between which lie the virtues of thrift and charity.

Following the proper path in life has been likened to walking a tightrope. If one leans too far to either side, the result is equally disastrous.

Neither gluttons nor ascetics practice moderation, but rather live in extremes. This is not the Divine wish, says the Rabbi of Kotzk. Too sweet and too sour are equally unacceptable.

NOTES

_____
_____
_____
_____
_____
_____
_____
_____
_____

CHESHVAN

26

חשון

Nov. 14, 1990
Nov. 3, 1991
Nov. 22, 1992
Nov. 10, 1993
Oct. 31, 1994
Nov. 19, 1995

... וְאֵרַשְׂתִּיךְ לִי לְעוֹלָם *From our Prayers*

I betroth you unto me eternally. I betroth you unto me with righteousness and justice, with loving-kindness and mercy. I betroth you unto me with faith, and you shall know G-d *(recitation upon putting on tefillin, Hoshea 2:21-22).*

The relationship of G-d and Israel is sometimes depicted as that of a father to a child, or a sovereign to a subject. Here it is depicted as a husband to a wife.

One cannot say that this marriage has not had its problems. Israel has tested G-d's patience countless times, and G-d's management of Israel has often resulted in outcries of anguish and bitterness. The moments of unperturbed conjugal bliss throughout history have been rather brief.

But this marriage has survived the test of time, and has withstood many ordeals. Perhaps the manifestations of righteousness, justice, mercy and loving-kindness have not always been evident to us, but faith has always prevailed. All the difficulties notwithstanding, Israel has never lost faith in G-d, nor G-d in Israel.

Perhaps this daily prayer was meant to alert us to what marriage should be. Too often these days, marriages that do not measure up to the popular fantasy of perfect bliss are terminated.

Where mutual faith prevails, all other problems can be overcome.

"Futility of futilities," said Koheles, "futility of futilities. All is futile!" *(Ecclesiastes 1:2).* *From the Scriptures*

In Ecclesiastes, Koheles dismisses all earthly pursuits as being futile and worthless, pure nothingness.

One of the commentaries points out that although zero has no value, and a thousand zeros are still nothing, they assume an astronomical value when the digit 1 is placed before them.

Similarly, all earthly pursuits are futile and worthless only if they are unassociated with anything of real substance. If we place spirituality, the oneness of G-d, in the fore of our earthly pursuits, they all take on a different character. Instead of being nothing, they add up to an immense value.

"Futility of futilities," but this is only when *all* is futile. Once true substance is introduced, whatever would otherwise have been futile now becomes purposeful and precious.

NOTES
_____
_____
_____
_____
_____
_____
_____
_____
_____

Nov. 15, 1990
Nov. 4, 1991
Nov. 23, 1992
Nov. 11, 1993
Nov. 1, 1994
Nov. 20, 1995

From our Prayers

וּמִי שֶׁמְיַחֲדִים בָּתֵּי כְנֵסִיּוֹת לִתְפִלָּה . . .

Those who dedicate the synagogue for worship, who provide for its upkeep, who provide food for the wayfarer and charity to the poor, and all those who work faithfully for the needs of the community, may G-d reward them, protect them from illness, heal their entire persons, forgive all their transgressions, and bless all their endeavors with success (*Shabbos morning service*).

While reward for performance of *mitzvos* is largely reserved for the eternal world, those who sincerely participate in the betterment of their community and who offer help to the needy may look forward to tangible rewards in their life on earth.

There is nothing so dear to G-d as a person who looks beyond his personal needs and desires, and devotes himself to the welfare of the community and to improving the lot of the less fortunate.

These are *mitzvos* whose "principle" is preserved for reward in heaven, but whose "interest" is given to us on earth.

From the Sages

Moses said to the Israelites, "I stood between you and G-d" (*Deuteronomy 5:5*). **Rabbi Michel of Zlotchow said, "It is the 'I', the ego, that stands as a barrier between man and G-d."**

Humility is the foundation of a close relationship between man and G-d.

A person must indeed have self-esteem, to be aware of his capabilities and know that there is so much that he can and should do. However, along with this self-esteem there must also be self-effacement, meaning that the person should not feel deprived by G-d, or feel that G-d has not dealt fairly with him by not rewarding him adequately for all good deeds.

Self-centeredness and self-righteousness lead to dissatisfaction and resentments against G-d for not giving one everything he feels he has coming to him. It is this kind of egoism that stands in the way of a relationship between man and G-d.

NOTES

_____
_____
_____
_____
_____
_____
_____
_____
_____
_____

. . . יַכִּירוּ וְיֵדְעוּ כָּל יוֹשְׁבֵי תֵבֵל *From our Prayers*

May all the inhabitants of the earth recognize and acknowledge that to You all knees must bend and all tongues swear. They will all accept the yoke of Your sovereignty (*daily service*).

Nov. 16, 1990
Nov. 5, 1991
Nov. 24, 1992
Nov. 12, 1993
Nov. 2, 1994
Nov. 21, 1995

Some people aspire to a state of uniqueness, wherein they hope to be accorded special recognition. Even if this were to come about as a result of their just deserts and accomplishments, it is nevertheless a selfish aspiration.

We pray that all the peoples of the earth will accept the sovereignty of G-d and abide by His commandments. Our aspirations should not be for our own aggrandizement, but rather for the greater glory of G-d. As Isaiah (*11:9*) said, the Messianic era will be characterized by "The land will be as abundant in the knowledge of G-d as the ocean basin is abundant in water."

These words that I have commanded you today shall lie on your heart (*Deuteronomy* 6:6).

From the Sages

Even if the words only lie on the surface of the heart, this too is of value, because at some point there will be a tiny opening into the heart, and they will be absorbed within it (*the Rabbi of Kotzk*).

Some people say that much of what they hear and learn does not effect any change in their lives. They say, "I understand these things intellectually, but they do not reach me emotionally."

We should not be discouraged if we do not immediately feel the impact of what we learn. We may have resistances to change and it may take time for these to be overcome.

Intellectual knowledge can be thought of as water accumulating behind a dam, because even a tiny crack in the wall will allow all the water to eventually flow through. Similarly, even a tiny crevice in our resistance can allow all the accumulated intellectual knowledge to be absorbed emotionally and influence our behavior.

NOTES

Although we must make every effort to refine our character, we must be patient with ourselves if desirable traits do not immediately become part of our personality. Many good things require time to mature, and some processes simply cannot be hurried.

Erev
Rosh Chodesh
[Eve of the
New Month]
Nov. 17, 1990
Nov. 6, 1991
Nov. 25, 1992
Nov. 13, 1993
Nov. 3, 1994
Nov. 22, 1995

From our Prayers

שְׁמַע קוֹלֵנוּ ... חוּס וְרַחֵם עָלֵינוּ ...

Hear our voice, O L-rd our G-d, spare us and have compassion upon us, and accept our prayer in compassion and favor, for You, O G-d, hear prayers and supplications ... Let us not return empty from Your presence, our King** (*daily Amidah*).

If the average person were given the opportunity to personally present a petition to the sovereign of the land, he would feel honored and privileged, even if for whatever reason his particular requests were not granted.

We should never walk away from prayer with a feeling of emptiness. We have been given the unique privilege of communicating directly and personally with the Sovereign of the universe, and we believe that He has heard our prayers.

Even if we are not granted what we have sought, we should appreciate that the very act of prayer is in itself a fulfillment.

From the Scriptures

You shall be sincere with the L-rd your G-d (*Deuteronomy 18:13*).

NOTES

_____
_____
_____
_____
_____
_____
_____
_____
_____

Rabbi Boruch of Medziboz once observed a man affecting piety.

"What do you plan to accomplish with your affectation?" asked Rabbi Boruch. "You certainly cannot deceive G-d, and you cannot consistently deceive others. The only one whom you can consistently deceive is yourself. Now what kind of triumph is it to deceive a fool?"

Sincerity is at the heart of man's relationship to G-d. I must realize that if I am insincere, the only one who will suffer from this deception is I.

But self-deception may be difficult to recognize. Confiding in a trusted friend and accepting constructive criticism from him may help reveal the truth.

שֶׁתְּחַדֵּשׁ עָלֵינוּ אֶת הַחֹדֶשׁ הַזֶּה . . . *From*
לְטוֹבָה וְלִבְרָכָה *our*

M ay it be Your will . . . to inaugurate the *Prayers*
coming month with goodness and
blessings, and give us long life . . . life in
which there is reverence of Heaven and
fear of sin (*blessing for Rosh Chodesh, recited
on the Shabbos preceding Rosh Chodesh*).

Long life is not always a goodness and blessing. People
who look back on years that were whiled away in idleness
or lack of accomplishment are likely to suffer, whether
consciously or unconsciously, the pangs of regret that so
much of their lives was wasted.

As we pray for the gift of long life, we should remember
to live in such a manner that when the present and future
become the past, we will be able to look back on a life of
dignity and achievement, a life that was dedicated to the
avoidance of wrong and devoted to the will of G-d.

G-d can grant us long life. It is in our hands to make long
life a blessing.

**How good are your tents, O Jacob, your dwelling
places, O Israel** (*Numbers 24:5*).

**"Tents," says the Talmud, refers to houses of
worship. These are wonderful when they are
"dwelling places," inhabited by worshipers. However, if they are merely great edifices that are devoid
of worshipers, they are of little value** (*Rabbi Yaakov
Yosef of Polnoah*).

The principal purpose of a synagogue is not to be an
architectural masterpiece to serve as a background for
pictures of tourists, or even as a monument of pride for the
community. For a synagogue to have value, it must be a
dwelling place, inhabited regularly and with great frequency by people who come to pray, to achieve a
closeness to G-d. It must be a house of study, where the
word of G-d is sought and taught with great frequency.

There is a reciprocal relationship between man and G-d.
If we dwell in His house, then He dwells in ours.

The synagogue must be a living place, a place with which
we identify, a place of life.

CHESHVAN

30

חשון

*First Day of
Rosh Chodesh
Kislev*

[*Most years Cheshvan
has only 29 days and
Kislev has only one
day of
Rosh Chodesh.*]

Nov. 7, 1991

Nov. 14, 1993

Nov. 23, 1995

*From
the Sages*

NOTES

————————
————————
————————
————————
————————
————————
————————
————————

KISLEV

1

כסלו

[Second Day of]
Rosh Chodesh
Nov. 18, 1990
Nov. 8, 1991
Nov. 26, 1992
Nov. 15, 1993
Nov. 4, 1994
Nov. 24, 1995

From our Prayers

רָאשֵׁי חֲדָשִׁים לְעַמְּךָ נָתָתָּ,
זְמַן כַּפָּרָה לְכָל תּוֹלְדוֹתָם

You have given Your people beginnings of new months, which are times of forgiveness for all their transgressions *(Mussaf service of Rosh Chodesh).*

Every beginning can be an opportunity to throw off the burdens of the past. The new month, the new year, and even each new day can be utilized as a fresh start.

But opportunities are just that. We can take advantage of them to do a moral inventory of our past and to rid ourselves of all inappropriate character traits. We can make the necessary changes that will allow us to be free of burdensome guilt. Or we can let the opportunities slip by, and plod along as we were, under the oppression and depression that prevents us from maximizing our potential and enjoying life to the fullest.

G-d gives us opportunities. Whether we utilize them or not is our choice.

From the Sages

You have been defiant with G-d *(Deuteronomy 9:24).*

The Rabbi of Rimanov points out that the Scripture does not say "defiant against G-d," but "defiant with G-d." Some people may unfortunately exploit religious practices in actual defiance of G-d.

History is replete with abominations and atrocities that have been committed under the guise of religion.

As repulsive as all crimes are, there is nevertheless a glimmer of hope that the perpetrator of a crime may achieve insight into his errant behavior and mend his ways. Not so when such behavior occurs in the name of G-d, because the pseudo-religious zeal prevents the perpetrator from realizing that he is wrong.

There are indeed situations when helping another person may require "tough love," but then one must be absolutely certain that his action is taken out of love, much as a loving mother subjects her infant to the pain and suffering of immunization.

If you feel that you must take aggressive action for someone's welfare, it is not enough to think twice. Think it over many times, and get some objective validation for your actions. We are too vulnerable to be "defiant *with* G-d."

NOTES

יְהִי רָצוֹן מִלְּפָנֶי אָבִינוּ שֶׁבַּשָּׁמַיִם *From*
לְקַיֵּם בָּנוּ חַכְמֵי יִשְׂרָאֵל . . . *our*

M ay it be the will of our heavenly Father *Prayers*
to perpetuate for us the wise scholars
of Israel, they and their loved ones and
their disciples, wherever they may be
(morning service for Monday and Thursday).

Nov. 19, 1990
Nov. 9, 1991
Nov. 27, 1992
Nov. 16, 1993
Nov. 5, 1994
Nov. 25, 1995

We pray for leadership by the wise and learned, because
responsible leadership is as vital to our well-being as all
other essentials of life.

Some people are unable to accept leadership and to defer
to authority. They set themselves up as the ultimate
authority, not realizing that they are prone to err, whether
as a result of lack of knowledge or self-serving interests
which can greatly distort their judgment.

The very act of prayer constitutes an acknowledgment of
a Higher Power. We should extend this deference to a
Higher Power to include the acceptance of authoritative
leadership, and we should have the humility to follow the
teachings of those who, by virtue of their knowledge,
experience, and character, are capable of guiding us.

You are cleaving unto G-d, and you are all living *From*
this day (Deuteronomy 4:4). *the Sages*

"What is the significance of the words 'this day'?"
asked Rabbi Elimelech of Lizensk. "It is to teach us
that although we may believe that we have lived
properly today, we should not be overconfident that
we will do so tomorrow. Each day has its own
challenges. We must renew our effort to do right
every day."

Humans are creatures of habit, and we tend to think that
the status quo will persist.

Rabbi Elimelech teaches us that this can give rise to a
treacherous false sense of security. Unless we are constantly
on the alert, our biological drives and temptations may gain
the upper hand and determine our behavior.

If we complete a day with what we feel to have been
proper behavior, we must be grateful to G-d for steering us
safely through the day that has past. But we must pray for
His continued guidance for the next day, being ever alert that
the forces that operate to bring about our undoing are never
at rest, and they constantly seek new ways to lead us astray.

Each day is both a new opportunity and a new challenge.

NOTES
_____
_____
_____
_____
_____
_____
_____
_____
_____

Nov. 20, 1990
Nov. 10, 1991
Nov. 28, 1992
Nov. 17, 1993
Nov. 6, 1994
Nov. 26, 1995

From our Prayers

הֲשִׁיבֵנוּ אָבִינוּ לְתוֹרָתֶךָ
וְקָרְבֵנוּ מַלְכֵּנוּ לַעֲבוֹדָתֶךָ . . .

Lead us back, our Father, to Your Torah, and draw us near, our King, to Your service, and cause us to return in complete repentance to Your presence. Blessed are You, G-d, Who takes pleasure in a repentant return *(daily Amidah)*.

As much as it distresses G-d when we deviate from His teachings, so does it greatly please Him when we return to them.

The natural reaction when one recognizes that he has done wrong is remorse, with agonizing guilt for one's behavior. But remorse should not be allowed to linger. Rather, as one determines to correct his ways and to eliminate those character defects that resulted in the transgression, one should be aware that G-d takes pleasure in his repentance and return, and one should feel joy in pleasing G-d.

A great Jewish ethicist said, "If you are not enjoying Jewishness, you are doing it wrong."

From the Sages

The Baal Shem Tov said, "Why do we say: 'G-d of Abraham, G-d of Isaac, and G-d of Jacob,' rather than 'G-d of Abraham, Isaac, and Jacob'? Because for Isaac and Jacob the searching and service of their father and grandfather was not enough. Each sought to extend his search for and service of G-d by his own efforts."

We must indeed begin our service of G-d with the tradition transmitted from the revelation at Sinai, but this is a beginning, and not the end.

Every person, in his own way and by his own diligence, must search for G-d. As we say in our prayers, "*My* G-d and G-d of my forefathers." King David instructed his son Solomon, "*Know* the G-d of your forefathers and serve Him" *(I Chronicles 28:9)*.

Although ultimate knowledge of G-d is beyond human grasp, we are nevertheless obligated to search for Him. Through the study of Torah in its most comprehensive sense, with dedication to the search for truth, and with sincere devotion, we must try to come to a greater awareness of G-d.

NOTES

_____
_____
_____
_____
_____
_____
_____
_____
_____

ה' חֲקַרְתַּנִי וַתֵּדַע . . . אָחוֹר וָקֶדֶם צַרְתָּנִי . . . *From our Prayers*

O G-d, You have searched me and You know me . . . You have confined me between the past and future, and have laid Your hand upon me . . . This knowledge is too high for me, I am not capable of it . . . I praise You for the wondrous way I have come to be, of this my soul is well aware *(Psalms 139:1,5-6,14).*

Nov. 21, 1990
Nov. 11, 1991
Nov. 29, 1992
Nov. 18, 1993
Nov. 7, 1994
Nov. 27, 1995

We can be aware of the mystery of Divinity, but we can never fully resolve it. As we look at our own miraculous formation, we can sense the existence of G-d. The Psalmist states that man's searching mind can try to understand G-d, but can never succeed. Yet there can be a close relationship between man and G-d, for although man's knowledge of G-d is meager, G-d's knowledge of man is complete.

If we find that we cannot relate to G-d as we understand Him, we can certainly relate to Him as He understands us.

The true service of G-d is the achievement of humility with joy. How can one rejoice in feeling humble? By knowing that thereby one is fulfilling the will of G-d. That alone is sufficient reason for joy *(Rabbi Meir of Apt).*

From the Sages

Humility does not mean that I must have a low opinion of myself. I can be fully aware of my G-d-given talents, and I should put them to use in the service of G-d.

Self-esteem consists of an awareness of what I am capable of doing, and this can lead me to constructive action. Vanity is expecting praise for what I have done. It is likely to result in a "holier-than-thou" attitude and in arrogance, especially if I do not receive the recognition I feel is my due. A vain person is actually likely to seek acclaim to compensate for his deep feelings of worthlessness.

If I can be aware of my capabilities and be humble in the knowledge that there is much that I must accomplish with them, I can be strengthened by self-esteem and can rejoice in my striving to fulfill the Divine will.

NOTES

_____
_____
_____
_____
_____
_____
_____
_____
_____

Nov. 22, 1990
Nov. 12, 1991
Nov. 30, 1992
Nov. 19, 1993
Nov. 8, 1994
Nov. 28, 1995

From our Prayers

אָנָה אֵלֵךְ מֵרוּחֶךָ, וְאָנָה מִפָּנֶיךָ אֶבְרָח . . .

Where can I go from Your spirit, or whither shall I flee from Your countenance? If I ascend into heaven, You are there, and if I make my bed in the nethermost depths, You are there ... Search me G-d, and know my heart . . . See if there be any way in me that is to be renounced, and lead me in the way of eternity *(Psalms 139:7-8, 23,24).*

Sometimes a person may be so depressed that he feels himself to be in the very depths of hell. Yet even if one were there, one need not feel abandoned, for there is no place that is devoid of the presence of G-d.

Wherever we are, G-d is always nearby, and from wherever we are we can open our hearts to Him and ask Him to remove any of our defects that stand in the way of our coming close to Him.

There is always hope, and this hope can banish the despair of depression.

From the Sages

The Divine spirit rests upon a person only amidst joy *(Shabbos 30b).*

What are the obstacles to attainment of joy? Ruminating about the past and being anxious about the future are certain to deprive us of joy.

Rabbi Nachman of Breslov says that some people are afraid to enjoy the present because they anticipate that their happiness will soon come to an end. They create their own misery either by worrying about their past or by being anxious that they will not be happy in the future, both periods of which are beyond their control. In this way they forfeit the enjoyment of the present.

Let us learn to rejoice each day, since joy is the essential element of both physical and spiritual well-being. Furthermore, the joy that emanates from performing a *mitzvah* is not only long-lasting in its own right, but also lends permanence to all other joy.

NOTES

_____
_____
_____
_____
_____
_____
_____
_____
_____

אַתָּה חוֹנֵן לְאָדָם דַּעַת . . . *From*
Y**ou favor man with perception, and teach** *our*
man moral insight. O favor us with *Prayers*
perception, insight, and wisdom from You.
Blessed be You G-d, gracious Giver of
perception (*daily Amidah*).

Nov. 23, 1990
Nov. 13, 1991
Dec. 1, 1992
Nov. 20, 1993
Nov. 9, 1994
Nov. 29, 1995

The above prayer is the first supplication of the daily
Amidah, taking precedence even over requests for life and
health. It is also known as *havdalah*, the prayer of
distinction, wherein we pray for the wisdom to distinguish
good from evil and right from wrong.

An existence that is without the capacity to perceive the
real nature of things, the insight to understand how things
relate to one another, and the wisdom to apply what we
have learned, is not the kind of existence a person should
seek. Perception, insight, and wisdom are the first order of
business.

What is insight? It is the awareness that the *From*
external world is but a mirror. Whatever you see *the Sages*
therein is but a reflection of yourself (*Baal Shem Tov*).

The Baal Shem Tov once happened to come upon a
person who was violating the Sabbath. He immediately
began a soul-searching as to how and when he had
transgressed the Sabbath himself, because he was convinced that he would never have noticed in someone else
any defect that was absent in himself.

This teaching can help us improve ourselves as well as be
more considerate of others. When I see faults in others, I
should direct my efforts to see if there are similar traits
within myself that need correction rather than being quick
to criticize others.

Simply in terms of conservation of energy, there is little
that I can do to change others, but much that I can do to
improve myself, if only I can be aware that improvement is
in order.

NOTES

. Nov. 24, 1990
Nov. 14, 1991
Dec. 2, 1992
Nov. 21, 1993
Nov. 10, 1994
Nov. 30, 1995

From our Prayers

אַתָּה חוֹנַנְתָּנוּ לְמַדַּע תּוֹרָתֶךָ . . .

You have favored us with knowledge of Torah ... You have made a distinction between holy and profane, between light and darkness, between Yisrael and other nations. Our Father, our King, let the approaching days begin in peace, removed from all sin and iniquity, and devoted to your worship (Amidah at the close of Shabbos).

This is an extension of the prayer for wisdom (see 6 Kislev), which stresses the importance for the capacity to distinguish.

All the knowledge in the world is useless if it is confused and chaotic. We therefore pray for wisdom to know the difference between things that may seem similar yet are in fact very different. We even admit to sometimes being unable to distinguish between such polar opposites as light and darkness.

The human capacity to rationalize is so great that we may sometimes convince ourselves of the validity of things that are not true. We therefore must pray for Divine guidance to know the truth.

From the Scriptures

Truth sprouts forth from the earth (Psalms 85:12).

The Baal Shem Tov said, "There is a folk saying that truth travels all over the world. What is meant by this is that truth is banished from one place after another, and it therefore must wander all over the world."

Rabbi Mendel of Rimanov once came across a child who was crying because he was playing hide-and-seek, but after he had hidden, none of his playmates tried to find him. Rabbi Mendel said, "How great is the Divine distress! G-d has concealed Himself in His works, but no one looks for Him."

The absolute truth is that G-d created the universe and His presence is evident in every bit of His creation. It is the Divine will and hence our obligation that we discover that truth. Too often we are so absorbed in our personal desires that the search for Divine truth is neglected.

Truth sprouts forth from the very earth, in every leaf and every blade of grass. Too often we fail to see it.

NOTES
_____
_____
_____
_____
_____
_____
_____
_____
_____

בְּיָדְךָ אַפְקִיד רוּחִי פָּדִיתָה אוֹתִי ה' קֵל אֱמֶת *From*

Into Your hands I entrust my soul. You *our*
have redeemed me, O G-d, the G-d of *Prayers*
truth *(prayer upon retiring; Psalms 31:6).*

Nov. 25, 1990
Nov. 15, 1991
Dec. 3, 1992
Nov. 22, 1993
Nov. 11, 1994
Dec. 1, 1995

Trust is an essential component of a wholesome personality. The person who cannot trust another must of necessity be totally self-reliant, but absolute self-reliance results in isolation and personal exhaustion. The person who cannot trust becomes a slave to himself.

Yet our trust in others is often limited because of concern that they may give priority to their own needs and neglect ours. Complete trust can therefore be only in G-d. But this requires a firm faith and the conviction that although we may perceive some experiences in life as bad, they are somehow good in the perspective of absolute truth, a truth which is known only to G-d.

The Psalmist prayed, "May goodness and kindness pursue me all the days of my life" *(Psalms 23:6).* "Why the need for pursuit?" asked the Baal Shem Tov. "Does anyone flee from goodness and kindness, so that they must pursue him?"

"Yes," answered the Baal Shem Tov. "Sometimes a person flees from something which he thinks is harmful, not knowing that it is really to his advantage."

From the Sages

I should learn from experience that many things that I thought to be great evils at the time they occurred, subsequently turned out to have been blessings in disguise. But since we come to such awareness only in retrospect, the Psalmist teaches us to pray, "If I flee from what is really good because I misperceive it as evil, may it pursue me relentlessly."

It is commonplace to pray for protection from our enemies. We should also pray to be protected from ourselves. Sometimes we can be our own greatest adversaries.

NOTES

———————
———————
———————
———————
———————
———————
———————
———————
———————
———————

Nov. 26, 1990
Nov. 16, 1991
Dec. 4, 1992
Nov. 23 ,1993
Nov. 12, 1994
Dec. 2, 1995

From our Prayers

כִּי אַתָּה שׁוֹמֵעַ תְּפִלַּת כָּל פֶּה . . .

For You hear the prayer of every mouth . . . Blessed are You, O G-d, Who hearkens to prayer *(daily Amidah)*.

At the Western Wall in Jerusalem I saw a blind man being led to the wall. He felt the stones with his fingertips, applied a gentle kiss to the sacred stones, and began speaking to G-d. Although he spoke very rapidly, I could catch some of the words. He was relating to G-d various things that had happened to him, and some of his requests.

At one point he stopped abruptly. "Oh, I'm sorry," he said. "I already told You that yesterday."

The sincerity of the man's prayer was electrifying. He had no doubt whatever that what he had said yesterday had been heard.

From the Scriptures

I will not give sleep to my eyes, nor slumber to my eyelids, until I have found a place for G-d, a dwelling place for the Mighty One of Jacob *(Psalms 132:4-5)*.

The above verse was spoken by King David, who aspired to construct a sanctuary for the service of G-d.

"However," said Rabbi Boruch of Medziboz, "this verse is a promise every person should make in every age.

"Man himself must become a sanctuary for the Divine spirit, as it is written in Scripture, 'They shall build for Me a sanctuary, and I shall dwell in *them*' *(Exodus 25:8)*. In *them*, rather than in *it*.

"We should never relax our efforts until we have so refined and cleansed ourselves of all moral impurities, that G-d would have an appropriate dwelling place within each of us. Through development of humility and unfaltering devotion to truth, every person can make himself into a sanctuary."

NOTES

_____
_____
_____
_____
_____
_____
_____
_____
_____

פָּדָה בְשָׁלוֹם נַפְשִׁי מִקְרָב לִי . . . *From our Prayers*

He has delivered my soul in peace from the battles that threatened me, even though those at my side were many indeed *(Prayer at the close of Shabbos, Psalms 55:19).*

Nov. 27, 1990
Nov. 17, 1991
Dec. 5, 1992
Nov. 24, 1993
Nov. 13, 1994
Dec. 3, 1995

We should recognize that our salvation is always from G-d, even when it may appear to us that our success was due to our own efforts or those of other people.

We must always be appreciative of the help we receive from others, but must recognize them as agents through whom G-d carried out His wish. Our ultimate trust should therefore be in G-d rather than in other humans, and our ultimate gratitude toward G-d.

"For thus said the L-rd, 'Cursed is the person who puts his trust in man, and whose strength is but flesh, and who turns his heart away from G-d . . . Blessed is the man who trusts in G-d' " *(Jeremiah 17:5,7).*

Keep your tongue from evil, and your lips from deceitful speech *(Psalms 34:14).* *From the Sages*

The Chafetz Chaim (Rabbi Israel Meir HaCohen) dedicated his life to teaching, preaching and writing about the gravity of gossip, slander, and evil talk.

Once on the train returning from a trip, he met another wayfarer. "Where are you heading?" asked the Chafetz Chaim.

"I am on my way to Radin to see the great *tzaddik*, the Chafetz Chaim," the man said.

The Chafetz Chaim, who was a paragon of humility, asked, "Why do you call him a great *tzaddik*? What is so special about him? He is a person just as any other."

"How dare you speak with such insolence about the great *tzaddik*!" the man said, accompanying his rebuke with a sound slap to the sage's face.

Upon being introduced to the Chafetz Chaim in Radin, the embarrassed man asked for forgiveness for his rudeness.

"There is no need to apologize," said the Chafetz Chaim. "After all, it was my honor you were defending. But this incident taught me something valuable. You must not speak badly of *any* person, even of yourself."

NOTES
_____
_____
_____
_____
_____
_____
_____
_____

Nov. 28, 1990
Nov. 18, 1991
Dec. 6, 1992
Nov. 25, 1993
Nov. 14, 1994
Dec. 4, 1995

*From
our
Prayers*

אֵין כָּמוֹךְ חַנּוּן וְרַחוּם . . .

There is none like You, O G-d, slow to anger and abundant in loving-kindness and truth. Help us in Your great compassion and deliver us from storm and rage *(morning service for Monday and Thursday).*

"Storm" refers to harm from forces external to us, and "rage" refers to the internal fury that we may experience. We should pray for deliverance from the latter as much as from the former. We may not truly realize that our own unbridled anger may be even more destructive to us than hostility from others.

We know that if we exert the necessary effort, we can control the *expression* of anger. But is it also possible to prevent provocative acts from eliciting the *emotion* of anger?

G-d is slow to anger because He is compassionate and abundant in loving-kindness. If we cultivate these traits, and are thereby able to look at another person's behavior in the best possible light, realizing that he may be acting under stresses unknown to us, we may be able to moderate the development of anger, and forestall its becoming rage.

*From the
Scriptures*

And you shall love your neighbor as your self *(Leviticus 19:18).*

Rabbi Elimelech of Lizensk took upon himself voluntary exile to atone for his sins. After wandering from village to village for two years he returned home, and on meeting the first townsperson he inquired as to the well-being of his family.

"Your son, Eliezer, is very ill," the man said.

Rabbi Elimelech hurried home and asked his wife, "What is wrong with Eliezer?"

"Nothing is wrong with Eliezer," she said. "He is well, thank G-d, and is at his lessons."

"But someone told me that Eliezer was sick," Rabbi Elimelech said.

"Oh, he must have confused our Eliezer with another Eliezer who lives down the street who is indeed sick," the wife said.

Rabbi Elimelech was momentarily relieved, but then sharply reprimanded himself. "So, Elimelech, if after two years of exile you feel a difference between your Eliezer and another person's child, then you have accomplished little spiritual growth in your exile." He then turned and left for another year of exile and wandering.

NOTES

_____
_____
_____
_____
_____
_____
_____
_____
_____

ה' שְׂפָתַי תִּפְתָּח וּפִי יַגִּיד תְּהִלָּתֶךָ *From* **our Prayers**

O G-d, open my lips, and let my mouth recite Your praise *(opening of the Amidah; Psalms 51:17).*

If we were truly aware that when we pray we stand in the immediate presence of G-d, we would understand the reason for the above prayer.

When someone is confronted by a sight that is awesome in might and of great majesty, he is literally rendered speechless. On approaching G-d in prayer, even with our limited grasp of His infinite greatness, we too should be rendered speechless. We need to pray in silence for the capacity to voice our prayers.

How can we praise G-d, Whose attributes are completely beyond our imagination? We are so incapable of composing appropriate praises to G-d, that if it were not that He put words in our mouths through the Divine revelations to the composers of our prayers, we would have to remain utterly silent.

Our Sages had to preface their verbal prayer with a silent prayer for the capacity to speak before G-d. The ease with which we pray should make us realize how little we understand of the greatness of G-d.

Nov. 29, 1990
Nov. 19, 1991
Dec. 7, 1992
Nov. 26, 1993
Nov. 15, 1994
Dec. 5, 1995

And you shall serve Him with all your heart, *(Deuteronomy 11:13).* **Service of the heart refers to prayer** *(Taanis 2a).*

From the Sages

One Rosh Hashanah Rabbi Levi Yitzchok of Berdichev delayed the beginning of service.

"There is a young shepherd," he explained, "who was orphaned as a child, and since no one provided for his schooling, he did not learn to read.

"This morning, when he saw everyone going to *shul* he was saddened because he could not join in the services. He turned his tearful eyes to heaven and said, 'Dear G-d, I do not know how to read the prayers to You. All I know is the alphabet, so I will recite the letters to You, and please, G-d, You put them together to make up the prayers.'

"So we must now wait with our prayers," Rabbi Levi Yitzchok said, "because G-d is busy putting together the letters for the young shepherd."

NOTES
_____
_____
_____
_____
_____
_____
_____
_____

Nov. 30, 1990
Nov. 20, 1991
Dec. 8, 1992
Nov. 27, 1993
Nov. 16, 1994
Dec. 6, 1995

*From
our
Prayers*

יְדִיד נֶפֶשׁ אָב הָרַחֲמָן
מְשֹׁךְ עַבְדְּךָ אֶל רְצוֹנֶךְ . . .

Love of my soul, merciful Father, draw Your servant to Your will. Your servant will hasten like a fleet deer to bow to Your glory. Your love will be sweeter to him than honey and all delicacies *(a Shabbos prayer).*

Since there is free will in issues of moral choice, how can we ask of G-d to draw us to His service? Serving G-d is something which man must choose to do.

The answer is that there is an intense attraction between the soul of man and its origin, which is G-d himself. There is an element of G-dliness within each of us. If man would only set aside his own desires which often constitute a barrier between man and G-d, then the natural attraction will prevail.

The pleasantness of physical gratifications is evident to us. We ask of G-d to allow us to perceive the sweetness of being close to Him, so that we may be able to eliminate those temptations that separate us from Him.

Ultimately, it is we ourselves who must choose to do moral right, and all that we ask of G-d is to give us a greater awareness of the delight of being close to Him, to help counteract the more tangible sensations of physical pleasures.

*From
the Sages*

A person must praise G-d when misfortune befalls him as well as when he enjoys good fortune *(Berachos 56b).*

A visitor to the Maggid of Mezeritch asked him, "How can we be expected to praise G-d for the bad things that happen to us?"

The Maggid directed him to Rabbi Zusia, who lived in abject poverty and who suffered constant pain as a result of various maladies.

Rabbi Zusia responded, "There must be some mistake. How could the Rabbi expect me to answer a question like that? I have never had anything bad happen to me."

Absolute trust in the benevolence of G-d, such as Rabbi Zusia had, can make one realize that nothing that is truly bad ever happens. When we suffer, we may be unable to understand how there could possibly be any good in what has befallen us. This is where an unfaltering faith can be our salvation.

NOTES

_____
_____
_____
_____
_____
_____
_____
_____

From our Prayers

לְכָה דוֹדִי לִקְרַאת כַּלָּה פְּנֵי שַׁבָּת נְקַבְּלָה *From*
Come, my Friend, to meet the bride; let
us welcome the Shabbos *(Friday evening
prayer)*.

In the Kabbalah, *Shabbos* is referred to as the bride and
the people of Israel as the bridegroom. The Friend is none
other than G-d himself, who brings the loving couple
together.

Shabbos is not merely a day of rest which enables one to
restore his energies for the following work week. *Shabbos* is
not a means, but rather an end.

For the devoted husband, who works to provide for the
needs of his beloved wife, work is the means, and the
happiness of his wife is the goal.

Shabbos, a day free of work and all diversions, is the day
when we can apply our faculties of thought and contemplation to bring us to a closer relationship with G-d.

How wisely it was said, "Even more than the Jews have
guarded the *Shabbos, Shabbos* has guarded the Jews."

Dec. 1, 1990
Nov. 21, 1991
Dec. 9, 1992
Nov. 28, 1993
Nov. 17, 1994
Dec. 7, 1995

From the Sages

And G-d completed the work of creation on the
seventh day *(Genesis 2:2)*.

Rashi asks, "But the work of creation was com-
pleted on the sixth day?", and answers, "After
everything was created, the world was still lacking
rest and peace. With the institution of Shabbos, there
was rest and peace, and the world was complete."

An old woman, who in her youth had been a servant in
the household of Rabbi Elimelech of Lizensk, used to say,
"During the week there were often cross words exchanged
in the kitchen, because servants are apt to quarrel with each
other.

"But on Friday night, something strange came over us.
We would embrace and say to each other tearfully, "Forgive
me for whatever wrong I may have done you during the
week. Have a joyful *Shabbos."*

The true spirit of *Shabbos* which prevailed in the
household of Rabbi Elimelech brought about the realization
that *Shabbos* is the ultimate goal of creation, since on
Shabbos one can more easily devote himself totally to the
Divine will.

When the will of G-d becomes our primary goal, the petty
differences that separate people from one another disappear, and there can be true peace.

NOTES
_____
_____
_____
_____
_____
_____
_____
_____

Dec. 2, 1990
Nov. 22, 1991
Dec. 10, 1992
Nov. 29, 1993
Nov. 18, 1994
Dec. 8, 1995

From our Prayers

תְּהִי יָדְךָ עַל אִישׁ יְמִינֶךָ . . .

May Your hand rest upon man ... we shall not retreat from You; sustain us and we will call in Your name. Almighty G-d of hosts, cause us to return, shine Your countenance upon us and we shall be saved *(Psalms 80:18-20).*

Man has the option to believe that the world is ruled by G-d, or that it is independent of G-d, functioning according to unguided laws of nature.

G-d acts with man accordingly. If man acknowledges G-d as the Master of the universe, then G-d provides for him. If man assumes that he is subject only to natural forces, then G-d abandons him to the consequences of these forces.

If we do not retreat from G-d, than He turns His attention to us. There can be no greater salvation than being under Divine Providence.

From the Sages

One of the beloved of G-d is a person who does not manifest anger *(Pesachim 113b).*

Rabbi Mordeka of Neschiz longed to acquire a *tzitzis* garment made of wool that was produced in the Holy Land. When the piece of wool was obtained, he gave it to one of his students to fashion into a garment. The overzealous student, in cutting out the hole to fit over the head, folded the material once too many, so that instead of one hole there were two, and the garment was ruined.

The trembling student tearfully approached the master with the ruined cloth. Rabbi Mordeka smiled and said, "Well, a *tzitzis* garment actually does need two holes. One is for an opening for the head, and the other is to test Mordeka whether he will lose his temper."

NOTES

_____
_____
_____
_____
_____
_____
_____
_____
_____

כִּי לִישׁוּעָתְךָ קִוִּינוּ כָּל הַיּוֹם . . . *From*
For it is Your salvation that we aspire *our*
each day and long for Your help. Blessed *Prayers*
are You, G-d, who makes sprout the trunk
of salvation (*daily Amidah*).

Some ask, why must we pray every day, three times
daily, and especially repeat the same prayer over and over
again?

One can also ask, why is there a need to pray at all?
Why doesn't G-d simply give us what we need?

It is important for man to recognize his dependence
upon G-d. Too often man becomes complacent or overconfident and believes that he can completely control his
own life. This is a grave error, which can lead to many
mistakes. We are all dependent on one another, and
together we are all dependent upon G-d.

We sing the praises of G-d, not to remind Him of His
greatness, but to help us be aware of our humbleness and
dependence, for therein lies our salvation.

Dec. 3, 1990
Nov. 23, 1991
Dec. 11, 1992
Nov. 30, 1993
Nov. 19, 1994
Dec. 9, 1995

Everything He made appropriate in its time
(*Ecclesiastes 3:11*).

*From the
Scriptures*

Rabbi Moshe Leib of Sasov asked, "Why did G-d create
man with the capacity to deny His existence? Since
everything was created with a purpose, what good can
there be in the capacity to deny G-d?"

Only half in jest, Rabbi Moshe Leib answered, "If faith
in G-d were absolute, then if you saw someone in need of
help, you might walk away from him thinking, 'No
problem here. G-d will certainly take care of him.'

"This is when denial of G-d can come in handy," said
Rabbi Moshe Leib. "When another person is in need of
help, make believe that there is no one around to help
him, and that if you do not help him, he will certainly fall
or perish.

"Have trust in G-d for yourself. When it comes to
helping others, do not rely on your faith in G-d and His
benevolence to free you from helping others."

NOTES
—————
—————
—————
—————
—————
—————
—————
—————
—————

Dec. 4, 1990
Nov. 24, 1991
Dec. 12, 1992
Dec. 1, 1993
Nov. 20, 1994
Dec. 10, 1995

From our Prayers

סְלַח לָנוּ אָבִינוּ כִּי חָטָאנוּ . . .

Forgive us, our Father, our King, for we have sinned . . . For You are a benign and forgiving G-d (*daily Amidah*).

In the Yom Kippur prayer we refer to G-d as "a Forgiver." One of the Chassidic masters explains that the term "Forgiver" indicates that G-d is a habitual forgiver, doing so many times, over and over again.

This Divine characteristic should not be abused, because if one says "I will do what I please, then repent it," such repentance is worthless. However, if one has sincerely repented, but subsequently slipped and repeated his mistake again, he should not despair of forgiveness. As long as a person's desire not to repeat his mistake is sincere, and as long as he backs up his good intentions with the necessary steps to avoid repeating a mistake, he must trust in G-d's infinite forgiveness, and should feel renewed in being able to continue life free of the burdens of the past.

From the Scriptures

For G-d knows the way of the just, but the ways of the wicked shall perish (*Psalms 1:6*).

The Rabbi of Apt cited the example of two people who were lost in a maze. One kept on blundering hopelessly, unable to find the path out of the maze. The other retraced his steps to the starting point, and each time marked the entrance with a prominent symbol to indicate that this path was one that does not lead to the outside, and that he must therefore try another way. By continuously eliminating the incorrect paths, he eventually found the path which did lead him to the exit.

Perhaps we are not always able to tell which is the right way to go in life, but we should be shrewd enough to enlist the help of others, and to recognize which ways are the ones *not* to follow. We may be unable to avoid new mistakes, but it is certainly possible to avoid repeating old ones.

NOTES

_____
_____
_____
_____
_____
_____
_____
_____
_____

יִתְגַּדַּל וְיִתְקַדַּשׁ שְׁמֵהּ רַבָּא *From*
בְּעָלְמָא דִּי בְרָא כִרְעוּתֵהּ ... *our*

May the name of the Lord be sanctified *Prayers*
and exalted, in the world which He
created according to His will and established His sovereignty (*Kaddish*).

The above prayer is the familiar *Kaddish*, which is
recited at various points during a communal service, and
is assigned to the mourner to recite during the year of
mourning as well as on a *yahrzeit* (annual memorial
service).

The *Kaddish* has no reference whatever to death, or
even to praying for the soul of the departed. Rather, it
refers to acknowledging the will of G-d and giving praise
to His name.

Even in relationship to death, Judaism stresses life and
the obligation upon the living to do the kinds of things
that will proclaim the glory of G-d. The grief over the loss
of loved ones can gradually be alleviated by the serenity of
knowing that G-d's judgment, even when painful, is true
and just.

Dec. 5, 1990
Nov. 25, 1991
Dec. 13, 1992
Dec. 2, 1993
Nov. 21, 1994
Dec. 11, 1995

There is no person that does not have his hour,
and no thing that does not have its place (*Ethics of the*
Fathers 4:3).

From
the Sages

"If everything has its place," asked the Rabbi of
Sadogura, "then every person, too, has his place. Why
then do people sometimes feel so crowded?"

And the Rabbi answered, "People feel crowded when
each feels dissatisfied with his own place and wishes to
occupy the place of another person."

There is an order in the universe, one which would
allow mankind to live in peace. It is only when one is
dissatisfied with whatever he has, and greedily covets that
which is not his, that the world order is upset, and one
feels oppressed and stifled.

We foolishly bring unnecessary distress upon ourselves
when we have insatiable desires. We then replace a sense
of peace with turbulent discomfort.

NOTES
_____
_____
_____
_____
_____
_____
_____

Dec. 6, 1990
Nov. 26, 1991
Dec. 14, 1992
Dec. 3, 1993
Nov. 22, 1994
Dec. 12, 1995

From our Prayers

. . . אֲשֶׁר בִּדְבָרוֹ מַעֲרִיב עֲרָבִים . . .

Blessed are You, O G-d . . . Who makes the evening fall, Who opens passages by His wisdom, and in His understanding alters the seasons and arranges the stars in the heavens according to His will (*daily evening service*).

Creation was not a historical incident following which G-d retreated from the universe which He designed. Rather, G-d continues to sustain the world, and the laws of nature are but expressions of His will.

When things happen with a regularity, we are prone to believe that they are the results of a process that was set in motion and which continues inexorably. Torah teaches that the hand of G-d is present in all natural phenomena no less than in miraculous occurrences.

From the Sages

You are born not of your own free will, and you will die not of your free will, and you will be held accountable before the great Judge, not of your own free will (*Ethics of the Fathers 4:29*).

The Maggid of Dubno responded with a parable to someone who asked, "Why should I be held accountable? I did not ask to exist. I never asked to participate in life. It was forced upon me."

A man had two daughters who could not find husbands. One had a vicious tongue, and the other was terribly homely. An itinerant matchmaker solved the problem by finding a deaf man for the first girl, and a blind one for the second. The two couples lived quite happily.

One day a doctor came through the town, and offered to treat the two men for a specified sum. His treatment was effective, but when he tried to collect his fee, the cured deaf man refused to pay on the grounds that his marriage was ruined because he was tormented by his wife's vile language. The other man said he was now repelled by his wife's ugliness. The dispute was brought to a judge.

The judge ruled that neither of them had to pay, provided they allow the doctor to render them once again deaf and blind. But now they refused to return to their previous conditions. "If so," said the judge, "then you do value your hearing and sight. You must therefore pay the doctor."

The Maggid said, "Perhaps you did not ask to be alive, but if your life were threatened, you would protect it zealously. Then you cannot say it is forced upon you, and you will therefore be held accountable for your deeds."

NOTES

_____
_____
_____
_____
_____
_____
_____
_____

From our Prayers קַוֵּה אֶל ה' חֲזַק וְיַאֲמֵץ לִבֶּךָ וְקַוֵּה אֶל ה'

Hope unto G-d, keep your heart coura-geous, and hope unto G-d (morning service; Psalms 27:14).

This is a rather strange sentence. Why is the phrase, "Hope unto G-d" repeated?

We sometimes pray for something, but we do not get what we prayed for. We may become disappointed or discouraged. "G-d is not listening to me. He is not paying attention to my needs. Perhaps I am not deserving of G-d's attention." Thoughts such as these are depressing, and may cause us to lose faith in prayer.

It is when our prayers appear to be unanswered that we need to strengthen our faith and to trust that G-d will provide for us that which is truly to our advantage. When our hopes are unfulfilled, we may think that we had better take things into our own hands. It is then that we must reinforce our resolve to hope unto G-d.

Dec. 7, 1990
Nov. 27, 1991
Dec. 15, 1992
Dec. 4, 1993
Nov. 23, 1994
Dec. 13, 1995

From the Sages

A person's feet are his guarantors. They take him wherever he is meant to be (Succah 53a).

Wherever you are at any given time, that is where you are supposed to be.

Of course, since we have freedom of moral choice, we can put ourselves in places we should not be, and this is not what the Talmud refers to.

However, there are many times when "things happen" that deter us from our plans. Circumstances that are beyond our control interfere with our plans. A flat tire or a broken radiator hose delay our travel. Inclement weather or equipment trouble cause cancellation of a flight. A sudden illness prevents our making a trip. How frustrated we get! How angry we become that our painstaking plans have gone awry.

At times like this we should have the serenity that although we may have no idea why we should not be where we wanted to be, it is nevertheless to our advantage that we are where we are. Years of history and experience have proven the Talmud to be correct. We must reinforce our trust in G-d, and rather than be angry and frustrated, we should be of good cheer in the realization that we are where we are supposed to be.

NOTES

_____
_____
_____
_____
_____
_____
_____
_____

Dec. 8, 1990
Nov. 28, 1991
Dec. 16, 1992
Dec. 5, 1993
Nov. 24, 1994
Dec. 14, 1995

From our Prayers

יִשְׂמְחוּ בְמַלְכוּתְךָ שׁוֹמְרֵי שַׁבָּת
וְקוֹרְאֵי עֹנֶג . . .

They shall rejoice in Your dominion, those who keep the Shabbos and delight in it. The people that sanctify the Shabbos, they shall all be satiated and take pleasure in Your bounty (*Shabbos morning service*).

Many people become so absorbed in their work, that they never have the opportunity to truly enjoy the fruits of their labor.

Many people continue to postpone the time for enjoyment, and too often this pattern of absorption in work and postponing enjoyment is brought to an abrupt halt only by a physical disability which interdicts work. However, this also severely restricts enjoyment, and brings on worry about one's health.

Shabbos compels a person to interrupt the hectic pace of the work week, and to enjoy what one has achieved. In addition, the compulsory restriction of activities is conducive to meditation, and facilitates a closer relationship with G-d.

From the Scriptures

Cast your burden upon G-d, and He will provide for you (*Psalms 55:23*).

Whereas there are many things which require our concern and planning, there is also much worrying that we do that is unnecessary. A woman once told the following story.

"One night, I was worrying about how my son would adjust to college. What if he did not do well in his courses? Would he despair of school and quit? What if he fell in with the wrong crowd and started using drugs? How would he adjust to being away from home?

"Then I heard him crying, so I went in and changed his diaper."

People who have a tendency to worry excessively should learn to place some of the burden of running the world onto G-d.

If we insist on controlling everything ourselves, we are apt to find ourselves indulging in unnecessary and premature worry that is as inappropriate as the woman's concern about how her infant son will adjust to college.

NOTES

_____
_____
_____
_____
_____
_____
_____
_____
_____

בּוֹרֵא רְפוּאוֹת נוֹרָא תְהִלוֹת . . . *From*
אֲדוֹן הַנִּפְלָאוֹת *our*

G-d creates remedies, He is awesome in *Prayers*
praise, and He is the Lord of wonders
(*daily morning service*).

KISLEV

22

כסלו

Dec. 9, 1990
Nov. 29, 1991
Dec. 17, 1992
Dec. 6, 1993
Nov. 25, 1994
Dec. 15, 1995

Why is "creation of remedies" listed first and given priority over the performance of miracles? "Because," said Rabbi Boruch of Medziboz, "G-d does not wish people to recognize His hand in only supernatural events. Nature does not operate on its own. The hand of G-d is as operative in natural events as in the supernatural."

Remedies are assumed to be purely natural phenomena, as when a particular medication cures a disease. But we must learn to appreciate the hand of G-d in nature as well as in miracles.

In prayer, we should be grateful to G-d for the many wonders He does for us, although they appear to be but "natural" phenomena.

Rabbi Yochanan ben Zakkai said, "If you have learned much Torah, do not take pride and become vain, for that is what you were created to do" (*Ethics of the Fathers 2:9*).

From the Sages

Having a healthy self-esteem means that we should be aware of our capabilities and not underestimate ourselves. However, a person should realize that his talents are G-d-given gifts, and should not consider himself superior to other people because of his achievements.

Our great Sages were well aware of their G-d-given abilities, but this made them feel humble rather than vain. They always felt that they had not achieved sufficiently, and had not fully utilized their great potential. This stimulated them to even greater achievement, yet they always remained humble, never resting on their laurels.

Having self-esteem is not at all the same as being vain. Self-esteem is a positive quality, which motivates one to action. Vanity is thinking that one has done so much that he deserves to be honored by everyone. Vanity is an abomination, which separates man from G-d as well as from fellow human beings.

NOTES

Dec. 10, 1990
Nov. 30, 1991
Dec. 18, 1992
Dec. 7, 1993
Nov. 26, 1994
Dec. 16, 1995

From our Prayers

. . . אֲפָפוּנִי חֶבְלֵי מָוֶת
. . . אָנָּה ה' מַלְּטָה נַפְשִׁי

When pains of death oppress me . . . when I face trouble and sorrow, then I call upon G-d, "O L-rd, deliver my soul." G-d is ready to grant grace and is just and merciful. G-d protects the simple. I had been brought low, and He grants me new life *(Hallel, Psalms 116:3-6)*.

Psalm 116 is a prayer of serenity.

In this beautiful psalm, we affirm that G-d hears our prayers, and that He "protects the simple." In other words, G-d looks after us when we lack the capacity to know what is truly in our best interest.

In this prayer, we express the highest degree of faith and trust that even when we are in anguish, G-d is with us.

Why, then, does G-d not intercede to prevent us from suffering?

The principle of faith is that G-d is just and compassionate. We are similar to the infant whose mother restrains him while the doctor administers the immunization. The tiny infant cannot possibly understand why his loving mother allows the doctor to hurt him. But we know that the mother is acting with true compassion.

So must we have faith in the compassion of G-d, which is beyond our understanding. Like the infant, we resent the pain. But unlike the infant, we can achieve serenity through the faith that although things may be bitter, they are not evil.

From the Sages

Rabbi Moshe Leib of Sasov said, "A human being who has not a single hour for his own every day is not much of a human being."

NOTES

These are very sharp words. According to Rabbi Moshe Leib, one can have an I.Q. in the genius range, operate sophisticated, high-technology equipment, solve intricate mathematical problems, and even perform complicated surgical procedures. Yet, if he does not have time *daily* to think about the meaning of life, to meditate about his ultimate goals and how he plans to attain them, he lacks something of humanity.

It is rather easy to lose ourselves in our work. Unfortunately, that may actually happen. We may be so engrossed in doing things that we lose our "selfs." We must be able to extricate ourselves from our activities, and devote some time to finding our "selfs."

לַעֲסוֹק בְּדִבְרֵי תוֹרָה . . . *From our Prayers*

Blessed are You, L-rd our G-d, King of the Universe, who has sanctified us with His commandments, and instructed us to engage in the words of Torah (*morning prayer*).

It is noteworthy that the prayer does not refer to the "study" of Torah, but rather to "engage" in the words of Torah.

Study of Torah is the greatest of all *mitzvos*, but only because it leads to proper behavior and worthy deeds. A pure, theoretical knowledge of Torah — regardless of how vast and profound it may be — which is not translated into action, is of little value.

To "engage" in Torah means to live by the Torah. We must relate to people according to Torah principles, transact business according to Torah principles, and conduct every phase of our lives according to Torah principles.

Erev Chanukah
[Eve of Chanukah] —
Dec. 11, 1990
Dec. 1, 1991
Dec. 19, 1992
Dec. 8, 1993
Nov. 27, 1994
Dec. 17, 1995
[the first candle is lit tonight.]

You shall have complete and honest weights, complete and honest measures (*Deuteronomy 25:15*).

A rabbi once observed an innkeeper, who had just put on his *talis* for the morning service, respond to a customer who had just entered to purchase a quart of beer. The rabbi was a bit distressed that the innkeeper would engage in business while wearing his *talis*.

After the innkeeper poured the beer, the customer began to haggle, whereupon the innkeeper returned the beer to the barrel, and continued with his prayers.

He later explained to the rabbi, "When the customer ordered the beer, I had the opportunity to fulfill the *mitzvah* of using honest measures. I felt it appropriate to fulfill the *mitzvah* while wearing the *talis*. But when he began to haggle, that meant I would have to engage in commerce with him, and I was not about to engage in commerce while wearing my *talis*."

Transacting honestly is performing a *mitzvah*. As in the prayer above, we can "engage" every facet of our lives in Torah.

From the Scriptures

NOTES

_____
_____
_____
_____
_____
_____
_____
_____
_____

Chanukah
Dec. 12, 1990
Dec. 2, 1991
Dec. 20, 1992
Dec. 9, 1993
Nov. 28, 1994
Dec. 18, 1995
[The second candle is lit tonight.]

From our Prayers

לְהַדְלִיק נֵר שֶׁל חֲנֻכָּה . . .

Blessed are You, L-rd our G-d, King of the Universe, who has sanctified us with His commandments and instructed us to kindle the lights of Chanukah (*Blessing for the Chanukah candles*).

Two great events occurred on Chanukah. The first was a military triumph of the Maccabees, a small group of warriors, over the mighty Syrian-Greek army. The second was the miracle of the oil, when one vial of oil burned for eight days.

The primary focus of the Chanukah celebration is not the military victory. We do not observe Chanukah with parades, speakers, and fireworks. The emphasis is on the *menorah*, the restoration of the Temple service, and the freedom to practice the faith of our fathers.

The military victory was but a means to the freedom to practice our faith, and that was its only true importance. The message of Chanukah is the *menorah*, and not the military conquest.

From the Sages

Upon entering the Sanctuary, the Maccabees found only one vial of oil that had not been defiled by the pagans. Although enough for only one day, this oil miraculously burned for eight days (*Shabbos 21b*).

There was certainly great disappointment when the Maccabees discovered that there was enough oil for only one day. No doubt there were those who pointed out that under such circumstances, the use of defiled oil in the *menorah* was permissible.

The Maccabees insisted on using the pure oil for the one day and not being concerned about what they would use the following day. They believed that they must do what is most proper today, and leave the future to G-d. This attitude merited a Divine miracle.

The Maccabees were true teachers of the principle, "Live one day at a time."

NOTES

_____
_____
_____
_____
_____
_____
_____
_____
_____

לְהַדְלִיק נֵר שֶׁל חֲנֻכָּה . . . *From*

Blessed are You, O G-d, King of the *our*
Universe, who has sanctified us with *Prayers*
His commandments and instructed us to
kindle the lights of Chanukah (*Blessing for
the Chanukah candles*).

Chanukah
Dec. 13, 1990
Dec. 3, 1991
Dec. 21, 1992
Dec. 10, 1993
Nov. 29, 1994
Dec. 19, 1995
*[The third candle
is lit tonight.]*

How can we say that G-d commanded us to light the Chanukah candles? All the Divine commandments of the Torah were given at Sinai, whereas Chanukah did not occur until many centuries later.

The Talmud explains that the Torah commands us to heed the teachings and instructions of the Torah authorities throughout the ages. "You shall not deviate from what they tell you" (*Deuteronomy 17:11*). Thus, since by following the Rabbinic instructions we are obeying the Divine commandment, and inasmuch as the Rabbis decreed that we are to observe Chanukah, we may refer to the latter as fulfilling the Divine wish.

This also indicates that we are not at liberty to make our own determinations of what is the Divine will, but we are to be guided by the Torah and by the Torah authorities.

Hillel says: On the first day of Chanukah, one candle shall be lit. Each subsequent night one candle is added, so that on the eighth night there are eight lights (*Shabbos 21b*).

*From
the Sages*

Why not light all eight candles every night?
Hillel teaches us two things. First, we must always seek to increase our enlightenment and not be stagnant. We should never be satisfied with whatever spiritual growth we have achieved, but should constantly seek to further our growth.

Secondly, it is a mistake to grasp too much too fast. Spiritual growth should be gradual, and we should adapt ourselves to each new level and integrate what we have achieved before going on to the next step. Overreaching can cause us to be top heavy, and our spirituality may be tenuous. Gradual growth provides us with a more firm foundation.

Eight lights the first night would be too much and too soon, and each night thereafter would show no increase in light.

NOTES
_____
_____
_____
_____
_____
_____
_____
_____

Chanukah
Dec. 14, 1990
Dec. 4, 1991
Dec. 22, 1992
Dec. 11, 1993
Nov. 30, 1994
Dec. 20, 1995
*[The fourth candle
is lit tonight.]*

*From
our
Prayers*

. . . שֶׁעָשָׂה נִסִּים לַאֲבוֹתֵינוּ
בַּיָּמִים הָהֵם בַּזְּמַן הַזֶּה

Blessed are You, L-rd our G-d, King of the Universe, who performed miracles for our forefathers in those days, at this season (*Blessing for the Chanukah candles*).

The literal translation of the last words of the above prayer is "in those days in this time." The commentaries tell us that "in *this* time" refers to our own time.

We tend to think that miracles occurred only in ancient times. Not so, say the Rabbis. We are frequent beneficiaries of Divine intervention on our behalf, but the miracles are disguised as natural phenomena.

Even if a person feels himself to be beyond all help, and can see no way out of a dilemma, he should never despair. Divine help is never to be abandoned, and we should pray for it.

*From
the Sages*

NOTES

_____
_____
_____
_____
_____
_____
_____
_____
_____
_____
_____

The mitzvah of Chanukah is to display the menorah prominently where it can be seen by all passersby, in order to publicize the great miracle (*Code of Law, Orach Chaim 671*).

The message of Chanukah is to be shared with everyone.

Chanukah teaches us that we should not yield our true faith even when confronted by overwhelming forces. The revolt of the Maccabees was against the tyranny of religious oppression. The ruling Syrian-Greeks did not seek to exterminate the Jewish people, rather to compel them to reject Jewishness and embrace Hellenism.

Those who suggest assimilation as a means for survival are in error. The Maccabees taught us that physical survival without spiritual survival is not worth having.

... וּלְךָ עָשִׂיתָ שֵׁם גָּדוֹל וְקָדוֹשׁ בְּעוֹלָמֶךְ *From*

For Yourself You made a great and holy *our*
name in Your world, and for Your *Prayers*
people You worked a great victory and
liberation *(Chanukah prayer).*

If we bear in mind that our goal and purpose is to do
the Divine will, then even our own salvation and survival
becomes secondary.

In expressing our gratitude for the miracles of
Chanukah, we therefore give first mention and priority to
the greater glory of G-d that was wrought by these
miracles, and only then for our own triumph.

This is a theme that should pervade the lives of those
who strive to be truly spiritual, to place the Divine will
above one's own, and the glory of G-d above one's
personal honor.

Chanukah
Dec. 15, 1990
Dec. 5, 1991
Dec. 23, 1992
Dec. 12, 1993
Dec. 1, 1994
Dec. 21, 1995
*[The fifth candle
is lit tonight.]*

**From all those who have taught me, I have learned
understanding** *(Psalms 119:99).*

One of the Chassidic masters used to say that one can
learn something from anyone or anything.

On Chanukah, when it was customary in some places
to play checkers as well as *dreidel*, the Rabbi remarked to
some checker players, "What have you learned from this
game?"

When they shrugged their shoulders, the Rabbi said,
"This game can teach you some rules of living: (1) You
may only move forward, never backward; (2) you can
only move forward one step at a time, and you may not
outdistance yourself; and (3) sometimes it is expedient to
give up something in order to gain more (i.e., surrender
one checker to set up a double jump)."

The rules of checkers can also be guidelines for
spiritual growth.

*From the
Scriptures*

NOTES

_____
_____
_____
_____
_____
_____
_____
_____
_____

Chanukah —
Erev Rosh
Chodesh
Dec. 16, 1990
Dec. 6, 1991
Dec. 24, 1992
Dec. 13, 1993
Dec. 2, 1994
Dec. 22, 1995
*[The sixth candle
is lit tonight.]*

*From
our
Prayers*

וְקָבְעוּ שְׁמוֹנַת יְמֵי חֲנֻכָּה אֵלּוּ
לְהוֹדוֹת וּלְהַלֵּל לְשִׁמְךָ הַגָּדוֹל

The Sages established these eight days of Chanukah to give gratitude and praise to Your great name (*Chanukah prayer in the Amidah*).

Whereas Purim is celebrated by feasting, Chanukah is observed by additional prayers and songs of praise to G-d.

The evil decree of Haman was to destroy the Jews physically, hence we celebrate Purim in a physical manner by feasting. The miracle of Chanukah was a spiritual salvation, because the decree for Jews to embrace paganism and Hellenism was one which threatened their souls rather than their bodies. Hence Chanukah is observed in a spiritual rather than physical modality.

*From
the Sages*

The menorah should be placed on the left side of the doorway. Since the mezuzah is on the right side, the person will be surrounded by mitzvos (*Shabbos 22a*).

When earthly pursuits and physical gratifications threaten one's spirituality, it is essential to surround oneself on all sides with *mitzvos*.

Our ethicists have referred to the *yeitzer hara,* or the evil inclination, as an enemy whose aim is to destroy the humanity or the spirituality of man. In doing battle with an enemy, we must protect all flanks, because any position that is left unguarded will be vulnerable to attack. It is immaterial to the enemy at which point he gains his access.

We can therefore not single out any part of our lives to be spiritual, but must rather sanctify every facet of our lives. We can do this by making certain that everything we do should be in the interest of fulfilling the Divine will. It is necessary to be totally immersed in spirituality if one wishes to have any spirituality at all.

NOTES

_____
_____
_____
_____
_____
_____
_____
_____

וְכָל שְׁמוֹנַת יְמֵי חֲנֻכָּה *From*
הַנֵּרוֹת הַלָּלוּ קֹדֶשׁ הֵם . . . *our*

A**ll these eight days of Chanukah, these** *Prayers*
lights shall be holy. We -shall not use
these lights for our own needs. They are
only to be observed, so that we are
reminded to praise You (*prayer following*
lighting of the candles).

KISLEV

כסלו

Chanukah —
First Day of Rosh
Chodesh Teves
[Some years Kislev
has only 29 days and
Teves has only one
day of Rosh Chodesh.
During those years
the 7th and 8th
candles are lit on
the nights following
1 and 2 Teves,
and the last day of
Chanukah is 3 Teves.]

Dec. 17, 1990
Dec. 7, 1991
Dec. 14, 1993
Dec. 3, 1994
Dec. 23, 1995
[The seventh candle
is lit tonight.]

Too often throughout history, man has exploited religion to suit his own needs. Territorial conquests have been made in the name of G-d. People have been oppressed in the name of G-d. This is religiosity rather than religion, and is antithetic to spirituality.

Paganism was a system whereby man created his own gods, and formulated rules that would please him. Pagan religion was religion in the service of man. The Maccabeean rejection of paganism was based on the principle that man is to serve G-d rather than the reverse.

The Chanukah candles, which symbolize the triumph of spirituality, are therefore not to be exploited for one's own needs. Their light is not to be used, but only observed. They are to remind us that Judaism is not to be exploited for personal gratification.

Chanukah candles which are twenty or more *From*
cubits above the ground are not valid, because they *the Sages*
are too high to be visible (*Shabbos 22a*).

NOTES

Some people think that spiritual principles are reserved for only those very lofty minds that can grasp very profound philosophies or for people who seclude themselves from others and live contemplative lives, but that everyday folk are unable to be truly spiritual.

The message of Chanukah is that spirituality is for everyone and is easily within every person's reach. In fact, if the Chanukah lights, which represent spirituality, are placed so high that they are out of reach, they have no validity whatever.

There is nothing terribly complex about spirituality. Keep it simple, and you will find it well within your grasp.

*Chanukah —
[Second Day of]
Rosh Chodesh
Teves*
Dec. 18, 1990
Dec. 8, 1991
Dec. 25, 1992
Dec. 15, 1993
Dec. 4, 1994
Dec. 24, 1995
*[The eighth (in some
years the seventh)
candle is lit tonight.]*

*From
our
Prayers*

מָעוֹז צוּר יְשׁוּעָתִי לְךָ נָאֶה לְשַׁבֵּחַ . . .

Rock of my salvation, praise to You is proper. **You will establish the house of my prayer, and there we shall offer thanksgiving** (*prayer following the lighting of the menorah*).

Although we are always grateful to G-d, we should be aware that our gratitude is incomplete, simply because we do not fully appreciate Divine benevolence.

As long as Jews are in exile, subject to the stresses and oppressions of other nations and cultures, we cannot achieve a full measure of gratitude, even with faith in Divine benevolence. We are much like a patient who undergoes a painful treatment. Although he knows it is to his own advantage, the pain nevertheless detracts from complete gratitude toward the physician.

We say to G-d that we are as thankful now as circumstances permit. When the Redemption occurs and we will be truly free and sovereign, our thanksgiving will be without bounds.

*From the
Scriptures*

Every day I will extol You and will praise Your name into the everlasting future (*Psalms 145:2*).

A renowned *tzaddik* stayed at an inn, and was treated very cordially by the innkeeper, who was not aware of the *tzaddik's* identity. When a traveler informed the innkeeper who his guest was, the innkeeper apologized to the *tzaddik* for not having accorded him his due respect.

"But you treated me very nicely," said the *tzaddik*. "Why do you apologize?"

"Had I only known who you were," the innkeeper said, "I would have treated you with even greater respect."

The *tzaddik* began to weep. "If only I had understood the greatness of G-d yesterday as I do today, how much more intensely would I have served Him yesterday."

Each day should bring us new spiritual growth, and each day we should therefore realize how much more we must do with our lives.

NOTES
_____
_____
_____
_____
_____
_____
_____
_____
_____

בִּזְכוּת מִצְוַת הַדְלָקַת נֵר חֲנוּכָּה . . . *From*

By merit of the mitzvah of the Chanukah *our* lights, may there be fulfillment of the *Prayers* promise, "My word shall not depart from your mouth, nor from the mouths of your children and children's children, from now unto all eternity" (*prayer preceding the lighting of the menorah*).

We pray that our children and descendants be spiritual people, loving and living by the word of G-d.

Values are transmitted not by teaching or preaching, but by example. Children are apt to esteem that which they see their parents hold dear. When parents are willing to sacrifice for the principles they espouse, the children see this as genuine, and are likely to accept these values in their own lives.

Lighting the Chanukah *menorah* should not be a mere ritual, but a dedication to the ideals of the Maccabees, self-sacrifice for one's faith, in the realization that a life devoid of spirituality is not worth living.

Chanukah
Dec. 19, 1990
Dec. 9, 1991
Dec. 26, 1992
Dec. 16, 1993
Dec. 5, 1994
Dec. 25, 1995
[In some years the eighth candle is lit tonight.]

This is my G-d and I shall beautify Him (*Exodus 15:2*). **How does one beautify G-d? By beautifying His mitzvos** (*Shabbos 133b*).

From the Sages

It has long been a practice among Jews to show their love for and esteem of *mitzvos* by embellishing them with precious metals, such as silver or gold *Kiddush* cups, *mezuzah* containers, Torah ornaments, candelabras, and *menoros*.

Such was not the practice of the *tzaddik* of Sanz. He believed that providing for the poor was far more important than owning expensive *mitzvah* objects.

When his followers bought him a silver Chanukah *menorah*, the *tzaddik* of Sanz promptly pawned it and divided the money among the poor.

"How can I light a silver *menorah* knowing that there are people who are hungry? As for adorning *mitzvos*, there is no finer ornament than *tzedakah* (charity)."

NOTES
_____
_____
_____
_____
_____
_____
_____
_____

[Last day of
Chanukah
in some years.]

Dec. 20, 1990
Dec. 10, 1991
Dec. 27, 1992
Dec. 17, 1993
Dec. 6, 1994
Dec. 26, 1995

*From
our
Prayers*

וּתְהֵא חֲשׁוּבָה מִצְוַת צִיצַת
לִפְנֵי הַקָּדוֹשׁ בָּרוּךְ הוּא . . .

May my performance of the mitzvah of tzitzis be accepted before the Holy One, Blessed is He, as though I had fulfilled it with all its details and ramifications *(prayer before putting on the talis).*

Sometimes people may neglect to perform a *mitzvah* because they do not understand its meaning.

The will of G-d is beyond the grasp of the human intellect. By our unaided efforts we cannot possibly understand the mind of G-d, or why He wills anything. Whatever understanding we do have of a *mitzvah* is a gift from G-d, an act of grace. We can merit such Divine enlightenment if we fulfill the Divine will as expressed in the teachings of the Torah.

Our forefathers at Sinai exclaimed, "We will do and we will understand" *(Exodus 24:7)*. Observance of the *mitzvos* precedes our understanding them.

*From the
Scriptures*

The conclusion after all has been heard is that you must have fear of G-d and observe His commandments, for that is all that man is *(Ecclesiastes 12:13).*

The Talmud interprets this verse to mean that the entire universe was created solely for the person who fulfills the Divine will *(Shabbos 30b)*.

It might appear presumptuous to state that the entire universe, with galaxies that are billions of light years in dimension, and stars that are beyond calculation, were all created for the purpose of a tiny human being, whose physical presence in the vast universe is even less than negligible. But that is precisely what Judaism teaches.

Once one accepts the existence of an infinite G-d, all dimensions become meaningless. In relation to infinity, there is no difference between a millimicron and a billion light years. Both are equally significant or insignificant.

After much contemplation the wise Solomon concludes that the being of ultimate significance in the entire universe is man. We must appreciate our significance, and live up to our responsibilities.

NOTES

_____
_____
_____
_____
_____
_____
_____
_____
_____

וְהָאֵר עֵינֵינוּ בְּתוֹרָתֶךָ וְדַבֵּק לִבֵּנוּ בְּמִצְוֹתֶיךָ *From* **E**nlighten our eyes with Your Torah, and *our* cause our hearts to cleave to Your *Prayers* commandments (*daily morning service*).

Dec. 21, 1990
Dec. 11, 1991
Dec. 28, 1992
Dec. 18, 1993
Dec. 7, 1994
Dec. 27, 1995

The greatest obstacle to living the ideal spiritual life is the inability to perceive truth. When a person's perceptions are distorted, his reasoning will lead him to erroneous conclusions, even if he has the keenest of intellects and a brilliant analytical mind.

"A bribe will blind the eyes of the wise" (*Deuteronomy 16:19*). When we are influenced by personal desires of any kind, we are essentially being "bribed". We are likely to make judgments that will result in our achieving the objects of our desires, rather than absolute truth.

We therefore pray to be enlightened so that our perceptions are valid, for then our reasoning can lead us to make the right choices in life.

The heart of this nation is fattened, its ears are hard of hearing, and its eyes are pasted; for if it sees with its eyes and hears with its ears and understands with its heart, it will repent and be healed (*Isaiah 6:10*).

From the Scriptures

If we do not see, hear, or understand the truth, it is because such perception and understanding would necessitate changes in our behavior, and we tend to resist change.

Habit is a powerful force. If any change in our usual way of doing things is likely to generate discomfort, we are likely to preserve the *status quo* to avoid the discomfort involved in change.

If we were to be aware that what we are doing is wrong, we would be compelled to change. It is therefore the strategy of the *yeitzer hora*, the force that deters us from righteous living, to distort our senses so that we do not perceive correctly.

A person should be aware of the hazards of misperception. Trusted friends and teachers, who are not biased by our particular desires and temptations, may help us correct our misperceptions.

NOTES
_____
_____
_____
_____
_____
_____
_____
_____

Dec. 22, 1990
Dec. 12, 1991
Dec. 29, 1992
Dec. 19, 1993
Dec. 8, 1994
Dec. 28, 1995

From our Prayers

... שׁוֹמֵעַ קוֹל שַׁוְעַת עֲתִירָה ...

May it be Your will, He who hearkens to the prayers of His people, that You prepare our hearts and thoughts to pray to You, and facilitate our prayers in our mouths** (*prayer before the morning service*).

What an interesting concept, a prayer before a prayer!

Prayer essentially consists of our asking G-d to provide for all our needs. But we must recognize that one of our vital needs is the ability to pray, because without prayer we have no way of directly relating to G-d.

Since prayer is so vital a human need, it is only logical that just as we pray for our other needs — health, sustenance, *nachas* — we should also pray for the ability to pray. This underscores for us that relating to G-d is at least on equal par with all other necessities of life.

From the Scriptures

Life and death I have placed before You, the blessing and the curse. And You shall choose life (*Deuteronomy 30:19*).

The Rabbi of Apt said, "The mission of man is to exercise freedom of choice, and to freely choose the correct way to live.

"However, in days of yore, there was no true freedom of choice. We had a court and penal system, which punished people who violated the Torah law. Even when we lost our political independence, there were social norms that were strictly observed. People were coerced to adhere to Torah law by social pressure, lest they be ostracized by the community. Observing the Torah by coercion, regardless of what form it may take, is not true freedom of choice.

"But today there is true freedom of choice. There certainly is no enforcement, and no one cares what anyone else does. One who violates Torah may still be considered a respected member of the community. Today there is no form of coercion whatever, and so the person who observes Torah today does so with true freedom of choice."

The Rabbi of Apt died in 1825. It is difficult to imagine that he was speaking of his own time, when the social structure of the *shtetl* was still a very potent deterrent of deviant behavior. The Rabbi of Apt prophesied for our day. Today we have true freedom of choice, and it may well be that it is the Torah observance today, in the midst of a decadent society, that will finally merit the Redemption.

NOTES

_____
_____
_____
_____
_____
_____
_____
_____
_____
_____

. . . From **our Prayers** . . . תַּעֲזוֹר לִי לְקַדֵּשׁ אֶת מַחְשְׁבוֹתַי

I beg of You, O G-d, inasmuch as the impact of harboring improper thoughts is so great, and evil thoughts can virtually detach a person from spirituality, that You protect me from all improper thoughts and feelings *(from the personal prayers of Rabbi Nachman of Breslov)*.

Dec. 23, 1990
Dec. 13, 1991
Dec. 30, 1992
Dec. 20, 1993
Dec. 9, 1994
Dec. 29, 1995

It was characteristic of Rabbi Nachman not only to formulate prayers of his own, but also to explain in his prayer why he was asking for something. Rabbi Nachman advocated personal prayer in addition to formulated prayers, and urged that we pray just as a child pleads with its parents for something that it wants.

When people are stricken, G-d forbid, with illness in themselves or their families, their prayers to G-d are sincere, and may be accompanied by tears of intense emotion, reflecting the deep pain and fears they experience as a result of the illness. This is not as likely to occur when we pray for wisdom, for the Redemption, and even for forgiveness. There may not be the same intensity of emotion.

Just as we feel the misery of serious illness and the fear that it may progress, G-d forbid, to loss of life, so we must come to realize that loss of spirituality is every bit as grave as physical illness. Our prayers for spiritual well-being should be no less fervent than for physical health.

And all the nation saw the sounds, the flames, the sound of the shofar, and the mountain in smoke, and the people saw and trembled, and stood from afar *(Exodus 20:15)*.

From the Scriptures

"What does it mean," asked the Rabbi of Rizhin, "that the people stood from afar?"

The Rabbi answered, "Miraculous and wondrous occurrences are for non-believers, to whom G-d must prove His existence by supernatural phenomena. True believers do not need any proof. Their faith is secure."

There is a popular cliche, "Seeing is believing." This is patently incorrect. Belief is when one does *not* see. When one sees something, there is no longer any need for belief.

Having faith in G-d is necessary precisely because we cannot see Him. Those who have such faith stand close to Him. Those who require miracles stand from afar.

NOTES
_____
_____
_____
_____
_____
_____
_____
_____
_____

Dec. 24, 1990
Dec. 14, 1991
Dec. 31, 1992
Dec. 21, 1993
Dec. 10, 1994
Dec. 30, 1995

From our Prayers

אַב הָרַחֲמִים הוּא יְרַחֵם עַם עֲמוּסִים . . .

May the Father of compassion have compassion upon a people so heavily laden. May He remember the covenant with the patriarchs, and may He deliver our souls from evil hours (*prayer prior to communal reading of the Torah*).

The history of the Jewish people abounds in suffering: enslavement, wanderings, economic oppression, pogroms, holocaust. How do we reconcile that with a G-d of compassion?

In the covenant with the patriarch Abraham, G-d said, "Know for certain that your children will be strangers in a foreign land, exiled and tortured ... but they will be delivered with great wealth" (*Genesis 15:13*).

It is beyond the capability of the human mind to fathom the wisdom of G-d. But there it is, spelled out in the beginning of our history: There will be suffering and there will be deliverance.

It is for us to have faith and trust that there is purpose to the Divine plan, and that G-d is indeed compassionate. Faith is most necessary when our senses would make us feel otherwise.

From the Sages

Hillel once saw a skull floating on the surface of the water. He said to it, "Even if they drowned you because you drowned others, nevertheless they will themselves be drowned (*Ethics of our Fathers 2:7*).

It is not good to do harm to others. The Talmud relates that although the Torah requires capital punishment for certain heinous crimes, the justices of the Sanhedrin (supreme court) would pray that they should not have to condemn anyone to death.

So many times in life there are incidents where we feel we have been wronged by others, and when the opportunity arises to retaliate, the urge to take revenge is intense.

The Torah forbids vengeance (*Leviticus 19:18*). This is in the portion in the Torah known as "*Kedoshim*" (sanctity), wherein we are told how to behave if we are to be a holy and spiritual people.

G-d has a perfect system of justice, even though with our limited human wisdom we may not appreciate this. It is not good to become an instrument of punishment, says Hillel. Even if one can justify his hostile acts, it can be destructive to oneself, just as it is to others.

NOTES

_____
_____
_____
_____
_____
_____
_____
_____
_____

הֹ׳ מְאֹד עָמְקוּ מַחְשְׁבֹתֶיךָ . . . *From*

O G-d, how infinitely profound are Your *our* thoughts. A man bare of reason does *Prayers* not understand, nor does a fool comprehend this, when the lawless spring up as the grass, and those who do wrong flourish . . . but You are most high forever, O G-d *(Shabbos service, Psalms 92:6-9).*

Dec. 25, 1990
Dec. 15, 1991
Jan. 1, 1993
Dec. 22, 1993
Dec. 11, 1994
Dec. 31, 1995

The corollary to the question, "Why do good people suffer?" is, "Why do the wicked prosper?"

Our sense of justice is perplexed when we see undeserving people prosper while the righteous so often suffer. Although various explanations have been given for this, the Psalmist essentially dismisses all attempts at logical understanding, and asserts that we must defer to a judgment that is most high, and is so far beyond our grasp that the human mind is comparatively considered to be "bare of reason."

One of the purposes of prayer as a whole is to surrender our lives to the transcendent will of G-d.

Behold I will give you bread (manna) from the heavens, and everyone will gather only one day's need, so that I may test you whether you walk in My ways *(Exodus 16:4).*

From the Scriptures

Rabbi Mendel of Rimanov remarked, "If you ask the average person whether he believes in G-d and that G-d created the world, he will answer, 'Of course. Even a simpleton knows that.' Then if you ask him whether he trusts that G-d will provide all his needs, he will answer, 'I haven't reached that level of trust yet.'

"But let us not deceive ourselves," Rabbi Mendel said. "Belief and trust are inseparable, if not identical. The person who does not have complete trust in G-d is lacking in belief as well."

That is why the Torah says that the *manna* was a test. Whoever took more than his needs for a single day, and did not rely on G-d to provide for him tomorrow, was manifestly incomplete in his belief in G-d.

Many of us are like Rabbi Mendel's "average person." We need to achieve a more profound trust in G-d, that will enable us to live one day a time and not be burdened with the worries of tomorrow.

Dec. 26, 1990
Dec. 16, 1991
Jan. 2, 1993
Dec. 23, 1993
Dec. 12, 1994
Jan. 1, 1996

From our Prayers

וְכֻלָּם מְקַבְּלִים עֲלֵיהֶם
עַל מַלְכוּת שָׁמַיִם זֶה מִזֶּה ...

They (the angels) take upon themselves the yoke of the kingdom of Heaven ... in unison they all proclaim holiness and declare in awe, Holy! Holy! Holy! is the L-rd of hosts. The fullness of all the universe is His glory *(daily morning service)*.

Countless heavenly angels give praise to the Almighty. Yet it is the devotion of the lowly human being that most pleases G-d. Angels are beings that were created in a state of perfection. They are pure of spirit, and are not subject to temptation. They have no inclination to do anything but the Divine will.

There is not much achievement in being holy if you were created holy and have no other option. The worship which G-d desires most is that of man, who is abundant in temptation and base desires, and who restrains himself, overcomes his powerful drives in deference to the Divine will, and makes himself into a spiritual being.

From the Sages

G-d assists those who come to purify themselves *(Avodah Zarah 55a).*

If one looks at the expectations and the requirements of Torah living, particularly the need of character development, it may appear to be so stringent and overwhelming that one may be discouraged from making even an attempt at it.

The Talmud assures us that there is no reason for discouragement. While there is no denying that the task of character refinement is formidable, we will receive more than adequate help to get it accomplished. All we have to do is be sincere in our intent, and do whatever is within our means, and G-d will assist us in completing the task.

But in order to merit Divine assistance, our intent must be genuine. Lip service will not work. G-d cannot be deceived. Sincerity of intent is demonstrated by how much effort we make on our own. G-d will assist those who will *come* to be purified. We have to come, because He will not come after us if we are lying in our hammocks.

NOTES

_____
_____
_____
_____
_____
_____
_____
_____
_____

עֲנֵנוּ ה' עֲנֵנוּ בְּיוֹם צוֹם תַּעֲנִיתֵנוּ ... *From*

Answer us, O G-d, answer us on this day *our* of our fast, for we are in great distress *Prayers* ... for You are G-d, who answers us in time of distress *(Amidah on days of fasting).*

A recovered alcoholic was telling a friend that on awakening each morning he prays to G-d for another day of sobriety, and that each night before retiring he thanks G-d for having granted him a day of sobriety.

"How do you know it was G-d who gave you the day of sobriety?" the friend asked.

"It had to be," the man responded. "He was the only one whom I had asked."

We often complain that our prayers have not been answered. Little do we realize how many more times our prayers *have* been answered. We take too many things for granted.

Some things are so simple if we only look at them sensibly.

Fast of Asarah B'Teves
Dec. 27, 1990
Dec. 17, 1991
Jan. 3, 1993
Dec. 24, 1993
Dec. 13, 1994
Jan. 2, 1996

The Ark of the Covenant, which contained the Tablets of the Ten Commandments, was carried on the shoulders of the Levites during the wanderings in the desert. The Talmud tells us that although it appeared to be carried, the Ark actually carried its bearers *(Sotah 35a).*

From the Sages

Rabbi Mendel of Rimanov said that when a person feels that he is not serving G-d adequately, and comes to a *tzaddik* for teaching and guidance in improving his devotion to G-d, the *tzaddik*, upon seeing the person's humility, feels, "This person is better than I am. He is more humble and is searching for closeness to G-d more diligently than I am." Consequently, the *tzaddik* becomes more humble.

The man who came to the *tzaddik* for help in his spiritual strivings thus helps the *tzaddik* achieve new heights in his own spirituality. In this way, "the Ark carries its bearers."

NOTES
_____
_____
_____
_____
_____
_____
_____
_____
_____

Dec. 28, 1990
Dec. 18, 1991
Jan. 4, 1993
Dec. 25, 1993
Dec. 14, 1994
Jan. 3, 1996

From our Prayers

אַהֲבַת עוֹלָם בֵּית יִשְׂרָאֵל עַמְּךָ אָהָבְתָּ . . .

With love everlasting You have loved the House of Israel Your people; the Torah and commandments, statutes and ordinances You taught us. Therefore, O L-rd our G-d, when we lie down and when we arise, we will meditate upon Your statutes and rejoice in the words of Your Torah and Your commandments forever (daily evening service).

All gifts which G-d may bestow upon a nation or an individual may not be permanent. But the Torah and its laws are our most precious possession, an eternal gift of G-d's everlasting love for Israel.

Empires have arisen, and empires have disappeared from the face of the earth. Many wealthy and powerful nations exist only in history texts, but the Jewish nation has survived. Even when driven from its homeland and subjected to unparalleled persecution, the Jewish people and nation survive.

The Torah is the Divine gift which has perpetuated our people, and for this gift we are grateful to G-d.

From the Sages

Do not stand idly by when your fellow man's life is in danger (Toras Kohanim; Rashi, Leviticus 19:16).

The Rabbi of Vorki was asked, ''The Talmud states that when Rabbi Zeira was asked by what virtue he had merited to live long, he answered that he had never rejoiced over anyone's misfortunes. To rejoice at another's misfortune is simply base, and one does not have to be a *tzaddik* to not rejoice at someone else's misfortunes. How could this be considered a virtue for Rabbi Zeira?''

The Rabbi of Vorki explained, ''You are not interpreting the Talmud correctly. What Rabbi Zeira said was that he could never rejoice in his own good fortune, in his own *nachas*, in those things that should have given him great joy, as long as he knew that others were suffering.

''We enjoy our meals, even though we know that there are many that are hungry. We enjoy the comfort of our warm homes even though we know that there are others that are homeless.

''Rabbi Zeira could not enjoy any of the good things of life while he knew that there were those that were suffering. That is why Rabbi Zeira was a *tzaddik*.''

NOTES

_____
_____
_____
_____
_____
_____
_____
_____
_____
_____

... אַל תִּבְטְחוּ בִנְדִיבִים *From*
אַשְׁרֵי שֶׁקֵּל יַעֲקֹב בְּעֶזְרוֹ *our*

*P*ut not your trust in nobles, in a human *Prayers*
who cannot help. If his spirit departs,
he will return to the earth, and on that day
all his plans are lost. Fortunate is he whose
help is the G-d of Jacob *(daily morning
service, Psalms 146:3-5).*

Dec. 29, 1990
Dec. 19, 1991
Jan. 5, 1993
Dec. 26, 1993
Dec. 15, 1994
Jan. 4, 1996

It is strange that people are sometimes obstinate in
refusing to learn from experience, much like the person
who had disastrous results every time he drank, yet
continued to drink under the delusion that "this time will
be different."

How often have we placed our trust in other people,
only to discover that even if they mean well, they are not
able to make good their promises. Even the might of
formidable resources is no assurance, as the failures of
mighty industrial empires have demonstrated. Yet we tend
to rely on humans, and our trust in G-d is so often only lip
service.

How fortunate is the person who sincerely trusts in
G-d.

**Rabbi Yonasan says, "He who fulfills the Torah
out of poverty will in the end fulfill it out of wealth.
He who neglects the Torah out of wealth will in the
end neglect it out of poverty"** *(Ethics of the Fathers 4:11).*

*From
the Sages*

The person who knows that true joy and fulfillment lie in
the study of Torah will continue that life even when his
material circumstances improve significantly. Indeed, he
will dedicate his resources toward the advancement of
Torah living for himself and for others.

NOTES

The person who neglects Torah under the delusion that
his abundance of material wealth can provide him with
happiness and security is totally without support if his
wealth diminishes. In desperation to save his wealth, which
he thinks he may accomplish by his own sagacity, he
squanders his energies and spends his health, and is likely
to end up in both spiritual and physical ruin.

How appropriately it is stated in today's prayer, "Fortunate is he whose help is the G-d of Jacob."

Dec. 30, 1990
Dec. 20, 1991
Jan. 6, 1993
Dec. 27, 1993
Dec. 16, 1994
Jan. 5, 1996

From our Prayers

וַאֲנַחְנוּ לֹא נֵדַע מַה נַּעֲשֶׂה . . .

As for us, we know not what to do, for our eyes are upon You. Remember Your compassion and Your kindness, O G-d (*morning service*).

The person who feels that he is confused or lost is likely to ask for guidance and directions. If a person is headed in the wrong direction, but is under the assumption that he is going in the *right* direction, he is not apt to discover his mistake until he has traveled far from his destination.

Those who, for whatever reason, have not stopped to ask for directions, can remember the frustration, anger, and self-recrimination when they discovered that rather than being closer to their destination, they had gone far in the opposite direction. "How could I have been so stupid?" they say.

Direction in life is of even greater importance than on the highway. If we listen carefully to the words of the prayer, "We know not what to do," we will ask for directions. A compassionate G-d has provided us with wise people who can direct us, but it is upon us to ask.

From the Sages

A person should be as humble and as flexible as Hillel, rather than as stern and strict as Shammai (*Shabbos 30b*).

Rabbi Chaim of Wolozin states that it is wrong to assume that Hillel and Shammai conducted themselves according to their temperaments. Our great Sages were not mere pawns at the mercy of their inborn traits. Hillel adopted an attitude of flexibility and humbleness because he felt that this is what Torah required of him. Shammai felt that when any principle of Torah is involved, there is no yielding whatever, and he was therefore "strict."

Rabbi Chaim says that if either Hillel or Shammai had been convinced that the other opinion was correct, they would have promptly changed their attitude one hundred and eighty degrees. Their entire lives were so dedicated to Torah that whatever they believed Torah required of them became their natural attitude.

Too often we allow attitudes to dictate for us what the Torah says. Rabbi Chaim teaches us that the correct way of Judaism is the reverse. It is Torah that must dictate attitudes, and not the other way around.

NOTES

_____
_____
_____
_____
_____
_____
_____
_____
_____

וְלִירוּשָׁלַיִם עִירְךָ בְּרַחֲמִים תָּשׁוּב *From*
וְתִשְׁכּוֹן בְּתוֹכָהּ | *our*

And to Your city Jerusalem return with *Prayers*
compassion, and may Your presence
dwell within it (*daily Amidah*).

Dec. 31, 1990
Dec. 21, 1991
Jan. 7, 1993
Dec. 28, 1993
Dec. 17, 1994
Jan. 6, 1996

The *tzaddik* of Sanz used to relate a parable of a prince
who was exiled. Having no manual skills, he became a
shepherd. Whereas other shepherds built huts to protect
them from the sun, the prince, not being handy with tools,
suffered in the intense heat.

Years later, the king visited the distant land, and peasants
threw petitions into the royal coach. The prince, too, wrote
a petition that he be given a little hut to protect him from
the sun.

When the king recognized his son's handwriting, he
wept. "How my son has forgotten who he is! He does not
ask to be recalled to the palace. His only aspiration is for
greater comfort as a shepherd."

The *tzaddik* of Sanz said, "We pray for our personal
needs, like the shepherd for his hut. We forget that we
belong in the Divine presence, under the immediate
providence of G-d."

**Rabbi Akiva, at the age of forty, had not learned
anything of Torah. One day he observed a hollow in
a rock that had been formed by flowing water, and
he reasoned, "If water can penetrate solid rock, the
Torah can penetrate into my heart"** (*Avos DeR' Nosson
6:2*).

*From
the Sages*

According to Rabbi Yisrael of Salant, it was not that
seeing the erosion of the rock by the water stimulated
Rabbi Akiva to study. Rather, said Rabbi Yisrael, Rabbi Akiva
had already begun to study, but was unable to comprehend
and retain anything he learned. Therefore, he quite logically
concluded that it was too late for him to absorb anything
new, and that he had passed beyond the age when new
learning was feasible.

The lesson of the water and the rock is that we are never
so inured that we are impenetrable to new knowledge.

That is, not unless we wish to be so.

NOTES

_____
_____
_____
_____
_____
_____
_____

LIVING EACH DAY / 105

Jan. 1, 1991
Dec. 22, 1991
Jan. 8, 1993
Dec. 29, 1993
Dec. 18, 1994
Jan. 7, 1996

From our Prayers

זְכוֹר ה' לְדָוִד אֵת כָּל עֻנּוֹתוֹ . . .

O G-d, remember unto David all his renunciations. How he swore to G-d ... "I will not enter into the tent of my house; I will not go up into the bed that is spread for me. I will not give sleep to my eyes ... until I shall have found a place for G-d" *(Shabbos afternoon prayer, Psalms 132:1-5).*

If we are sincere in our quest for spirituality, then we must accord it priority. We cannot be primarily physically oriented people for whom spirituality is but an afterthought. By definition, spirituality must be primary, the most important aspect of our lives.

Our actions testify as to our priorities. How much do we invest in our homes, and how much in our houses of study and worship? How much are we willing to spend on our children's spiritual training, and how much on their secular education?

The Psalmist had his priorities in order. Not until the Sanctuary was built to the glory of G-d was David willing to dwell in his palace.

From the Scriptures

The mighty One, His deeds are perfect, all His ways are just. He is a G-d of trust and there is no iniquity, for He is righteous and fair *(Deuteronomy 32:4).*

The Rabbi of Tchortkov said, "When my brother (the Rabbi of Sadogura) prays the Psalms, he does so with such fervor and devotion that the Almighty says to him, 'Avraham Yaakov, my child, I place the entire world in your hands. You are free to do with it whatever you desire.'

"But my brother is a faithful and trusted servant, and he returns the world to G-d just as it was given to him.

"If only G-d would turn over operation of the world to me for a while," the Rabbi of Tchortkov said with a smile, "then we would see some changes."

The ultimate of faith is when one has the capacity to make changes, yet is so absolute in his trust in the compassion of G-d that one sets aside his judgment in deference to the Divine wisdom.

NOTES

TEVES

16

טבת

Jan. 2, 1991
Dec. 23, 1991
Jan. 9, 1993
Dec. 30, 1993
Dec. 19, 1994
Jan. 8, 1996

ה' מָה רַבּוּ צָרָי רַבִּים קָמִים עָלָי ... *From our Prayers*

O G-d, how many are our oppressors; many are they who rise up against me. Many are there that say of my soul: "There is no more help for him from G-d." But You, G-d, remain a shield about me, You are my glory, and even now You raise my head *(prayer before going to sleep, Psalms 3:2-4).*

This prayer was said by David in one of the bitterest moments of his life. His son, Absalom, had led a rebellion against him, and had driven him from Jerusalem. Although David knew he was fighting for his very life as well as his throne, he feared triumph every bit as much as defeat, because victory might come at the cost of Absalom's life, as indeed it did.

The Talmud states that David was forewarned that evil would befall him as punishment for his liason with Bathsheba (*Samuel* II 12). Although David confessed his sin and repented, he did not turn against G-d when the Divine retribution occurred.

Anyone of lesser stature than David would have been bitter toward G-d. But David, in the moment of his most profound anguish, found it possible to sing praises to G-d. He humbly accepted the Divine punishment, and prayed for salvation.

Little wonder we say, "David, king of Israel, lives on forever." He lives on as our mentor and teacher.

Behold, I come to you in the thickness of a dark cloud *(Exodus 19:9).* *From the Scriptures*

Rabbi David Moshe of Tchortkov said, "The presence of G-d is often contained in the thickness of darkness. Although the world is full of the glory of G-d, His presence is accentuated in the darkness of distress."

"I dwell among the humble and oppressed," says G-d *(Isaiah 57:15).* The acknowledgment of G-d, the faith and trust in Him, is more likely to be found in those who are deprived rather than those who abound in plenty.

Moses knew where to find G-d. "And Moses approached the dark cloud, wherein was the presence of G-d" *(Exodus 20:18).*

How foolish we are to overlook the presence of G-d when He is with us in the darkest moments of our lives.

NOTES

_____
_____
_____
_____
_____
_____
_____
_____

Jan. 3, 1991
Dec. 24, 1991
Jan. 10, 1993
Dec. 31, 1993
Dec. 20, 1994
Jan. 9, 1996

*From
our
Prayers*

וְהִנְנִי מוֹחֵל בִּמְחִילָה גְמוּרָה
לְכָל מִי שֶׁחָטָא נֶגְדִּי . . .

I forgive everyone who may have offended me in any way, and just as I forgive others, please let me find favor in the eyes of others, that they may forgive me *(Tefillah Zakkah of Rabbi Avraham Danzig).*

"Just as water reflects the image, so is the heart of one person to the other" *(Proverbs 27:19).* The wise Solomon's statement is a psychologic law of nature. Emotions are not unidirectional. If you want to know how someone else feels about you, just analyze how you feel about that person, and you will have your answer.

But what about unrequited love? Do we not often see that one person may love another without a like response?

There may be feelings that simulate love but are not true love, just as a zircon simulates a diamond but is not really a diamond. Solomon is correct. True love is reciprocated. "Pseudo-love" can be unidirectional.

If you wish others to feel kindly toward you, this is simple to achieve. Feel kindly toward them, but genuinely so.

*From the
Scriptures*

See, this alone I have discovered. G-d made humans straight, but they have sought a multitude of calculations *(Ecclesiastes 7:29).*

Life is really not that complicated, unless one makes it so.

The Divine plan was a simple one. Man was to act according to the dictates of G-d. Truth was to prevail, and truth is simple because there is only one truth. Falsehood is complicated, because there are many, many lies.

We seem to have developed a love for complexity. We spend time and effort on myriads of calculations. Give a person a rather simple situation, and he will worry enough about it and approach it in a variety of devious ways, until it does become a very thorny problem.

Llfe does not have to be very complicated. Keep things simple. You will be pleasantly surprised to find that there are simple solutions if you do not complicate problems.

NOTES
_____
_____
_____
_____
_____
_____
_____
_____
_____

ה' מוֹרִישׁ וּמַעֲשִׁיר מַשְׁפִּיל אַף מְרוֹמֵם . . . *From* *our* *Prayers*

G-d impoverishes and enriches; He casts down and elevates. He lifts the poor from the dust, and out of refuse He raises the needy, to place them among the nobility and bestow upon them positions of honor *(I Samuel 2:7-8; Haftarah first day of Rosh Hashanah).*

Jan. 4, 1991
Dec. 25, 1991
Jan. 11, 1993
Jan. 1, 1994
Dec. 21, 1994
Jan. 10, 1996

This prayer is from the song of thanks of Channah, mother of Samuel. After years of being childless and incessant prayers for bearing a child, her prayers were answered, and she gave birth to one of the greatest of prophets. As she had promised in her prayers, she dedicated the child to the service of G-d.

Channah's maternal instincts were intense, but she prayed for a child whom she could raise in sanctity and donate to the service of G-d. Channah's prayers were not for herself, but for the greater glory of G-d.

On the day that she brought her only, beloved child to the Sanctuary and left him there to serve the High Priest, she expressed her gratitude in prayers. Channah dismisses her personal gain and asserts that when we are the beneficiaries of G-d's grace, we should be moved more by the honor this brings to G-d than the pleasure it brings to us. This is prayer at its finest.

And G-d blessed the seventh day and hallowed it, for on it He rested from all the work that G-d created to be done *(Genesis 2:3).* *From the Scriptures*

The last phrase, "to be done," indicates that it was only the work of initial creation that was completed. G-d indeed created all the components of the world, but these were only the raw materials of which the ultimate world was to be fashioned.

The completion of the world is the duty of mankind. We are nothing but laborers who have been given the materials, and we are to put together the desired structure according to the plan of the Designer. If we do not do so, we are severely remiss.

Each day we must ask ourselves, "What have I done today to bring the world to its state of completion?"

NOTES

_____
_____
_____
_____
_____
_____
_____
_____

Jan. 5, 1991
Dec. 26, 1991
Jan. 12, 1993
Jan. 2, 1994
Dec. 22, 1994
Jan. 11, 1996

From our Prayers עִבְדוּ אֶת ה' בְּשִׂמְחָה בֹּאוּ לְפָנָיו בִּרְנָנָה . . .

Serve G-d with gladness, come before Him with exultation. Know that G-d is G-d, He has made us and we are His *(daily morning service, Psalms 100:2-3).*

What kind of statement is, "Know that G-d is G-d?"

Note that the psalm began by telling us to serve G-d with gladness. Is it always possible to be in a state of gladness? How are we to be glad when we suffer? How are we to exalt G-d in a state of happiness when we do not feel happy? Can we manipulate happiness and gladness at will?

The answer is simple. If man is man and G-d is G-d, then we can be perpetually happy. We must do all that is in our human means, and if things do not turn out the way we wished, that is not our fault. We need not hold ourselves responsible for things that are beyond our control.

Much human misery results when man thinks himself to be G-d-like. We often fail to see our own limitations, and we think we can control the world, We are then unable to make peace with a world that is not to our liking. If we only knew that G-d is G-d, we could worship Him with gladness.

From the Sages

A wise man is greater than a prophet *(Bava Basra 12a).*

"In what way is a wise man greater than a prophet?" asked the Rabbi of Ropshcitz. "Because a prophet foresees the future, and a wise man sees the present."

If one has the capacity to foresee the future, then it is no great achievement to do so correctly. But when one has the capacity to see the present, it is still a major feat to do so.

There is little likelihood that our perception of the future will be distorted, because we are not affected by things that have not yet happened. If we are not emotionally involved, we can see clearly and objectively.

It is the present that is so difficult to see correctly, because in the present we are deeply affected by our pride, our desires, our frustrations, and our resentments. These can alter our perception because we are unable to see things except through emotionally tinted lenses.

We can always benefit from asking others' opinions. We may not be wise enough to recognize our own distortions.

NOTES

אֵלֶּה בָרֶכֶב וְאֵלֶּה בַסוּסִים *From*
וַאֲנַחְנוּ בְּשֵׁם ה' אֱלֹקֵינוּ נַזְכִּיר . . . *our*

Some [see G-d] in chariots, and others in *Prayers*
horses, but as for us, we remember our
G-d by the name "Hashem." When they
knelt, they fell down; but we have always
risen again and have constantly kept
ourselves upright. O G-d, grant us salvation; the King will answer us on the day on
which we call upon Him *(daily morning
service, Psalms 20:8-10)*.

Some nations see G-d in their arsenals, and when they
are defeated, they fall and are destroyed. We see our
strength and survival in G-d and not in our own might, and
therefore, although we indeed reel under the impact of the
blows dealt to us, we continue to get up and keep ourselves upright.

What is true of us as a nation is also true of the
individual. The person who trusts in his own power is
crushed when his power fails him. The person who trusts
in G-d may indeed totter, but is never destroyed. With G-d
at his side, he can always rise again.

True salvation is only with G-d.

If you have wisdom, then what do you lack? If you | *From*
lack wisdom, then what do you have? *(Nedarim 41a).* | *the Sages*

Rabbi Simchah Zisl Ziv states that man will not be held
accountable simply because he gratified his passions.

A person who is very thirsty may drink out of a dirty
cup, and if his thirst is very intense, he may even drink
dirty water. However, if he drinks salt water, which will
only intensify rather than quench his thirst, he is being
extremely foolish.

A person with intelligence should realize that some
passions are stimulated rather than satiated by gratifying
them. A person will therefore be held accountable for not
using his intellect, and for allowing himself to indulge in
behavior which could only cause him even greater cravings.

Unless we utilize our intellect and wisdom, what can we
possibly acquire? All acquisitions will only give us greater
desire rather than more satisfaction.

TEVES

20

טבת

Jan. 6, 1991
Dec. 27, 1991
Jan. 13, 1993
Jan. 3, 1994
Dec. 23, 1994
Jan. 12, 1996

NOTES

——————
——————
——————
——————
——————
——————
——————
——————

Jan. 7, 1991
Dec. 28, 1991
Jan. 14, 1993
Jan. 4, 1994
Dec. 24, 1994
Jan. 13, 1996

*From
our
Prayers*

כִּי זוֹכֵר כָּל הַנִּשְׁכָּחוֹת אַתָּה

For You remember all that is forgotten (*Rosh Hashanah prayers*).

Rabbi Tzvi Yehudah of Rosdvil said. "What man forgets, G-d remembers. What man remembers, G-d forgets."

If a person has done something wrong, is sincerely remorseful, asks forgiveness, and remembers never to repeat the act, then G-d forgets this sin and forgives him. If, however, he simply dismisses his transgressions and quickly forgets them, then G-d will remember them.

If a person forgets that he has done good deeds, and constantly thinks that he has not yet begun to fulfill his duties, then G-d will remember all his good deeds. If the person remembers all his good deeds and believes that he has done so much that everyone should appreciate and honor him, then G-d does not remember his deeds.

What man remembers, G-d forgets.

*From
the Sages*

Just before Rabbi Yochanan ben Zakkai's death, his students asked for his blessing. Rabbi Yochanan responded, "May your fear of G-d be as great as your fear of man" (*Berachos 28b*).

Some people may consider themselves to be G-d-fearing. Their actions, however, reveal the truth of their convictions.

During his wanderings, the Rabbi of Berdichev came to a village. He was approached by a local resident who asked, "Rabbi, are you perhaps a *shochet* (ritual slaughterer)?"

"Yes," replied the Rabbi. "I am a *shochet*."

"Wonderful!" exclaimed the man. "Our local *shochet* is ill, and I have no meat for my customers. Come with me to the slaughterhouse, and I will pay you well for your work."

"Very well," the Rabbi said. "But first I must ask a favor. I must marry off my daughter, and I desperately need a loan of two hundred rubles. I promise to repay within three months."

NOTES

"What! Two hundred rubles?" the man exclaimed. "You expect me to lend such a huge sum to a total stranger whom I just met a few minutes ago?"

"How strange," said the Rabbi. "Although you do not know me, you are willing to trust me as a *shochet*, and if I am not competent, you risk feeding non-kosher meat to the community. But whereas you trust me with something that affects your soul, you will not trust me with your money."

Let us examine our own values in the light of the Rabbi's remarks. Do we guard our own spiritual welfare as much as we do our material interests?

הַמּוֹצִיא לֶחֶם מִן הָאָרֶץ . . . *From*

B lessed are You, L-rd our G-d, King of the *our* universe, Who brings forth bread from *Prayers* the earth (*Blessing for bread*).

Jan. 8, 1991
Dec. 29, 1991
Jan. 15, 1993
Jan. 5, 1994
Dec. 25, 1994
Jan. 14, 1996

On a visit to Israel, I shared a table with a man who recited the blessing for bread, and then kissed the bread before he ate it. This seemed rather strange to me, and I asked the man why he kissed the bread.

The man looked at me with bewilderment. "Do you not kiss the Torah? Do you not kiss sacred objects to show your reverence for them? Bread, too, is sacred. It is the handiwork of G-d. Do we not say, 'He brings forth bread from the earth?' "

I felt so foolish. Of course the man was right. We are so accustomed that when one plants wheat it grows, that we assume this to be a "natural" phenomenon.

A seed is buried in the ground, decomposes, and sprouts a new plant. What is really natural for a decomposed object is to remain decomposed. That it can sprout life is a direct act of G-d, whose handiwork should be seen in every stalk of wheat and every blade of grass.

This blessing now reminds me of this man's teaching. Bread is sacred.

For I will not forsake you, (but I will be with you) until I have done all that I have spoken to you (*Genesis 28:15*).

From the Scriptures

NOTES

A destitute man came to the Rabbi of Apt for a blessing that his fortune should improve. The Rabbi blessed him and assured him that G-d would help him.

'But what am I to do until G-d helps me?'' the man asked in desperation.

"Do not worry," said the Rabbi. "G-d will help you even before He helps you. That is what He promised our forefather, Jacob. 'I will not forsake you before I have fulfilled My promise to you.' "

If we do not receive what we want in answer to our prayers, we should know that G-d will give us the strength and the ability to do without what we think we need.

TEVES

טבת

Jan. 9, 1991
Dec. 30, 1991
Jan. 16, 1993
Jan. 6, 1994
Dec. 26, 1994
Jan. 15, 1996

From our Prayers

וּבִרְצוֹנְךָ . . .

שֶׁלֹּא תְהֵא צָרָה וְיָגוֹן וַאֲנָחָה . . .

By Your favor, O L-rd our G-d, grant us rest so that there be no distress, no grief, or sighing on this day of our rest *(addendum for Shabbos to Blessings after meals).*

The Talmud says, "Prayer accomplishes half" *(Vayikra Rabbah 10:5),* which means that when there is something that the person himself can do to achieve his wish, the response to the prayer will be only for that part which the person cannot do himself.

We do indeed need Divine help that our *Shabbos* rest not be disturbed by grief or distress. But whether it is disturbed by sighing may well be in our own hands.

No doubt we accumulate all kinds of worries during the week. In the true spirit of *Shabbos,* we should be able to set them aside. As we testify in *Kiddush* to G-d's creation of the universe in six days, and His blessing of the seventh day on which He rested, we, too, should be able to rest on the seventh day, and leave all the weekday worries behind us.

We need not disturb the peace and tranquility of *Shabbos* by sighing. But that depends on our own attitude.

From the Sages

And Moses said, "Eat it (the manna) today, for today is Shabbos unto G-d" *(Exodus 16:25).*

The Rabbi of Rimanov commented, "'Eat it' refers to Shabbos itself. Ingest the Shabbos, for it can be your nourishment."

NOTES

It is a practice among the chassidim to serve *farfel-tzimis* on Friday night.

The origin of this custom is ascribed to the Baal Shem Tov, who is alleged to have said that the word "farfel" is similar to the Yiddish word "farfallen," which means "bygone." Eating the *farfel* on Friday night is thus symbolic that as the week comes to a close, we should let bygones be bygones, and not carry the heavy baggage of the past week into the new one.

In this way *Shabbos* can indeed be an important source of nourishment.

פּוֹקֵחַ עִוְרִים . . . *From*

Blessed are You, L-rd our G-d, King of the *our* universe, who opens the eyes of the *Prayers* blind *(prayer upon arising)*.

Customary things are often taken for granted. Judaism teaches us not to take things for granted. The marvelous capacity to see is a gift, and upon opening our eyes each morning, we must give thanks to G-d for the precious gift of vision.

Our ethicists point out that if you gave someone a very expensive gift, such as a set of golden tableware, and later noted that the person was using the golden utensils to dig holes in the ground, you would conclude that this person had either taken leave of his senses and had no awareness of what he was doing, or if he did, was expressing his contempt for you by abusing your gift.

If we understand our visual sense to be a precious gift from G-d, how could we abuse this gift by looking at things that are not suitable for us to see? The daily blessing of gratitude for vision should remind us to use our sight properly.

Jan. 10, 1991
Dec. 31, 1991
Jan. 17, 1993
Jan. 7, 1994
Dec. 27, 1994
Jan. 16, 1996

There are mitzvos whose fruits are enjoyed in this world while their principal is reserved for the world to come *(Pe'ah 1:1)*.

From the Sages

One of the Chassidic masters approached a person engaged in amassing great wealth, who was known to indulge in physical pleasures.

"Tell me," he said, "why do you not have any earthly rewards?"

"What do you mean, Rabbi?" the man responded. "I have abundant earthly rewards. Can you not see? I am wealthy, I have a beautiful home with lavish furnishings and many of my heart's desires."

"Yes, I see all that," the Rabbi said. "But that is because you are using up your heavenly rewards. I am asking you, where are your *earthly* rewards?"

If you have savings and you squander them foolishly, you will have nothing left for things that you may truly need at a later date. Therefore, it is important that we avail ourselves of *mitzvos* whose merits will be preserved for us so that we do not arrive in the eternal world empty-handed.

A study of the Talmud and ethical works will show us that just as with financial investments, there are *mitzvos* that are "high-income" producers, whose principal will remain untouched.

NOTES

_____
_____
_____
_____
_____
_____
_____
_____

Jan. 11, 1991
Jan. 1, 1992
Jan. 18, 1993
Jan. 8, 1994
Dec. 28, 1994
Jan. 17, 1996

From our Prayers

סוֹמֵךְ ה' לְכָל הַנֹּפְלִים וְזוֹקֵף לְכָל הַכְּפוּפִים

G-d upholds all that fall, and raises upright those that are bent over *(daily service, Psalms 145:14)*.

The initial letters of this psalm contain an acrostic of the Hebrew alphabet, the first verse beginning with *aleph*, the second with *beis*, and so on. However, the letter *nun* is conspicuously absent.

The Talmud states that David omitted *nun* because it stands for *nophel* (falling), and he did not wish to imply that G-d causes anyone to fall. He did include the *nun* in the verse cited above, "G-d upholds all that fall (*nophlim*)."

Isn't is strange that we tend to ascribe only terrible happenings to G-d, but not good occurrences? It is common practice to refer to a flood, a fire, or an earthquake as an "act of G-d," but a bumper crop, discovery of an oil well, or winning a sweepstakes is not usually thought of as an "act of G-d."

David teaches us otherwise. When a person falls, it is generally of his own doing. When those who have fallen arise, that is where Divine intervention should be recognized.

From the Scriptures

And I saw that there is nothing better than for a person to rejoice (simchah) with his deeds, for that is his portion. For who can bring him to see what will occur after him? *(Ecclesiastes 3:22)*.

All the works of Torah ethics, both chassidic and *mussar*, are replete with the importance of *simchah*, joy or happiness.

Yet it is evident that modern man knows little about joy or happiness. In an era of unprecedented affluence, when science and technology have so vastly improved the quality of life, the use of alcohol, tranquilizers, anti-depressants, and drugs is extremely widespread. People do not take these emotional anesthetics because they are happy. No one wants to get rid of a good feeling. Our society is one in which people do not know how to be happy.

The wise Solomon tells us not to worry about the future, not to postpone enjoying what we have, and not to let greed or envy prevent us from enjoying our portion in life.

Be happy with your deeds also means to live in a manner that your deeds bring you happiness rather than become the cause of your remorse.

NOTES

_____
_____
_____
_____
_____
_____
_____
_____
_____

. . . וְלֹא יַעֲלֶה קִנְאַת אָדָם עַל לִבֵּנוּ . . . *From*

May there not be envy by one person of *our* another, and direct our hearts that each *Prayers* one of us see the virtues of our fellow humans and not their defects and faults *(prayer of Rabbi Elimelech of Lizensk).*

Jan. 12, 1991
Jan. 2, 1992
Jan. 19, 1993
Jan. 9, 1994
Dec. 29, 1994
Jan. 18, 1996

Is it appropriate to ask of G-d to direct our hearts to do right and avoid wrong? Isn't this our responsibility, something we must accomplish by our own efforts?

There are several answers to this question. One approach is that the essence of prayer is to ask for something that we desire. The more intense our desire for something, the more fervent the prayer, and the more fervent and sincere the prayer, the more likely it is to be answered. If we pray fervently not to see other people's character defects because of an intense and sincere desire to see only the good in others, we are very apt to achieve that. Getting ourselves to have this intense desire *is* the effort we make.

One thing have I asked of G-d, only this do I seek: my peaceful sojourn in the House of G-d all the days of my life *(Psalms 27:4).*

From the Scriptures

Rabbi Moshe Teitelbaum (author of *Yismach Moshe*) told of a dream wherein he was admitted to *Gan Eden* (Paradise). All that he saw there were Sages studying Torah. Having fantasized that Paradise was something more elaborate, he was disappointed.

A heavenly voice then called out to him, "Moshe son of Channah! You are in error. It is not that the Sages are in Paradise. Rather, it is Paradise that is in the Sages."

We often contemplate about what it would take to make us happy. We each have lists of things that we feel would fulfill our desires.

The dream of the Yismach Moshe tells us that happiness is not dependent on anything external to us. Our Paradise must be within ourselves, rather than our seeking to be in it.

Do not deceive yourself. If you do not have inner happiness, if you are not happy without the long list of your desires, then getting what you want will not bring you happiness.

We must look for happiness within ourselves, and not in the external world.

NOTES

_____
_____
_____
_____
_____
_____
_____
_____
_____

TEVES

טבת

Jan. 13, 1991
Jan. 3, 1992
Jan. 20, 1993
Jan. 10 ,1994
Dec. 30, 1994
Jan. 19, 1996

From our Prayers

אֱמֶת וֶאֱמוּנָה חֹק וְלֹא יַעֲבֹר . . .

It is a truth and an unchangeable conviction, a statute which will not pass away. It is a truth that You are our L-rd, our G-d and the G-d of our fathers, our King and the King of our fathers . . . our redeemer and deliverer — such has been Your name forever (daily morning service).

We assert our belief that the word of G-d is eternal and binding upon us in all eras. The belief in G-d and the teachings of the Torah are as valid in the day of space travel as at the Revelation at Sinai.

A couple who had been married for many years was traveling. The wife reminisced, "Do you remember how, when we were just married, we were so much closer?"

The husband, sitting behind the steering wheel, nodded. "Yes," he said, "and I have not moved."

We read about the quality of life of previous generations and wonder why the generations appear to have been more spiritual than we are.

We should realize that G-d has not drifted away from us. He is eternal and unchanging. It is we who have moved, and it is we who must make the effort to re-establish the closeness we crave.

From the Scriptures

As east is distant from west, so has G-d removed our sins from us (Psalms 103:12).

One of the Rabbis noted that if a person is facing east, all he must do to face west is simply turn around. He does not have to exert himself to orient himself toward the west rather than toward the east.

With the very same ease, we can have our sins removed. All that is required is a sincere change in attitude. Whereas a person may have previously looked favorably upon an improper behavior, he can repudiate it with simple determination, without necessarily going through severe acts of penance.

Rejecting erroneous ways is not as difficult as one might think. You just have to want to do so.

NOTES

_____
_____
_____
_____
_____
_____
_____
_____
_____
_____

הַשָּׁמַיִם מְסַפְּרִים כְּבוֹד קֵל *From*
וּמַעֲשֵׂה יָדָיו מַגִּיד הָרָקִיעַ . . . *our*

The heavens recount the glory of G-d and *Prayers*
the firmament tells the work of His
hands ... The Torah of G-d is all-encompassing; it responds to the soul ... The
mandates of G-d are upright; they gladden the heart *(Shabbos morning service,
Psalms 19:2-9).*

Jan. 14, 1991
Jan. 4, 1992
Jan. 21, 1993
Jan. 11, 1994
Dec. 31, 1994
Jan. 20, 1996

In this psalm, David places the natural law and the
Divine law side by side.

Whereas thoughtful observation of design in the universe attests to its being created by an all-wise Designer,
and we can thus reason logically to the existence of G-d, we
do not yet know from this what it is that G-d asks of us. For
this we must have recourse to the Torah, which contains
the Divine mandates.

Juxtaposing the natural law and the Divine law also
indicates that neither are subject to change by humans. Just
as no legislature or sovereign can abrogate the law of
gravity or alter the movements of the planets, neither can
anyone tamper with the Divine law.

We must subject ourselves to the will of G-d, and not
attempt to adapt His will to our desires.

Find favor and wisdom in the eyes of G-d and man
(Proverbs 3:4).

*From the
Scriptures*

NOTES

The Sages tell us that we should act in a manner that will
not only be pleasing to G-d, but will also earn the respect of
others *(Ethics of the Fathers 2:1).*

Why should we be concerned about the opinions of
others?

Firstly, if we are careless in our behavior, others may
misinterpret our actions and wrongly assume that it is
permissible to do something that it is actually improper.

Secondly, we should not act in a manner that will cause
people to think badly of us and speak derisively of us, for
we will thereby be the indirect cause of their sin of gossip.

It is not false pride to be above suspicion. We should be
examples of integrity.

Erev
Rosh Chodesh
[Eve of the
New Month]
Jan. 15, 1991
Jan. 5, 1992
Jan. 22, 1993
Jan. 12, 1994
Jan. 1, 1995
Jan. 21, 1996

From our Prayers

. . . מִנְהַג בֵּית דִּינְךָ הַצֶּדֶק
. . . לֹא כְמִנְהַג בָּתֵּי דִינִין שֶׁל בְּנֵי אָדָם

Master of the universe! The custom of Your righteous court of justice is not like that of human courts. Among humans, the person who admits a debt must pay, and if he denies it, he goes free. But Your court is otherwise. If one denies his acts, woe is to him; but if he admits and repents, You have mercy on him (*special prayer on the day preceding Rosh Chodesh*).

We must take advantage of every opportunity to begin a new segment of life free of the burdens of the past: a new week, a new month, a new year.

The key to unburdening ourselves of the past is a sincere repentance for whatever wrongs we have committed. But in order to repent we must recognize that something we did was wrong. Too often our defense mechanism of denial precludes such recognition.

We must make a concerted effort to overcome this denial. Our only salvation before the Divine tribunal lies in recognizing and admitting our mistakes.

From the Sages

NOTES

Whoever is merciful towards others merits mercy from Heaven (*Shabbos 151b*).

The Or Hachaim (*Deuteronomy 13:18*) states that mercy, which is essentially a suspension of absolute justice, is granted only to those who are merciful towards others.

Many times we may feel justified in bearing grudges toward people who have offended or harmed us. In our anger, we are unlikely to consider that there may have been mitigating circumstances in their behavior.

Even if we think we are right, or better yet, even if we are in fact right, we should think about how we wish to be judged ourselves. We always seem to have ample explanations to justify our actions. We should grant this courtesy to others.

If we hope to be forgiven, we must learn to forgive.

בָּרְכִי נַפְשִׁי אֶת ה' . . . *From*
our

Bless G-d, O my soul. My G-d, You are
very great. You have clothed Yourself *Prayers*
with majesty and with the glory of might
(Psalms 104:1, recited on Rosh Chodesh).

Psalm 104 is a masterpiece of poetry. It has been said
that it is worthwhile learning Hebrew if only to read this
psalm in the original. David describes nature lovingly. In
every facet of nature — the rain, the winds, the mountains,
the springs, the trees, the dwelling places of animals — in
everything David sees the hand of G-d.

"The glory of G-d will endure forever; may G-d take
delight in His creations" *(104:31).*

G-d has indeed created a beautiful world, but will He
have the delight He wished? That depends on the deeds of
mankind, because G-d has left man free to choose his
moral actions.

David exhorts us to live in a way that will not mar the
beauty of the world, and will provide G-d the delight He
sought in its creation.

Rosh Chodesh
Jan. 16, 1991
Jan. 6, 1992
Jan. 23, 1993
Jan. 13, 1994
Jan. 2, 1995
Jan. 22, 1996

**The sinners will at last cease to be from the
earth, and the lawless will be no more** *(Psalms 104:35).*

**The correct interpretation, says the Talmud, is
that sins and lawlessness will be eradicated, but not
the people who commit them** *(Berachos 10a).*

This interpretation was given by Beruria, wife of Rabbi
Meir, who disagreed with her husband's prayer that the
wicked should perish.

"Do not pray for their death," she said. "Rather pray that
they recant their errant ways. It is the sinfulness that should
be eradicated, not the sinner."

Beruria believed in the inherent goodness of man.
Granted that social order requires punishment for unacceptable behavior, but if one prays for Divine intervention,
the wish should be to remove evil, not those who do evil.

If one prays for people to cease doing wrong, one will be
stimulated to teach them and to help them do right.

There is much that we can learn from Beruria.

*From
the Sages*

NOTES
——————
——————
——————
——————
——————
——————
——————

SHEVAT

שבט

Jan. 17, 1991
Jan. 7, 1992
Jan. 24, 1993
Jan. 14, 1994
Jan. 3, 1995
Jan. 23, 1996

*From
our
Prayers*

קָרָאתִי מִצָּרָה לִי אֶל ה' וַיַּעֲנֵנִי
מִבֶּטֶן שְׁאוֹל שִׁוַּעְתִּי שָׁמַעְתָּ קוֹלִי . . .

Out of my anguish I called to G-d and He answered me. From the midst of the grave I prayed, and You heard my voice . . . I had thought I had been banished from before Your eyes, but I will still look upon Your holy Sanctuary *(Jonah 2:3,5).*

Jonah, the immortal story of the man who tries to run away from G-d because he disputes G-d's judgment.

Why is Jonah not severely punished for his defiance?

While it is true that we must at all times accept the sovereignty of G-d and defer to His judgment, there are times that a person may feel so intensely that G-d has wronged him, that he is tempted to turn against G-d.

The Talmud states that a person is not held liable for what he says when he is suffering *(Bava Basra* 16b). G-d knows our nature very well. When circumstances cause a person to feel angry with G-d, this is not a denial of G-d. Quite the contrary, it is an expression of belief in His existence and in His absolute control and mastery over the world.

A Chassidic master is alleged to have said, "You can be for G-d, and you can be against G-d. You just cannot be without G-d."

*From the
Scriptures*

And Pharaoh said, "Who is G-d, that I must obey him? I do not acknowledge G-d" *(Exodus 5:2).*

The Rabbi of Kotzk said, "Some people call themselves non-believers. How ridiculous! Let them just suffer a severe headache, and there they are, standing before the Ark of the Torah, praying for relief.

"Pharaoh was a non-believer. Miracle after miracle before his very eyes, punishment after punishment, yet he refused to acknowledge G-d."

There are some people who profess that they do not believe in G-d. There are some who have sought alternatives to Torah-observant Judaism. If you want to know what they really believe, observe what they do when they are in anguish. Their prayer, how they pray and where they pray, betrays their true belief.

It is time that people stop deluding themselves that they do not have faith. The Rabbi of Kotzk was right. All Jews are believers.

וַאֲנִי בְּרֹב חַסְדְּךָ אָבוֹא בֵיתֶךָ *From*
אֶשְׁתַּחֲוֶה אֶל הֵיכַל קָדְשְׁךָ בְּיִרְאָתֶךָ *our*

And I, by the grace of Your kindness, shall *Prayers*
enter Your house. **I will bow down to
Your holy Sanctuary in Your reverence**
(Psalms 5:8, prayer upon entering the syna-
gogue).

Jan. 18, 1991
Jan. 8, 1992
Jan. 25, 1993
Jan. 15, 1994
Jan. 4, 1995
Jan. 24, 1996

The Talmud states that the pious men of earlier days
would meditate for an hour before beginning to pray
(Berachos 30b).

A person who is going to do something which he feels is
of great consequence, whether it is a surgeon who is going
to perform a difficult operation, or an artisan who is going
to fashion a delicate piece of jewelry, will first study the
project and make certain that all his instruments are in
proper order before beginning his task.

Our instruments of prayer are our minds and our
mouths. If we took prayer seriously, we would devote some
time to thinking about what we are about to do. To whom
are we praying? What is it that we will be saying? Have we
properly cleansed our tools — our minds and our mouths
— for prayer? Are we cautious that our minds and our
mouths not be contaminated by improper thoughts and
speech?

The fact that we have "introductory" prayers such as that
above should call our attention to the quality of our prayers.

You shall love your G-d, and you shall serve Him *From*
with all your heart *(Deuteronomy 11:13).* *the Sages*

**Rashi notes that "service of the heart" refers to
prayer.**

As a child, I used to watch my grandfather pray. I was
surprised that during the *Amidah*, which is usually recited
by heart with one's eyes closed to avoid distraction, NOTES
Grandfather kept his eyes open.

One time I gathered enough courage to ask him why he
kept his eyes open during the *Amidah*.

Grandfather looked at me with bewilderment. "I do
what?" he asked.

I then understood that his devotion and absorption in
prayer were so absolute that he was not even aware that his
eyes were open!

The Talmud is correct when it states that the pious men
of yore knew how to pray.

SHEVAT

שבט

Jan. 19, 1991
Jan. 9, 1992
Jan. 26, 1993
Jan. 16, 1994
Jan. 5, 1995
Jan. 25, 1996

From our Prayers

חָנֵּנִי אֱלֹקִים כְּחַסְדֶּךָ
כְּרֹב רַחֲמֶיךָ מְחֵה פְשָׁעָי . . .

Favor me, O G-d, according to Your loving-kindness. With the fullness of Your mercy, blot out my transgressions. Wash me thoroughly from my iniquities, and cleanse me from my sins. For my transgressions are known to me, and my sins are ever before me *(Psalms 51:3-5).*

This prayer of David followed his reprimand by the prophet, Nathan.

David did not deny that he had done wrong. He did not try to justify his act. He promptly admitted that he had sinned, and was therefore granted forgiveness.

David knew that he must yet atone for his sin, and that in the cleansing process he would suffer. He did not ask for a Divine dispensation, but rather not to be cast away from G-d.

David teaches us that as long as we can feel a closeness to G-d, even severe suffering is bearable.

From the Scriptures

The ways of a simpleton seem proper to him, but he who accepts counsel is wise *(Proverbs 12:15).*

NOTES

_____
_____
_____
_____
_____
_____
_____
_____

The Talmud states that before creating man, G-d sought the counsel of the angels, not because He needed their wisdom, but to teach us that even the great and mighty should listen to advice from those who are of a lesser stature.

Many costly mistakes may result if one considers himself to be above everyone else, and rejects the counsel of those whom he considers to be less wise. Although we must make our own decisions, we should keep an open mind to other opinions, because even if we are wiser than others, their opinions may not be affected by those biases or desires to which we are subject, and others can therefore provide us with another perspective.

Only a fool is absolutely certain that his way is right.

הַרְאֵנוּ ה' חַסְדֶּךָ וְיֶשְׁעֲךָ תִּתֶּן לָנוּ . . . *From our Prayers*

O G-d, let us behold Your loving-kindness, and grant us Your salvation (Psalms 85:8). **Arise to our aid and redeem us for the sake of Your loving-kindness** (Psalms 44:27, morning service).

Jan. 20, 1991
Jan. 10, 1992
Jan. 27, 1993
Jan. 17, 1994
Jan. 6, 1995
Jan. 26, 1996

Although we trust that everything G-d does is just, and even that our sufferings are somehow for our ultimate good, the Psalmist prays, "Let us *see* Your loving-kindness." We may pray for blessings that are not in disguise, but are visibly good.

Even though we pray for our own welfare, this is not an exclusively selfish prayer. If what happens to us is not visibly good in our own limited perception, then others cannot see the Divine beneficence either. It is thus for the greater glory of G-d that we ask that His kindnesses come to us in an undisguised form. Hence we pray, "Come to our aid for the sake of Your loving-kindness," so that all may clearly observe the mercy and bounty of G-d.

A person may tend to deliberate whether he should or should not give tzedakah (charity). That is why the Torah exhorts, "Do not close your hand to the poor" (Rashi, Deuteronomy 15:7).

From the Sages

A follower of Rabbi Nachum of Czernobl presented him with a gift of three hundred rubles. Earlier that day, a man had described his plight to Rabbi Nachum: He was in arrears in his rent to the *poritz* (the feudal lord) for three hundred rubles, and unless he paid promptly, his family would be evicted.

When Rabbi Nachum received the three hundred rubles, his first impulse was to give the money to this needy man. Subsequently, he began to reflect that there were other needy people in the community. Why give the entire sum to one person? Perhaps it would be better to give one hundred rubles to this man, and divide the remainder among other needy people.

NOTES

Rabbi Nachum decided that his after-thought was the machinations of the *yeitzer hara* (the evil inclination) rather than the *yeitzer hatov* (the good inclination).

"This is always the way the *yeitzer hara* operates," Rabbi Nachum said. "Once you decide to do something that is right, he comes along with all kinds of logical arguments why you should do otherwise."

He then gave the entire sum to the needy man.

Jan. 21, 1991
Jan. 11, 1992
Jan. 28, 1993
Jan. 18, 1994
Jan. 7, 1995
Jan. 27, 1996

From our Prayers

וְתַגִּיעֵנוּ לִמְחוֹז חֶפְצֵנוּ
לְחַיִּים וּלְשִׂמְחָה וּלְשָׁלוֹם . . .

Bring us to our desired destination in life, gladness and peace, and protect us from all enemies, from ambush, wild beasts, and from all sorts of mishaps *(prayer of the traveler).*

In ancient times, travel was indeed hazardous. There was always the danger of being robbed by highwaymen, attacked by ferocious beasts, or injured in a violent storm.

Today's travel is, or course, much safer. But there is one journey that remains hazardous, and that is the journey throughout life, until we arrive at our final destination.

Awareness of the presence of danger is in itself a safeguard, because we can then be alert and on guard. One can take protective and evasive measures, or enlist the necessary help to overcome the danger.

If we bear in mind that life is a journey to an ultimate destination, we may then be alert to exercise the necessary precautions so that nothing should interfere with our arriving at our desired goal.

From the Sages

Remember whence you came, where you are headed, and before whom you must give an account of your life *(Ethics of the Fathers 3:1).*

The Baal Shem Tov was born in the village of Tlust in Russia, yet often signed his name "Yisrael of Okup."

Rabbi Shneur Zalman of Liadi explained that the village of Tlust once had a fortress that was destroyed in one of the wars. The Baal Shem Tov's parents were extremely poor, and they lived in a cave formed by the moat of the fortress. The Russian word for "excavation" is *okupi*. In order to always remember his humble origin, the Baal Shem Tov always referred to himself as one who had grown up in the "ditch."

When success threatens to turn our heads, it is important to remember that we are all really of humble origin.

NOTES

_____
_____
_____
_____
_____
_____
_____
_____
_____

וְזַכֵּנוּ לְקַבֵּל שַׁבָּתוֹת מִתּוֹךְ רוֹב שִׂמְחָה *From*
וּמִתּוֹךְ עֹשֶׁר וְכָבוֹד וּמִתּוֹךְ מִעוּט עֲוֹנוֹת *our*

Grant us that we may welcome many *Prayers*
Shabbosos amidst much joy, with
abundance and honor, and with a minimum of sins *(prayer before Kiddush on Shabbos eve).*

Jan. 22, 1991
Jan. 12, 1992
Jan. 29, 1993
Jan. 19, 1994
Jan. 8, 1995
Jan. 28, 1996

Why pray for a minimum of sins? Why not pray to be
completely free of sin?

Sins are our mistakes in life, and no person goes
through life without making any mistakes.

Mistakes can be valuable experiences and can teach us
a great deal, but only if we are open minded and willing to
learn, willing to accept both reprimand and guidance.

We can learn just as well from minor mistakes as from
very serious mistakes. If we do learn from minor mistakes, we may well be able to prevent major ones. If we
dismiss minor mistakes as trivia, as insignificant, then we
learn nothing from them, and we render ourselves vulnerable to more serious mistakes.

So we pray for "minimal" mistakes. But we must be
wise to know how to benefit from them.

**I constantly place the presence of G-d before my
eyes** *(Psalms 16:8).* **This is a fundamental rule in Torah
and behavior of the righteous who walk in the path
of G-d** *(Shulchan Aruch Orach Chaim 1:1).*

*From
the Sages*

Someone asked Rabbi Nachum of Kosov, "How is it
possible to consistently keep the presence of G-d before
one's eyes? During the day, a person is involved in work,
in business transactions, and in so many other distracting
things, that it is simply impossible to always think of the
presence of G-d."

Rabbi Nachum shrugged. "During prayers and the
reading of the Torah you often think about your business
affairs, don't you? If you can think about business when
you should be meditating about G-d, then you can also
meditate about G-d when you are engaged in business."

It really comes down to how important something is to
us. Our thoughts tend to gravitate to that which we
consider most important.

NOTES
_____
_____
_____
_____
_____
_____
_____
_____
_____

SHEVAT

8

שבט

Jan. 23, 1991
Jan. 13, 1992
Jan. 30, 1993
Jan. 20, 1994
Jan. 9, 1995
Jan. 29, 1996

*From
our
Prayers*

שַׂבְּעֵנוּ בַבֹּקֶר חַסְדֶּךָ
וּנְרַנְּנָה וְנִשְׂמְחָה בְּכָל יָמֵינוּ

Satisfy us with Your loving-kindness in
the morning, and we will sing and
rejoice all of our days *(Psalms 90:14, Shabbos
morning service).*

If in the "morning," or in the early days of our lives, we
can be the beneficiaries of manifest Divine loving-kindness, then we are more likely to be free of emotional
distress the rest of our days.

This would seem to be a prayer that we say for our
children's sake, because as grownups, the "morning" of
our lives is behind us.

While we pray to G-d to show His loving-kindness to
our children, we must remember that as parents, we also
bear a great measure of that responsibility. We should
provide a secure and wholesome environment, being
particularly cautious not to take out our personal frustrations on them.

*From
the Sages*

**Israel, the Torah, and the Holy One, Blessed is
He, are all one** *(Zohar, Acharei Mos).*

Rabbi Yaakov Yosef of Polnoah said that G-d is absolute
unity, a pure oneness, rather than a composite unit. The
Torah is the word of G-d and the wisdom of G-d, and
since the wisdom of G-d is inseparable from G-d himself,
anyone who embraces Torah, or who embraces a *mitzvah*, which is the word of G-d, is embracing G-d himself.

NOTES

_____
_____
_____
_____
_____
_____
_____
_____
_____

This is nothing less than mind boggling. Mortal man,
with all his frailties and limitations, has the capacity not
only to serve G-d, but to become one with G-d!

Because man has free will, he can choose to transgress
the Divine commandments. But one should be aware that
in doing so, he not only is remiss in the service of G-d, but
also detaches himself from Him.

Rabbi Shneur Zalman points out that no rational person
would willingly separate himself from G-d. Sin occurs only
because man is unaware that it will bring about this
separation.

בָּרְכֵנוּ בַּבְּרָכָה הַמְשֻׁלֶּשֶׁת . . . *From*
בַּתּוֹרָה הַכְּתוּבָה עַל יְדֵי מֹשֶׁה עַבְדֶּךָ . . . *our*

Our G-d and G-d of our fathers, bless us *Prayers*
with the tripartite blessing that is contained in the Torah, and that is recited by
Aaron and his children, the priests, Your
sacred congregation *(daily Amidah)*.

Jan. 24, 1991
Jan. 14, 1992
Jan. 31, 1993
Jan. 21, 1994
Jan. 10, 1995
Jan. 30, 1996

Belief in G-d can be obtained in two ways: (1) A person believes because he accepts the principles of faith from his ancestors; or (2) he cogitates and comes to the conclusion that there is a G-d who rules the universe.

The strength of the first method is that it is not vulnerable to challenge by philosophical argument, but its weakness is that it is a very shallow kind of faith. The second method has the strength of logical conviction, but its weakness is that it is subject to challenge.

The ideal faith is therefore a combination of both methods: "Our G-d and G-d of our fathers." We accept the teachings of our ancestors, but reinforce them with our own learning.

G-d looked down from heaven upon the children of man, to see whether there were any who were using their reason in search of G-d *(Psalms 14:2)*.

From the Scriptures

Rabbi Simchah Zisl Ziv notes that people seem to have an innate curiosity to learn something new, to hear of a new discovery. We rarely miss a news program or a newspaper, lest we remain unaware of a new happening.

"Where," he asks, "is the curiosity to learn about G-d? Why are people not coming in droves to those who can teach them and direct them to learn about G-d?"

Perhaps the answer to this question is that learning anything else that is new does not obligate us, whereas coming to a greater knowledge of G-d will make us more subservient to G-d. Perhaps people are apprehensive that if they know more about G-d, they will be more compelled to accept His sovereignty, and this might necessitate changing their way of living.

NOTES

The Psalmist says that G-d looks down from heaven to see if anyone is interested in learning more about Him. But apparently no one wishes to change. "Every man was depraved. None was a doer of good, not even one" *(Psalms 14:3)*.

Jan. 25, 1991
Jan. 15, 1992
Feb. 1, 1993
Jan. 22, 1994
Jan. 11, 1995
Jan. 31, 1996

From our Prayers

רַבּוֹת מַחֲשָׁבוֹת בְּלֶב אִישׁ
וַעֲצַת ה' הִיא תָקוּם . . .

Many are the thoughts in the heart of man, but the counsel of G-d will prevail *(Proverbs 19:21).* **The counsel of G-d endures forever, the thoughts of His heart throughout all generations** *(Psalms 33:11, morning service).*

The true prayer is that we may be shown the will of G-d and helped to achieve it.

The Torah tells us that Joseph had a prophetic dream, but his envious brothers sought to defy the Divine will by selling him into slavery. But rather than thwarting the Divine will, this act actually led to its fulfillment, for it was out of slavery that Joseph became a viceroy, and thus the prophecy was realized.

We would be wise to recognize how powerless we really are, and that the will of G-d will prevail. This is why so many prayers begin with "May it be Your will . . . ," because if it is not the will of G-d, all our efforts are futile.

From the Scriptures

Do not give your money in usury, and for interest do not give your food. I am your G-d who has delivered you from the land of Egypt, to give you the land of Canaan, to be your G-d *(Leviticus 25:37-38).*

Rabbi Yeruchim Levovitz said that the halachic prohibition of interest has an important teaching.

When you do a favor for someone, you should do so because it is the right thing to do. We are to emulate G-d, in that He does things for us without expectation of return, because there obviously is nothing that we can do for Him. Similarly, we should not be motivated by expectation of return when we do things for others. If we should ever be in need, then others should help us because it is the proper thing for them to do, and not because they are in any way obligated to us.

Taking interest for lending someone money is a return on a favor. The strictness of the Torah prohibition on interest indicates how important it is to do for others without obligating them to us.

If we would only apply this teaching in everyday life, how many resentments and disappointments could be avoided!

NOTES

_____
_____
_____
_____
_____
_____
_____
_____

From אֶת צֶמַח דָּוִד עַבְדְּךָ מְהֵרָה תַצְמִיחַ
our וְקַרְנוֹ תָּרוּם בִּישׁוּעָתֶךָ ...

Speedily cause the offspring of David, *Prayers*
Your servant, to sprout, so that his
strength may be uplifted by Your salvation, for we hope for Your salvation all the
day *(daily Amidah)*.

Jan. 26, 1991
Jan. 16, 1992
Feb. 2, 1993
Jan. 23, 1994
Jan. 12, 1995
Feb. 1, 1996

How do we have the audacity to say before G-d, the
Searcher of all hearts, that all day long we aspire for His
salvation, when the fact is that we think of it so rarely? Our
thoughts during the day are totally occupied with our work
and business affairs.

When a devoted mother puts her infant in the crib and
goes about her housework, her conscious mind is occupied
by what she is doing; but just beneath the surface of her
conscious mind, the thought of her infant is always present.
The slightest whimper puts her into immediate, conscious
contact with the baby, who is thus never really out of her
thoughts for one moment.

While we may be concentrating on whatever it is that we
are doing, the hope for Divine salvation should always be
present in our minds.

You shall teach and reprimand your friend *(Leviti-*
cus 19:17).

*From the
Scriptures*

The Rabbi of Porisov overheard his nephew, Rabbi
Pinchas, berating himself in a soliloquy.

"Young man," the Rabbi of Porisov said, "if someone
else would have said of you one tenth of what you said of
yourself, you would have certainly been insulted and
resentful of him."

NOTES

"Of course," said Rabbi Pinchas. "Anyone else saying
these things about me would hardly be a friend of mine,
and it is unlikely that his intentions would be for my
betterment. I am not insulting myself. I am merely pointing
out my character defects, so that I can improve upon
them."

It is rare to have friends that we know are so devoted to
us that we would accept their criticisms of us without
resentment. We may therefore have to act as our own best
friends.

Jan. 27, 1991
Jan. 17, 1992
Feb. 3, 1993
Jan. 24, 1994
Jan. 13, 1995
Feb. 2, 1996

*From
our
Prayers*

וְטַהֵר לִבֵּנוּ לְעָבְדְּךָ בֶּאֱמֶת

Purify our hearts to serve You with truth
(Shabbos Amidah).

A disciple of the Maggid of Mezeritch complained that he could not pray with pure devotion because of improper thoughts that were intruding during his prayer. The Maggid referred him to Rabbi Wolf of Zhitomir for help with this.

On arriving in Zhitomir, the man sought out Rabbi Wolf's house and knocked on the door, but there was no answer. After repeatedly knocking on the front door, rear door, and shutters, the man concluded that Rabbi Wolf was not at home. He sat in the doorway to wait for him and fell asleep. Hours later, Rabbi Wolf opened the door and invited him into the house.

"Have you learned anything yet, young man?" Rabbi Wolf asked. The man shook his head in bewilderment.

"You knocked incessantly on my doors and shutters seeking entrance. But since I am master of my house, I chose to refuse you entrance.

"You can be master of your mind. If you are determined to keep some thoughts out of your mind, you can do so. You can refuse them entrance, regardless of how much they try to intrude."

*From the
Scriptures*

When you come into the land, and plant trees of fruit, you shall hold the fruits three years forbidden, not to be eaten. The fourth year, its fruit shall be sacred to G-d *(Leviticus 19:23-24).*

Whereas we can never know the Divine intent of any *mitzvah*, we can derive many teachings from them.

Forbidding the early fruits of the tree may be telling us that the ideas of childhood are immature. And just as the first mature fruits must be sacred and taken to Jerusalem, so must we process our transition to adulthood, from immaturity to maturity, through Torah and the Divine service.

Immaturity is not limited to age. Some grown people retain childish ideas. Some people are arrested in their emotional development similar to people who early in life use alcohol or drugs, and whose bodies continue to develop while their emotions remain juvenile.

We need the help and guidance of wise and experienced people to help us recognize the residuals of childish thought and behavior. By living a Torah-true life, we can convert these juvenile feelings into mature feelings, and we can then enjoy their fruits in a healthy manner.

NOTES

_____
_____
_____
_____
_____
_____
_____
_____

אַשְׁרֵי שֶׁקֵּל יַעֲקֹב בְּעֶזְרוֹ שִׂבְרוֹ עַל ה' אֱלֹקָיו *From*

Fortunate is the person in whose help is *our*
the G-d of Jacob, whose hopes are in the *Prayers*
L-rd, his G-d *(Psalms 146:5, morning services).*

A childless woman pleaded with Rabbi Nachum of Cze nobl to bless her that she may have a child, but the Rab'ji refused to yield to her, and she left in tears. The Rat bi's assistant could not contain himself, and asked the Ral'bi why he had refused the woman his blessing.

'Go after the woman and bring her back," said Rabbi N..chum.

On her return, Rabbi Nachum asked, "What did you do after you left my study?"

The woman replied, "'I raised my hands to Heaven and said, 'Dear G-d, even the Rabbi refuses to help me. Now the only one I can turn to is You.' "

Rabbi Nachum smiled and said, "Go home in good cheer. Your prayers will be answered." To his assistant he said, "This woman was placing her belief in me, as though I could work some magic for her. I had to turn her away, so that she would place her trust in G-d, where it belongs."

Jan. 28, 1991
Jan. 18, 1992
Feb. 4, 1993
Jan. 25, 1994
Jan. 14, 1995
Feb. 3, 1996

Rabbi Yitzchak Meir of Gur said, "The spies reported to Moses that the inhabitants of Canaan were such giants, that, 'We appeared to them as grasshoppers, and that is how we felt' (Numbers 13:33). This teaches us that the esteem you receive from others depends on how much you value yourself."

From the Sages

This is a profound psychological truth. If we do not have self-respect, we cannot expect others to respect us.

Having self-respect and self-esteem is not the same as vanity. One can have a healthy self-esteem and yet be very humble. I developed this theme in *Let Us Make Man* (*Traditional Press*, 1986).

A person must know the truth, and if we deflate ourselves so that we do not recognize our true value, we distort the truth. Torah certainly does not expect us to distort the truth. We must recognize our strengths and capabilities, but such awareness should cause us to be humble with the recognition of how much we have yet to do, rather than vain with pride about how much we have already achieved.

NOTES
_____
_____
_____
_____
_____
_____
_____
_____
_____

Jan. 29, 1991
Jan. 19, 1992
Feb. 5, 1993
Jan. 26, 1994
Jan. 15, 1995
Feb. 4, 1996

From our Prayers

הָשִׁיבָה שׁוֹפְטֵינוּ כְּבָרִאשׁוֹנָה וְיוֹעֲצֵינוּ כְּבַתְּחִלָּה וְהָסֵר מִמֶּנּוּ יָגוֹן וַאֲנָחָה . . .

Restore our judges as before, and our counselors as at the beginning. Remove from us sorrow and sighing . . . Blessed be You, G-d, King who loves righteousness and justice *(daily Amidah).*

We pray for justice, or better yet, for restoration of justice.

This prayer for Divine help in restoring justice is particularly relevant in an age when it has become so evident that the unguided human intellect, even though its intentions are noble, may so distort the process of attaining justice, that there is a virtual breakdown of law and order.

Under guise of protecting the rights of persons accused of crime, criminals have often been given free reign, and it is the victims of crime who have lost their rights. Under guise of protecting human liberty, some abominations have received the sanction of law.

If there is to be true justice, it will come only with Divine guidance.

From the Sages

Rabbi Pinchas of Koritz said, "The world is like a book that can be read in either direction. There is the power of creation, making something out of nothing; and there is the power of destruction, making nothing out of something."

Science teaches us the principle of conservation, that neither matter nor energy can be created or destroyed, only converted from one form to another.

Torah teaches us that creation began with G-d bringing substance from absolute nothingness. Man also has the capacity to create. The Talmud says that with each *mitzvah* that a person does, he *creates* a new angel, a new force for good.

Any transgression of the will of G-d is destructive. It is taking substance which G-d created to be used for good, and using it for evil. This results in its becoming a spiritual "nothingness."

Man can thus continue the work of creation, or he can bring about its destruction. Why destroy when you can create?

NOTES

_____
_____
_____
_____
_____
_____
_____
_____
_____
_____

שֶׁלֹא חִסַּר בְּעוֹלָמוֹ דָּבָר . . . *From*
וּבָרָא בוֹ בְּרִיּוֹת טוֹבוֹת וְאִילָנוֹת טוֹבִים *our*
לְהַנּוֹת בָּהֶם בְּנֵי אָדָם *Prayers*

Blessed be You, L-rd our G-d, King of the universe, Who has withheld nothing from His world and has created beautiful creatures and beautiful trees in it, so that people may delight in them *(blessing on seeing trees blossoming for the first time in the year).*

Tu BiShvat
[Rosh Hashanah la'eelan — New Year for the trees]
Jan. 30, 1991
Jan. 20, 1992
Feb. 6, 1993
Jan. 27, 1994
Jan. 16, 1995
Feb. 5, 1996

The fifteenth day of Shevat is designated in the Talmud as the "new year" for trees. On seeing trees burst into blossom, we are required to recite a prayer of gratitude to remind us that the beauty in the world is a Divine gift. It is something which must be not only appreciated, but used with reverence, reminiscent of its Giver.

The beauty of the blossom should call forth the realization that G-d did not withhold anything in His world. The original world was the Garden of Eden, where man and all creatures could have lived in physical and spiritual delight.

In our own limited way, we can partake of a "perfect" world, even as it is now with all its apparent imperfections, which are the result of man deviating from the will of G-d. If we have full trust and faith in G-d, and come closer to Him in spirituality, we become less vulnerable to the effects of the present world's defects.

What is atonement? It means that the person should reject his sinful ways *(Maimonides, Laws of Repentance, 2:2).*

From the Sages
NOTES

A petitioner asked the Rabbi of Rizhin for instruction on how to accomplish atonement. "How come you did not need to ask for instruction on how to sin?" the Rabbi asked.

"Sin occurred spontaneously," the man answered. "I did what I did, and then I discovered it was sinful."

"Well, then just reject what you did, and atonement will come spontaneously," the Rabbi answered. "First abandon your sinful behavior, and then you will discover that this constitutes atonement."

Jan. 31, 1991
Jan. 21, 1992
Feb. 7, 1993
Jan. 28, 1994
Jan. 17, 1995
Feb. 6, 1996

*From
our
Prayers*

לָמָה ה' תַּעֲמֹד בְּרָחוֹק
תַּעְלִים לְעִתּוֹת בַּצָּרָה

O G-d, why do You stand afar off? Why do You hide Your presence in times of trouble? *(Psalms 10:1)*

Several years ago, I visited an eight-year-old child who had just undergone open-heart surgery. When the physicians took the child for treatment to clear the lungs of secretions, I accompanied the child into the treatment room, and the doctor suggested that the father remain outside.

I could see the father peeking through the crack in the doorway. The treatment was uncomfortable, and the child cried and tried to fight off the doctors. "Daddy! It hurts. Don't let them do this to me!" he screamed.

Then I understood. Like the child, we may feel the pain of adversity and try to fight off what is happening to us. Like the child, we are unable to understand that the process which causes us suffering is essential to our lives and health. Our Father has not abandoned us. He watches and shares in our pain, but He knows what we do not know. He knows how and why this suffering is going to make us better.

All we need to know is that our loving Father is there, watching over us, even in our suffering.

*From
the Sages*

Envy, lust, and vanity are nothing but three taverns *(Rabbi Mendel of Kotzk).*

The prophet Isaiah refers to the people of his time as being "drunk, albeit not with wine" *(Isaiah 29:9).*

For the active alcoholic, no amount of drink is enough. He is not satisfied until he drinks himself into a stupor. The drinking, and his way of getting his drink, dominate his life and distort his thoughts and behavior in a very destructive manner.

NOTES

The Rabbi of Kotzk elaborates on the words of Isaiah. Envy, lust, and vanity are like alcohol to the alcoholic. There is no point at which we have enough, and in our attempts to satisfy these insatiable drives, we may bring ruin to ourselves and others.

Recovery for the alcoholic requires realization that his behavior is sick. Recovery from envy, lust, and vanity also require realization that these drives are sick.

שָׁאֶזְכֶּה לְהִסְתַּכֵּל עַל עַצְמִי תָּמִיד **From**
מַה אֲנִי עוֹשֶׂה בָּעוֹלָם הַזֶּה **our**

Please, O G-d, have mercy upon me that **Prayers**
I should not live a life of futility. May I
always reflect upon myself, "What am I
doing in this world?" *(Personal prayer of
Rabbi Nachman of Breslov).*

Feb. 1, 1991
Jan. 22, 1992
Feb. 8, 1993
Jan. 29, 1994
Jan. 18, 1995
Feb. 7, 1996

A man was once sentenced to twenty-five years of hard
labor. His hands were chained to the handle of a great
wheel that was set into a wall, and, for many hours each
day, he had to turn this massive wheel. He would often
wonder what he was accomplishing. Perhaps the wheel
turned a grindstone in a flour mill, or perhaps he was
generating energy that was being converted for some
purpose.

When his sentence expired and the shackles were
removed, the man, broken both in body and spirit,
immediately ran to the other side of the wall. To his
horror, there was nothing there! He collapsed with bitter
disappointment.

Our greatest need is to have purpose, to know what we
are doing in this world.

**For You, G-d, are merciful. You repay a person
according to his deeds** *(Psalms 62:13).*

**From the
Scriptures**

A *tzaddik*, accompanied by a disciple, passed a house
and heard sounds of a scuffle. Looking in, they saw a man
dragging his elderly father to evict him from the house.
The *tzaddik* stood in silence, and the disciple was
bewildered why his master did not intervene to stop this
atrocity.

When the man had his father at the threshold, the
tzaddik rushed in, seized him, and gave him a sound
thrashing. "You scoundrel," he said. "How dare you treat
your father this way?"

The *tzaddik* later explained to his disciple, "When this
father was young, he had dragged *his* father to throw him
out of the house, but he only managed to drag him to the
threshold. Therefore, that much he had coming to him."

If we are not at the point where we can be kind to
others altruistically, we should do so selfishly. There is a
system of justice.

NOTES

Feb. 2, 1991
Jan. 23, 1992
Feb. 9, 1993
Jan. 30, 1994
Jan. 19, 1995
Feb. 8, 1996

From our Prayers

אִם כְּבָנִים רַחֲמֵנוּ כְּרַחֵם אָב עַל בָּנִים . . .

If we are like children to You, have compassion on us like a father to a child. If we are like servants to You, our eyes turn to You, until You be gracious to us *(Rosh Hashanah prayer).*

The Talmud relates that Rabbi Yochanan ben Zakkai asked Rabbi Chanina ben Dosa to pray for his sick son, and Rabbi Chanina's prayer was promptly answered *(Berachos 34b).*

Rabbi Yochanan's wife asked him, "Is Rabbi Chanina indeed greater than you?" to which he replied, "I am like an officer in the palace of the king, and must follow protocol. Chanina is like a servant, who has unlimited access to every part of the palace at any time."

Rabbi Yochanan recognized that although he was the greater scholar of the two, Rabbi Chanina's self-effacement before G-d was more complete. Rabbi Chanina was not only profoundly humble, but had no will of his own. His only desire was to fulfill the wishes of his Master.

The more we turn our lives over to the Will of G-d, the more profound and sincere our prayers will be.

From the Sages

The Divine spirit is present only amidst joy *(Shabbos 30b).*

There is a legend that Satan and the angel Michael pleaded their respective causes before G-d. Michael argued that Jews were performing many *mitzvos*, and Satan contended that they also committed many sins.

Michael responded, "When Jews do *mitzvos*, they celebrate. They make a feast for their child's *bar mitzvah*, or when they complete a volume of the Torah, or when they celebrate *Shabbos* or the Festivals. Granted that they may occasionally sin, but then it is only when they cannot withstand temptation. No one throws a party for a sin. See what they celebrate, and You will see what they truly value."

There is joy in doing *mitzvos*. We should not fail to rejoice when we have the opportunity to do a *mitzvah*.

NOTES

_____
_____
_____
_____
_____
_____
_____
_____
_____

... הוֹשַׁע ה' אֶת עַמְּךָ אֶת שְׁאֵרִית יִשְׂרָאֵל *From*

O G-d, save Your people, the remnant of *our* Israel. Even if they deviate from You, *Prayers* may their needs always be before You (*from the abridged Amidah*).

Feb. 3, 1991
Jan. 24, 1992
Feb. 10, 1993
Jan. 31, 1994
Jan. 20, 1995
Feb. 9, 1996

The abridged *Amidah* is to be recited if a person finds himself in dangerous circumstances at the established time of prayer, and cannot take the time to say the complete version of the *Amidah*.

It is important to note that the format of the prayer to be recited in time of danger is not for one's personal salvation, but for the salvation of all. Even when one's own life is in peril, prayer should not be selfish, and even under such duress, we are expected to think of others as well as ourselves.

The Talmud says that when we set our own needs aside and pray for others, such prayers are more readily answered. Devotion to one another elicits Divine grace.

I will judge you harshly for your saying, "I have not sinned" (*Jeremiah 2:35*).

From the Scriptures

Repentance is a unique, Divine gift to mankind. With appropriate repentance, there is not only forgiveness, but an actual eradication of the transgression, so that in the eyes of G-d, it did not occur.

Repentance is impossible unless we have an awareness that we did wrong. Yet we have a propensity to defend our behavior when it is wrong, and to fabricate a multitude of rationalizations to convince ourselves as well as others that what we did was actually right.

NOTES
————
————
————
————
————
————
————
————

G-d is more than willing to forgive, in a manner that far surpasses human forgiveness. But if we refuse to consider that we may have done wrong, we are not apt to change our errant ways.

Without recognition of our mistakes, there can be no change, and hence, no forgiveness.

Feb. 4, 1991
Jan. 25, 1992
Feb. 11, 1993
Feb. 1, 1994
Jan. 21, 1995
Feb. 10, 1996

From our Prayers

ה' אֱלֹקַי שִׁוַּעְתִּי אֵלֶיךָ וַתִּרְפָּאֵנִי . . .

O G-d, my G-d, I prayed to You and You healed me. You raised me from the depths, and preserved me from being lowered to the grave *(Psalms 30:3-4, daily morning service).*

There are many times in life when we experience distress, when our fortunes appear so dismal that we become severely depressed.

We cannot possibly fathom the reasons for suffering, and belief in G-d in the face of intense misery is the acid test of faith. What we must remember at all times is that regardless of how dismal things may appear to be, we are never without hope.

"Even when a sharp sword is at a person's throat, he must not despair of Divine mercy" *(Berachos 10a).* Why we are put through so severe a test is beyond us. We may be unable to avoid severe stress, but it is within our capacity to avoid despair. We must never abandon hope.

From the Sages

Breaking things in a fit of rage is as severe a transgression as worshiping idols *(Shabbos 105b).*

The Sages of the Talmud were well aware that a person may be provoked to anger. But to lose control over oneself and to become physically or verbally abusive is inexcusable, even if the anger itself can be justified.

Our great teacher, Moses, was denied his fondest wish, to enter the Promised Land, because he did not control his anger *(Numbers 20:10),* and was reprimanded by G-d, "You did not believe in Me" *(ibid., 12).*

A person whose faith in G-d is absolute can have the strength to restrain himself even when provoked. The provocation may be only the ultimate test, whether he believes that everything in the world happens with just cause.

The greater our faith, the less apt we are to lose ourselves when stressed.

NOTES

_____
_____
_____
_____
_____
_____
_____
_____
_____

שֶׁתְּזַכֶּה אוֹתִי וְאֶת כָּל בְּנֵי בֵיתִי *From*
לִמְצוֹא חֵן וְשֵׂכֶל טוֹב בְּעֵינֶיךָ . . . *our*

Grant me and all of my household that *Prayers*
we find favor in Your eyes and in
the eyes of all who behold us, that we
may better serve You (*prayer before Kiddush
Shabbos Eve*).

Feb. 5, 1991
Jan. 26, 1992
Feb. 12, 1993
Feb. 2, 1994
Jan. 22, 1995
Feb. 11, 1996

It is only natural for a person to wish to be liked and
respected by others.

To the person who has sincerely dedicated his life to the
Divine will, there are no personal desires of a purely
self-gratifying character. Everything he wishes is in order to
better serve G-d.

We do many things to attract others to us. Why do we
desire their friendship? May we sometimes be influenced
by ulterior motives to associate with people whose
influences on our spiritual lives may not be desirable?

We pray that we find favor in the eyes of others so that
we may better serve G-d. This attitude will help us choose
proper friends.

**Rabbi Eliezer of Bartosa said, "Give Him of His
own because both you and all that you have are His"**
(*Ethics of the Fathers* 3:8).

*From
the Sages*

The Rabbi of Hornostipol had followers who gave him
large donations, yet he never had enough for the expenses
of his household, because he divided all his money among
the needy.

When his wife complained that she did not have enough
money for household expenses, and could he not keep a bit
more for himself, the Rabbi answered, "Why do you think
that people give me money? It is because there are those
who are wealthier and those who are poorer, and I have
been chosen as the conduit to see that some of the wealth
of the rich should find its way to the poor. In this way, I am
but a servant, carrying out G-d's wish.

"If I keep money for myself, I would essentially be
embezzling. G-d does not want servants who embezzle. If
I keep more for myself, he will dismiss me from His
service, and then we will have nothing at all."

NOTES

_____
_____
_____
_____
_____
_____
_____

Feb. 6, 1991
Jan. 27, 1992
Feb. 13, 1993
Feb. 3, 1994
Jan. 23, 1995
Feb. 12, 1996

From our Prayers

מַתִּיר אֲסוּרִים . . .

Blessed are You, O L-rd our G-d, King of the universe, who releases those who are bound *(prayer upon arising).*

This prayer is recited after awakening, when one begins to move about volitionally.

Each day we execute millions of muscular movements without the slightest thought that each move we make is a marvelous phenomenon. The coordination of the muscular system by the brain defies description. A study of the anatomy and physiology of the brain and its extensions reveals the many billions of messages that go to and fro when we move a limb, or even change the position of a tiny muscle.

When things happen with regularity, we fail to see their miraculous character. Perhaps the Israelites of the Exodus were so accustomed to supernatural events that their attitude upon the division of the Red Sea might well have been, "So what else is new?"

Our capacity to use our limbs and muscles should be appreciated with a prayer of deep gratitude. Just ask any stroke victim, and he will tell you.

From the Sages

Because G-d desired to bestow great favor on Israel, He gave them Torah and laws in abundant measure *(Makkos 23b).*

The Talmud states that performance of one *mitzvah* leads to another *mitzvah*. This should be understood as a law of nature. Much as a magnet attracts iron filings, one *mitzvah* attracts another.

That there are so many *mitzvos* is therefore a Divine gift. Many *mitzvos* are simple to perform. It is a *mitzvah* to avoid theft and murder, to avoid eating insects, to affix a *mezuzah* to a door. If one adheres to these things because they are the Divine wish, he thereby performs a *mitzvah*, and this will facilitate performance of other *mitzvos*, which may be more difficult to perform.

When confronted with temptation to do things which are in violation of the Torah, and if one fears that he may lack the strength to withstand the temptation, one can facilitate the struggle by doing a *mitzvah* of any kind. For example, one may keep a *pushkah* (charity-collection box) handy and add a few coins for a deserving cause. Or recite a verse of *Psalms.* Do an easy *mitzvah*, any *mitzvah* at all, and this will make observance of the more difficult *mitzvos* so much easier.

NOTES

_____
_____
_____
_____
_____
_____
_____
_____
_____

Blessed are You, our G-d and G-d of our forefathers ... who is the great One, the mighty One, the awesome One, the Most High *(daily Amidah).*

. . . הָקֵל הַגָּדוֹל הַגִּבּוֹר וְהַנּוֹרָא . . . *From our Prayers*

Feb. 7, 1991
Jan. 28, 1992
Feb. 14 1993
Feb. 4, 1994
Jan. 24, 1995
Feb. 13, 1996

The Talmud states that when the prophet Jeremiah and Daniel saw the oppression of Jews and the destruction of Jerusalem, they omitted the attributes "mighty" and "awesome" from their prayers. "Where is His might and where is His awesomeness, if His people can be so oppressed?" *(Sotah 68b).* Although their belief in the might and awesome greatness of G-d had not diminished, they knew that G-d values truth above all, and since their observation of reality conflicted with their convictions, they felt that in asserting their convictions they would be less than truthful.

The Sages of the Great Assembly restored these attributes, commenting that if a weak lamb survives in a pack of hungry wolves, that is the greatest miracle of all. The fact that Jews have survived unprecedented and unparalleled persecutions can be due only to Divine intervention, and this phenomenon testifies to the might and awesome greatness of G-d even more than would the existence of a mighty empire of Israel.

We can learn much from Jeremiah and Daniel, and we can learn from the Sages of the Great Assembly. We must learn to love truth, but also to recognize that truth is not always what we think it to be.

From the Scriptures

Of all the fruits of the trees of the Garden (of Eden) you may eat, but of the Tree of Knowledge of good and evil you shall not eat *(Genesis 2:16-17).*

"How is it," asked the Maharal of Prague, "that man acquired the valuable capacity to discern between good and evil as a result of transgressing the commandment of G-d?"

The Maharal explains that prior to disobeying G-d, man could avoid wrong not because he intellectually knew it to be wrong, but because he would be instinctively repelled by wrong, just as animals instinctively avoid eating poisonous plants.

Operating by instinct is far more efficient than analyzing things intellectually. Man did not gain by disobeying G-d, but rather lost a precious capacity.

Sometimes we think that we may gain something by transgressing a Divine commandment. This is a delusion. What appears to be a gain is actually a loss. G-d cannot be outsmarted.

NOTES

_____

_____

_____

_____

_____

_____

_____

_____

SHEVAT

24

שבט

Feb. 8, 1991
Jan. 29, 1992
Feb. 15, 1993
Feb. 5, 1994
Jan. 25, 1995
Feb. 14, 1996

From the
Scriptures

NOTES

_____
_____
_____
_____
_____
_____
_____
_____
_____
_____

From
our
Prayers

חָנֵּנוּ מֵאִתְּךָ דֵּעָה . . .
הֲשִׁיבֵנוּ . . . סְלַח לָנוּ . . .

Grant us wisdom . . . Return us to You . . .
Forgive us . . . Heal us . . . Bless us . . .
(daily Amidah).

All our prayers are in the plural. We do not say forgive
me, heal *me*, bless *me*. It is always *us*.

No person is an island. We are all interdependent. A loss
for one person is a loss for humanity. A triumph for one
person is a triumph for humanity.

The idea that we can profit at the expense of others is the
work of Satan, the evil force whose aim is to bring about
the destruction of the world. But since he finds it rather
difficult to coax us into overt self-destruction, he tries to
accomplish his nefarious plans by deluding us, and by
leading us to think that we can gain by being destructive to
others.

Our prayers should remind us how false this is.

**And you shall remember G-d, for it is He who
gives you the capacity to accomplish things**
(Deuteronomy 8:18).

Rabbi Levi Yitzchok of Berdichev walked through the
market place one day, and saw the multitude of people
running to and fro, busily engaged in commerce.

The Rabbi climbed to the top of a pillar in midst of the
market square and called out, "My dear children! G-d's
holy people! You are all busily engaged in your commerce,
and each of you knows exactly why he or she is here, what
you are doing, and why you came. But you forget why you
are here, in the world, in the first place, and what you are
really supposed to be accomplishing with your existence."

It is so true. We become so absorbed with what we are
doing at any moment that we forget what we are here for
altogether.

But there is help. During your busy day, when you drink
a cup of tea or coffee, eat a snack, or even drink water,
there is a blessing to be said. "Blessed are You, O G-d, King
of the universe, for everything came into being with His
word." After eating or drinking, we say, "Blessed are You,
G-d, King of the universe, Who has created many living
things and provided for all their needs."

We need to remember to say these blessings, and we
need to think about what we are saying.

144 / LIVING EACH DAY

יוֹצֵר אוֹר וּבוֹרֵא חֹשֶׁךְ ... *From*
עֹשֶׂה שָׁלוֹם וּבוֹרֵא אֶת הַכֹּל *our*

B lessed are You, O L-rd our G-d, King of *Prayers*
the universe, who fashions light and
creates darkness; He makes peace, and
creates all (*morning service*).

Feb. 9, 1991
Jan. 30, 1992
Feb. 16, 1993
Feb. 6, 1994
Jan. 26, 1995
Feb. 15, 1996

The Talmud states that this prayer was designed to refute
the belief in dualism that asserted that there were two
gods, one who ruled over light and good, the other who
ruled over darkness and evil. In this prayer we affirm our
belief in the one true G-d, who is sovereign over
everything.

Although dualism as a formal religion no longer exists,
we must be careful to avoid dualistic thinking. Those who
try to explain why there is evil in the world and why
innocent people suffer, by saying that G-d has lost control
over the world, are essentially dualists.

"He makes peace," says the prayer. The word *"shalom"*
means not only peace, but also "completion." There is a
harmony in the universe which encompasses all space and
time. One cannot pick up a tiny fragment of the universe
and try to understand it. Although it may make absolutely
no sense by itself, this little fragment fits into the complete
and comprehensive design of the universe, which can
never be known to man.

Adam was so tall he reached from the earth to the
sky (*Chagigah 12a*).

From
the Sages

The Maggid of Mezeritch explained this Talmudic
statement. Although man is physically earthbound with his
feet planted in the soil, his spirit is far reaching, and can
extend into the heavens.

The uniqueness of man, hence his very essence, is his
spirit. Man's physical body is quite similar to that of other
animals. The definition of man is thus in his spirit, his ability
to think, to feel, and to imagine.

NOTES

Wherever man's spirit happens to be, that is where he
himself is. If his thoughts, feelings, imagination, and wishes
are all earthy, then he is confined to earth. If his spirit
carries him into contemplation of the greatness of G-d, into
unselfish love of mankind, and into searching for the will of
G-d for him, then his spirit and hence his very essence is in
the heavens.

We can be spiritual. We can reach up into the sky.

Feb. 10, 1991
Jan. 31, 1992
Feb. 17, 1993
Feb. 7, 1994
Jan. 27, 1995
Feb. 16, 1996

*From
our
Prayers*

יִהְיוּ לְרָצוֹן אִמְרֵי פִי וְהֶגְיוֹן לִבִּי לְפָנֶיךָ
ה׳ צוּרִי וְגֹאֲלִי

May the words of my mouth and the thoughts of my heart be accepted by You, O G-d, my strength and my Redeemer *(Psalms 19:15; prayer upon completion of the Amidah).*

Earlier (5 Teves) we noted that there was a prayer before prayer, and now we see that there is also a prayer after prayer.

If prayer is something that we complete in an allotted time and then go about our activities as usual, then it is not much of a prayer. If prayer has not had an impact upon us, and has not made us feel different than before we prayed, then it has fallen short of its mark.

Sometimes we pray only with our lips and not with our hearts. We may say words without thought. Such prayer is very superficial, and is not absorbed and integrated into our being.

But if at the very last moment we realize that we did not internalize our prayer, and that we only said words which did not penetrate us, it is not too late. This moment of realization is invaluable, and we can actually salvage our entire prayer with this momentary awareness. It is akin to spreading a layer of gold on a surface, and then striking it with a hammer which drives it in.

That is why we have a prayer after prayer.

*From
the Sages*

This world is but a vestibule before the world to come *(Ethics of the Fathers 4:21).*

A *tzaddik* was once visited by a wealthy merchant. Upon seeing the *tzaddik's* meager living quarters, with one room serving as the bedroom, kitchen, dining room, and study, the merchant offered to acquire more spacious accommodations for him.

"Why, in my home," said the merchant, "I have separate rooms for eating, sleeping, receiving guests, and so on."

"And when you are on the road," asked the *tzaddik*, "do you also have separate rooms for each function?"

"No," answered the merchant. "When I am on the road, I have only one room in a hotel."

"I, too, have spacious accommodations in my permanent home," said the *tzaddik*. "But I am only a traveler in this world, and while on the road, one room is sufficient."

NOTES
_____
_____
_____
_____
_____
_____
_____
_____
_____

From our Prayers

אֲשֶׁר קִדְּשָׁנוּ בְּמִצְוֹתָיו . . .
וְצִוָּנוּ לְהַפְרִישׁ תְּרוּמוֹת וּמַעַשְׂרוֹת

Blessed are You, O L-rd our G-d, King of
the universe, who has sanctified us with
His commandments, and instructed us to
tithe *(prayer upon separation of the offerings to
the Kohanim and Levites)*.

Feb. 11, 1991
Feb. 1, 1992
Feb. 18, 1993
Feb. 8, 1994
Jan. 28, 1995
Feb. 17, 1996

In ancient Israel, the priestly tribe, the *Kohanim* and the Levites, were supported by tithes. They owned no property, and were to be free of financial worries so that they might fully devote themselves to the teaching of Torah. They were the teachers in Israel.

Too often, we wish our rabbis to be something other than teachers of Torah. We wish them to be community organizers, fund raisers, performers of weddings, *bar mitzvos*, and funerals. We wish them to do everything, except, perhaps, to teach us Torah. We prefer, perhaps, that they *not* teach us or tell us what we should do.

The primary functions of the rabbi today should be that of the *Kohanim* or the Levites of yore: to teach Torah, and to help us understand what G-d wants of us. We should value these functions sufficiently so that we should support students and teachers of Torah adequately, that they may learn and convey the Divine wisdom to us.

We can do so only if we are willing to listen, and, when necessary, make the changes in our style of living that Torah requires.

Accustom your tongue to say, "I do not know"
(Berachos 4a).

From the Sages

If there is any barrier that stands in the way of our progress in developing our character and fulfilling the will of G-d, it is our reluctance to admit ignorance.

If one already "knows it all," there is no chance of learning. If we "know it all," then there is no need to change.

We begin each day with a prayer for the study of Torah. We would do well each night to reflect on the day gone by. "Have I learned anything new today?" If we find that we have not acquired any new knowledge that day, we should recognize this as a lost opportunity, and make certain that the next day be more productive.

The awareness of how much we do not know is the royal road to knowledge and wisdom.

NOTES
_____
_____
_____
_____
_____
_____
_____
_____

SHEVAT

שבט

Feb. 12, 1991
Feb. 2, 1992
Feb. 19, 1993
Feb. 9, 1994
Jan. 29, 1995
Feb. 18, 1996

From our Prayers

שִׁיר הַמַּעֲלוֹת מִמַּעֲמַקִּים קְרָאתִיךָ ה'

A song of ascents. From the depths have I called to You, O G-d *(Psalms 130:1-2)*.

We call to G-d from the depths. This refers to two types of depths: a lowering and humbling of oneself before G-d, and an immersion into deep meditation.

In ancient synagogues, there was actually a depression in the floor before the lectern where the reader stood, to symbolize the concept of praying "out of the depths."

Deep meditation in prayer, a feeling of communion with G-d and an absorption into the Divine Presence requires the self-effacement of humility. One must come to understand that the only true reality is G-dliness, and one must surrender oneself completely to the will of G-d.

This self-effacement is totally distinct from the feelings of worthlessness that characterize depression. Rather, it is a feeling that one is not a separate entity distinct from G-d, but very much united with G-d. This self-effacement gives rise to *simchah* (elation) rather than depression.

From the Sages

A person should always provoke his good inclination to overpower his evil inclination *(Berachos 5a)*.

Rabbi Yeruchim Levovitz stated that it is a mistake to assume that the struggle between the two opposing forces within us is one of logic, and that our actions are determined by whichever logic prevails.

Not so, says Rabbi Yeruchim. The battle is one of sheer force. Whichever force has the greater strength dominates. It is as simple as that.

However, we do have the capacity to influence the magnitude of force present in each. Every time we do something which is the expressed will of G-d, we add energy and strength to our good inclination. Every time we do anything which is not in any way in the service of G-d, we add strength to the evil inclination.

Thus, the Rabbi says, when we do things that are permissible, but without sincere intent to direct these intentions toward the service of G-d, we increase the strength of the evil inclination, and render ourselves more vulnerable to its dominance. "In *all your ways*, you can know G-d" *(Proverbs 3:6)*. We can eat to nourish ourselves so that we have the energy to do the Divine will. We can sleep to be rested, and take recreation to be refreshed, so that we can be in optimum condition to do the will of G-d. Nothing need be excluded from fulfilling the will of G-d.

SHEVAT

29

שבט

From our Prayers

... בַּמֶּה אֲקַדֵּם אוֹ מָה רְפוּאָה אֲבַקֵּשׁ

How can I approach You and how can I expect to be healed? ... That which You have forbidden I permitted; and that which You permitted, I forbade. That which You rejected, I embraced; and that which You embraced, I rejected *(prayer on day preceding Rosh Chodesh).*

As we prepare to begin a new segment of life, and we seek to disencumber ourselves from the mistakes of the past, we must recognize what it is that led us to deviate from proper behavior. Simple regret of mistakes is not sufficient, because unless we know whence they originated, they are likely to be repeated.

A major source of error is the value system by which we judge right and wrong. Many serious mistakes arise as a result of misguided lenience, as well as overzealous strictness.

Torah ethics provide guidelines for love, kindness, and mercy, as well as for firmness and stern judgment. Unaided by Torah values, our judgments are vulnerable to serious distortion by our emotions. We may end up permitting what should be forbidden and vice-versa.

Erev
Rosh Chodesh
[Eve of the New Month]

Feb. 13, 1991
Feb. 3, 1992
Feb. 20, 1993
Feb. 10, 1994
Jan. 30, 1995
Feb. 19, 1996

For on every action G-d will bring judgment, even if it is concealed *(Ecclesiastes 12:14).*

The Chafetz Chaim said that modern technology should help us in the observance of the *mitzvos*. Prior to invention of the telephone and phonograph, a person might have treated speech very casually. Now we have concrete evidence how far reaching a word can be, and that it may be recorded for posterity.

We have now progressed to video photography. Let us imagine that on our judgment day, we will stand before the Heavenly tribunal, and a video recording of our entire lives will be shown to us. Everything we ever did will be played back before our eyes, with the tribunal looking on. Nothing will be omitted, nothing.

Can we imagine a punishment any more severe than having to watch a replay of our lives with others looking on?

So let us live our lives with the knowledge that everything is being recorded for replay.

From the Scriptures

NOTES

_____
_____
_____
_____
_____
_____
_____
_____
_____
_____

**First Day of
Rosh Chodesh
Adar**

Feb. 14, 1991

Feb. 4, 1992

Feb. 21, 1993

Feb. 11, 1994

Jan. 31, 1995

Feb. 20, 1996

*From
our
Prayers*

. . . חַיִּים שֶׁאֵין בָּהֶם בּוּשָׁה וּכְלִמָּה

May it be Your will, O G-d, that You renew the coming month for us . . . and grant us a life that is free of shame and embarrassment *(prayer for blessing Rosh Chodesh).*

Shame is a feeling that has no redeeming features. Correctly defined, shame is not the same as guilt. Guilt is for what I do, shame is for what I am.

Guilt can be constructive if it is the result of having done something wrong. Healthy guilt leads us to make amends for what we have done wrong, to ask for forgiveness, and to avoid doing the same thing again.

Shame is when we feel there is something inherently bad about us, regardless of what we do. Shame destroys self-esteem, and discourages a person from trying to accomplish things and to improve himself.

Just as we pray to be spared from disease, injury, and other harmful things, we pray to be spared from shame. This should also put us on the alert that we should never do anything that will arouse feelings of shame in others.

*From the
Scriptures*

Remember, and do not forget, how you angered G-d in the desert [with worship of the golden calf] *(Deuteronomy 9:7).*

The episode of the golden calf almost defies comprehension. How could a people that had just witnessed with their own eyes an unprecedented intervention by G-d, with countless miracles, and that had experienced the Divine revelation at Sinai, how could they have so precipitous a spiritual decline, to resort to pagan idolatry?

The answer is that the Israelites achieved their spirituality too rapidly. Having had a slave mentality for generations, and having been immersed in a heathen culture, their sudden emergence to freedom and their embracing the lofty concept of G-d and spirituality was a radical change that had come about not through their own long, arduous efforts, but as a Divine gift.

What this teaches us is that if spirituality is to become an integral part of our lives, we must work toward its achievement diligently and patiently. Sudden flashes of insight into spirituality may be dramatic, but may not be able to withstand the tests of time and stress.

In an era when technology has given us so many ''instant'' things, we should be aware that ''instant'' spirituality may be of little value.

NOTES

_____

_____

_____

_____

_____

_____

_____

_____

_____

_____

He is the One who sends forth springs *Prayers*
into brooks, that they may run between
the mountains, to give drink to every beast
of the fields, and the creatures of the
forest quench their thirst *(Psalms 104:10-11,
recited on Rosh Chodesh).*

*Second Day of
Rosh Chodesh
Adar*

*[During Hebrew leap
years a thirteenth
month called Adar
Sheni (the second
Adar) is added to the
calendar. For those
years, two sets of
corresponding dates
are given below,
the first for Adar,
and the second for
Adar Sheni.]*

The Baal Shem Tov and a disciple were enroute, when the
disciple was seized by a sudden, intense thirst, but there
was no water anywhere near.

"Do you not believe that G-d sees the needs of all
mankind and provides for them?" asked the Baal Shem Tov.

"I believe," the disciple answered.

"If you do believe with absolute faith, then your needs
will be provided," said the Baal Shem Tov.

Shortly thereafter, they saw a water-carrier with his
buckets. They beckoned to him, and gave him a few cents
for water.

"Why are you carrying water out here?" asked the Baal
Shem Tov.

"My master has gone mad," the man answered. "Every
day, I fetch water from a nearby well. Today, he got it into
his head that he wants water from a distant well, and he sent
me all the way here."

The Baal Shem Tov turned to his disciple. "The beasts of
the field turn to G-d for water, and He provides for them. If
only man turned to G-d for all his needs, he would lack
nothing."

Feb. 15, 1991

Feb. 5, 1992

Feb. 22, 1993

Feb. 12, 1994

Feb. 1, 1995

Feb. 21, 1996

Adar Sheni

March 6, 1992

March 3, 1995

**As the month of Adar enters, one should increase
in joy** *(Taanis 29a).*

*From
the Sages*

The increase in joy is in anticipation of celebration of
Purim and Passover. We now enter into a season of
salvation and deliverance.

But how does one increase joy? Joy is an emotion which
is usually a consequence of the circumstances in which we
find ourselves. Joy is hardly subject to control as if with a
rheostat.

That is precisely the point. The Talmud says, "For a
tzaddik, his emotions are in his hands." We need not be
passive subjects of circumstances. We should indeed be
capable of intensifying our joy.

Analysis of the full significance of Purim and Passover,
and appreciation of freedom and Divine deliverance, should
elevate our spirits and increase our joy.

NOTES

_____
_____
_____
_____
_____
_____
_____
_____
_____

ADAR

2

אדר

Feb. 16, 1991
Feb. 6, 1992
Feb. 23, 1993
Feb. 13, 1994
Feb. 2, 1995
Feb. 22, 1996

Adar Sheni

March 7, 1992
March 4, 1995

From our Prayers

קְצוּבָה הִיא זֹאת לְשׁוֹעִים וְקַלִּים
קְצִינִים וְרָשִׁים יַחַד בָּה שְׁקָלִים

Out of Your love for Your people . . . You commanded that they donate shekalim for forgiveness . . . An equal gift from the rich and poor alike *(prayer on the first of the four special Shabbosos preceding Passover).*

The initial donation for the Sanctuary in the desert was commemorated by an annual gift of a half-*shekel* for the daily offerings in the Temple. These donations are referred to as the "silver of forgiveness."

The outstanding feature of this gift was that all Jews contributed an equal amount, the richest of the rich giving no more than the poorest of the poor.

The reality is that there is no equal distribution of wealth. But a person's worth should never be measured in terms of his possessions.

True forgiveness can be attained only when people respect one another for what they *are*, and not for what they *own*.

Forgiveness is contingent upon recognizing everyone else as equal.

From the Scriptures

Your people, when altogether, are righteous. They shall inherit the eternal land *(Isaiah 60:21).*

Brotherhood among Jews is so dear to G-d that it obscures individual defects. "Your people, *when altogether* are righteous." Collective righteousness depends on a feeling of equality.

One of the Chassidic masters, when being taught Hebrew as a young child, was told that when two *yuds* are written together (יי) they should be read as the name of G-d.

When the child came to the end of a sentence, which was marked by two vertical dots (:), he pronounced the name of G-d.

"No, no!" said the teacher. "When the two *yuds* (Jews) stand alongside each other, then it represents G-d. If one *yud* is above the other, then this is not G-d. This shows that things have come to an end."

And so it is. When we stand alongside each other, G-d is with us. If we consider ourselves to be above another, we have reached the end.

NOTES

_____
_____
_____
_____
_____
_____
_____
_____
_____
_____

אוֹר פָּנֶיךָ עָלֵינוּ אָדוֹן נְסָה *From*
וְשֶׁקֶל אֶשָּׂא בְּבֵית נָכוֹן וְנִשָּׂא *our*

Give us a sign of the light of Your *Prayers*
countenance, our Master, and we will
again donate our shekels in Your supreme
Temple *(prayer on the first of the four special
Shabbosos preceding Passover).*

Feb. 17, 1991
Feb. 7, 1992
Feb. 24, 1993
Feb. 14, 1994
Feb. 3, 1995
Feb. 23, 1996

Adar Sheni

March 8, 1992
March 5, 1995

The Torah specifies that the gift of the *shekels* must be a half-*shekel* per person.

"Why a half-*shekel*?" asked the Rabbis. "Because," they answer, "we must recognize that without another person to complement us, we are all incomplete. No person, regardless how well endowed he may be, is self-sufficient. We all need one another."

The Talmud says that we lost our national independence because of our divisiveness. As we pray for the restoration of our nation and the return of the Temple, we must remember the symbolism of the half-*shekel*, that we are whole only when together.

When G-d told Moses that the gift of the shekel *From*
would be an atonement for the sin of the golden calf, *the Sages*
Moses was bewildered, until G-d showed him a
shekel of fire *(Midrash Tanchuma).*

The Rabbi of Kotzk explained the bewilderment of Moses; he could not understand how a donation of money could expunge a sin so grievous as the worship of the golden calf.

Then G-d showed him a *shekel* of fire. It is not the dollar value of the donation that elicits forgiveness, but the spirit of the gift. When *tzedakah* is given with warmth and consideration for the needy, when the spirit of the humble recipient is uplifted by encouraging words of the giver, this merits forgiveness.

In the past, charity was given personally. The giver had an opportunity to accompany his alms with words of comfort.

NOTES

Today, in our mechanized society, the giving of *tzedakah* has fallen victim to bureaucracy. Too often, charity is restricted to a single large donation to a federation, an agency. Even this is sometimes done grudgingly. There is no personal contact, no giving of oneself.

For *tzedakah* to bring about forgiveness, a *shekel* is not enough. It must be a fiery *shekel*, one accompanied by personal warmth.

Feb. 18, 1991
Feb. 8, 1992
Feb. 25, 1993
Feb. 15, 1994
Feb. 4, 1995
Feb. 24, 1996

Adar Sheni

March 9, 1992
March 6, 1995

From הֲשִׁיבֵנוּ ה' אֵלֶיךָ וְנָשׁוּבָה חַדֵּשׁ יָמֵינוּ כְּקֶדֶם
our **B**ring us back to You, O G-d, and we shall
Prayers return. Restore our days as those of old
(Lamentations 5:21, prayer upon return of the
Torah to the ark).

One of the obstacles to changing our behavior and
correcting our character defects is the sense of remorse
that often persists and plagues us. We continue to feel
shame and guilt for the wrongs we have done. We
therefore may think, "What's the use? I can never achieve
peace of mind, even if I change."

In our own experience, when one person forgives
another, one can never undo what has been done. We have
no way of eradicating the past. Hence, as penitents, we
tend to feel remorseful and subdued. We are unable to
experience feelings of joy because of the burdens of our
past.

We must realize that forgiveness by G-d is otherwise.
When we do proper *teshuvah* (atonement), G-d removes
our sins as though they never existed. While we should
always maintain humility, we need not feel shame, we need
not feel crushed.

"Restore our days as those of old." When we return to
G-d, we are then as we were before we ever sinned.

From
the Sages

"And man became a living spirit" *(Genesis 2:7)*. **"A**
creature with will," said the Rabbi of Pshis'cha. **"To**
have a spirit means to have a will."

The uniqueness of the human being is his will. That is
what is meant by "spirit."

Animals are living creatures that have no will. Animals
are slaves to their internal drives, being totally dominated
by their physical impulses. When an animal experiences an
impulse, it must seek its gratification. An animal cannot
decide to abstain or to delay gratification.

The human being is unique in that he can be free to
choose. A person can be subject to various drives and
intense cravings, but he has the capacity to deny these if he
considers them to be improper. Hence only a human being
is truly free.

Freedom consists of mastery over oneself, of exercising
the dominion of the spirit over one's bodily desires.

Freedom, humanity, spirituality. They are one and the
same.

NOTES

_____
_____
_____
_____
_____
_____
_____
_____
_____

From our Prayers

לְהַקְדִּישׁ לְיוֹצְרָם בְּנַחַת רוּחַ
בְּשָׂפָה בְרוּרָה וּבִנְעִימָה . . .

(The heavenly angels) hallow the Creator with a pleasant spirit, with clear expression, and with a holy sweetness. In unison, they respond in awe, and amidst great fear they say, "Holy! Holy! Holy! is the G-d of hosts" *(daily morning prayer).*

"What is it that angels fear?" asked Rabbi Yeruchim Levovitz. "Man fears that he may succumb to temptation and transgress the will of G-d. But angels are pure spirit and have no temptation, no evil inclination. What is there for them to fear?"

Rabbi Yeruchim answers, "The angels know that somewhere in the universe evil does exist. Even though they know themselves to be far above vulnerability to evil, nevertheless, they fear it.

"At no time should anyone consider himself immune from sin." Regardless of how spiritual we may become, we must always be on guard. The force of evil is treacherous. We must never consider ourselves safe from its machinations. That is what the heavenly angels teach us.

Feb. 19, 1991
Feb. 9, 1992
Feb. 26, 1993
Feb. 16, 1994
Feb. 5, 1995
Feb. 25, 1996

Adar Sheni

March 10, 1992
March 7, 1995

When a person comes to his eternal world, all of his earthly actions are enumerated before him *(Taanis 11a).*

From the Sages

Rabbi Zusia said, "If they ask me on judgment day, 'Why were you not as great as Moses, as the prophets, as the Sages of the Talmud, or as the Baal Shem Tov?' I will not feel threatened.

"But if they say to me, 'Zusia, why were you not Zusia?' woe is to me! I will have no answer."

Every person has his or her own unique potential. We can each maximize our potential, and that is our obligation.

We may not have been endowed with some particular personality assets which were given to others, and we will not be answerable for not having achieved what others achieved. But we will be held accountable for not realizing our own potential.

It is of utmost importance that we come to know who we are and what we are, because only then can we achieve our fulfillment (see my *Let Us Make Man*, Traditional Press, 1986).

NOTES

_____

_____

_____

_____

_____

_____

_____

_____

Feb. 20, 1991
Feb. 10, 1992
Feb. 27, 1993
Feb. 17, 1994
Feb. 6, 1995
Feb. 26, 1996

Adar Sheni

March 11, 1992
March 8, 1995

From our Prayers

וּבַעֲבוּר אֲבוֹתֵינוּ שֶׁבָּטְחוּ בְךָ וַתְּלַמְּדֵם
חֻקֵּי חַיִּים לַעֲשׂוֹת רְצוֹנְךָ בְּלֵבָב שָׁלֵם . . .

Just as You taught our forefathers the laws of life to do Your will with a complete heart, so may You be gracious to us and teach us *(morning service)*.

I was once challenged by a woman who had been addicted to drugs for twenty years, and whose many attempts to stop had been unsuccessful.

"How can you believe there is a G-d?" she asked. "If there were a just G-d, would He let you do something foolish when you are too young to know better, and then allow you to suffer for the rest of your life? What did I know when I was sixteen and someone introduced me to drugs? Now I cannot escape from the terrible mistakes I made when I was so young."

I must admit that I questioned the Divine wisdom. Why, indeed, does G-d grant us maximum wisdom when we are much older and our lives are essentially behind us? Why does He not give us wisdom when we are young, when we make the decisions that will decide our entire lives?

The answer is that sedate wisdom and youthful ambition are essentially incompatible. The only solution is for the young, energetic people to accept guidance from their elders who have accumulated wisdom through both learning and experience.

That is why we pray for the grace to have the wisdom of our elders.

From the Sages

Rabbi Akiva said, "The verse 'G-d is the hope (mikveh) of Israel,' can also mean that G-d is the purifying pool (another meaning of mikveh) for Israel. Just as a mikveh purifies, so does G-d purify Israel" *(Yoma 85b)*.

NOTES

One of the Chassidic masters added, "And just as purification in a *mikveh* does not occur unless there is total immersion, so that the water covers every part of the person, so is purification by G-d contingent upon one's total immersion into G-dliness. One cannot separate and give to G-d what is His and to Caesar what is his."

In Judaism, there is no dichotomy. Everything in life must be directed toward G-dliness, toward fulfilling the Divine will.

Half-measures avail us nothing.

. . . וּמֵעוֹלָם עַד עוֹלָם אַתָּה קֵל . . . *From*
A prayer of Moses, a G-dly man . . . From *our*
all the past into all the future, You are *Prayers*
the Almighty. You allow an amoral man to
sink back until he is crushed, and You say,
'Return, O sons of man" *(Psalms 90:1-3,*
Shabbos morning service).

Feb. 21, 1991
Feb. 11, 1992
Feb. 28, 1993
Feb. 18, 1994
Feb. 7, 1995
Feb. 27, 1996

Adar Sheni

March 12, 1992
March 9, 1995

Indeed, G-d is all powerful, but He has relinquished control over man insofar as He allows man the freedom to make moral choices.

When man sins and chooses wrongly, G-d calls upon him to repent. But man often hesitates to repent, for repenting would mean giving up some pleasurable behaviors. There-fore, man often rationalizes his actions, and ingeniously constructs myriads of logical-sounding arguments to justify them.

Man's denial of his errant behavior may be overcome only when he begins to feel its consequences. G-d therefore allows man to sink back until he feels crushed, until the denial is overcome, and the call, "Return to me," can be heard.

We could avoid much misery if we would only heed the Divine call earlier.

Every day there is a Heavenly voice that emanates from the mountain of Sinai, proclaiming these words: "Woe to mankind for their disregard of the Torah" *(Ethics of the Fathers 6:2).*

From
the Sages

The Baal Shem Tov asked, "Of what good is this Divine call from Sinai if it is inaudible? No one has ever reported hearing this heavenly voice."

The Baal Shem Tov answered, "The Divine voice is not audible to the ear, but is perceived by the *neshamah*, the soul. Every time a person has a twinge of conscience which arouses him to examine his ways and to repent the wrongs he has done, it is because his *neshamah* has heard the Divine call."

Perhaps years ago, it was difficult to understand this. Today, we know that there are actual sounds which are beyond the range of perception of the human ear, and that can be perceived by more sensitive ears, such as some animals, or by special instruments.

The Divine call is very real. Our sensitive *neshamah* hears it every day. Every single day, G-d beckons to us and begs us to return to him. How foolish of us to ignore this call!

NOTES
_____
_____
_____
_____
_____
_____
_____
_____
_____
_____

Feb. 22, 1991
Feb. 12, 1992
March 1, 1993
Feb. 19, 1994
Feb. 8, 1995
Feb. 28, 1996

Adar Sheni

March 13, 1992
March 10, 1995

From the
Scriptures

NOTES

_____
_____
_____
_____
_____
_____
_____
_____
_____
_____

From זְכוֹר . . . טוֹב שׁוֹמֵעַ תְּפִלָּה הַפְלָה תְּפִלָּתוֹ בְּבֶהָלָה
our **R**emember how Amalek attacked Your
Prayers people, who had just emerged from
bondage . . . In Your goodness, You heard
Israel's prayer and destroyed their attack-
ers *(prayer on the second of the four special*
Shabbosos before Passover).

In Jewish history, the attack by Amalek on the defense-
less people who had just emerged from crushing enslavement is an incident that lives on in infamy.

The Torah relates that during the battle with Amalek,
when Moses raised his hands to heaven in prayer, the
Israelites triumphed, and when he lowered his hands, the
Amalekites triumphed.

The Talmud emphasizes the obvious implications. Regardless of how outnumbered and outarmed, Israel triumphs when it turns for help to its true source of strength.

When battle with an aggressor is necessary, our strength
on the battlefield is proportional to the intensity of our
prayers.

When Moses raised his hands, the Israelites
triumphed, and when he lowered his hands, Amalek
triumphed. But Moses' hands were heavy, so Aaron
and Chur supported his hands in prayer *(Exodus*
17:11-12).

Were Moses' hands indeed so heavy that he could not
keep them raised? Furthermore, is there really that much
significance to a person's posture in prayer?

The Rabbi of Gur explains that the strength of a leader is
but a reflection of the strength of the nation. The Talmud
says that the Israelites were vulnerable to the attack by
Amalek because they were lax in their spirituality. The
triumph of the Israelites was therefore contingent upon
their renewed commitment to spirituality.

Moses' hands could not be raised beyond the degree
representing the nation's trust in G-d. In spite of his own
spiritual greatness, when the Israelites' faith in G-d
weakened, Moses' hands grew heavy, and could not reach
to the heavens.

Sometimes we contend that if we had greater leaders
who were more spiritual and more learned, they would
inspire us to greater spirituality. Not so, says the Rabbi of
Gur. The spirituality of the leader varies proportionately
with the spirituality of the people rather than the reverse.

... תְּזַכֵּנִי לִשְׁפֹּךְ שִׂיחִי לְפָנֶיךָ ... *From*
our
Prayers

M aster of the universe, open the mouth
of one as mute as I am, and illuminate
my words. Help me explain myself so that
I can pour out everything in my heart to
You *(prayer of Rabbi Nachman of Breslov).*

Rabbi Nachman stressed the importance of personal prayers in addition to the mandatory daily prayers. He said that the *yeitzer hara*, the evil inclination, tries to obstruct our prayers from reaching heaven, and it is therefore necessary to outmaneuver the *yeitzer hara*.

If one is afraid that highwaymen will rob him of his possessions, one can eliminate this danger by avoiding the well-traveled routes and blazing a new trail, because it is along the well-traveled roads that robbers lie in wait for their victims.

Similarly, the *yeitzer hara* attacks during the scheduled prayers. If one takes another path, a private path, the *yeitzer hara* does not suspect this, and one can safely get by.

That is why it is important — in addition to the regular prayers — to pray many times during the day, in whatever language one understands, and pour out one's innermost feelings to G-d. The *yeitzer hara* is thus caught off guard, and will not obstruct these prayers.

Feb. 23, 1991
Feb. 13, 1992
March 2, 1993
Feb. 20, 1994
Feb. 9, 1995
Feb. 29, 1996

Adar Sheni

March 14, 1992
March 11, 1995

For G-d is high above all nations; His glory is beyond the heavens. He looks down so low unto the heavens and upon the earth *(Psalms 113:4,6).*

From the Scriptures

"The mistake of heresy," said Rabbi Yisrael of Koznitz, "is explained by Maimonides, that people thought that G-d is so supreme, that it is beneath His dignity to tend to the affairs of mere, lowly humans, and that He occupies Himself only with the host of heaven.

"The fallacy here is that relative to G-d's infinite greatness, the entire expanse of the universe is no greater than a single grain of sand. As the Psalmist says, G-d looks down on *both* heaven and earth. In relationship to G-d, both heaven and earth are equal.

"We therefore must believe that the Creator of the universe is as concerned about the slightest movement of the lowliest being as with the actions of the heavenly host. What every human being does is important to Him, and He watches over every individual with deep concern. Before G-d, there is no trivia."

NOTES
_____
_____
_____
_____
_____
_____
_____
_____
_____

Feb. 24, 1991
Feb. 14, 1992
March 3, 1993
Feb. 21, 1994
Feb. 10, 1995
March 1, 1996

Adar Sheni

March 15, 1992
March 12, 1995

From our Prayers

קוֹלִי שָׁמָעְתָּ אַל תַּעְלֵם אָזְנְךָ לְרַוְחָתִי לְשַׁוְעָתִי From **You have heard my voice. Do not hide Your ears from my prayer, and grant me relief** *(Lamentations 3:56).*

Since prayer for one's needs, as in the *Amidah,* is to be said silently, why does the prophet use the term, "You have heard my voice?"

We sometimes mistake decibels for content, and think that the louder we say something, the more impact it has. The truth is just the opposite. A valid point can be conveyed quietly. Shouting is only needed when the argument is weak.

The Torah states that when Pharaoh's daughter found the infant Moses in the reeds, she opened the chest and she *saw* the infant crying, and said, "This must be a child of the Jews" *(Exodus 2:6).* A more correct expression would be that she *heard* the infant crying. Rabbi Bunim of Otwoczk said, "A Jew can cry silently. She *saw* the child crying but did not hear him, and therefore concluded that it must be a Jewish child."

Our silent prayer can be very vocal. We can scream loudly without it being audible. G-d hears our silent voices.

From the Scriptures

(Following the worship of the golden calf) Moses returned to G-d and said, "I beg of You, O G-d, this nation has sinned grievously, and made for themselves an idol of gold" *(Exodus 32:31).*

What kind of plea for forgiveness is it to describe the sin as grave? Why did Moses not try to minimize the sin?

In my practice with people who have problems with alcohol or drugs, I have seen some people behave completely out of character. It is very obvious that when they did some of their actions, they were not in their right minds or in full possession of their faculties. Their behavior was therefore "sick" rather than "bad," and for this they needed treatment rather than punishment.

This was Moses' plea. If the people had committed a minor offense, they could be considered sinful. But for them to turn to idolatry within days after the revelation at Sinai was not sinful, but sick. They needed help, not punishment.

We should recognize when things we do are out of character for us, and take appropriate steps to be healed from our spiritual sickness. As one recovering alcoholic appropriately said, "I am not responsible for my disease, but I *am* responsible for my recovery."

NOTES

_____
_____
_____
_____
_____
_____
_____
_____
_____
_____

קֵלִי קֵלִי לָמָה עֲזַבְתָּנִי *From*
רָחוֹק מִישׁוּעָתִי דִּבְרֵי שַׁאֲגָתִי *our*

M y G-d, my G-d, why have You forsaken *Prayers*
me? You have distanced Yourself from
my salvation, from the words of my prayer
(Psalms 22:2).

Feb. 25, 1991
Feb. 15, 1992
March 4, 1993
Feb. 22, 1994
Feb. 11, 1995
March 2, 1996

Adar Sheni

March 16, 1992
March 13, 1995

The Talmud states that this was the prayer of Esther
when she approached the throne to plead for her people.

The first twenty-two verses of this chapter are a painful
cry of anguish. Why does G-d not respond? Why did He
come to the aid of our ancestors, but now abandons us to
evil forces? Why does G-d, who has sustained us from our
birth to this very day, now allow us to perish?

Then, in verses twenty-three to thirty-two, there is an
abrupt change. G-d never turns away the cry of the
afflicted. We will yet sing His praises and tell of His
salvation.

This is a powerful prayer. We may be feeling hopeless and abandoned, but we must remember that there
are never any grounds for despair. There is always
hope. Regardless of our distress, we shall yet live to tell
of the greatness of G-d. That is the history of the Jews,
and what is true of the nation is true for each individual
person.

You stand today before G-d, your G-d (Deuteronomy 29:9).

*From the
Scriptures*

We can stand before G-d if we concern ourselves only
with this day.

Rabbi Nachman of Breslov said, "Yesterday and
tomorrow are man's downfall. Today, you may be devoted to G-d but your yesterdays and tomorrows pull you
back."

NOTES

We have within us a *yeitzer hara*, a destructive force,
which does not operate exclusively by inciting us
toward actual commitment of sin. If it can paralyze a
person, and prevent his being constructive, it accomplished its goal.

We can do nothing about the past, and usually very little
about the future. Preoccupation with the past and future,
which deters us from constructive action today, is thus a
machination of the *yeitzer hara*.

To be with G-d, we must concentrate on today.

Feb. 26, 1991
Feb. 16, 1992
March 5, 1993
Feb. 23, 1994
Feb. 12, 1995
March 3, 1996

Adar Sheni

March 17, 1992
March 14, 1995

From our Prayers

תְּשׁוּעָתָם הָיִיתָ לָנֶצַח
וְתִקְוָתָם בְּכָל דּוֹר וָדוֹר . . .

You have been their salvation throughout eternity, and their hope in every generation. This makes known that those who trust in You shall not perish (prayer of Purim).

There have been many eras when Jews were exiled, banished, and persecuted. In each generation, we have had our Hamans, and in each generation, we have placed our trust in G-d.

Sometimes those who trusted in G-d did not live to witness His salvation. When we do not see the Divine salvation, our faith is strained. Why did G-d not come to our assistance?

But if we ever have moments of doubt as individuals, we cannot have any serious doubt as a nation throughout history. No people could possibly have survived as the Jews did without Divine providence.

"The hope of every generation and their salvation throughout eternity."

Even if a particular generation does not get to see the salvation of G-d, the persistence of the Jewish people throughout history testifies to His watchfulness over us.

From the Scriptures

For if you will keep your silence at this time, our salvation shall come from some other source, but you and yours shall perish (Esther 4:14).

NOTES

There are occasions when we may be able to do a kindness for another person, but we may be reluctant to do so because we may be placing ourselves at some risk.

Mordechai's message to Esther clarifies this for us. If you can intercede for another person, but you are concerned that in doing so you would be exposing yourself to a personal risk, do not fear. Quite the contrary, reluctance to help another person may be to your own disadvantage. Trust in G-d that fulfilling the mitzvah of coming to the aid of another person will never bring you harm.

From our Prayers

רַבֵּץ תְּנוֹקוֹת לְפָנָיו . . . בְּקוֹל יַעֲקֹב לַחֲלוֹשׁ . . . From Mordechai assembled small children to pray ... and their voices rose to heaven. "What is this sound I hear?" G-d asked. "These are Your holy children," Mordechai answered. "Save them from their bitter foe" (prayer for the Fast of Esther).

The purity of the prayer of children, who are innocent of wrongdoing, occupies a special place in Jewish liturgy. "Out of the mouths of children and sucklings You have fashioned an invincible might" (Psalms 8:3).

Rabbi Samson Raphael Hirsch explains that even if those who wish to deny G-d would try to expunge the idea of Divine morality, they could never succeed. Each new child is a pure neshamah (soul), capable of G-d-consciousness.

We are witness today to the efforts of communism to stamp out the name of G-d. We also know that at the risk of their very lives, young children in communist countries learn Torah and pray.

We who enjoy the freedom of prayer should join in spirit with the children who pray to G-d amidst religious oppression. G-d will certainly hear our prayers.

The Midrash says that Mordechai asked children to quote verses from their studies. They responded, "Do not fear a sudden threat, nor the storm of the wicked. They will plot, but it will be spoiled; they will plan, but it will not come to be; for G-d is with us" (Esther Rabbah 7:17).

Very often our problem is that we think too much, and that we complicate that which is simple.

Pure faith and trust in G-d have been our salvation throughout history. Yet, we often become overwhelmed by the problems confronting us. They appear so insurmountable. How can we ever emerge from the thicket of problems that are so complicated?

If only we learned from our past experiences. Simple solutions have often emerged as if out of the blue. Simple solutions to complicated problems are not likely to come about by human endeavor, but rather by Divine intervention. Children have a simple faith and trust. That is why their prayers are so precious.

We should learn from them.

Fast of Esther

[During Hebrew leap years the fast is observed in Adar Sheni. When 13 Adar falls on the Sabbath the fast is observed on the preceding Thursday.]

Feb. 27, 1991

Feb. 17, 1992

March 6, 1993

Feb. 24, 1994

Feb. 13, 1995

March 4, 1996

Adar Sheni

March 18, 1992

March 15, 1995

From the Sages

NOTES

Purim

[During Hebrew
leap years Purim is
celebrated in
Adar Sheni.]

Feb. 28, 1991

Feb. 18, 1992

March 7, 1993

Feb. 25, 1994

Feb. 14, 1995

March 5, 1996

Adar Sheni

March 19, 1992

March 16, 1995

From ... לְהַשְׁמִיד לַהֲרֹג וּלְאַבֵּד אֶת כָּל הַיְּהוּדִים

our
Prayers **W**hen the wicked Haman sought to annihilate all Jews, young and old ..., You in Your infinite mercy thwarted his plans and frustrated his intentions, and caused that which he sought to do to recoil on his own head** (*prayer on Purim*).

According to many authorities, the miracle of Purim surpasses in significance the great Biblical wonders.

Whereas the plagues of Pharaoh and the dividing of the Red Sea were indeed great miracles, leaving no doubt as to the wondrous actions of G-d, they represented supernatural phenomena. People still might have thought that Divine intervention is present only when the laws of nature are abrogated, but when things proceed naturally, they do so according to fixed physical laws, detached from Divine providence.

The miracle of Purim was a happening totally within natural boundaries. A king gets drunk at a party, and in his intoxication orders the queen's execution. The successor to the queen is a Jewess, a cousin to one of the nobility, who conceals her ethnic origin. A palace plot against the king is discovered by the Jewish nobleman, and this is recorded in the royal chronicles. An anti-Semitic viceroy plots against the Jews, and wishes to execute the Jew who had saved the king's life. The queen reveals that she is a Jewess, and turns the king against his viceroy.

No flashes from the sky. No upheavals. No suspension of the laws of nature. But at every step, there is G-d's providence for the salvation of His people.

From the
Scriptures

NOTES

The month that was converted from distress to joy, from grief to a holiday, shall be days of feasting, exchanges of gifts, and alms to the poor (*Esther 9:22*).

The Talmud states that even when Jews deviated from observance of the Torah, as long as they were united, they merited Divine salvation.

Too often, it is only the threat of an aggressor that binds Jews together. In absence of an external threat, petty factionalism separates us from one another.

Nothing is so dear to G-d as to see His children united. We can merit the most bountiful Divine blessings if only we cling together.

It is time that we resolve whatever differences among us that set us apart from one another.

From our Prayers . . . בְּךָ בָּטְחוּ אֲבֹתֵינוּ בָּטְחוּ וַתְּפַלְּטֵמוֹ

Our forefathers trusted in You; they trusted and You rescued them; they cried unto You and they escaped evil; they trusted in You and they were not disgraced *(Psalms 22:5-6, prayer of Esther).*

In our moments of greatest need, our prayers always refer to our forefathers.

It is not only that we plead for Divine grace by virtue of our forefathers' merits. It is also that we need to be reminded of the faith and trust in G-d which characterized our ancestors' lives.

While there is no denying that science and technology have given us powerful tools and methods to master our environment, we should not be deceived that we are masters of our fate. Our culture has paid a heavy price for the alienation from G-d that was spawned by the "G-d is dead" era. Science is indeed marvelous, but when it was enthroned as god, it soon became the god that failed. Science can only provide some wherewithals for living, never a reason for living.

Our forefathers, unaffected by the deceptive radiance of science, had a more sincere faith. They trusted, and they were not abandoned. Even with the advance of science and technology, we can have that faith.

They shall go from strength to strength, and show themselves before G-d in Zion *(Psalms 84:8).*

Two *chassidim* were discoursing.

"How do you define a *chassid*?" asked the first.

"A *chassid* is someone who aspires to be a *chassid*," the other answered.

"Well, what person would not want to become a *chassid*?" the first asked.

"That's simple. Anyone who thinks that he already is one," the other replied.

Spirituality is a rather strange entity, in that we only have it as long as we think we do not have it. Once we believe we already have attained spirituality, we have actually lost it.

Spiritual growth can occur only when we feel ourselves to be lacking in spirituality.

ADAR

15

אדר

Shushan Purim
[During Hebrew leap years Shushan Purim is celebrated in Adar Sheni.]

March 1, 1991
Feb. 19, 1992
March 8, 1993
Feb. 26, 1994
Feb. 15, 1995
March 6, 1996

Adar Sheni

March 20, 1992
March 17, 1995

From the Scriptures

NOTES
_____
_____
_____
_____
_____
_____
_____
_____

March 2, 1991
Feb. 20, 1992
March 9, 1993
Feb. 27 ,1994
Feb. 16, 1995
March 7, 1996

Adar Sheni

March 21, 1992
March 18, 1995

From our Prayers

אָמַר רַבִּי אֶלְעָזָר אָמַר רַבִּי חֲנִינָא
תַּלְמִידֵי חֲכָמִים מַרְבִּים שָׁלוֹם בָּעוֹלָם . . .

Rabbi Elazar quoted Rabbi Chanina, "Torah scholars promote the cause of peace in the world, as the Scripture says, 'All Your children are learned of G-d, and there is abundant peace among Your children' *(Isaiah 54:13)*. 'Children' refers to disciples of learning" *(morning service)*.

How does a Talmudic comment fit into the prayer service?

Our most fervent prayer is for peace. We pray for peace in the world, peace within our communities, peace in our households.

It is not enough to ask G-d for peace. Yes, He will give us this precious blessing, but we must prepare ourselves to receive it. The seeds of peace will not take root except in fertile soil.

The *sine qua non* for peace is open-mindedness, a willingness to listen, to learn, to consider another person's point of view.

For peace to prevail, we must be "students" of wisdom. We should not consider ourselves already wise, because then our learning ceases. Once we think we know it all, we close our minds to everyone and everything.

As we pray for peace, we must realize what we must do ourselves to have this prayer fulfilled.

From the Sages

A fool believes everything *(Proverbs 15:14)*. **It is better to be called a fool all my life, rather than to be wicked for a single moment before G-d** *(Eduyos 5:6)*.

Rabbi Nachman of Breslov said that if we had to make a choice between being credulous or universally skeptical, it would be better to be credulous. If one believes everything, even that which is false and foolish, then he will also believe the truth, and that will save him. One who scoffs at everything will deny even the truth.

The very first verse of Psalms warns us against associating with scoffers.

Hopefully, we can believe intelligently. But if we must err, then it is better to err on the side of believing too much rather than denying too much.

NOTES

_____
_____
_____
_____
_____
_____
_____
_____
_____
_____

בּוֹרֵא מִינֵי בְשָׂמִים . . . *From*

B**lessed are You, L-rd our G-d, King of the** *our*
universe, who creates many kinds of *Prayers*
fragrance (Blessing on fragrant spices, recited at
Havdalah, marking the end of Shabbos).

The Talmud states that the reason we use fragrant spices
at the *Havdalah* service is to comfort the soul, and relieve
the gloom that comes when *Shabbos* ends.

Our *neshamah*, our soul, is distressed that *Shabbos* is
over, and that we are plunged into the hectic pace of the
work week, which leaves us so little time to provide the
soul with its spiritual nourishment.

Why do we not feel the anguish of the soul? Indeed, are
we not sometimes impatient for *Shabbos* to be over so that
we can return to the pressing needs of our work, which has
been curtailed by *Shabbos*?

Perhaps our priorities are out of order. Spirituality is
what we should be living for. The work of the weekdays
should be only the method whereby we sustain ourselves
so that we can achieve spirituality.

The blessing of the fragrant spices reminds us of what we
should be feeling.

March 3, 1991
Feb. 21, 1992
March 10, 1993
Feb. 28, 1994
Feb. 17, 1995
March 8, 1996

Adar Sheni

March 22, 1992
March 19, 1995

All the diseases which I inflicted upon Egypt, I
will not inflict upon you, for I am G-d, your healer
(Exodus 15:26).

From the
Scriptures

A man who had been advised to undergo a somewhat
hazardous medical procedure came to the Rabbi of
Czernobl for advice and his blessing.

"I suggest that you consult the professor in Hanipole,"
the Rabbi said. (In Europe, the most competent physicans
were those who held professorships in medical schools.)

Hanipole was a small village, and when the man arrived
there, he discovered that not only was there no medical
school in Hanipole, but there was not even a single doctor
in the entire village. He returned to Czernobl in bewilderment.

"There is no professor in Hanipole," he said to the
Rabbi. "They have no doctor at all."

"Then what do the residents of Hanipole do when they
get sick?" the Rabbi asked.

"What *can* they do?" the man replied. "All they can do is
pray and trust in G-d to heal them."

"You see? That is what I meant. Seek help from the One
who heals the people of Hanipole."

NOTES

_____
_____
_____
_____
_____
_____
_____
_____

March 4, 1991
Feb. 22, 1992
March 11, 1993
March 1, 1994
Feb. 18, 1995
March 9, 1996

Adar Sheni

March 23, 1992
March 20, 1995

From our Prayers

וְכֻלָּם פּוֹתְחִים אֶת פִּיהֶם בִּקְדֻשָּׁה וּבְטָהֳרָה
בְּשִׁירָה וּבְזִמְרָה . . .

And they (the heavenly angels) all open their mouths in holiness and purity with song and psalm, and they bless and praise, glorify and declare the might, holiness, and majesty of the name of G-d *(morning service).*

One of the Chassidic masters said, "There is an angel that has a thousand heads. Each head has a thousand tongues. Each tongue has a thousand voices. Each voice a thousand melodies. Imagine the indescribable beauty of this angel's song!

"But with all its beauty, this angel cannot give a morsel of bread to a hungry person.

"A human being may lack the beauty of this angel's hymn, but when he helps another person, his prayer surpasses that of the angel."

In the Yom Kippur service, we describe the greatness of the heavenly angels as contrasted to the frailties of mortal man. Yet, it is the prayer of mortal man that is most dear to G-d.

From the Scriptures

And G-d said, "Let us make man" *(Genesis 1:26).*

The entire work of creation was done by G-d alone. In the creation of man, G-d sought participation of others. "Let *us* make man." Who is this *us*?

Everything else in the universe was created complete and essentially in a state of perfection. Angels do not change at all. Animals change only in size and mass. All growing things change only according to the preordained pattern inherent in their genetic structure.

Man is the only being whose perfection is not preordained. Man must participate in his own perfection.

G-d created man incomplete and imperfect, and He wishes man to work toward that perfection which will make him the being G-d wished him to be. Therefore, G-d said, "Let *us* make man. You and I together. I give you the potential. You use your freedom of choice to become perfect."

Spirituality is not what you are, but what you make of yourself. In this sense, the heavenly angels are not spiritual. Only man can be spiritual.

NOTES

_____
_____
_____
_____
_____
_____
_____
_____
_____

תְּפִלָּה לְעָנִי כִי יַעֲטֹף וְלִפְנֵי ה' יִשְׁפֹּךְ שִׂיחוֹ *From* **our Prayers**

The prayer of the poor man who is faint with weakness. His desire is to pour out his thoughts before G-d *(Psalms 102:1).*

The Baal Shem Tov explained this verse with a parable. A king announced that on a specific day he would grant any requests made of him. People thronged about the palace, and each person submitted his request for whatever he wished.

One wise man did not ask for riches or a prestigious position. Rather, he requested that he be allowed to have an audience with the king every day. This not only provided him the incomparable thrill of being in the presence of the king daily, but also enabled him to eventually have many of his other requests satisfied.

Similarly, said the Baal Shem Tov, we are the spiritually impoverished who pray out of our frailties. Our requests of G-d should not be for our immediate needs, but to be allowed in His presence daily to pour out all our thoughts to Him. For then, not only will we have the exquisite joy of being in the Divine presence, but we will also have access to present our other requests to Him.

Our most fervent prayer in times of need should be that we should be able to pray.

March 5, 1991
Feb. 23, 1992
March 12, 1993
March 2, 1994
Feb. 19, 1995
March 10, 1996

Adar Sheni

March 24, 1992
March 21, 1995

Serve G-d with reverence, and rejoice with trembling *(Psalms 2:11).*

From the Scriptures

Rejoice with trembling? How can one rejoice if one is in a state of fear? Are these two emotions not mutually exclusive?

A follower of Rabbi Shneur Zalman of Liadi once presented him with a petition enumerating his many needs. The Rabbi studied the petition and then remarked, "It seems you have given a great deal of thought to all that you need. Have you given equal thought to why you are needed?"

This comment sent the man reeling. The Rabbi had sharply reprimanded him for indulging in what he would like to get out of life, but not giving adequate thought to what he must contribute to life. What was he to give to the world, and what measures had he taken to fulfill this obligation?

While the man trembled with this admonishment, he was also elated. He had been reminded that his life has a purpose. He has a great value. There is something unique about him, some special mission that he must complete. His life has meaning, and that is an elating thought.

He trembled, but with joy.

March 6, 1991
Feb. 24, 1992
March 13, 1993
March 3, 1994
Feb. 20, 1995
March 11, 1996

Adar Sheni

March 25, 1992
March 22, 1995

From our Prayers

בְּכֵן אֵין לַעֲמוֹד בְּסוֹדָהּ
וְאֵין לְהַגִּיעַ יְסוֹדָהּ וְאֵין לַחֲקוֹר חֻקָּה . . .

There is no way to understand the mystery of this mitzvah (of the red cow), nor to investigate its reason, nor to minimize its importance, nor to know its value. Only G-d Himself understands its ways *(prayer on the third of the four Shabbosos preceding Passover).*

The Talmud cites the ritual of the red cow as a *mitzvah* which is completely beyond human understanding, and which must be accepted on sheer faith. As explained in *Numbers* 19:1-22, a person who had come in contact with a dead body remained in a state of ritual contamination until he was cleansed by having the ashes of a sacrificial red cow sprinkled on him.

The importance of this *mitzvah* is precisely that it is beyond logic. We can think of many reasons and advantages of other *mitzvos*, but this *mitzvah* defies understanding. Its observance thus represents our acceptance of the sovereignty of G-d and our deference to His infinite wisdom, with absolute effacement of our will before His.

Why is this concept included in prayer? Because unless we achieve this surrender of our will and judgment to the Divine wisdom, we are removed from G-d, and we are not in a relationship where prayer can be effective. Sincere prayer requires that we turn our lives and will over to G-d.

From the Scriptures

Anyone who comes in contact with the ashes of purification (of the red cow) shall become tamei (ritually contaminated) *(Numbers 19:21).*

One of the mysteries of the ritual of the red cow is that whereas its ashes purify a person who is in a state of *tumah* (contamination), they contaminate a person who is "clean."

This should teach us that what can be beneficial to one person can be detrimental to another person. We must consider ourselves as individuals, and not assume that what is good for one is necessarily good for all.

A classic example is alcohol. "Wine will gladden a person's heart" *(Psalms 104:15)* may be true for a person who can consume alcohol safely and use it judiciously. But for the person who has a problem with alcohol, drink can be most destructive. While wine may gladden the heart of one person, it may take the life of another.

NOTES

_____
_____
_____
_____
_____
_____
_____
_____
_____

From our Prayers

רֹעֵה יִשְׂרָאֵל הַאֲזִינָה נֹהֵג כַּצֹּאן יוֹסֵף . . .

O Shepherd of Israel, hearken to us. You Who leads Joseph like a flock of sheep, Who dwells in the cherubim, shine forth to us *(Psalms 80:2).*

Why does the Psalmist refer to all Israel as "Joseph," who was but one of the twelve tribes?

Joseph represents three important pillars of Judaism which, we remind ourselves in our prayer, are crucial to our survival.

Joseph maintained his Jewish identity in an alien culture. Although immersed in Egyptian society, and indeed achieving the highest office in the land, Joseph nevertheless remained a loyal son of Abraham, Isaac, and Jacob. Maintaining our identity in the face of powerful forces of assimilation is essential to Judaism.

The second characteristic of Joseph is that he was uncompromising in his morality, even at enormous personal cost *(Genesis 39:7-20).*

Finally, Joseph had ample reason to bear resentments against the brothers who had sold him into slavery. But Joseph overcame his resentments, forgave, and reunited the family of Israel.

If we as a people are to be deserving of Divine salvation, we must adhere to these principles of Joseph.

March 7, 1991
Feb. 25, 1992
March 14, 1993
March 4, 1994
Feb. 21, 1995
March 12, 1996

Adar Sheni

March 26, 1992
March 23, 1995

From the Sages

The caravan that carried Joseph into bondage transported fragrant spices *(Genesis 37:25).* **Usually this was a trade route for malodorous merchandise such as resins and pitch. To spare Joseph the irritation of offensive odors, G-d provided these merchants with a cargo of fragrant spices** *(ibid., Rashi).*

Of what consequence is it to a young boy, being ruthlessly sold by his envious brothers into a slavery from which he may never escape, whether the air is filled with fragrance of perfumes, or annoying odors of resinous vapors?

The *mussar* authorities explain that the decrees of G-d are precise to a hairsbreadth. A person will not experience even one insignificant iota more than has been decreed upon him.

The Divine wisdom decreed that Joseph was to be enslaved and that was fulfilled. The least discomfort beyond that was not permitted to occur.

Although we cannot understand many things that happen to us, we should realize that nothing occurs haphazardly. Whatever the reason for our distress may be, it is all carefully calculated. No suffering is in vain.

NOTES

March 8, 1991
Feb. 26, 1992
March 15, 1993
March 5, 1994
Feb. 22, 1995
March 13, 1996

Adar Sheni

March 27, 1992
March 24, 1995

From our Prayers

הַקְשִׁיבָה לְקוֹל שַׁוְעִי
מַלְכִּי וֵאלֹקָי כִּי אֵלֶיךָ אֶתְפַּלָּל

Hearken to the voice of my prayer, my King and my G-d, for it is to You that I pray *(Psalms 5:3).*

The Jerusalem Talmud comments, "Do not pray to the angel Michael, nor to Gabriel. Pray unto Me, and I will answer promptly" *(Berachos 9:1).*

Why then do so many of our prayers appear to be unanswered when we do pray only to G-d and not to any intermediary?

The admonition not to pray to an intermediary applies not only to angels or saints, but also to placing one's trust in humans. "Do not place your trust in noblemen, nor in mortals with whom help is naught" *(Psalms 146:3).* The farmer who puts the seed in the ground should know that he is going through the necessary motions, but that he cannot convert the seed into grain or fruit. That requires an act of G-d.

Perhaps we do not pray to angels or saints, but we must remember that absolute trust in G-d means just that. To the degree that we believe that our needs can be provided by humans or by any source other than G-d, to that degree our prayer is lacking. Others may be the instruments of G-d, but the source of all help is G-d alone.

From the Sages

The patriarch Abraham observed all the commandments of the Torah, even though they had not yet been revealed *(Yoma 28b).*

How could Abraham have fulfilled commandments which were unknown to him?

The Chassidic masters explain that the Talmud correlates the six hundred thirteen Divine commandments with six hundred thirteen components of the human body. Each part of the human body corresponds to a specific *mitzvah*.

The patriarch Abraham had completely turned his life to the will of G-d. As demonstrated by the ultimate test, he was ready to sacrifice his beloved son when he thought this to be the will of G-d.

This total surrender to the Divine will resulted in each part of his person being naturally attracted to its corresponding *mitzvah*, and having intrinsic resistance to anything that would not be in keeping with the Divine will. In this way, his entire person intuitively fulfilled the will of G-d.

Let us remember that we are descendants of Abraham, and that we should turn our lives over to the will of G-d.

NOTES

_____
_____
_____
_____
_____
_____
_____
_____
_____

From our Prayers ··· וְיִשְׂמְחוּ כָל חוֹסֵי בָךְ לְעוֹלָם יְרַנֵּנוּ

All those that put their trust in You shall rejoice. They will ever be of good cheer, and You will protect them. They that love You will exult in You (*Psalms 5:12*).

How does prayer work? When we ask G-d for something, do we change His mind? Is G-d subject to change?

The answer is that G-d does not change. The Divine emanations are beneficent and consistent. However, just as the rays of the sun can darken one object yet bleach another, and heat can melt one substance while solidifying another, thus indicating that varied results are a function of the receiving object rather than the force at work, so it is with the Divine emanations.

That is why prayer does not always consist of asking for something. Prayer may be an expression of hope, of trust, of the awareness of G-d's majesty, or of acceptance of G-d's sovereignty. Such prayer can bring about changes in ourselves, and as *we* change, the effects of the Divine emanations may be more favorable to us.

March 9, 1991
Feb. 27, 1992
March 16, 1993
March 6, 1994
Feb. 23, 1995
March 14, 1996

Adar Sheni

March 28, 1992
March 25, 1995

Evil talk (lashon hara) is so grievous a sin because it kills three people: the one who speaks evil, the one who listens to evil talk, and the one who is being slandered (*Erechin 15b*).

From the Sages

Gossip and slander are grievous sins, yet unfortunately are frequently transgressed. People who would never consider violating any other law of Torah may fall prey to a sin which is considered as grievous as the cardinal sins of idolatry, adultery, and murder, all taken together.

How can one avoid *lashon hara*? The Baal Shem Tov provided a simple formula. Simply do not talk of any other person for any reason whatsoever. If you are in a mood to praise someone, praise G-d instead. If you are in a mood to be critical of someone, be critical of yourself. A bit of soul-searching should help you find things about yourself which could stand correction.

Just never talk about anyone else.

NOTES

_____
_____
_____
_____
_____
_____
_____
_____

March 10, 1991
Feb. 28, 1992
March 17, 1993
March 7, 1994
Feb. 24, 1995
March 15, 1996

Adar Sheni

March 29, 1992
March 26, 1995

From our Prayers

חַטֹּאת נְעוּרַי וּפְשָׁעַי אַל תִּזְכֹּר . . .

Remember not the sins and transgressions of my youth. For the sake of Your goodness, O G-d, remember me with Your loving-kindness (*Psalms 25:7, morning service*)

It is perfectly reasonable to ask forgiveness for behavior that resulted from immaturity, provided that we behave more responsibly as mature grownups. However, if we persist in behaving in a juvenile manner when we have the capacity to do otherwise, we can hardly put forth immaturity as a defense.

Maturity involves learning from experience, giving consideration to the consequences of our actions, postponing gratification of one's desires when necessary, and seeking and accepting counsel from those who are wiser and more experienced. Maturity is characterized by sober deliberation rather than impulsive action.

If, as mature people, we do not repeat the folly of our youth, then we have achieved true *teshuvah* (repentance) and our transgressions can then be forgiven.

From the Sages

If a person wished to do a mitzvah but circumstances beyond his control prevented him from carrying out his intention, G-d will consider it as though it had been done (*Berachos 6a*).

Among people, good intentions are not enough. The popular aphorism is that "the road to hell is paved with good intentions."

However, between man and G-d it is otherwise. Man's responsibility is to make a sincere effort to do that which is right. Once we have done all that is within our means, we have done our share. Obviously, if the results are beyond one's control, one cannot be held responsible for them. When we reach the stage that we are powerless over something, we must then turn it over to G-d.

The Psalmist says, "O G-d, bring things to a conclusion for me" (138:8). We must not delude ourselves that we can control everything and bring things to the conclusion we desire. Our responsibility is to do whatever we can. Beyond that, G-d takes over.

NOTES

_____
_____
_____
_____
_____
_____
_____
_____
_____
_____

From our Prayers

מִי שֶׁעָשָׂה נִסִּים לַאֲבוֹתֵינוּ . . .
חֲבֵרִים כָּל יִשְׂרָאֵל וְנֹאמַר אָמֵן

May He Who performed miracles for our fathers and redeemed them from slavery to freedom speedily redeem us and gather our dispersed people from the four corners of the earth. All of Israel is united. Amen *(Blessing of Rosh Chodesh).*

March 11, 1991
Feb. 29, 1992
March 18, 1993
March 8, 1994
Feb. 25, 1995
March 16, 1996

Adar Sheni

March 30, 1992
March 27, 1995

As we pray for Divine salvation, for miracles like those our ancestors merited, for redemption from oppression, we assert that all Israel is united.

The Talmud states that the enslavement of Egypt was a consequence of the tribes selling their brother Joseph into slavery.

The Torah refers to the Egyptian bondage as a purifying process. It was the common suffering that united Jews. The sin of envy which had set one brother against another was expunged when their descendants, enslaved and tortured, came closer together to help and comfort one another. The Egyptian ordeal was indeed a purifying process.

A major obstacle delaying our ultimate redemption is our divisiveness. Let all Israel be united, and we will be speedily redeemed. We have the capacity to make our prayers come true.

From the Scriptures

Fortunate is the person who derives strength from You. They cherish in their hearts the paths that lead to spiritual heights *(Psalms 84:6).*

The Seer of Lublin called attention to the apparent inconsistency in this verse, in that it begins with the singular and ends in the plural.

"There are two ways to spread the word of G-d," he said. "One is to go out and preach. This is exhausting and also diverts you from your own continued growth.

"The other is to lead a Torah-true life yourself, with total devotion to the will of G-d. This will bring you a measure of happiness and peace so great, that others will seek to emulate you, in order to achieve that which they see you have achieved."

The person who derives his strength from G-d can thus influence the multitude who observe him. We can disseminate the teaching of G-d by attraction rather than by promotion.

NOTES

_____
_____
_____
_____
_____
_____
_____
_____

ADAR

אדר

March 12, 1991
March 1, 1992
March 19, 1993
March 9, 1994
Feb. 26, 1995
March 17, 1996

Adar Sheni

March 31, 1992
March 28, 1995

From our Prayers

אֲחֵינוּ . . . הַנְּתוּנִים בְּצָרָה וּבְשִׁבְיָה . . .

As for our brethren, the entire house of Israel, who still remain in distress and captivity, whether on the sea or on land, may G-d have compassion upon them and lead them from oppression to relief, from darkness to light, from slavery to redemption, at a near time, Amen (morning service).

The entire house of Israel is in captivity?

This prayer teaches us the true sense of *achdus*, of oneness amongst Jews. Just as when one feels intense pain in any part of the body, it is the whole person that is in pain, so it is with the house of Israel. If there is one Jew that is suffering because he is a Jew, then the entire Jewish people suffer. As long as even one Jew is oppressed anywhere in the world, then no Jew is free anywhere in the world.

When we pray for the house of Israel, we are really praying for ourselves. Indeed, when we pray for any other person, we are praying for ourselves.

And it shall be when you hearken to these laws and observe them, G-d will keep for you the promise and the kindness that He swore to your ancestors. He will love you, bless you, and increase you. He will bless the fruit of your womb (Deuteronomy 7:12-13).

From the Scriptures

A woman came before the Maggid of Koznitz asking him to pray for her that she have a child.

"My mother too was as unhappy as you are," said the Maggid. "Then one day she met the Baal Shem Tov and presented him with a beautiful cape. One year later I was born."

The woman's eyes brightened. "I will make you the most beautiful cape in the world!" she said.

NOTES

The Maggid smiled and shook his head. "I am afraid that will not work," he said. "You see, my mother did not know this story."

A gift given to a *tzaddik* because of genuine admiration of his sanctity, without expectation of reward, indeed merited a reward. This was a gift generously given to another person. However, a gift which is given with anticipation of reward is actually a gift to oneself, and does not carry the same merit.

G-d has indeed promised us many blessings. But His rewards should not be our prime reason for observing His commandments.

לָכֶם הוּא רִאשׁוֹן נְצוּרֵי כָאִישׁוֹן . . . *From* **U**nto you (people of Israel) this month *our* shall be the first month, you who are *Prayers* so dear to G-d, so that you can proclaim the majesty of G-d Who is the first and the last *(prayer for the fourth of the four special Shabbosos preceding Passover).*

March 13, 1991
March 2, 1992
March 20, 1993
March 10, 1994
Feb. 27, 1995
March 18, 1996

Adar Sheni

April 1, 1992
March 29, 1995

The Jewish calendar, according to the Torah, is not a fixed instrument. In the days of the Sanhedrin (supreme court), months could vary in their length and leap years could be declared according to the discretion of the court. The Talmud later developed a formula for a fixed calendar.

The principle of the Jewish calendar varying according to the discretion of the court is interpreted to symbolize that man can be master over time, rather than be subject to it.

The technology of modern civilization has, in some ways, made man a slave to time. Some people essentially worship time. Deadlines and competition for quick results have given rise to pressures and tensions that tax human physiology and strain emotional tolerance.

"The months shall be yours to declare." The only power that we should recognize as being above us is the majesty of G-d.

Everything has its time. There is a time for every desire beneath the heavens . . . G-d made everything favorable in its appropriate time *(Ecclesiastes 3:1,11).*

From the Scriptures

NOTES

One of the most frequent sources of error is impatience. In our haste to satisfy our desires, we may fail to see some long-term disadvantages. We may then pay a heavy price for failing to properly assess things under the urgency of desire or passion.

Much of Judaism has to do with learning to postpone. Even as small children, we learn to postpone for a period of time the ice cream we crave following consumption of meat. The message is clear: There is nothing wrong with ice cream, but it must wait its time. As we mature, we must learn how to delay.

March 14, 1991
March 3, 1992
March 21, 1993
March 11, 1994
Feb. 28, 1995
March 19, 1996

Adar Sheni

April 2, 1992
March 30, 1995

From our Prayers

עַל הַצַּדִּיקִים וְעַל הַחֲסִידִים
וְעַל זִקְנֵי עַמְּךָ בֵּית יִשְׂרָאֵל . . .

Toward the righteous and toward the devoted, toward the elders of Your people, toward the surviving remnant of scholars, toward sincere proselytes and toward ourselves, may Your compassion be moved, O G-d, our G-d (*daily Amidah*).

The destiny and strength of Judaism is in its spirituality and morality. True, the Jewish nation has given the world some of its greatest scientists, philosophers, physicians, and mathematicians. But the charge given to us at Sinai was not to produce a nation of scientific geniuses. "And you shall be unto me a kingdom of priests and a sacred nation" (*Exodus 19:6*). That is how it all began, and that is how it was meant to be. The Jewish nation was meant to be a beacon of *kedushah*, illuminating righteousness and morality for all mankind.

We pray for our sustenance and for our welfare. We pray for ourselves as individuals and as a community. But we must never forget our primary obligation, which requires the wisdom, guidance, and teachings of Torah scholars, and we pray for their well-being.

We must not lose sight of our mission.

From the Sages

Open for me the tiniest portal of teshuvah (repentance), even like the eye of a needle, and I shall expand it like the doors of a great palace (*Shir HaShirim Rabbah*).

All we are asked to do is to make a beginning in *teshuvah*, and G-d will then assist us in broadening it.

"But," said the Rabbi of Kotzk in explanation of this Midrash, "it must be a thorough beginning. It may be the tiniest in magnitude, like the eye of a needle, but it must penetrate the personality through and through."

A disciple of the Rabbi of Karlin complained to him that whereas his colleagues were all making progress in their spiritual growth, he seemed to be getting nowhere.

"Alas," said the Rabbi. "I have not yet found the key to your heart."

"A key?" cried the disciple in anguish. "Who needs a key? Open my heart with an axe!"

"No need," said the Rabbi. "It has just been opened."

All that is needed is a single moment of spiritual awakening, but it must be sincere, permeating every fiber of one's being.

NOTES

_____
_____
_____
_____
_____
_____
_____
_____
_____

R**emember for us, O G-d, the love of our forebears, Abraham, Isaac, and Jacob, Your servants** (daily morning service).

... וְזָכַר לָנוּ ... אַהֲבַת הַקַּדְמוֹנִים

From our Prayers

ADAR

29

אדר

As we know, G-d does not need to be reminded of anything because there is no forgetfulness before Him. Our prayer is rather that He help us remember what we may tend to forget.

A person may have a blood test performed to determine if he harbors an infectious germ in his system. The presence of a microscopic bacteria or virus means that he may develop an infectious disease, because even a single germ may proliferate. Some viruses may lie dormant for years, and unexpectedly erupt and multiply, causing serious illness.

The forces of good surpass those of evil, just as the forces of health are greater than those of disease, else we could not survive in an environment of bacteria.

In every drop of our blood there is a particle of Abraham, Isaac, and Jacob. In every soul there is a fragment of the souls of the patriarchs. If we would only allow these elements to proliferate, we could achieve spirituality similar to that of the patriarchs. All that is necessary is that we remove the "antibodies", those character defects that inhibit such proliferation.

Help us, O G-d, to remember whence we derive, to recognize who we are, and to know what we can achieve.

See, I set before you this day a blessing and a curse ... The blessing if you will obey ... and the curse if you will disobey (Deuteronomy 11:26-28).

The text of Deuteronomy consists essentially of Moses chastising the Israelites. In what way are these verses an admonishment?

The Rabbi of Lelov explained that in order to teach a small child proper behavior, it may be necessary to resort to reward and punishment, becuase the child cannot grasp the inherent values of right and wrong. A mature adult, however, should understand that doing what is right and avoiding wrongdoing should not be dependent on external reward or punishment.

This, then, is Moses' reprimand. "After forty years of trying to teach you the essence of good and evil, I must still have recourse to reward and punishment. Are you not ashamed that you have not progressed beyond juvenile motivation?"

We achieve maturity when we no longer need external reward or punishment to behave properly.

Erev
Rosh Chodesh
[Eve of the
New Month]
March 15, 1991
March 4, 1992
March 22, 1993
March 12, 1994
March 1, 1995
March 20, 1996

Adar Sheni
April 3, 1992
March 31, 1995

From the Scriptures

NOTES

**First Day of
Rosh Chodesh
Adar Sheni**

*[During most years
Adar has 29 days.
During Hebrew
leap years Adar has
30 days, while
Adar Sheni has 29.]*

March 5, 1992

March 2, 1995

*From
our
Prayers*

רַחֲמָנָא, אִדְכַּר לָן קְיָמֵהּ דִּי אַבְרָהָם . . .

Merciful One! Remember for us Your promise to Abraham . . . to Isaac . . . to Jacob . . . to Joseph . . . to Moses . . . *(prayer on the day preceding Rosh Chodesh).*

This prayer is recited in Aramaic rather than Hebrew. The reason, says Rabbi Yaakov of Emden, is because the heavenly angels do not understand Aramaic and will not obstruct this prayer, for otherwise they might find fault with each of the patriarchs, and find reason to argue that the Divine promise be rescinded.

How strange! Our adversaries not only find fault with us, but also try to malign the patriarchs as well.

This prayer teaches us a historical lesson: Whoever seeks to find fault with us will stop at nothing.

We say this prayer in Aramaic, and bypass even the heavenly host. We appeal directly to G-d, because only He understands us.

"Israel, trust only in G-d. He is your salvation and protection" *(Psalms 115:9).*

*From the
Scriptures*

The jewels of the ephod (the breastplate of the High Priest) shall be according to the names of the children of Israel *(Exodus 28:11).*

Among the followers of Rabbi Sholom Dov of Lubavitch was a diamond merchant who was present when the Rabbi extolled the virtues of many of the townspeople, who, although not learned, were pious and sincere.

"Why do you praise them so highly?" the merchant asked. "They are quite simple people, and I see nothing special about them."

The Rabbi asked the merchant to show him his diamonds. He showed the Rabbi a number of jewels and, pointing to one particular diamond, the merchant was ecstatic, "This diamond, Rabbi, is most unusual and extremely valuable."

"I see nothing special about this stone," the Rabbi said. "It looks quite like all the others."

"Aha!" the merchant said. "For this you have to be a *mayvin* (connoisseur). Not everyone can tell the stone's value without knowing how to look and what to look for."

"Exactly," said the Rabbi. "And no one can tell how precious these simple, pious folk are unless one knows how to look and what to look for."

If sometimes we do not hold others in high regard, let us remember that the fault lies in us. We may not know where to look and what to look for.

NOTES

_____
_____
_____
_____
_____
_____
_____
_____
_____

He is a worker of truth whose deeds are
true. And to the moon he instructed
that she renew her glory to His chosen
people, for they too will be renewed (*prayer
on seeing the new moon*).

Whereas the secular calendar is based on the sun, the
Jewish calendar is based on the moon. Many commentaries
remark that there is a symbolism in the lunar calendar. After
reaching its maximum brightness, the light of the moon
begins to decrease until it disappears completely. Then, out
of the darkness, a bright new crescent appears.

This is something to remember when circumstances in
life are such that we find ourselves in utter darkness,
without any visible sign whence our salvation may come.
We should know that out of the depths of darkness, a new
brightness can appear.

Our history as a nation more than confirms this. As
individuals, too, we should remember that even at times
when everything seems bleak, there is always hope. From
virtually out of nowhere, light always reappears.

Rosh Chodesh
March 16, 1991
April 4, 1992
March 23, 1993
March 13, 1994
April 1, 1995
March 21, 1996

**This month (Nissan) shall be for you the head of
the months. It shall be the first of the months of the
year** (*Exodus 12:2*).

*From the
Scriptures*

The Torah refers to Nissan in two ways: It is the first
month of the year and it is the head of the year.

Just as the head is the master control of the body, and not
even the slightest movement can occur without it being
processed through or registered in the head, so it must be
with our lives all year round. They must be processed
through Nissan, the head of the year.

The very word Nissan means "miracles." We should
always remember that we are not accidental objects floating
around in a self-governing world, but that we are at every
moment under the watchful eye of G-d. We are constant
beneficiaries of countless miracles.

Secondly, Nissan is the month of freedom. Our actions of
all year round should be actions of a free people, actions of
true choice rather than compulsive behavior of people
driven by internal impulses, addictions of any kind, or
external pressures.

In the month of Nissan we became free. We must never
allow ourselves to be enslaved by our actions.

NOTES

March 17, 1991
April 5, 1992
March 24, 1993
March 14, 1994
April 2, 1995
March 22, 1996

From our Prayers ... וַיְהִי הַמַּקְרִיב בַּיּוֹם הָרִאשׁוֹן אֶת קָרְבָּנוֹ

The first day the prince of the tribe of Judah brought the following offering ... On the second day the offering was brought by the prince of the tribe of Isachar ... On the third day it was the prince of the tribe of Zebulun ...

May it be Your will, O L-rd my G-d and G-d of my forefathers, that if I, Your servant, am from this tribe (of that day), that the sanctity of that tribe illuminate my life to do Your will *(the Prince's offering, recited daily from 1-12 Nissan).*

The Sanctuary in the desert was dedicated during the first twelve days of Nissan, with the prince of each of the twelve tribes bringing an offering each day.

It is of interest that although each of the twelve offerings was identical in composition, the Torah, which assiduously avoids even a single superfluous letter, enumerates in detail the offerings of each prince *(Numbers 7:1-83).*

The teaching inherent in this is that dedicated service to G-d calls for a personal commitment and a personal conviction. Even if what we do is proper, it should not be done out of conformity or simply to mimic others.

Judaism is fiercely individualistic. "I am the L-rd, *your* G-d" *(Exodus 20:2)* was said in the singular. Each person's relationship with G-d is a highly personal one.

From the Scriptures

I will teach transgressors Your ways, and those who have been sinful how they may return to You *(Psalms 51:15).*

NOTES

Rabbi Bunim of Pshis'cha said that although committing sin is wrong, a person may plead in his defense that he was overwhelmed by temptation and just did not have the strength to resist. However, if he subsequently fails to repent his sin, that is a more grievous offense, for here one cannot even plead overwhelming temptation.

In addition to repenting for whatever wrong we may have committed, we can also take precautions not to put ourselves in those circumstances of vulnerability, where temptation would be great. It is well within our means to insulate ourselves from some temptations, and we certainly may be held responsible if we fail to do so.

ה' מִי יָגוּר בְּאָהֳלֶךָ מִי יִשְׁכֹּן בְּהַר קָדְשֶׁךָ . . . *From our Prayers*

O G-d, who shall dwell in Your Taberna-
cle, who shall rest upon the mountain
of Your Sanctuary? He that walks in moral
integrity and practices righteousness and
speaks the truth within his heart. He who
has borne no slander upon his tongue, nor
done evil to his fellow, nor tolerated an
aspersion cast upon his neighbor *(Psalms
15:1-3).*

March 18, 1991
April 6, 1992
March 25, 1993
March 15, 1994
April 3, 1995
March 23, 1996

Earlier (5 Teves) we referred to the idea of a prayer
before praying. The above psalm is found in many prayer
books as an introductory prayer to the morning service.

One can attend the house of G-d every day, yet be only
a visitor, essentially a stranger or an onlooker who is not
really a participant, or one can be a dweller, someone who
belongs there.

Becoming a dweller or gaining a membership in the
house of G-d is not achieved by paying dues. It is earned
only by developing one's character to own the traits listed
in psalm 15.

Before we begin our prayer, we should examine whether
our character indeed complies with the above psalm, and
resolve to make those changes in ourselves that will qualify
us as "dwellers" in the house of G-d.

**It is customary to buy wheat to distribute to the
poor for Passover needs** *(Orach Chaim 29:1).* *From the Sages*

In just two weeks we will open the *Seder* service with the
declaration, "Let all who are hungry come and eat. Let all
who are needy come and join our Passover feast."

At that point in time it is a bit too late to be hospitable,
for then we are sitting in our own homes, in the privacy of
our own dining rooms. No one can hear our invitation, and
no one can take advantage of it.

If our offer at the *Seder* is to have any meaning, we must
put our intentions to work well in advance of Passover. We
must inquire within our communities about families that
are needy, and make certain that they have the means to
provide adequately for Passover. We must inquire which
agencies distribute funds to needy people, whether in Israel
or in any other country.

Let our noble words at the *Seder* not be vain utterances.

NOTES

March 19, 1991
April 7, 1992
March 26, 1993
March 16, 1994
April 4, 1995
March 24, 1996

*From
our
Prayers*

אֱלֹקִים נִצָּב בַּעֲדַת קֵל . . .

G-d stands in every Divine tribunal; He judges in the midst of judges. "How much longer will you enforce violence in your judgment, and respect the persons of the lawless? Help him who has been brought low and the orphan to obtain their rightful due, and proclaim the right of those bereft of wealth and station" *(Psalms 82:1-3, Tuesday morning prayer).*

We often pray for justice in the world.

The Psalmist reminds us that the establishment of justice is often in our own hands.

Much of the injustice that prevails is because of man's own doing. The people we elect to draft our laws, and those we elect to execute and to adjudicate them are, in final analysis, extensions of ourselves.

Judges are corrupt if they take bribes. But if the public perpetuates unjust people in office because they will look after their own specific interests, then it too is accepting a bribe, and it too is corrupt.

Before complaining to G-d about the injustices in the world, let us ask ourselves, "What have we done to promote justice and fairness?"

*From
the Sages*

Rabbi Eliezer says that the world was created in Tishrei. Rabbi Joshua says the world was created in Nissan *(Rosh Hashanah 10b-11a).*

It is axiomatic that in the Talmud both sides of an argument are true, even if only one can be adopted as law.

But this Talmudic argument seems to be a difference in fact. Was the world created in Tishrei or in Nissan? Obviously, it cannot be both.

Nissan is the season of liberation. In Nissan it was declared that man should be the servant of G-d, and not enslaved by another human being; and that man's thoughts and wills should be his own, and not dominated by any authoritarian system.

A world in which there is no freedom is not deserving of existence. The physical creation of the world indeed occurred in Tishrei, when we celebrate Rosh Hashanah. But the real world did not come into being until Nissan, when freedom was proclaimed, and man took the first steps toward the spirituality which was later achieved in the Divine revelation and the giving of the Torah at Sinai.

NOTES

_____
_____
_____
_____
_____
_____
_____
_____

From ‏‏. . . וְדִבְרֵי שִׂנְאָה סְבָבוּנִי וַיִּלָּחֲמוּנִי חִנָּם

T hey surround me with words of hatred, *our* and wage war against me for no reason. *Prayers* In return for my love, they despise me, and I am a prayer *(Psalms 109:3-4).*

March 20, 1991
April 8, 1992
March 27, 1993
March 17, 1994
April 5, 1995
March 25, 1996

The last phrase is sometimes translated, "and I pray," but the literal translation is, "I am a prayer."

Rabbi Bunim of Pshis'cha said that when someone approaches you clad in rags and obviously poorly nourished, he does not have to make his request known to you. His very being speaks for itself.

In this psalm, David's anguish is profound and intense. It is so intense that he cannot verbalize it. "I cannot even pray. I *am* a prayer. Just look at me, O G-d, and You will see all my needs."

Sometimes the distresses of life are such that words fail us. All we can do is stand before G-d in silence, and simply turn ourselves over to Him.

Deliver me out of the mire so that I shall not sink *(Psalms 69:15).*

From the Scriptures

The Rabbi of Rizhin once met Rabbi Meir of Premishlan on the road. The Rabbi of Rizhin, who lived in splendor, was riding in a coach drawn by several pairs of horses. Rabbi Meir had one horse, an old nag that limped along slowly.

The two *tzaddikim* exchanged greetings and words of Torah. Then the Rabbi of Rizhin remarked, "You wonder, no doubt, why I travel with several pairs of horses. That is so that in case we go off the road into the swamp, the horses will be able to pull us out and get us on the road again."

NOTES

Rabbi Meir, who was wont to refer to himself by his first name, shrugged. "Meir cannot afford many strong horses," he said. "Meir has only this frail nag. Therefore Meir must take great caution not to deviate from the road."

If we realize how limited our energies are, we will take great caution not to deviate from the correct path. We may not have adequate strength to pull ourselves out of the mire.

NISSAN

נִיסָן

March 21, 1991
April 9, 1992
March 28, 1993
March 18, 1994
April 6, 1995
March 26, 1996

From our Prayers

. . . עַל שֶׁהִנְחַלְתָּ לַאֲבוֹתֵינוּ
. . . אֶרֶץ חֶמְדָּה טוֹבָה וּרְחָבָה

We thank You for giving to our forefathers a good and abundant land; for delivering us from bondage; for teaching us Torah; for giving us life, grace, and sustenance. Above all, O G-d, we are grateful to You (*Grace after Meals*).

The Maggid of Mezeritch interpreted this prayer to read, "We are grateful to G-d for many things, but above all, we are grateful that He is our G-d."

There was once a Jew who, upon seeing his house consumed by flames, recited the blessing thanking G-d for not having made him a heathen.

When asked about the relevance of this prayer, he said, "Just think, if I were a pagan, I would have been worshiping idols, and even my gods would have been destroyed in the fire along with my other possessions. But because I am a Jew and have a spiritual G-d, I will never be without Him, even though everything else I own may be lost."

How true are the words of the Psalmist, "Fortunate is the person whose strength is in You" (*Psalms 84:6*)."

From the Sages

And if listening you will listen to the voice of G-d (*Deuteronomy 28:1*). **The Talmud says that the verb "listen" is repeated to indicate that, "If you have listened to the old, you will be able to learn the new"** (*Succah 46b*).

The Rabbi of Rizhin's son was engaged to the daughter of Rabbi Hirsh of Rimanov.

At the engagement, the Rabbi of Rizhin — who was of a proud lineage, a descendant of many *tzaddikim* who traced his ancestry to King David — asked Rabbi Hirsh about his forebears.

Rabbi Hirsh responded, "My parents were simple folk, and both died when I was a child. I was apprenticed to a tailor, a simple but G-d-fearing man who taught me the principles of being a good worker. 'Do your best to mend any flaws in an old garment, and be careful not to make any defects in a new garment.' That is my heritage."

This is a simple but beautiful rule for living. Correct the mistakes of the past, and try to avoid mistakes in the future.

NOTES

_____
_____
_____
_____
_____
_____
_____
_____
_____

הוּא נָתַן לֶחֶם לְכָל בָּשָׂר
כִּי לְעוֹלָם חַסְדּוֹ . . .

He gives bread to all flesh, for His kindness is eternal. And in His great beneficence He has not deprived us and will not deprive us of sustenance for ever and ever (*Grace after Meals*).

March 22, 1991
April 10, 1992
March 29, 1993
March 19, 1994
April 7, 1995
March 27, 1996

The Rabbi of Kotzk commented that because of the serpent's seduction of Adam and Eve, he was cursed to "eat earth all the days of your life" (*Genesis 3:14*).

"What kind of curse is that?" the Rabbi asked. "The serpent will never go hungry. His food is always plentiful."

The Rabbi explained, "All living creatures must turn to G-d for food. 'He gives animals their food, to the young of the raven, who call upon Him' (*Psalms 147:9*). But G-d so despised the serpent that He said, 'You will never lack for food. Do not call upon Me. Do not pray to Me. I do not wish to hear your voice.' "

When we ask G-d to provide our needs, it is a privilege. We thank Him both for providing for us, and for making it necessary that we pray to Him. We are honored by the knowledge that He wishes to hear our voices in prayer.

Whoever observes the lighting of the Shabbos candles will have honorable children (*Shabbos 23b*).

Ushering in the *Shabbos* with the lighting of candles is not only a beautiful but also a most meaningful ritual.

Creating light is the prototype of an unselfish act, because even if you create light for yourself, the light shines for others as well. And if you create light altruistically, it illuminates your own world as well.

In our family, as in many others, the custom is to add an additional candle with the birth of each child. It was most edifying for me to know that our home was brighter simply because of my existence, regardless of my performance and achievements.

As we end a week and begin a new one, the symbolism in the candle-lighting ceremony can greatly enrich our spirit.

March 23, 1991
April 11, 1992
March 30, 1993
March 20, 1994
April 8, 1995
March 28, 1996

From our Prayers

הוֹדוּ לַה׳ כִּי טוֹב כִּי לְעוֹלָם חַסְדּוֹ

Give thanks to G-d for He is good. His **kindness endures forever** (Psalms 107:1, Grace after Meals).

The theme of gratitude to G-d is repeated many times in daily prayer: A song of thanksgiving (Psalms 100:1); Give thanks to G-d; Call in His name (Psalms 105:1), and various other places in the daily service.

Indeed, the Talmud gives us the formula for prayer as "Give thanks for the past, and pray for the future." It has also been said that if one thanks G-d for the day of life one just had, one has thereby bought for oneself another day of life for tomorrow.

It would almost appear that G-d is hungry for our gratitude, for having us acknowledge Him as our benefactor. Yet this is absurd, because G-d has no need for anything. Why then all the emphasis on gratitude?

Because the foundation of being a *mensch*, a decent human being, is being appreciative, and acknowledging what others do for us. But since some people see gratitude as being tied to obligation or dependence, they do not wish to feel obligated to or dependent on anyone. Therefore, they erect barriers to gratitude. They think of themselves as independent and self-sufficient, and this may in turn lead to arrogance and conceit. It is not easy to feel humble.

That is why we need to be reminded so often to be thankful to G-d. It helps us to learn gratitude, which we then can apply in a broader sense.

From the Scriptures

For the day is Yours, as is the night. You have established the light and the sun (Psalms 74:16).

One of the Chassidic masters read this verse somewhat differently. "For with You it is day, *even* when it is night. Light and sun are with You."

The unaided human eye sees light when it is light, and only darkness when it is dark. It sees good only when good is clearly evident, and sees things as bad when they appear to be bad.

The person with the deep trust in G-d knows that there is light even in darkness, and that there is good even when things appear to be bad. Light does not have its origin in the sun. The sun is only an emissary of G-d to reveal physical light to the world. The origin of the sun itself is in G-d, and if one is with Him, then light does not fade with sunset.

With sincere trust in G-d, we can see brightness even in the thick of night.

NOTES

_____
_____
_____
_____
_____
_____
_____
_____
_____
_____

הַטֵּה אֱלֹקַי אָזְנְךָ וּשְׁמַע *From*
פְּקַח עֵינֶיךָ וּרְאֵה שֹׁמְמֹתֵינוּ ... *our*

O G-d, bend Your ear and hear, open *Prayers*
Your eyes and see our desolation
(Daniel 9:18, morning service). **Awake, why do
You slumber, O G-d?** *(Psalms 44:24).*

NISSAN

9

ניסן

March 24, 1991
April 12, 1992
March 31, 1993
March 21, 1994
April 9, 1995
March 29, 1996

How are we to understand such phrases, which refer to
G-d as if He were unable to hear and see, or as if He were
asleep?

The Baal Shem Tov interprets the verse, "G-d is Your
shadow," *(Psalms 121:5)* as indicating that just as a person's
shadow corresponds to his movements, with the shadow
moving just as the person does, so does G-d relate to us
according to our behavior and our attitudes. If we act kindly
to others, He is kind to us. If we forgive others, He forgives
us. If we insist on absolute and stern judgment, exacting
from others everything that is justly due us and show no
lenience or consideration, then that is how G-d will act
toward us.

G-d is always awake. He hears and sees all. But if we
render ourselves deaf to the pleas of others, or blind to their
plights, or if we are lazy and sleep away our days, then that
is how G-d will act toward us.

If we desire Divine attention, we must merit it.

**Those who come to me in secret to speak evil of
others, I will destroy** *(Psalms 101:5).*

*From the
Scriptures*

In this psalm, King David teaches us an important rule of
life. Whereas many kings would have elaborate spy systems
to detect dissension and report anyone who speaks critically
of them, David acted otherwise. Not only did he not
advocate such a system of intelligence gathering, but if
anyone came to speak badly about others, David was ready
to destroy him. It soon became known that to this king, one
does not carry tales.

Many people will accept gossip about what others have
said of them. They think that those who alert them to what
others are saying about them are their true friends. Carriers
of gossip are not friends, but mortal enemies. We should
think well enough of ourselves and not suspect that others
speak badly of us, and we should trust in G-d that He will
protect us even if others do design against us.

NOTES

_____
_____
_____
_____
_____
_____
_____
_____
_____

NISSAN

10

נ יסן

March 25, 1991
April 13, 1992
April 1, 1993
March 22, 1994
April 10, 1995
March 30, 1996

From our Prayers

כִּי גָדוֹל ה' וּמְהֻלָּל מְאֹד
וְנוֹרָא הוּא עַל כָּל אֱלֹהִים . . .

For G-d is great and highly praised. He is awesome above all the mighty. For all the idols of all the nations are naught, whereas G-d created the heavens (*I Chronicles 16:25-26; morning service*).

On the tenth day of Nissan, our ancestors, who were enslaved in Egypt, acquired lambs from their Egyptian masters, for the expressed purpose of bringing the Passover Lamb as a sacrificial offering. This was their manifest repudiation of Egyptian idolatry, since the lamb was worshiped in Egypt.

Idolatry, whether it is the worship of a lamb or any other idol, is essentially a system wherein man seeks his personal gratification, and believes that he can placate the gods so that they will grant him his wishes.

Judaism is not only a repudiation of the embodiment of the deity in images and icons, but even more, a surrender of man to the will of G-d. We do not seek a relationship with G-d so that He will grant us our desires, but rather that we become spiritual, and that we do that which He desires.

From the Scriptures

In vain do they speak falsely, one to another, saying, "May G-d destroy those who speak with forked tongues," while their hearts are insincere (*Psalms 12:3-4*).

NOTES

_____
_____
_____
_____
_____
_____
_____
_____
_____

This is how Rabbi Moshe Alschich interprets this verse, explaining that people who are insincere, and speak one way while thinking otherwise, may believe that they are successfully deceiving the other person. Not so, says the Alschich. Their deceptive efforts are in vain. There is a non-verbal communication that supersedes their words, and in spite of their best efforts, their true thoughts and feelings do get communicated.

We should refrain from lying not only because it is wrong and sinful, but also because it is futile. Truth will prevail much sooner than we may realize.

מִמַּסְגֵּר אַסִיר בְּצֵאת לְחוֹפֶשׁ ... *From*
סְגֻּבְתָּם חֹק מַרְגּוֹעַ וָנוֹפֶשׁ *our*

W hen the prisoner [Israel] left his dun- *Prayers*
geon [Egypt] for freedom . . . You en-
vigorated them with the law of Shabbos, a
day of rest (*prayer of the Shabbos preceding*
Passover).

March 26, 1991
April 14, 1992
April 2, 1993
March 23, 1994
April 11, 1995
March 31, 1996

The *Shabbos* preceding Passover is referred to as *Shabbos*
Hagadol, or the Great *Shabbos*.

The Midrash states that in Egypt Moses succeeded in
securing a weekly day of rest for the enslaved Jews, arguing
that this would enable them to be more productive the other
days of the week. The Jews thus observed *Shabbos* while in
Egypt, and it was known as "The Day of Moses."

But *Shabbos* is much more than a day of physical rest.
Shabbos is a day of prayer and meditation, a day on which
a person who is free from the preoccupation of work can
contemplate the purpose of his existence, and what it is that
he wishes to do with his life.

These are concepts that are appropriate for a free person.
Slaves do not have the luxury of choosing their goals and
determining their purposes. Their fates are determined by
their masters.

The *Shabbos* on the eve of liberation was different from
previous *Shabbosos*. This was no longer to be a day of rest
for weary slaves, but a day of spiritual uplifting for people
who are free. This indeed was a Great *Shabbos*.

What is man that You should be mindful of him, *From the*
what is the son of mankind that You should take *Scriptures*
account of him? You have withheld from him but
little of the Divine (*Psalms 8:5-6*).

These verses appear contradictory. The first appears to
speak of the insignificance of man, and the second of his
greatness.

There really is no contradiction. Physical man indeed is
frail. His being is less than an infinitesimal subatomic particle
in an immense universe. But spiritual man is great. He was
given a spirit that enables him to achieve a spirituality far
superior to that of the heavenly angels. The spirituality of
angels is fixed, it never progresses. However, man's
spirituality can grow, and man can achieve a spiritual growth
that will bring him closer to G-d than even the heavenly host.

It is our unique privilege to grow in spirituality. This is a
rare gift which we dare not neglect.

March 27, 1991
April 15, 1992
April 3, 1993
March 24, 1994
April 12, 1995
April 1, 1996

From our Prayers

וִיהִי נֹעַם ד' אֱלֹקֵינוּ עָלֵינוּ . . .

May it be the will of G-d that His presence rest in the work of your hands. And may the bliss of G-d come to us. Establish upon us the work of our hands *(blessing of Moses upon completion of construction of the Sanctuary, Psalms 90:17, Shabbos morning service).*

The Chassidic masters write that man's purpose on earth is to reveal the G-dliness that is present in everything. In the spiritual realm of the heavens, the glory of G-d is manifest. Here on earth, where everything is physical, where living things are motivated by physical desires, and where things appear to operate according to fixed physical laws of nature, G-dliness is concealed. We live in a world where it is possible for man to deny G-d.

It is our mission to remove the cloak of concealment and reveal the Divine presence in everything, so that the Name of G-d is sanctified on earth, just as it is in the heavens above *(Kedushah prayer of the daily Amidah).*

The method whereby this is accomplished is the observance of the *mitzvos* of the Torah. Fulfillment of our mission draws down upon us the bliss of G-d, a measure of true happiness which is not obtainable any other way.

From the Sages

A person must be very patient, even with himself *(Rabbi Nachman of Breslov).*

NOTES

It is surprising that people who can have endless patience with others are often extremely harsh and impatient with themselves. Just as some people are extremely short with others but will find many justifications for their own behavior, other people go to the opposite extreme.

Neither extreme is constructive. If we deny our character defects and rationalize all our actions, we will never correct them. If we are overcritical of ourselves, we will not grant ourselves adequate time to make the necessary changes in our character. If we expect ourselves to change faster than actually possible, we are apt to despair of our efforts.

As with all traits, the golden path of virtue is the median, and not either extreme.

וְצִוָּנוּ עַל בְּעוּר חָמֵץ . . . *From our Prayers*

H e has instructed us on the removal of
chametz [leavened bread] *(Blessing when
searching for chametz).*

NISSAN

ניסן

March 28, 1991
April 16, 1992
April 4, 1993
March 25, 1994
April 13, 1995
April 2, 1996

*[The search
for chametz
takes place tonight.]*

The requirement to dispose of every fragment of *chametz*
from our premises is unique. For none of the other food
items that are forbidden is possession proscribed. Why is
chametz so different?

Tosafos (Pesachim 2a) explains that *chametz* is something that is normally used, and except for the week of
Passover, is perfectly permissible. And since our habitual
use of *chametz* might result in our inadvertently eating it
during the forbidden period, we have to put it beyond our
reach.

The message is clear. To rid ourselves of a bad habit —
whether it is the unhealthy use of alcohol, violent anger out-
bursts, overpossessiveness, or any other undesirable behavior — simply deciding not to continue it is not sufficient.
To stop unwanted behavior, two steps are necessary. First,
we cannot retain any part of the objectionable behavior. It
must be completely avoided. Second, we must take
extraordinary precautions to prevent relapse. Success is
possible only if both steps are fully implemented.

**Matzah dough becomes chametz if the process of
the dough rising is even permitted to begin** *(Orach
Chaim 459).*

*From
the Sages*

The symbolism of *matzah*, says Rabbi Tzvi Elimelech,
is that it has no spontaneous activity, having only the
consistency and shape given it by the baker. *Chametz*,
however, rises on its own. *Chametz* thus indicates a
process occurring without the formative guidance of its
maker.

The Passover commemoration of our liberation requires
an absolute restriction of *chametz*. This is to teach us that
freedom is complete only when we are not pawns in the
hands of fixed and unguided natural forces. Everything that
occurs in the universe, everything that occurs to us, with the
sole exception of moral decisions which are of our own
choice, occurs at the discretion of Divine Providence.

G-d has a constant interest in every human being, and
everything we do is of significance to G-d. We must direct
our lives according to this principle. Hence, on the festival
of freedom, the most minute crumb of *chametz*, a substance which has "spontaneous" activity, is forbidden.

NOTES

Erev Pesach
[Eve of Passover]
March 29, 1991
April 17, 1992
April 5, 1993
March 26, 1994
April 14, 1995
April 3, 1996

*From
our
Prayers*

כָּל חֲמִירָא וַחֲמִיעָא דְּאִכָּא בִרְשׁוּתִי
דַּחֲזִתֵּהּ וּדְלָא חֲזִתֵּהּ . . .

All the chametz that may be in my possession, whether I am aware of its presence or not . . . I hereby disown and declare it to be of no value to me *(prayer upon burning chametz).*

Following last night's search for *chametz*, we now burn whatever *chametz* we have found in our search, and then declare that whatever may have remained in our possession that is unknown to us is also null and void.

When one makes a personal moral inventory, he must search out whatever character defects he has, and he must do his utmost to correct them. However, regardless of how thorough the inventory is, a person invariably overlooks some character defects, perhaps because he may not recognize them as such.

If one's intentions at character improvement are sincere, he then declares that he repudiates any character defects which are beyond his awareness, which means that, as in the case of *chametz*, as soon as they become known to him, he will promptly get rid of them.

With sincere soul-searching and a dedication to improve ourselves, G-d will assist us in the removal of any remaining character defects which are unknown to us.

*From the
Scriptures*

Though he who bears the measure of seed goes on his way weeping, he shall surely come home with exultation, bearing his sheaves of grain *(Psalms 126:6).*

Searching into one's soul and discovering one's character defects can be depressing. How can we distinguish the feelings of sadness, that are the result of discovering one's faults, from the dejection of pathological depression?

Rabbi Boruch of Medziboz quoted the above verse of *Psalms* as the answer to this question.

If one continues to progress and improve himself as he rids himself of his character defects, much as the farmer laboriously weeds his land and plants seeds which will bear fruit, then his weeping will surely turn to joy. The dejection of depression is characterized by despair, as one resigns oneself to inactivity. The disappointment of discovering objectionable character traits in oneself should lead to their elimination and to personality growth.

Tears of repentance lead to song and jubilation.

NOTES

―――――――
―――――――
―――――――
―――――――
―――――――
―――――――
―――――――
―――――――

W**e were slaves to Pharaoh in Egypt, and G-d delivered us with great might . . . And if G-d had not delivered us, we would still be enslaved . . .** (Haggadah).

עֲבָדִים הָיִינוּ לְפַרְעֹה בְּמִצְרָיִם . . . *From our Prayers*

Would we indeed be enslaved today had G-d not delivered us? Is history not replete with accounts of enslaved peoples who somehow managed to gain their freedom? Perhaps we, too, could have gained our political freedom. But in Judaism political freedom is not the ultimate goal. The goal is spiritual freedom, and this could not have been achieved without Divine intervention.

Many nations have their heroes, and the Jewish nation is not deficient in this respect. But the names that have been perpetuated in Jewish history are not those of generals, statesmen, or even great scientists.

The people who represent Judaism from Moses down to this very day are those who teach spirituality and live spiritually. In the footsteps of Moses, they are G-dly people.

Passover is not a mere independence day, but the first step in man's relationship to G-d.

First Day of Pesach
March 30, 1991
April 18, 1992
April 6, 1993
March 27, 1994
April 15, 1995
April 4, 1996

For who is like Your nation, like Israel, a unique people on earth (II Samuel 7:23).

From the Scriptures

One Passover eve, during the period when Russia and Turkey were at war, the Rabbi of Berdichev asked his townspeople to bring him some Turkish tobacco.

"But Rabbi," they argued, "That is contraband. Possession of any Turkish merchandise is punishable by imprisonment and even death!"

The Rabbi insisted, and before long some Turkish tobacco was brought. He then asked for some Turkish wool. Again the people protested that it was not to be had, again the Rabbi insisted, and again some was found.

"Now bring me a piece of bread from a Jewish household," the Rabbi said. After hours of search, the people returned empty handed.

The Rabbi raised his hands in prayer. "Dear G-d, do Your people not deserve better than You have treated them? Here stands the czar with his armies and police. Those who violate his law can be shot on sight. Yet, I could get Turkish contraband from people who defied the czar's edict.

"But although You have no army and no police, and do not threaten imminent punishment, Your decrees are faithfully observed. Not a single piece of bread is to be found in any Jewish household! Who else is like Your people, G-d? Their devotion merits better treatment.'"

NOTES
_____
_____
_____
_____
_____
_____
_____
_____
_____

Second Day of Pesach

[In the Land of Israel this is the first day of Chol Hamoed, the Intermediate Days.]

March 31, 1991
April 19, 1992
April 7, 1993
March 28, 1994
April 16, 1995
April 5, 1996

From our Prayers

בְּכָל דּוֹר וָדוֹר
חַיָּב אָדָם לִרְאוֹת אֶת עַצְמוֹ . . .

In every generation a person should consider himself as though he was personally liberated from Egypt *(Haggadah)*.

Jewish liturgy is replete with references to the Exodus. The *Shabbos,* the Festivals, and numerous *mitzvos* are all considered to commemorate the deliverance from Egypt.

The Chassidic masters explain that the Hebrew word for Egypt, "Mitzraim," can also be read phonetically as "metzarim." This word means boundaries, restrictive limitations. They explain that to the extent that a person does not fulfill his potential, to that extent he is restricted, and as it were, in bondage. Just as there can be an external bondage that stifles political and civil liberties, and prevents a person from exercising his rights, there is an internal bondage. This internal bondage can stifle a person's potential.

The enslavement of *Mitzraim* and the deliverance therefrom was a historical event of many hundreds of years ago. The enslavement of *metzarim,* of our own oppression of our potential, occurs in every generation, and we must struggle to liberate ourselves from these restrictive limitations to our creativity and productivity.

From the Scriptures

Speak to the children of Israel, that they shall take for themselves a lamb for each household *(Exodus 12:3).*

The first *mitzvah* of the newly liberated people, the Passover offering, was a ritual to be observed by the entire household, a family oriented *mitzvah*.

The foundation of this new nation, one formed out of a people broken in body and spirit by decades of torture and dehumanization, was to get together as a family. Family cohesiveness is the secret of the origin of the Jewish people, and is the secret of its survival.

The deterioration of the family that has occurred in modern Western civilization, and has affected the Jewish people as well, is a greater threat to our survival than all of our mortal enemies combined. The Passover *Seder* is but a residual of the traditional gathering of the family to commemorate the emergence of our people as a spiritual nation. Whatever we can do to strengthen family cohesiveness and to avoid those tragic incidents that divide families will contribute to the perpetuation of Israel.

NOTES

_____
_____
_____
_____
_____
_____
_____
_____
_____

וְצִוָּנוּ עַל סְפִירַת הָעוֹמֶר . . . *From*

Blessed are You, L-rd our G-d, King of the *our* universe, who has sanctified us with His *Prayers* commandments and instructed us on the counting of the Omer (*daily blessing between Passover and Shavuos*).

Among the many miracles of the Exodus, not the smallest was the transformation of a people who had been in bondage for centuries, living with a slave mentality, into a people who were a "kingdom of priests and a sacred people" (*Exodus 19:6*). How was this transformation accomplished?

From the Exodus to the revelation at Sinai, seven weeks elapsed. Paralleling that, we have the mitzvah to count the Omer from the day after the celebration of the Exodus until the day on which we celebrate the revelation at Sinai. For seven weeks we count each day: Today is the first day of the Omer, today is the second day of the Omer, etc.

Developing a spiritual nation out of a group of newly emancipated slaves is a task that appears to border on the impossible.

But it is only impossible if one tries to embrace too much too soon. If one can work on spirituality "one day at a time," and accomplish today only that which needs to be accomplished today, the impossible becomes possible.

As with the generation of the Exodus, so it is with us. We must divide time into manageable segments, and live one day at a time.

Chol Hamoed Pesach

April 1, 1991
April 20, 1992
April 8, 1993
March 29, 1994
April 17, 1995
April 6, 1996

Lift your eyes above and see who created these (*Isaiah 40:26*).

From the Scriptures

When Rabbi Shmuel of Lubavitch was a boy of seven, he received a letter from his father, Rabbi Menachem Mendel, who was away on a trip.

"G-d did a great kindness with man," he wrote, "in that He made him unique among all living things. All other creatures walk with their eyes directed toward the earth, whereas man walks upright. Therefore he can easily direct his eyes toward the heavens."

Rabbi Menachem Mendel expected his child of seven to develop his spirituality, to break away from things that bind one to the earth, and to aspire to reach the heavens.

Some people who are many times seven fail to take advantage of their upright posture. To be truly human we must exercise our uniqueness. We must look upward, and we must strive toward G-dliness.

NOTES

_____
_____
_____
_____
_____
_____
_____
_____
_____

NISSAN

18

נִיסָן

Chol Hamoed
Pesach
April 2, 1991
April 21, 1992
April 9, 1993
March 30, 1994
April 18, 1995
April 7, 1996

*From
our
Prayers*

אֶחָד חָכָם וְאֶחָד רָשָׁע וְאֶחָד תָּם
וְאֶחָד שֶׁאֵינוֹ יוֹדֵעַ לִשְׁאוֹל

Blessed be G-d, blessed is He who gave the Torah to His people, Israel. The Torah responds to the four types of children: the wise, the defiant, the simple, and the ignorant *(Haggadah)*.

Throughout history there have been people who have challenged the authenticity of Torah. There have been intellectuals whose infatuation with their own intellect prompted them to reject any suprarational system. There have been the defiant, who refused to accept any restrictions on their behavior. There were the simple, who followed any and all types of leaders, and the ignorant, who defended their ignorance by scoffing at the learned.

It has been said that those who do not learn from history must pay the price of learning from their own experience. How foolish!

Judaism has survived for three thousand years. Every challenge to Torah Judaism has already been raised and has been answered. The Torah remains unchanged and eternal.

Blessed is He who has given the Torah to the people of Israel, the same Torah to the people of the Exodus and to their descendants of today.

*From
the Sages*

This maror (bitter herbs) that we eat is to commemorate the bitterness that our ancestors suffered during their enslavement in Egypt *(Haggadah)*.

The Torah refers to the ordeal of Egypt as being in an "iron-smelting furnace" *(Deuteronomy 4:20)*. This was a purifying furnace, which cleansed the people of contaminants and molded them into a nation.

No one who experienced the suffering of the Egyptian bondage could have envisioned any good emerging from it. Yet for reasons known only to G-d, this was the process necessary to bring about the formation of an eternal nation.

In everyone's life, there are moments, and sometimes years, of bitterness. *Maror* teaches one to believe that even that which is so bitter now will result in future sweetness.

The *Seder* service notes that Hillel combined the *maror* with the *matzah*. Bitterness can be tolerated if we understand the significance of the *matzah* (see 13 Nissan); if we know that we are not victims of inexorable physical laws, but that everything we experience, regardless of how distressful, is under the vigilance of a loving and merciful G-d.

NOTES

_____
_____
_____
_____
_____
_____
_____
_____
_____
_____

לְפִיכָךְ אֲנַחְנוּ חַיָּבִים לְהוֹדוֹת לְהַלֵּל . . . *From our Prayers*

It is therefore incumbent upon us to give thanks and praise to the One who did all these wonders for us. He brought us out from slavery to freedom, from bondage to deliverance, from grief to joy, from darkness to great light, and we will sing new praises to Him, Hallelujah! *(Haggadah).*

The theme of Passover is freedom. But there is a great difference between freedom and recklessness. Freedom does not mean, as some like to think, rejection of authority and doing whatever one pleases. This is recklessness rather than freedom. Freedom means being responsible, and responsibility begins with gratitude.

Gratitude is a most logical feeling. It consists of acknowledging what has been done for us and expressing our appreciation, whether in word or deed. Gratitude must also take into account the totality of the favor one has received, as is indicated in the above prayer. Why is gratitude difficult for some people? Because feeling gratitude obligates, and people do not like to feel obligated, even if only to verbally express their gratitude.

This Passover prayer teaches us what freedom means. It teaches us how to be a *mensch.*

Chol Hamoed Pesach

April 3, 1991
April 22, 1992
April 10, 1993
March 31, 1994
April 19, 1995
April 8, 1996

For with You, O G-d, there is kindness, for You reward a person according to his deeds *(Psalms 62:13).*

From the Scriptures

One of the Chassidic masters was once asked, "Why is it that in rewarding a *mitzvah*, G-d considers all the good consequences that evolve from that *mitzvah*, whereas in punishing a sin, only the immediate action itself is considered? Is that really justice?"

"It is very simple," the Rabbi answered. "If one gives *tzedakah* to sustain a poor man through a crisis, and as a result he is able to provide for his children, who then grow up to be healthy and productive, certainly the donor would have wanted all these fine things to come about.

"But if a person yields to temptation and steals, and as a result of the theft the owner is heartbroken and becomes ill or some other bad thing occurs, this was certainly not the thief's intent. He stole only because of his greed, but did not wish the bad consequences to occur."

So in our relating to others' reactions toward us, we must abound in gratitude for favors we receive, but hold little resentment when we are offended.

NOTES

Chol Hamoed
Pesach
April 4, 1991
April 23, 1992
April 11, 1993
April 1, 1994
April 20, 1995
April 9, 1996

*From
our
Prayers*

הָא לַחְמָא עַנְיָא דִי אֲכָלוּ אַבְהָתָנָא . . .

This matzah is the bread of affliction which our forefathers ate in Egypt. Let all the needy come join in our feast . . . Today we are slaves, in the year to come we shall be free *(opening prayer of the Haggadah).*

When Moses came with the tidings of the forthcoming liberation, he was repudiated by some of the people. They had become accustomed to slavery. They were tolerant of their degradation, and had no aspiration for freedom. Even after leaving Egypt, whenever they considered themselves to be in peril, they opted for return to the security of Egypt, their enslavement notwithstanding.

In every age we must do a careful soul-searching. Have we perhaps resigned ourselves to a lesser status than one which we can achieve? Have we perhaps become tolerant of conditions that stifle our personality growth, and prefer to remain in a rut rather than exert ourselves to become something greater than what we are?

The *matzah* is a bread of affliction, not only the affliction of being slaves, but even more so the affliction of making peace with being enslaved.

*From the
Scriptures*

And yet, for all that, even when they are in the land of their enemies, I have not despised them nor abhorred them to make an end of them, to break My covenant with them, for I, G-d, remain their G-d *(Leviticus 26:44).*

Rabbi Zev Kitzes, a disciple of the Baal Shem Tov, was an ardent traveler. On one of his excursions, he met a man dressed in oriental clothes, who inquired about the situation of Jews in Europe.

"G-d does not forsake them," Rabbi Zev answered.

Upon his return, he related this encounter to the Baal Shem Tov. The Baal Shem Tov began weeping.

"We lost an opportunity for the redemption," he said. "Every so often, the patriarch Abraham comes down to earth to inquire as to the welfare of his descendants. Had you told him of our distress, of our persecution, of our spiritual impoverishment and our longing to return to Jerusalem to live in the radiance of the Divine presence, he would have interceded to hasten our Redemption.

"But no, you had to reassure him that all was well!"

Of course it is true that G-d does not forsake us, but that should never satisfy our spiritual aspirations.

NOTES

From our Prayers מַלְכוּתְךָ רָאוּ בָנֶיךָ בּוֹקֵעַ יָם לִפְנֵי מֹשֶׁה . . .

Your children witnessed Your majesty as You divided the sea before Moses. In unison they all praised and enthroned You and responded, "G-d is our King forever!" (*daily evening service*).

How strange that those who witnessed the miraculous dividing of the Red Sea could so soon deny G-d, as the account of the Torah attests.

The Rabbi of Kotzk, upon hearing of a *tzaddik* who allegedly saw the seven patriarchs in his *succah*, said, "I did not see them, but I believed they were there. Belief is superior to seeing."

These days when laboratory proof is often considered the only test of validity, some who do not believe say, "Prove G-d's existence to me. I believe only what I can see."

The Red Sea disproves this argument. People who saw it divide miraculously were not immune to denying G-d.

The acceptance or the denial of G-d is contingent upon our willingness to accept our own powerlessness and turn our lives over to G-d. Those who can do so will have no difficulty believing in G-d. Those who refuse to do so will deny Him even with incontrovertible proof of His existence.

If we sometimes have difficulty with our prayers or with our faith, we should ask ourselves, "How reluctant are we to accept our own powerlessness and the sovereignty of G-d?"

Seventh Day of Pesach
[In the Land of Israel this is the last day of Pesach.]
April 5, 1991
April 24, 1992
April 12, 1993
April 2, 1994
April 21, 1995
April 10, 1996

On that day G-d saved the Israelites from the hands of the Egyptians . . . And Israel saw the mighty hand of G-d that He wielded over Egypt, and they believed in G-d (*Exodus 14:30,31*).

From the Scriptures

A man once came to a *tzaddik*, relating his desperate plight and asking for the *tzaddik's* blessing.

"Have no fear," the *tzaddik* said. "Have faith in G-d, and He will certainly help you."

The man shook his head. "That is not what it says in the *siddur*," he said, quoting the above verse in Exodus. "First G-d must help, and then we believe."

The *tzaddik* smiled. "Go home in peace," he said. "Your prayers will be answered."

To his disciples, the *tzaddik* said, "This man's simple piety and the sincerity of his belief warranted salvation. Very simplistically, he held G-d accountable for what is said in the Torah. That is an argument to which G-d must yield."

NOTES

_____
_____
_____
_____
_____
_____
_____
_____
_____

*Eighth Day
of Pesach
[Yizkor]*

April 6, 1991
April 25, 1992
April 13, 1993
April 3, 1994
April 22, 1995
April 11, 1996

*From
our
Prayers*

כִּי בָא סוּס פַּרְעֹה בְּרִכְבּוֹ וּבְפָרָשָׁיו בַּיָּם . . .

As Pharaoh and his chariots came into the sea, G-d returned the waters of the sea upon them, and the children of Israel walked on dry land through the sea *(daily morning service, Song of Moses).*

The sequence of events appears reversed, for the Israelites walked through the dry land first, and later the waters returned.

One of the Chassidic masters pointed out that for the person who sincerely believes that G-d maintains continuous control of the universe even when He operates it through natural laws, for this person miracles and natural phenomena are identical. Both are actions of G-d.

To the true believer, walking on dry land is no less miraculous than walking on the dry bed of a sea that has just divided. Every move we make is miraculous in its own right. The term "supernatural" means nothing more than the term "unusual."

For those who became true believers on witnessing the division of the Red Sea, their subsequent travels on dry land were no less miraculous than their crossing the dry bed of the divided sea.

Perfect faith converts every natural phenomenon into a miracle.

*From the
Scriptures*

Honor your father and mother, so that G-d will be benevolent toward you and you will live long *(Deuteronomy 5:16).*

Rabbi Shmelke of Nikolsburg would preface the performance of every *mitzvah* by studying the laws pertaining to that particular *mitzvah*.

Every day before breakfast he would study the laws relating to honoring one's parents.

Rabbi Shmelke explained that as a young man he would frequently fast to atone for his sins. His mother was concerned for his health, and commanded him, on the basis of the *mitzvah* to respect one's parents, that he should eat breakfast every day.

Although Rabbi Shmelke preferred to fast, he did not wish to transgress his mother's instructions. Eating breakfast was thus out of respect for her wish, and was therefore a *mitzvah*.

That is why he prefaced breakfast with the study of the laws of parental respect.

זָכַרְתִּי לָךְ חֶסֶד נְעוּרַיִךְ ... *From*
אַהֲבַת כְּלוּלֹתָיִךְ ... *our*
Prayers

Thus said G-d, "I remember for you the
kindness of your youth, the love of your
betrothal to Me, when you followed Me
into the wilderness of the desert, into a
barren land" *(Jeremiah 2:2, Rosh Hashanah
liturgy)*.

April 7, 1991
April 26, 1992
April 14, 1993
April 4, 1994
April 23, 1995
April 12, 1996

A woman complained to the Maggid of Koznitz that her
husband said he was leaving her. "He said that I am old and
unattractive, and that he no longer loves me."

The Maggid sighed. "What can I do for you, my dear
woman? Some foolish men are interested only in physical
attractiveness."

"But where is justice and fairness?" the woman cried.
"When he married me, I *was* young and beautiful. Does
he not owe me his allegiance even if I have lost my
beauty?"

The Maggid's eyes filled with tears. He raised his hands
in prayer to heaven. "Dear G-d, where is justice and
fairness? In our youth we too were beautiful. When You
took us out of Egypt, we followed You blindly into a desert
where there was no food, no water. We trusted in You and
You loved us for our faith. Even if we now no longer have
that beauty, do You not owe us Your allegiance? Have you
not stated so yourself?"

The fact is, however, that we are different than the
woman. We *can* restore our faith and trust. We can reclaim
every bit of the beauty of our youth.

**If not that Your Torah was my delight, I would
have perished in my affliction** *(Psalms 119:92).*

*From the
Scriptures*

The Rabbi of Rizhin made a frightening prediction. "A
day will come," he said, "when ignorance will reign.
Mediocre men will feel at ease on earth and above, while
men of spirit and conscience will be alienated. The most
pious Jew will be incapable of reciting a verse of Psalms. I
tell you this so you will know, because that is how it will
be."

But we can thwart this prophecy. We can overcome
illiteracy and ignorance. The Torah is at our very fingertips,
and we have more educational aids than ever before in
Jewish history.

We must dedicate our efforts to the study of Torah for
young and old alike. It is our only salvation.

NOTES

_____
_____
_____
_____
_____
_____
_____
_____
_____

From our Prayers

הָרַחֲמָן הוּא יְפַרְנְסֵנוּ בְּכָבוֹד . . .

May the Merciful One sustain us in dignity. May the Merciful One remove the yoke of oppression from our necks and lead us in pride to our homeland . . . May the Merciful One bless my parents, my spouse, and my children (*Grace after Meals*).

What relevance do these prayers have to the blessings after the meal? The Chafetz Chaim explained that performance of any *mitzvah* brings a person into a closer relationship with G-d, and this enables his prayers to be more profound and more meaningful. Furthermore, performance of a *mitzvah* bestows a state of merit upon a person.

Reciting the blessings after the meal is a *mitzvah*. "You shall eat and be satisfied, and give thanks to G-d" (*Deuteronomy* 8:10). Having just completed a *mitzvah*, it is an opportune moment for praying for our needs.

In addition to being a *mitzvah*, the recitation of blessings after the meal is also a step toward character refinement. Whenever we are appreciative of anything and express our gratitude for what we have received, we become more considerate, more sensitive, and more humble. If we can be grateful for having our own needs met, we are more likely to be cognizant of the needs of others. Such refinement of character makes us more deserving of Divine blessing.

From the Scriptures

Rejoice, young man, in your youth, gratify your heart's wishes when you are young, and go in the ways of your desires and what your eyes see. But know for certain that for all these you will be answerable to G-d on judgment day (*Ecclesiastes 11:9*).

We are a society that lives on credit cards. We buy now and pay later, even though the cost of credit may be exorbitant. Our economy is based on mortgaging our future to satisfy our desires of the present period.

Solomon warns us against indulging ourselves for the momentary gratification without considering the ultimate consequences of our actions.

The goods of the world were given to us as means to sustain ourselves so that we can do the will of G-d. Judicious enjoyment of Divine blessings is appropriate, but excesses are not.

Let us use, as our guideline, that on Judgment Day we will be answerable for all that we do.

NOTES

_____
_____
_____
_____
_____
_____
_____
_____
_____
_____

From אַהֲבַת עוֹלָם . . .

With eternal love You have loved us, *our* O L-rd our G-d (*daily service*). *Prayers*

We begin each day and we close each day with a reminder that G-d's love for us is eternal and unconditional.

We need never feel alone. There is no way that G-d will ever desert us. Even if our behavior is not in accordance with His wishes, even if we cause Him to be angry with us, His love for us remains.

A parent who has a rebellious child may have to deal harshly with him, yet this does not diminish the parent's love for the child. The parent always longs for the child to return so that he can embrace him. How much more so with G-d, whose love is infinite both in time and quality.

An infant cradled in the parent's strong and protective arms feels the warmth and security of the parent's presence and feels that no harm can befall him. That is how we should feel the presence of G-d: ever-loving, ever-protecting, never abandoning.

When we begin the day with its many ordeals and challenges, we know that G-d loves us; and when we entrust our souls to Him each night, we know that G-d loves us, with a love that is unconditional and eternal.

April 9, 1991
April 28, 1992
April 16, 1993
April 6, 1994
April 25, 1995
April 14, 1996

Do not trust in yourself until the day of your death (*Ethics of the Fathers 2:5*).

From the Sages

It is important that we understand that our lives are one long struggle to resist temptation and to triumph over the forces that incite us to do wrong.

Our greatest single danger is overconfidence. We may feel so secure in our convictions that we consider ourselves beyond vulnerability to do wrong. This causes us to lower our guard, and at that moment we are at greatest risk.

The Talmud relates that Yochanan, the High Priest, devoted and dedicated himself to the service of G-d for eighty years, only to succumb to heresy in his advanced years.

There is no laying down the arms in the struggle against evil. We must guard ourselves particularly for the unguarded moment.

NOTES

_____
_____
_____
_____
_____
_____
_____
_____
_____
_____

April 10, 1991
April 29, 1992
April 17, 1993
April 7, 1994
April 26, 1995
April 15, 1996

From our Prayers

מְנוּחָה וְשִׂמְחָה אוֹר לַיְּהוּדִים . . .

Tranquility and joy, a brightness for the Jewish nation; a day of rest, a day of pleasantness. Those who observe it and commemorate it thereby testify that in six days G-d created the universe (*Zemiros of Shabbos*).

Shabbos: a testimony to the creation of the universe. The message of creation is twofold. Firstly, the universe was brought into creation for a purpose. In a purposeful universe, man can have a goal and a purpose to achieve, and life can have meaning.

Secondly, the Divine process of creation came to an end on the sixth day. By *Shabbos*, G-d completed His work. "For on the seventh day G-d rested from all His work that He had created, *to be done*" (*Genesis 2:3*). Where G-d's work ends, man's work begins.

If life has no purpose, then everything is futile, and there can be no joy. Without a reason for existence, the anxiety of living in a meaningless world would be overwhelming.

Joy and tranquility can be only with *Shabbos*.

From the Sages

All of a person's earnings are preordained from one Rosh Hashanah to the following Rosh Hashanah (*Beitzah 16a*).

A man complained to Rabbi Meir of Premishlan that someone opened a competitive business near him, and he was fearful that his earnings would suffer.

Rabbi Meir told him that when a horse drinks water from a river, he thumps with his hoof.

"Do you know why he does this?" Rabbi Meir asked. "Because when he sees his reflection in the water, he thinks there is another horse there, and he tries to frighten him away, lest the other horse drink all the water and not leave enough for him.

"The horse does not have enough sense to understand that there is ample water in the river. But as a human being you should understand that competition will not diminish your income. Whatever you are destined to earn, you will earn."

How different our lives would be if we did not exhaust ourselves trying to increase our earnings, and believed that while it is our responsibility to work to earn our sustenance, there is nothing we can say nor do to alter whatever was decreed for us, and no one will take from us that which is meant for us.

NOTES

_____
_____
_____
_____
_____
_____
_____
_____
_____
_____

קַדֵּשׁ אֶת שִׁמְךָ עַל מַקְדִּישֵׁי שְׁמֶךָ . . . *From*
Sanctify Your name upon those who *our*
hallow You, and sanctify Your name in *Prayers*
Your world (*daily morning service*).

Rabbi Yerucham Levovitz notes that on various occasions the Talmud refers to the person who lives according to the dictates of G-d as "one who is a partner in the creation of the world" (see, for example, *Shabbos 10a*).

A partner, says Rabbi Yeruchim, is not an employee, but rather an owner. A partner has a right to express an opinion on the operation of a business, and whereas his opinion may be overruled, he is not like a hired worker, who cannot insist on his opinion being heard.

Rabbi Yerucham states that the reason the great *tzaddikim* were able to make things happen with their prayers was because they had achieved a status of being "partners with G-d" in the operation of the world. As partners, they had an authoritative position. In those instances where we find the prophets to have taken issue with G-d, it is because they felt that they had an owner's share in the world, and had a right to express their opinion.

If we think our prayers are not effective enough, perhaps we should think of doing those things that will bestow upon us a status of "partnership." This is not an easy achievement, and the responsibility is awesome. But we are then in a position to not only pray, but actually demand of G-d that He reveal His glory in the world, and openly sanctify His name so that all living things can see His majesty.

April 11, 1991
April 30, 1992
April 18, 1993
April 8, 1994
April 27, 1995
April 16, 1996

When a person insults someone else, it is his own defects that he is revealing (*Kiddushin 70a*).

Rabbi Meir Malbim had some bitter enemies in his community. On Purim, when it was customary to send the Rabbi a gift, one of his adversaries sent him a pig.

Rabbi Meir responded by sending the man a photograph of himself, with a note that read, "I received your gift. Since you chose to send me a likeness of yourself, I am returning the favor and sending a likeness of myself."

When overcome by anger, a person may berate someone, thinking that he will thereby punish the other person by insulting him. The Talmud cautions us that not only is this a juvenile character defect, but it is also self-defeating. People do not respect anyone who insults, even if there were justifications for resentment.

Proper character development requires learning how to overcome resentments, and handling personal insults gracefully.

From
the Sages

April 12, 1991
May 1, 1992
April 19, 1993
April 9, 1994
April 28, 1995
April 17, 1996

From our Prayers

הוֹדוּ לַה׳ קִרְאוּ בִשְׁמוֹ

Give thanks to G-d, declare His Name *(daily morning service; I Chronicles 16:8).*

One Thanksgiving Day, I received a letter from a woman who had recovered from alcoholism.

"There were so many Thanksgiving Days that I did not feel that I had anything to be thankful for. I was resentful, angry at the whole world, and I let everybody know it.

"This Thanksgiving Day is different. I can feel again, real feelings. I can cry and even laugh sometimes. I know I am alive, and I am grateful to be alive and to feel it."

This is clearly not a letter from someone who is experiencing undisturbed bliss. This woman is struggling with life, and may well be crying more often than laughing. Having lost the capacity to feel while she was anesthetized by the alcohol, she is now grateful to be able to feel, even if the feelings are not always pleasant.

Even without alcohol, some people turn their feelings off, and lose the capacity to experience the world. We should be thankful for the capacity to be able to feel. With proper faith and trust in G-d, many feelings can be pleasant.

From the Sages

Make a fence for the Torah *(Ethics of the Fathers 1:1).*

This is the origin of the many Rabbinic laws that we are required to observe, whose purpose is to protect us from transgressing any of the Torah prohibitions.

A simple, unlearned man came to a bookstore, asking to purchase a *siddur*. He rejected all the *siddurim* he was shown, and finally chose a mammoth, encyclopedic *siddur*, which had many pages of commentary.

The salesman was puzzled why a person who was clearly unable to understand such a complicated work would insist on buying it.

NOTES

"You see," the buyer said, "I have small children at home, and when they get hold of my *siddur*, the first page often gets torn out, and there goes my *Adon Olam* (the prayer "Master of the universe," which is on the first page of many *siddurim*).

"With this *siddur*, there are many pages of commentaries. They can tear out that many pages, and I will still have my *Adon Olam* intact."

The purpose of the Rabbinic laws, the fences, is to make certain that if we slip and transgress, we do not immediately lose our relationship with the *Adon Olam*.

בּוֹרֵא מִינֵי מְזוֹנוֹת . . . *From our Prayers*

Blessed are You, O G-d, King of the universe, who creates various forms of nutrition *(Blessing over grain foods).*

Erev
Rosh Chodesh
[Eve of the
New Month]

April 13, 1991
May 2, 1992
April 20, 1993
April 10, 1994
April 29, 1995
April 18, 1996

Modern advances in nutrition have identified various food substances, such as vitamins and amino acids, that are specific for certain functions of the body. Lack of one of these essential substances may cause serious dysfunction in one of the body's systems, and this may occur even though the person appears robust and healthy in every other way.

Just as there are specific nutrients for particular body functions, there is a specific nutrient for the *neshamah* (soul), and that is the observance of the Divine will as taught in the Torah. Failure to supply the *neshamah* with its essential nutrients may cause it to be very frail and dysfunctional, even though the person may appear physically healthy.

The function of the *neshamah* is to provide direction through life. It is the vehicle through which a person can achieve his purpose in existence. Failure to nourish the *neshamah* properly results in a life that misses its goal.

G-d has provided us with various forms of nutrition. It is our responsibility to see that all our health needs are met, our spiritual needs just as well as our physical ones.

"One should not say 'I cannot stand the meat of swine.' Instead one should say, 'I desire it, but my Heavenly Father has forbidden it' " *(Toras Kohanim cited by Rashi, Leviticus 20:26).*

From the Sages

NOTES

If one abstains from forbidden foods because they are repulsive, then if something would bring about a change in one's attitudes and tastes, one may likely eat them.

Furthermore, if one abstains from things that are forbidden because they are not appealing, one is essentially fulfilling one's own will. It is only when we abstain *against* our will and out of deference to the Divine commandment, that we are fulfilling the Divine will.

The fundamental requirement in Judaism is to do the will of G-d rather than our own will.

**First Day of
Rosh Chodesh
Iyar**

*April 14, 1991
May 3, 1992
April 21, 1993
April 11, 1994
April 30, 1995
April 19, 1996*

*From
our
Prayers*

חַיִּים שֶׁיִּמָּלְאוּ מִשְׁאֲלוֹת לִבֵּנוּ לְטוֹבָה

Bless us with a life wherein all the desires of our hearts that are truly good will be fulfilled *(Blessing of the Shabbos before Rosh Chodesh).*

Why do we specify that G-d fulfill only those of our wishes that are truly good? Can we not rely on His judgment that He will not fulfill a request which He knows to be to our detriment?

Like many other prayers, this is not primarily to apprise G-d of something, but to impress ourselves with the limitations of our understanding. A person may have an intense desire for something and pray very fervently for it, and then be disappointed that his prayers are not answered.

Parents must often refuse their child's request when their mature judgment tells them that it may be harmful to the child, such as ice cream before a meal or a toy that has sharp edges.

G-d will not grant a wish when He knows it to be harmful to us, but we need to be reminded of this frequently, because at the time that we have a burning desire, like the child, we are unlikely to consider that not all of our wishes are truly wise.

*From
the Sages*

Whatever the partriarch Abraham did personally for his guests was repaid to his children directly by G-d. Whatever Abraham did via an intermediary was repaid by G-d via an intermediary *(Baba Metzia 86b).*

After his marriage, Rabbi Levi Yitzchok of Berdichev lived with his father-in-law, who was a man of means.

One evening some wayfarers stopped by, and were invited to spend the night there. Rabbi Levi Yitzchok attended to their needs himself, serving their meals and preparing their lodgings.

"Why are you doing all this yourself?" his father-in-law asked. "You could have asked for one of the servants to take care of this."

"What?" remarked Rabbi Levi Yitzchok. "You expect me to give away the precious *mitzvah* of hospitality to a servant, and then pay him on top of that? That foolish I am not."

This is an important point to bear in mind in a culture that delegates charitable deeds to agencies that are funded. The greatest virtue in benevolent deeds is when we do them ourselves.

NOTES

_____
_____
_____
_____
_____
_____
_____
_____
_____

מִזְבֵּחַ חָדָשׁ בְּצִיּוֹן תָּכִין ... *From*

You will set up a new altar in Zion, and *our* upon it we will bring the elevation *Prayers* offering for the new month, symbolizing the surrender of our own will ... You will bring them eternal love, and you will remember the covenant of the fathers for the children *(Mussaf prayer of Rosh Chodesh).*

Rabbi Samson Raphael Hirsch interprets the above prayer to mean that through the symbolic expression of high resolve, such as by an elevation offering, we ourselves become deserving of G-d's love, and become the beneficiaries of His promise to our ancestors.

Love among humans, even when most intense, cannot bring about complete fusion. All members of a love relationship remain distinct individuals, the partners being separate from one another, and certainly one generation being separate from one another.

The love of G-d for Israel permits an absolute fusion. "Just as you have declared Me a oneness in the universe, so I will make you into a single entity" *(Berachos 6a).*

With a total surrender to the will of G-d we can achieve a unique oneness, that spans both space and time, so that Jews the world over, and all Jews from beginning of time to the end of time, are one.

What divides us is only our individual wills and desires. If we all surrender our individual wills to the will of G-d, we are molded into one.

Rosh Chodesh

April 15, 1991
May 4, 1992
April 22, 1993
April 12, 1994
May 1, 1995
April 20, 1996

If someone tells you, "I tried but I did not achieve," do not believe him *(Megillah 6b).*

From the Sages

Some commentaries interpret this to mean: Do not believe the person when he says that he tried, for had he indeed made the effort, he would have succeeded.

One of the Chassidic masters explained otherwise. "Do not believe" means do not accept the person's conclusion that he did not accomplish. Although the person may not have achieved his desired goal, just the fact that he tried is a major achievement in itself.

People often castigate themselves for not achieving a particular goal. The Talmud says, "It is not up to you to complete the work, yet you are not free to desist from it *(Ethics of the Fathers 2:21).* We can only make a maximum effort, and the effort is our achievement. Ultimate outcomes are in the hands of G-d.

NOTES

_____
_____
_____
_____
_____
_____
_____
_____

April 16, 1991
May 5, 1992
April 23, 1993
April 13, 1994
May 2, 1995
April 21, 1996

From our Prayers

וְלֹא נְתַתּוֹ ה' אֱלֹקֵינוּ לְגוֹיֵי הָאֲרָצוֹת . . .

And You did not give it (Shabbos) O L-rd our G-d, to the peoples of the lands . . . But to Israel, Your people, You gave it in love . . . The people that sanctify the seventh day shall all be satisfied and delight in Your goodness (*Shabbos morning service*).

Shabbos is far more than mere rest. As opposed to creative labor, says Rabbi Samson Raphael Hirsch, in which man seeks to dominate the world by his strength and power, the observance of *Shabbos* expresses man's subordination of himself and his world to G-d.

This unique concept of *Shabbos* is not for masses of humanity. *Shabbos* was given to Israel as a gift of love, not as a burden. One who turns over to G-d all his earthly activities and who submits all his week's work, both success and failure, to the trust of G-d, will be satisfied with whatever portion G-d allots him. Though a person's strength may be feeble and his tangible achievements small, he can always feel that he has made a contribution to the fulfillment of G-d's will on earth.

From the Scriptures

It is not good for a person to eat and drink, and think that all this comes to him as a result of his efforts (*Ecclesiastes 2:24*).

The Maggid of Dubno provided the following parable.

A laborer came to a town where there lived a very generous man whose home was always open to wayfarers. In the same town there also lived a notorious miser.

The laborer, looking for a day's work, was hired by the miser to work for him in return for room and board. After completing a hard day's work, the miser directed him to the home of the benevolent local citizen, where he received ample food and comfortable lodging.

NOTES

On the following day the laborer discovered that what he had received was the bounty of his host's generosity, and that it had nothing to do with his hard work.

"How foolish I was to exhaust myself," he said, "when all this would have been given to me anyway."

We must work, said the Maggid, because the Torah decrees that man must do something to earn his bread. But let us not think that how much we do determines our earnings. These are a gift from G-d, and we would therefore do well to spend more time in spiritual pursuits and less time on the futile task of trying to increase our earnings.

מַה יָּקָר חַסְדְּךָ אֱלֹקִים *From*
וּבְנֵי אָדָם בְּצֵל כְּנָפֶיךָ יֶחֱסָיוּן ‧‧‧ *our*

Prayers

How precious is Your loving-kindness which You show as a G-d of judgment. The children of man find assurance in the shadow of Your wings. They satisfy themselves from the abundance of Your house ... Defer Your loving-kindness to those that know You, and grant Your righteousness to those that are upright in heart *(daily morning service; Psalms 36:8-11).*

April 17, 1991
May 6, 1992
April 24, 1993
April 14, 1994
May 3, 1995
April 22, 1996

This is the translation given by Rabbi Samson Raphael Hirsch, who interprets this psalm as an expression of man's faith and trust in Divine benevolence.

We assert our belief that G-d's kindness is abundant and that we are under His Providence. When we see things that appear to us to be unjust, it is because our perspective is limited and incomplete. Only in the Divine light can the truth be seen.

We further affirm our belief that G-d may defer granting rewards, but this can be understood only by those who know G-d. Those who are upright in heart can appreciate G-d's righteousness.

This is a psalm composed by David who, with all his recurrent and intense suffering, never faltered in his belief in G-d's kindness.

I am a stranger upon earth. Do not conceal Your commandments from me *(Psalms 119:19).*

One of the Chassidic masters explains that since the Torah is the word of G-d, He too is obliged to observe it.

Since the Torah says that you must show love, kindness, and consideration to strangers, we therefore have the right to ask G-d that He be kind to us, for we are "strangers" upon earth. He must observe His own commandments.

This is an appeal we can justly make only if we conduct ourselves as strangers on earth, if we know that our permanent home is the spiritual one in the eternal world, and that we are but sojourners in this earthly life. What we truly believe is evidenced by how much investment of time and effort we make in the physical aspect of our lives, and how much in the spiritual aspect.

If we live as though this earthly world is all there is to life, we lose this compelling argument to merit Divine grace.

From the Scriptures

NOTES

_____
_____
_____
_____
_____
_____
_____
_____

April 18, 1991
May 7, 1992
April 25, 1993
April 15, 1994
May 4, 1995
April 23, 1996

From our Prayers

קֵל מִסְתַּתֵּר מֵעֵינֵי כָּל חַי . . .

O G-d, who is concealed from the eyes of all living things, who is sublime and wonderful beyond sight of all creatures; the many heavens cannot contain You, but all those who seek You can find You in their hearts, and all who meditate upon You can find You in their thoughts *(morning prayer of Rabbi Saadya Gaon).*

Rabbi Bunim of Pshis'cha once asked, "Where can one find G-d?" and he answered, "Wherever one allows Him entrance."

The Torah says that man was created "in the image of G-d." Since G-d has no form, this term can mean only that man is comprised of a spirit of G-d. The kabbalists point to the verse, "And He blew into his nostrils a spirit of life" *(Genesis 2:7),* and note that when one blows into something, one exhales something from within oneself.

Rabbi Nachman of Breslov told the story of a poor man who dreamt that in a faraway city there was a buried treasure. After great effort, he reached the site and began digging. An observer asked him what he was doing, and upon hearing the dream remarked, "How strange! I dreamt that a treasure was buried in a far-off village under the floor of this peasant's hut (referring to the man who was digging)!"

We frequently look for treasures elsewhere, when they are really within ourselves. We look for G-d everywhere, when He is right within each of us. The great ethical works of Torah teach us how to find G-d within ourselves.

From the Scriptures

And G-d separated between the waters beneath the firmament and the waters above the firmament, and it was so *(Genesis 1:7).*

The Midrash states that on the second day of creation the Torah does not say "and G-d saw that it was good," as it does on the other days of creation, because on the second day there was a separation, and separation is not good.

However, later Sages comment that on the fourth day the Torah states that G-d separated between light and darkness, and yet says that "G-d saw it was good!"

The difference is that on the fourth day the separation was between opposites, and separation between opposing forces can be good. On the second day, however, the separation was between water and water, and separation among likes is not good.

Kindred should remain close to one another.

NOTES

_____
_____
_____
_____
_____
_____
_____
_____

From our Prayers

... יָתְקוּ ... שֶׁבִּזְכוּת סְפִירַת הָעוֹמֶר ... *From*

May it be Your will that by virtue of my counting the Omer this day, there be a correction of the defects I have caused, and that I be purified and sanctified by the Holiness from above *(prayer following counting of the Omer).*

April 19, 1991
May 8, 1992
April 26, 1993
April 16, 1994
May 5, 1995
April 24, 1996

We recognize that as humans we have many imperfections, and that it is our responsibility to improve upon our character traits.

When we realize how far we are from the ideal, we may exclaim, "What an order!" We may be so overwhelmed by the enormity of the challenge of improving ourselves that we may despair of accomplishing it, and simply do nothing.

As we count the *Omer* one day at a time, we are helped to realize that the task is not as overwhelming as we thought. We are not required to achieve perfection, and what we do, we can do in daily installments. Improvement of character can be in morsels, and need not be in bundles.

Although we can not achieve perfection by our own efforts, if we sincerely do that which we can, *all* that which we can, the perfection we strive for will be given to us as a gift from above.

From the Scriptures

And G-d said, "Behold, I will make bread rain for them from the heavens, and the people shall gather each day only the provisions for that day" *(Exodus 16:4).*

To children born and raised during the forty-year sojourn of the Israelites in the desert it was perfectly natural for fresh food to fall from the heavens daily. When they entered the Promised Land, and for the first time saw food growing from the ground, they considered this a wondrous miracle. "You put a seed in the ground, and it actually grows into food, just like the food that regularly fell from the sky."

What we consider natural or miraculous depends entirely on what we are accustomed to. The fact is that bread from the sky is no more of a miracle than bread from the earth.

With the *manna*, the Divine blessing was meant to be harvested each day, with trust in G-d that He would provide for tomorrow. This was perfectly natural. We also need to take G-d's gifts each day, and trust that He will again take care of us tomorrow. This too is perfectly natural.

NOTES

IYAR

אייר

April 20, 1991
May 9, 1992
April 27, 1993
April 17, 1994
May 6, 1995
April 25, 1996

From our Prayers

וֶאֱמֶת ה' אֱלֹקִים כִּי בְּרֹב רַחֲמֶיךָ . . .

And in truth, O G-d, in Your abundant mercy for Your children, You have granted us a Torah of kindness and mitzvos of truth. You have taught us laws of fairness and just edicts, to guide us in straight paths, to purify our souls, and to redeem our souls from the pressures of the time *(prayer of Rabbi Bachya).*

Not only does Torah observance refine our character, but, Rabbi Bachya adds, Torah living protects us from the pressures of one's time.

In an era when there is so much emphasis on stress management, Rabbi Bachya's observation is of the greatest importance. Sincere dedication to Torah living — which in addition to being a code of conduct entails a trust in G-d and an acceptance of the vicissitudes of life with equanimity — can provide a stability and tranquility which can counteract the "pressures of the time." Indeed, character improvement and optimum adaptation to stress go hand in hand.

Torah is as relevant today as in times past, and its salutary effect on stress is as valid in the jet age as in the days of the camel caravan. The only caveat is that Torah living must be complete. Half measures avail us nothing.

From the Sages

"And Noah planted a vineyard, drank of the wine, and became drunk" *(Genesis 9:20-21).* **The Midrash states that on the same day that Noah planted the grapes, they miraculously grew, and produced wine, and on that same day he became drunk.**

The Maggid of Dubno explains with a parable.

A man once came to a *tzaddik* and asked him for a blessing for success. The *tzaddik* responded, "May your first venture flourish and multiply many times over."

The man ran home elated, and asked his wife for their money box. The wife, fearful that he would squander the money, refused to give it to him, and they began to argue. The argument escalated into abuse and violence.

The *tzaddik* later told the man, "You let the blessing go to waste. You chose as your first venture to fight with your wife, and indeed, it flourished and escalated."

Similarly, after the flood, Noah received the Divine blessing. Instead of using the blessing for spiritual ends, Noah sought to make wine, which led to his undoing.

We are frequent recipients of Divine blessings. We must make sure not to use them to our own detriment.

NOTES

הַנּוֹטֵעַ אֹזֶן הֲלֹא יִשְׁמָע *From*
אִם יֹצֵר עַיִן הֲלֹא יַבִּיט . . . *our*

H e that implants the ear, should He not *Prayers*
hear? He that shapes the eye, should
He not see? He that restrains the nations,
should He not correct? He that teaches
man knowledge? But G-d knows the
thoughts of man, that they are vanity.
Forward strides the man whom You, O
G-d, train by discipline, and whom You
teach out of Your law (*Song of the day for
Wednesday, Psalms 94:9-12*).

April 21, 1991
May 10, 1992
April 28, 1993
April 18, 1994
May 7, 1995
April 26, 1996

When we see some just people suffer while some wicked
people prosper, our sense of justice is offended, and our
faith in Divine fairness is put to the test.

According to Rabbi Samson Raphael Hirsch, the Psalmist
says that we are foolish to question G-d. Certainly He is
aware of all that transpires, and has the power to intervene
in the affairs of the world.

Why then does G-d tolerate injustice? First, we see only
a small fragment of history, whereas G-d, in His infinite
wisdom, knows that all wrongdoing will end in nothingness.
The eventual demonstration of the futility of evil will be the
most emphatic way to bring mankind to this realization.

Second, man's endurance of suffering is part of his
discipline and training. Woe is to him whom G-d does not
test, because that person is unable to grow in character and
in spirituality.

The fear of G-d is a precious wealth (*Isaiah 33:6*). *From the
Scriptures*

The Rabbi of Karlin said, "If a person fears G-d, then all is
well. If a person does not fear G-d, then he really has cause
to be in fear."

There is a disease which effects the nervous system in a
way that causes the person to be unable to feel pain.
Without pain, victims of this disease may sustain injuries
without being aware that they have been injured.

Pain is a safeguard. The natural avoidance of pain helps us
to avoid those things that may harm us.

The fear of G-d protects a person from doing things which
could harm him spiritually. If a person has no fear of G-d, he
is unprotected. He may do things that are ruinous to himself
without being aware of what is happening.

In human affairs, we have nothing to fear except fear itself.
In relation to morality, we should fear the absence of fear.

NOTES

April 22, 1991
May 11, 1992
April 29, 1993
April 19, 1994
May 8, 1995
April 27, 1996

*From
our
Prayers*

אֲנִי מַאֲמִין . . . בְּבִיאַת הַמָּשִׁיחַ . . .

I believe with perfect faith in the coming of the Messiah, and even though he may tarry, nevertheless I shall await him every day *(the Thirteen Principles of Faith, morning service).*

The world that G-d created in perfection, and which has been the scene of so much distress, suffering, and injustice, will yet one day return to the state of perfection that G-d intended.

"When will the Messiah come?" asked the Talmud. "It can be today, if only we would listen to the word of G-d *(Psalms 95:7)."*

Judaism posits that there will be a coming of the Messiah, and that mankind will not be allowed to degenerate into hopeless decadence. But that longed-for day can be hastened. Man can bring about his own redemption. One is not permitted to absolve himself from responsibility and say, "If G-d wishes to have a perfect world, then let Him bring it about." It is man's task to work toward perfection.

There is hope for mankind. There will be redemption. It can be today, if we are ready to listen to the word of G-d.

*From
the Sages*

Hillel said, "If I am not for myself, then who will be for me? But if I am only for myself, what am I? And if not now, when?" *(Ethics of the Fathers 1:14).*

These words have come down through the centuries as a beacon of light for spiritual living.

Improvement of one's character must begin with a diligent search, and with the assumption that we are far from perfect and hence there is a great deal of work to be done. We cannot depend on others to make us aware of our character defects, because people are polite and tend to give compliments rather than the truth, which they think may offend us. Therefore, we must begin the work ourselves.

But since we are very likely to be blind to our own shortcomings, we may be unable to find them if we search alone. We must therefore enlist the help of others. We must also, in a considerate and benevolent manner, try to help others in their spiritual growth. Both of these concepts are contained in "If I am only for myself, what am I?"

Hillel recognized the resistances we have to changing our character, and the ubiquitous tendency to postpone any changes until tomorrow, a tomorrow that is always receding. Therefore, "If not now, when?"

NOTES

_____
_____
_____
_____
_____
_____
_____
_____
_____

IYAR

9

אייר

April 23, 1991
May 12, 1992
April 30, 1993
April 20, 1994
May 9, 1995
April 28, 1996

From
our
Prayers

The empty space for today's prayer represents a prayer that has been deleted from the *siddur*.

The morning service in the Temple included recitation of the Ten Commandments *(Tamid 32b)*. This special prominence given to the Ten Commandments was distorted by some to mean that only the Ten Commandments were of Divine origin, and the remainder of the Torah was compiled by humans. To avoid this misinterpretation, the recitation of the Ten Commandments was deleted from the service.

In every age there have been those who have selected those portions of the Torah of which they approved, and rejected those portions that did not suit them. They would designate the first as being "authentic," and the latter as fabricated and hence dispensable.

Torah is not a smorgasbord from which one can choose according to one's taste. This approach makes Torah a handmaiden of man, whereas in reality the Torah is the vehicle whereby man is to serve G-d.

Mesiras nefesh is the highest degree of devotion to G-d. It is most often translated as "martyrdom." In fact, however, the words taken literally mean *turning one's life over to G-d*, and one can do this admirably while still living.

Thus, by a somewhat circuitous route, the deleted prayer represents this concept of *mesiras nefesh*.

From the
Scriptures

If a person in need of discipline is obstinate and resistive, he may suddenly crumble, and there will be no healing for him (Proverbs 29:1).

The wise Solomon knew human nature so well.

Man is subject to temptation, and may be unable at times to resist his drives. But as long as he is receptive to guidance and respects the words of those who are wiser that himself, he need not have a precipitous fall. He can be helped to see the folly of his behavior and can be returned to correct living.

The person whose arrogance leads him to reject any opinions other than his own has no safety net. His desires and passions are unrestrained, and he is likely to become so decadent that restoration to healthy spiritual living is virtually impossible.

If one listens to constructive criticism and retains an open and receptive mind, one is likely to avoid spiritual deterioration.

NOTES

_____
_____
_____
_____
_____
_____
_____
_____
_____

LIVING EACH DAY / 219

April 24, 1991
May 13, 1992
May 1, 1993
April 21, 1994
May 10, 1995
April 29, 1996

From our Prayers

אֲנִי מַאֲמִין . . . שֶׁהַבּוֹרֵא יִתְבָּרֵךְ שְׁמוֹ . . .

I believe with perfect faith that G-d is the Creator and the One who conducts all living things, and that He alone has done, does, and will do, all that is done (the *Thirteen Principles of Faith, morning service*).

To believe with *perfect* faith is to believe with *simple* faith, a faith that is superior to logic and that is unassailable by argument. Simple faith is the most difficult hurdle in Judaism.

One of the most tragic figures in Jewish history is Elisha ben Avuyah, who was a Talmudic scholar of the highest rank, but who became a heretic.

The Talmud gives two reasons for Elisha's apostasy. The first is that he was stunned by the Roman execution of pious scholars, and the second is that he fell prey to secular philosophy. The two reasons are actually one. Gross injustices were not a new phenomenon even in ancient times, and the mystery of why the innocent and righteous suffer was known to have baffled even Solomon. The only approach to this unanswerable question is to accept with suprarational faith the infinite judgment of G-d.

But Elisha's enchantment with secular philosophy and his admiration of the greatness of the human mind prevented him from making the surrender to faith. To Elisha, a mind that can know so much could know all, and anything that was not within grasp of his great intellect was rejected; hence his inability to accept the harsh and incomprehensible Divine judgment on his beloved colleagues.

As we pray, we must try to achieve an attitude of complete faith, one to which we can adhere to even in defiance of our logical considerations.

From the Scriptures

NOTES

_____
_____
_____
_____
_____
_____
_____
_____

The superiority of man over animals is naught (*Ecclesiastes 3:19*).

The Rabbi of Kotzk said, "The superiority of man over animals is that man can have an awareness that he is naught; i.e., he can be humble, and be aware of his nothingness. This is a concept which an animal cannot achieve."

A person who is not humble, who is vain and arrogant and who does not perceive his nothingness, is bereft of the primary distinction between man and lower forms of life.

Perhaps it is these people that science justifiably classifies as *Homo sapiens*, or gorillas with intellect, for all they are are animals with higher intelligence.

From our Prayers

טוֹב לְהֹדוֹת לַה' וּלְזַמֵּר לְשִׁמְךָ עֶלְיוֹן . . .

It is good to praise G-d and to sing to Your name, the Most High. To tell each morning Your kindness, and Your trust in the evening *(Shabbos service, Psalms 92:2-3).*

April 25, 1991
May 14, 1992
May 2, 1993
April 22, 1994
May 11, 1995
April 30, 1996

The significance of this prayer is not apparent until it is compared to a statement by the philosopher Francis Bacon, "Hope is a good breakfast, but a bad supper." According to this secular philosophy, a day in which one's efforts have not been successful — and especially a day in which one suffered failure — is a bad day, one which justifies one's feeling depressed at its close. Bacon would have us hope only in the morning and express gratitude (if at all) in the evening if and only if the day were successful. This is an attribute which reflects the thinking of the market place, where good and bad are measured in terms of success and failure.

Torah values are different. We can only put forth effort, but we cannot control outcome. Good and evil have nothing to do with success or failure, only with effort or lack of effort.

We express gratitude to G-d in the *morning*, before the day's work is begun, for His giving us another day of opportunity. At night we express hope, the hope and trust that He will give us yet another chance tomorrow.

The serpent said to the woman, "You shall not die (if you eat of the forbidden fruit)" *(Genesis 3:4).*

From the Scriptures

The Midrash states that the serpent pushed Eve to make contact with the tree, and said, "You see how harmless it is. Just as contact with the tree is not harmful, so will eating of its fruit not be harmful."

That is the methodology of seduction to do what is wrong or harmful to our spirituality. We are duped into believing that things that are in fact injurious are harmless, and in our desire to gratify our temptation, we succumb to patently false reassurances.

Ask any alcoholic who has relapsed into drinking. He will tell you that after a period of sobriety, he began drinking small amounts of alcohol, and to his pleasant surprise, none of the dreaded anticipated consequences occurred. This led him to conclude that indeed he could drink safely again, and it was only a short time before the inevitable disasters of uncontrolled drinking occurred.

We would be wise to trust the teachings of the Torah, and not deceive ourselves into believing that we can emerge unscathed if we defy the word of G-d in any way, even in what may appear to us to be trivia.

NOTES

April 26, 1991
May 15, 1992
May 3, 1993
April 23, 1994
May 12, 1995
May 1, 1996

From our Prayers

אָבִינוּ מַלְכֵּנוּ זָכְרֵנוּ בְּזִכָּרוֹן טוֹב לְפָנֶיךָ

Our Father, our King! Remember us with good memories *(Avinu Malkeinu prayer).*

May we not take the liberty of interpreting this passage as asking G-d to help us have pleasant memories?

Our minds are a storehouse of memories. Virtually everything that we have experienced in our lives is filed away in our memory bank.

Is it not strange that we so often recall unpleasant memories, and dwell on our failures and on the mistakes we have made? Only infrequently do we reflect on the pleasant times we have enjoyed.

Memories of failures are depressing. They deflate us, rob us of our self-confidence, and drain our ambition. They cast a specter of anticipation of failure on everything we plan to do.

Memories of our successful accomplishments can be very encouraging. They need not at all make us conceited. Rather, they should help us realize that we have the capacity to succeed, and thereby encourage us to keep trying.

If the *yeitzer hara* (evil inclination) wishes to disable us, all he needs to do is remind us of the failures of our past. If we succumb to this ruse, we may indeed fail. We must keep our focus on our good memories.

From the Scriptures

G-d said to Cain, "Why are you angry, and why have you lost face? If you will repent, then you will be forgiven. If you do not repent, then sin awaits you at your doorstep" *(Genesis 4:6-7).*

Even the most grievous sin can be forgiven if there is sincere repentance, and a progressive chain of destructive behavior can be avoided. If one does not repent the mistakes of the past, they become the seeds for mistakes in the future.

What was the indication that Cain had not repented? He was angry and he was depressed. He had lost all faith in himself. His sin continued to consume him and drain him of all hope.

We cannot avoid the initial reaction of disappointment in ourselves when we realize that we have done wrong. But our depression will be relieved if we admit our wrong, and resolve to make whatever amends we can.

If we fail to repent, and instead try to justify our behavior, the sin will persist and manifest itself by persistent anger and depression.

NOTES

From our Prayers

אָבִינוּ מַלְכֵּנוּ זְכוֹר כִּי עָפָר אֲנָחְנוּ *From our*

Our Father, our King, remember that we are but dust *(Avinu Malkeinu prayer).*

April 27, 1991
May 16, 1992
May 4, 1993
April 24, 1994
May 13, 1995
May 2, 1996

As with many other prayers, the words should be directed toward ourselves as much as to G-d.

We should understand what it is that we are comprised of, so that we will be prepared to guard ourselves against the temptation that our composition can lead us to, and also know that temptation *per se* is not a sin. It is only the yielding to temptation that is sinful.

Some people may disown thoughts or feelings that they consider to be alien to them. Denial of such feelings is not a virtue. Bringing them under control is a virtue.

The Midrash says that the heavenly angels argued that they, rather than lowly humans, deserved to be given the Torah. Moses pointed out to them that the Torah forbids acting out one's greed, envy, lust, and other traits which are unique to humans.

We need the Torah precisely because we are made of dust, and we need to achieve mastery over our physical urges. Angels are created spiritual. We need the Torah to help us become spiritual.

The woman whom You gave to me, it was she who gave me of the tree and I ate *(Genesis 3:12).*

From the Scriptures

Rashi notes that the Hebrew verb in this sentence is not in the past tense, but in the present, and that what Adam really said was, "I ate of the fruit, and I shall continue to eat of it."

How does one speak so defiantly to G-d?

The entire episode of the sin of the forbidden fruit is a lesson in human psychology, and being that it is virtually the first incident reported in the Torah, this indicates the primacy of the message.

Adam and Eve sinned, and they were punished. It is clear that their punishment was not for their transgression, but for their refusal to admit that they had sinned. We do not find even one word of repentance in the story of Adam and Eve.

Eve blamed the serpent. Adam blamed Eve. Furthermore, Adam argued with G-d that he did *not* do wrong. Adam was obstinate. "Yes, I have eaten, and I will continue to eat." This is not so much defiance as it is rationalization; continuing errant behavior is one way of reinforcing one's conviction that one has not done wrong.

As humans, we are vulnerable to mistakes. But when they happen, we should promptly admit them and not be obstinate and justify our wrong actions.

NOTES

April 28, 1991
May 17, 1992
May 5, 1993
April 25, 1994
May 14, 1995
May 3, 1996

From our Prayers

... הַגּוֹמֵל ... שֶׁגְּמָלַנִי כָּל טוֹב ...

Blessed are You, L-rd our G-d, Who grants His beneficence even to those who are undeserving *(Blessing upon emerging from a perilous situation).*

Some people are tormented with anxiety, fearing that something terrible is going to happen to them. A mother is afraid to enjoy her baby, thinking that if she enjoys it, she may lose it. These expectations of doom are generally the result of one's concept of G-d as harsh and punitive, and of themselves as somehow evil and deserving of punishment.

The above prayer should help disperse such unnecessary, destructive torment. Although we see tragedies altogether too often, it is a mistake to conclude that these are acts of an angry and punitive G-d. There is much about the operation of the universe of which we are ignorant, and few of us have been made privy to G-d's grand designs.

For purposes of everyday living, the above prayer should guide us. G-d is beneficent, even to those who may not be deserving. He has given us more blessings than we are aware, and His goodness to us will continue.

From the Sages

G-d holds righteous people responsible for even a hairsbreadth deviation *(Bava Kamma 50a).*

Rabbi Elimelech of Lizensk often reprimanded himself for being derelict in his devotion to G-d. A disciple who knew his master's extreme piety, asked, "How can you be so critical of yourself? Are you really unaware of your spiritual achievements?"

Rabbi Elimelech answered, "A king built a new palace, complete with a new throne and crown jewels. One of the laborers digging the foundation was negligent and dug several meters off course. When the mistake was discovered, he was made to fill in the hole and then continue on.

"The jeweler cutting the crown diamond was also careless, and cut the stone a fraction of a millimeter off the mark. He was given a severe punishment for his dereliction.

"In terms of measurement, the laborer's deviation was thousands of times greater than the jeweler's, yet the latter's dereliction was much more serious because he was dealing with the crown jewels and not with shovelfuls of earth.

"The more a person grows, the greater are the demands that he behave according to his elevated position. Our responsibilities are proportional to our level of spirituality."

Why then should a person strive for spirituality if it brings with it so great a responsibility? Because a person should become all that he can, and not settle for anything less.

NOTES

_____
_____
_____
_____
_____
_____
_____
_____
_____

... · לְכָל יוֹם וָיוֹם מֵחַיֵּינוּ דֵי מַחְסוֹרֵנוּ ... *From*

May it be Your will, to provide me and my *our*
household with our necessities for each *Prayers*
day in sufficient amounts, and for each
hour of our hours what is sufficient for our
needs *(prayer following recitation of the chapter
of the manna, Exodus 16:4-36).*

April 29, 1991
May 18, 1992
May 6, 1993
April 26, 1994
May 15, 1995
May 4, 1996

When children are young, parents provide for their needs.
They prepare their meals, because left to their own devices,
the children would fill themselves with sweets that would
satisfy their desires, but leave them nutritionally lacking.

Responsible parents choose proper clothing for their
small children, giving consideration to providing them
maximum warmth and protection. They choose sizes that
will serve for a longer period, rather than be rapidly out-
grown. Parents know the child's present and future needs
better than the child does.

If we truly believe, as Judaism requires, that G-d will
provide for us, why do we not place greater trust in Him? Has
experience not adequately demonstrated that what we once
thought to be essential later on turned out to be useless?

Our needs change from day to day, and even from hour
to hour. We cannot always anticipate them, because we do
not know what the future holds. G-d does, and He can anticipate our needs, but only if we will entrust ourselves to Him.

**Three sinners are doomed to eternal damnation.
One who takes another man's wife, one who
humiliates someone in public, and one who calls
someone a foul name (even if this does not result in
public humiliation). It is better that one throw
himself into a fiery furnace than humiliate someone
publicly** *(Bava Metzia 58b, 59a).*

*From
the Sages*

The Talmud does not use the term "eternal damnation"
loosely. Even grievous sins can be forgiven, and "all Jews
have a share in the eternal world."

Notable exceptions to this are the mortal psychological
assaults that one inflicts on another person, which are
characterized by adultery, public humiliation, and insult.
Unless the offender is forgiven by the offended person, there
is no remedy for the soul of the sinner. Man was created in
the image of G-d. To humiliate another person is to sin
against G-d Himself.

Let every person's honor be as dear to you as your own
(Ethics of the Fathers 2:10).

NOTES

_____
_____
_____
_____
_____
_____
_____
_____
_____

April 30, 1991
May 19, 1992
May 7, 1993
April 27, 1994
May 16, 1995
May 5, 1996

From ... לְעוֹלָם יְהֵא אָדָם יְרֵא שָׁמַיִם בְּסֵתֶר וּבַגָּלוּי

our A person should always be G-d-fearing in
Prayers private as in public, acknowledge the
truth, and speak the truth in his heart. Let
him arise early and say, "Master of the
universe . . . *(daily morning service).*

What is the proper attitude for prayer? To be genuine,
espousing in private what one declares in public, admitting
the truth to others, and being truthful with oneself. Then and
only then can one arise and address G-d.

This is not easily achieved. Many people present a benevolent face to the world but a tyrannical one to their families.
Some may be able to admit their wrongs when confronted
by others, but when there is no external challenge, cannot
be truthful with themselves.

"G-d is close to those who call upon Him, to all who call
upon Him *in truth"* *(Psalms 145:18).* The essence of prayer
is sincerity and truth.

From
the Sages

**One who does charitable deeds is greater than
one who brings sacrifices, as it says, "He who does
justice and charity is more dear to G-d than one who
brings burnt offerings on the Altar"** *(Succah 49b).*

One of the Chassidic masters failed to appear at the
pre-dawn *Selichos* services prior to Rosh Hashanah. His
followers explained his absence as, "He ascends to heaven."

One man scoffed, and was determined to prove that the
Rabbi's absence was due merely to his sleeping late. He
came to the Rabbi's home posing as a wayfarer, and asked
for lodging.

In the early morning hours he secretly observed the Rabbi
don a woodsman's clothes and leave the house carrying an
axe. Curious, he followed the Rabbi into the woods and saw
him fell some trees. The Rabbi then carried the wood to the

NOTES

_____
_____
_____
_____
_____
_____
_____
_____
_____
_____

hut of an old, feeble woman. "Do you need any firewood
today?" the Rabbi asked.

"Yes, I do," she said, "but I have no money to pay you."

"Do not worry," the Rabbi said. "I am willing to trust you.
And that should be a lesson to you. If I am willing to trust you,
even though you are old and frail, then you should certainly
be willing to trust in G-d, who is mighty and eternal."

The Rabbi then arranged the wood and ignited it, while
humming the tunes of the *Selichos* prayers.

The scoffer later told the townspeople, "You think the
Rabbi is absent because he ascends to heaven? You are
wrong. He ascends much higher."

M aster of the universe! I am Yours, and my dreams are Yours ... May it be Your will that all my dreams portend good for me and others (prayer for benign interpretation of dreams). ... רִבּוֹנוֹ שֶׁל עוֹלָם אֲנִי שֶׁלָּךְ וַחֲלוֹמוֹתַי שֶׁלָּךְ *From our Prayers*

May 1, 1991
May 20, 1992
May 8, 1993
April 28, 1994
May 17, 1995
May 6, 1996

Dreams have fascinated man from time immemorial. Countless books have been written about dreams, and there are many theories on the meaning of dreams.

Sometimes dreams are terrifying, and leave a person tormented with worry about their portent. The Talmud composed the above prayer to relieve a person from the anguish of frightening dreams.

The prayer's essence is in its opening words, "I am Yours, and my dreams are Yours." This is a statement of absolute surrender to G-d's care. A person who believes he can control his own destiny may be distressed by a dream which portends that his life will take a direction other than the one he chooses. However, one who believes that his life is in the hands of G-d, that G-d will do with him whatever is His wish, and that the Divine will is always for an ultimate good, will not be upset by a dream.

"May it be Your will" — if our concern is only to do the Divine will — then "all my dreams portend good."

Know the G-d of your ancestors and serve Him with a complete heart (I Chronicles 28:9).

From the Scriptures

Rabbi Shlomo Eger was a great Talmudic scholar who opposed the Chassidic movement. He was most disturbed, therefore, when his son, Rabbi Laibele, became a disciple of the Rabbi of Kotzk, a fiery Chassidic leader.

After several years in Kotzk, Rabbi Laibele returned home. "What have you learned in Kotzk?" Rabbi Shlomo asked.

"I came to know that G-d is in charge of the world," Rabbi Laibele answered.

"What!" Rabbi Shlomo exclaimed. "For that you studied for years?" He then called in the cleaning woman. "Do you know who runs the world?" Rabbi Shlomo asked her.

"Of course," she answered. "G-d runs the world."

Rabbi Shlomo turned to his son. "There, you see! Everyone knows that G-d runs the world. This unlearned young woman knows it."

Rabbi Laibele smiled. "No, Father," he said. "She does not know it. She only says it. I *know*."

We are sometimes satisfied with our meager concept of Divinity. Only by pursuing the study of Torah philosophy can we really know what it is that our faith consists of.

NOTES

_____
_____
_____
_____
_____
_____
_____
_____
_____

IYAR

אייר

Lag B'Omer

May 2, 1991
May 21, 1992
May 9, 1993
April 29, 1994
May 18, 1995
May 7, 1996

הִנֵּה אָנֹכִי שֹׁלֵחַ מַלְאָךְ לְפָנֶיךָ . . .

From our Prayers

Behold, I am sending an angel before you to guard you in the path, and to bring you to the place I have destined *(Exodus 23:20, prayer for the traveler).*

In Jewish lore, life is often referred to as a "journey." I was therefore impressed when a recovering alcoholic said, "Today I will remember that it is the reward of the journey itself, and not the destination that I seek."

The recovering alcoholic provides an excellent model. His major challenge is to go through life, encountering many stresses and difficulties, without succumbing to the urge to drink. If he achieves this, he has succeeded regardless of whether or not he has amassed wealth or achieved fame. Whether the struggle is with the urge to drink or with any of the many human temptations, success consists of making it through the journey triumphantly.

As any recovering alcoholic will testify, success is impossible without the help of a Power greater than ourselves. G-d is ready to assist us, if only we ask Him. That is the essential requirement: We must ask for His help, and we must ask sincerely.

From the Scriptures

If you will follow My laws and do My judgments, I will provide rain in its proper time, and the land will give its fruit . . . And you will eat to satiety and live in peace *(Leviticus 26:3-4).*

How does this promise of earthly reward conform with the Talmudic dictum that rewards for observance of the *mitzvos* is reserved for the eternal world *(Kiddushin 39b),* and are not given to us in our earthly existence?

The answer is that the conditions and supplies that an employer provides for his workers are not the compensation for their work. That is not paid until the end of the assignment. But the worker must have the necessary materials and tools for the job. He must have a reasonably comfortable work environment to achieve maximum productivity. And even some coffee breaks and appropriate vacation periods.

The earthly goods G-d gives us are not the rewards for *mitzvah* observance. The Sages state that the reward for even a single *mitzvah* is beyond earthly compensation. What we are given is the means to get our assignments done.

It stands to reason that someone who clearly has no interest in doing the assigned task may not be well provided. This is just another reason, albeit a selfish one, why we should be diligent in doing His will.

NOTES

... דְּמוּ אוֹתְךָ וְלֹא כְּפִי יֶשְׁךָ *From*

Wｅ imagine You, not in Your essence, but *our* according to Your deeds. Although we *Prayers* think of You in many ways, You are One, regardless of all our conceptions ... You appear as one who is old when You judge, but as a young hero in time of battle (*Hymn of Glory*).

May 3, 1991
May 22, 1992
May 10, 1993
April 30, 1994
May 19, 1995
May 8, 1996

What does one mean when saying "G-d"?

The essence of G-d is beyond human grasp. The name of G-d which refers to His essence is ineffable, and we are not permitted to pronounce it. It is referred to as "the Name of Being," and indicates that G-d is eternal; He is, was, and always will be. The concept of infinity is something which is alien to human experience, and since we cannot properly think of it, the very word is not pronounced.

Therefore, we refer to G-d by various appellations: the Mighty, the Master, the L-rd of Hosts, the Sovereign of the universe.

We can have only a vague understanding of the manifest attributes of G-d, and even this feeble understanding varies from time to time.

Judaism conceives of G-d as the Creator of the universe, the Power that brought the world into being and maintains its existence, and that supervises everything in the universe, from the most grandiose and the mightiest to the tiniest and lowliest being.

While we thus relate to G-d according to His attributes, as He reveals Himself to us, we must realize how limited this concept is, because He is beyond all understanding.

Correct yourself first, and then you can correct others (*Bava Metzia 107b*).

Rabbi Levi Yitzchok of Berdichev said, "When I became aware that the townsfolk were not heeding my words, I began to examine my own actions. Then I saw that my own family members were not behaving respectfully toward me. I intensified my soul-searching, and by the grace of G-d, I discovered various defects in my character, and that others' attitudes toward me were my fault, not theirs.

"I began making efforts to improve myself. Gradually my family's attitudes changed, and then the townsfolk began listening to me."

How wise are the words of the Talmud. "If you wish to influence others, begin by making changes in yourself."

May 4, 1991
May 23, 1992
May 11, 1993
May 1, 1994
May 20, 1995
May 9, 1996

From our Prayers

הַצֵּל אֶת תְּפִלָּתִי מִכָּל מִינֵי עִרְבּוּב הַדַּעַת

Grant us clarity of thought, a pure mind, and that our minds be tranquil, without any confusions whatever *(personal prayer of Rabbi Nachman of Breslov).*

One of the purposes of prayer is to make us aware of what it is that we lack. Obviously, if we pray for something, it is for something that we do not have.

How often do we stop to think whether our thought processes are really functioning properly? The average person probably has his automobile engine tuned more frequently than his brain. Yet the automobile engine is a relatively simple apparatus, a mere tinker-toy compared to the unbelievably complex apparatus that constitutes our mind.

I once asked an alcoholic why he decided to enter treatment. He said that after many attempts at stopping on his own had failed, "I realized that it is absolutely impossible for me to stop on my own, maybe." He did not see that the terms "absolutely impossible" and "maybe" are contradictory. I have repeated this sentence to many people, and I am surprised how many fail to grasp its internal absurdity.

This shows that we are capable of thinking chaotically without being aware of it. That is why we must pray sincerely for the gift of clarity of thought.

From the Sages

Rabbi Chanina said, "A person does not suffer even a small injury to his finger unless it was so ordained from heaven" *(Chullin 7b).*

The brothers, Rabbi Elimelech and Rabbi Zusia, the great Chassidic masters, took upon themselves the torment of exile to atone for their "sins." They wandered from hamlet to hamlet, surviving under the most meager circumstances.

One cold evening, the two brothers lay down on the benches in an inn. At night, some of the townspeople gathered to drink, and while in their cups, began to sing and dance in a circle. Each time one of the drunks passed by the reclining Jews, he delivered a solid blow to Rabbi Zusia.

After several minutes, Rabbi Elimelech said, "Zusia, why do you get all the beatings? I deserve some too. Let us change places."

The next time around, just as the drunkard was about to land a blow, his friend stopped him. "Why do you always beat this Jew?" he asked. "You should beat the other one too." Again the blow landed upon Rabbi Zusia.

"You see, Elimelech," Rabbi Zusia said. "You cannot outsmart G-d. What is coming to Zusia, Zusia will get."

NOTES

_____
_____
_____
_____
_____
_____
_____
_____
_____

... וְתֵן בְּלִבִּי בִּינָה לְהָבִין וּלְהַשְׂכִּיל ... *From our Prayers*

Help me to succeed, and grant me the wisdom to understand and to fulfill the words of Your Torah. Protect me from inadvertent mistakes, and cleanse my mind and thoughts to serve You *(prayer at the completion of the Priestly Blessing).*

May 5, 1991
May 24, 1992
May 12, 1993
May 2, 1994
May 21, 1995
May 10, 1996

"Protect me from inadvertent mistakes." The importance of this prayer lies in the realization that only G-d can accomplish this for us. Man cannot avoid all errors.

Someone said that when one cannot tolerate criticism, one learns to be a perfectionist. While it is important that we always try to do our best at whatever it is we do, we must realize that as humans we are prone to mistakes, and they will occur.

People who feel very inadequate may have a fear that making a mistake will devastate them. There are only two ways to avoid making a mistake: (1) Do nothing, and then one cannot fail, except that failure by inaction can be a very serious failure; or (2) be perfect. The problem with the latter solution is that it is beyond human capability, and insistence on perfection will lead to utter exhaustion.

While mistakes are not pleasant, they need not be devastating. We should think well enough of ourselves to live with our mistakes and accept constructive criticism.

When we ask G-d to protect us from mistakes, we realize the reality of our humanness.

Who is a wise person? He that learns from everyone. Who is strong? He who subdues his impulses. Who is wealthy? He who is satisfied with what he has. Who is honorable? He who honors others *(Ethics of the Father 4:1).*

From the Sages

Torah values are so different from secular values. Most people think that the wise person is the one who can teach; the strong person is the one who dominates others; the wealthy person is the one who has many possessions, and that the honorable person is the one who receives acclaim.

The Torah says the reverse. True wisdom is the capacity to learn. Strength is mastery over oneself. Wealth is enjoying whatever one has. Honor is recognizing others.

Living with Torah values can produce happiness. Secular values result in our trying to fill bottomless pits, and they bring exhaustion and frustration rather than happiness.

NOTES

May 6, 1991
May 25, 1992
May 13, 1993
May 3, 1994
May 22, 1995
May 11, 1996

From our Prayers

סוֹמֵךְ נוֹפְלִים וְרוֹפֵא חוֹלִים וּמַתִּיר אֲסוּרִים

He supports the fallen, heals the sick and unchains the bound *(daily Amidah)*.

Human beings were meant to grow. Indeed, life should be one long period of growth. Whereas physical growth comes to a halt in adulthood, spiritual growth should never stop.

Numerous incidents in everyone's life can temporarily interrupt the growth process. Physical illnesses, emotional illnesses, loss of loved ones, financial reversals — all these can temporarily arrest the growth process. But all these can and should be overcome, and indeed, surmounting these hurdles can accelerate spiritual growth.

The major impediment to growth is being bound to old habits and old patterns which we refuse to change. Some lifestyles can be a millstone around one's neck which precludes any forward motion. Traits such as self-righteousness, obstinacy, escaping instead of coping, blaming others when things go wrong, drinking or drugging away our problems, are all impediments to growth. We must be able to let go and abandon old established patterns.

G-d unchains those who are bound. He can release us from the bondage of engrained habits, if we ask Him to. But in order to do that, we must be willing to let go.

From the Scriptures

G-d has chastened me heavily, but has not given me over to death *(Psalms 118:18)*.

These are the words of David, who, as the Midrash says, did not experience one day free of suffering during his entire life.

For reasons unknowable to us, some people suffer intensely. It is the nature of suffering to cast a person into despair and hopelessness.

Rabbi Nachman of Breslov says that a person must bring himself to know as an absolute certainty that hopelessness does not exist. When a reasonable person sees a chimera — a centaur, a pink elephant with green spots, a sea monster on his front lawn — he knows that what he sees is not real. Either someone is engaging in theatrics, or he is hallucinating, but he knows that what he sees simply does not exist in reality, even if his senses tell him it is there.

This is how we must think of hopelessness. Regardless of how convincing the feeling of hopelessness may be, says Rabbi Nachman, we must recognize that it is a delusion. If we feel despair, it is our minds playing tricks on us. Hopelessness simply does not exist. There is always hope, always.

NOTES

_____
_____
_____
_____
_____
_____
_____
_____
_____

חָנֵּנִי ה' כִּי אֻמְלַל אָנִי רְפָאֵנִי ה' . . . *From our Prayers*

Favor me, O G-d, for I am bowed down. Heal me, O G-d, for my bones are afflicted . . . Return, O G-d, free my soul *(Psalms 6:3,5)*.

IYAR

אייר

May 7, 1991
May 26, 1992
May 14, 1993
May 4, 1994
May 23, 1995
May 12, 1996

We pray for relief from oppression of all types. We should realize that the worst form of oppression is that of our own ego, and we should pray for freedom of our soul from our own oppressiveness.

Self-centeredness can ruin anyone. When a person sees himself at the center of the world, he interprets all things as pertaining to him. When a person feels crushed, when he thinks of himself as unworthy, he is apt to misinterpret other people's actions and attitudes as being belittling or even hostile toward him. His need for reassurance can be insatiable, and he may so torment others to provide him with constant reassurance that he becomes unbearable, and indeed others turn away from him.

We pray for the release of our soul from our own tyranny. We must do our share in bringing about this freedom. That consists of working toward a healthy self-esteem, so that we do not become our own worst enemies.

When a person is brought before the heavenly tribunal, he is asked, "Did you look forward for salvation?" *(Shabbos 31a).*

From the Sages

Rabbi Ber of Rodshitz once stayed at an inn. In the morning, he asked the innkeeper, "Where did you get your chime clock? Every time I heard it strike the hour I was overcome with elation. I felt that wonderful things were going to happen."

The innkeeper responded, "That clock was given to me as a pledge by a guest who could not pay his bill."

"Could that guest have been related to the Seer of Lublin?" Rabbi Ber asked. The innkeeper then remembered that he had indeed heard the man speak of the Rabbi of Lublin.

"Then I understand," Rabbi Ber said. "Usually, the chime of a clock is depressing, because it indicates that another hour of our lives has gone, never to return.

"But with the Seer of Lublin it was otherwise. He saw every passing hour as bringing us that much closer to the Redemption."

We can look at the passing of time either with depression or elation. The choice is ours.

NOTES

May 8, 1991
May 27, 1992
May 15, 1993
May 5, 1994
May 24, 1995
May 13, 1996

From our Prayers

שֶׁתַּצִּילֵנִי הַיּוֹם וּבְכָל יוֹם מִיֵּצֶר רָע . . .

May it be Your will, O G-d, to spare me today and every day . . . from evil temptation *(daily morning service).*

The *tzaddik* of Sanz once stood at his window and called in a passer-by. "What would you do," he asked, "if you found a purse with a large sum of money, and the name of its owner was in it?"

"What kind of question is that?" the man responded. "I would immediately return it."

"You speak foolishly," the *tzaddik* said. He then called in another man and repeated the question, to which this man replied, "A large sum of money? Why, I would keep it."

"You are a scoundrel," the *tzaddik* said.

The next person to whom the question was put said, "Rabbi, how can I tell you now what I would do under those circumstances? I might say one thing now and act otherwise under temptation. Right now I can only hope that if I am put to the test, G-d will help me overcome temptation."

"Wisely spoken," said the *tzaddik*.

It is wrong to plan to do wrong, but if we become overconfident and think that we will never do wrong, we are at a great risk. We must recognize our vulnerabilities and guard against them.

From the Sages

Rabbi Akiva said, "Love your neighbor as you do yourself" *(Leviticus 19:18).* **This is a great principle of Torah** *(Jerusalem Talmud, Nedarim 9:4).*

Rabbi Mordechai Dov of Hornostipol developed a severe hiccup which persisted several days and threatened to aggravate his heart condition. When all remedies failed, he consulted a neurologist in Kiev.

After studying the case, the doctor said there was only one effective method: to deliver a shock to the spinal cord. This was accomplished by scalding it with a hot poker.

The doctor was surprised when the Rabbi did not move nor utter a sound upon being scalded. Thinking that perhaps the poker had not made skin contact, he repeated the process. When again there was no response, the doctor exclaimed, "I cannot believe this! Why, the other day I had another patient like this, and I had barely reached for the poker when he jumped out the window."

The Rabbi smiled. "When someone comes to me with a problem, and I am unable to help them, that hurts much worse. If I do not jump out the window then, I will certainly not do so now."

NOTES

_____
_____
_____
_____
_____
_____
_____
_____
_____

IYAR
25
אייר

O **. . . הֲלֹא כָּל הַגִּבּוֹרִים כְּאַיִן לְפָנֶיךָ . . .** *From*
G-d, before You all the mighty men are *our*
like naught, famous people as though *Prayers*
they never were, the wise as though they
were without knowledge . . . and the superiority of man over beasts is naught, except
for the pure soul *(daily morning service).*

May 9, 1991
May 28, 1992
May 16, 1993
May 6, 1994
May 25, 1995
May 14, 1996

The uniqueness of man and his superiority over lower
forms of life is not in his strength, fame, or even intellect. It
is in his soul, which is G-dlike. To the extent that a person
drifts away from G-d, to that extent he diminishes his
humanity.

How is one G-dly? The Talmud states that being G-dly
means to emulate the attributes of G-d. Just as He is
merciful, kind, forgiving, selfless, tolerant, and truthful, so
must we live and act according to these characteristics.

Since the soul within us is Divine, it possesses all of these
qualities. Each of us has within himself an infinite capacity
for goodness. Each of us has these noble traits of character.

Too often we are unaware of the good that exists within
us. Perhaps we are so preoccupied with what is external to
us, what lies before us and behind us, that we are unaware
of what lies within.

Our souls are pure G-dliness. That is a fact. We need only
discover it.

**Isachar, an agile beast of burden . . . saw that
leisure was a good thing . . . so he bowed his
shoulder to bear** *(Genesis 49:14-15).*

*From the
Scriptures*

Rabbi Bunim of Pshis'cha asked, "If he saw that leisure
was a good thing, why did he bow his shoulder to bear a
burden?"

Rabbi Bunim answers, "Leisure is enjoyable only if one
can bear a burden. The person for whom the burdens of life
are intolerable cannot have any leisure either. He never
knows peace."

There are some things in life which are unchangeable and
they are the burdens we must bear. The reasons for these are
known only to G-d. But if we can accept them with faith, then
we can enjoy serenity. If we defiantly refuse to accept the
unchangeable, we can never know a moment's rest, because
as long as we are struggling to throw off an inescapable
burden, we can never be at rest.

NOTES

_____
_____
_____
_____
_____
_____
_____
_____

May 10, 1991
May 29, 1992
May 17, 1993
May 7, 1994
May 26, 1995
May 15, 1996

From our Prayers

וְנֶאֱמָן אַתָּה לְהַחֲיוֹת מֵתִים . . .

You are trusted to awaken the dead. Blessed are You, O G-d, Who will resurrect the dead (*daily Amidah*).

In the Thirteen Principles of Faith, Maimonides includes as an essential principle of Judaism the belief in resurrection. He lists this as the last of the Thirteen Principles, perhaps because he considers it the most difficult to accept, something which no human has ever witnessed except for the few incidents related in the Scriptures. This is where faith must supersede experience and override logic.

Resurrection is the ultimate rejection of hopelessness. In human experience, people will cling to hope against all odds as long as there is life. But once death occurs, all hope is gone. Death is the absolute finality.

This is true in human experience. For the person who trusts in G-d, there is no absolute finality, and there is never a loss of hope. With G-d, nothing is impossible, and for those who trust in G-d there is never any despair.

We pray for our Redemption with the words, "Make the seed of David sprout" (*daily Amidah*). A seed does not grow until it first disintegrates in the soil. Our faith teaches us that there is always hope in life and growth, even when we may feel that we have totally disintegrated.

The Thirteenth Principle of Faith: There is always hope.

From the Scriptures

And G-d said to Solomon, "This house that you are building, if you will follow My decree and obey My laws and observe My mitzvos . . . then I will dwell in the midst of the children of Israel" (*I Kings 6:11-13*).

As beautiful as the ornate gold and silver and fine woods of Solomon's Temple were, that was not what attracted the Divine presence. "This house that you are building . . . if you follow My decree." We merit G-d's immediate presence among us when we fulfill the Divine will, and not by erecting elaborate buildings.

Beautifying a place of worship is indeed commendable, just as it is meritorious to beautify any *mitzvah*. But if one attractively decorates a room, one must first have a firm foundation, a solid floor, and sturdy walls. Decorative wallpaper in absence of a solid structure is of no value.

The structure of a Sanctuary is its spiritual composition. When people observe the Divine will, the edifice is a Sanctuary. If they turn away from G-d, it is just another attractive building.

NOTES

_____
_____
_____
_____
_____
_____
_____
_____

אֵלֶיךָ ה' נַפְשִׁי אֶשָּׂא *From*

To You, O G-d, I lift my soul *(Psalms 25:1,* our
daily morning service).

Prayers

To the average person, one might give a gift of silver. To
a wealthier person, one would give a gift of gold. To a king,
a gift of diamonds. What then is an appropriate gift to
Almighty G-d? One's soul, one's very own self *(Commentary on the Psalms).*

In bringing ourselves closer to G-d, we become more
spiritual. In prayer, we ask of G-d to fulfill our desires. But
we should not lose sight of the fact that G-d *desires* to hear
our prayers. The Talmud says that the reason the patriarchs
and matriarchs did not have children earlier in their lives is
because G-d wished to hear their prayers. Prayer refines a
person and enhances his spirituality.

We give ourselves to G-d as our gift to Him. How
precious we must be that we are an appropriate gift to the
Almighty! How precious our prayers must be that G-d
desires to hear them. If ever we tend to denigrate ourselves
and think of ourselves as unworthy, let us remember that
G-d thinks of us as most precious.

May 11, 1991
May 30, 1992
May 18, 1993
May 8, 1994
May 27, 1995
May 16, 1996

**So will those who defy G-d be destroyed, but
those who love G-d will be like the sun when it
shines forth with all its strength** *(Judges 5:31).*

*From the
Scriptures*

"Who are those that love G-d and who will shine with the
brightness of the midday sun? They are those who, when
offended, do not return an insult, and who, when they hear
themselves berated, do not respond" *(Gittin 36b).*

If we were asked to define what constitutes love of G-d,
we might come up with other criteria. The Talmud,
however, sums it up in a few words. Love of G-d consists of
character development and, particularly, of being sufficiently in control of one's emotions to be able to refrain
from reacting even when one is wrongly offended.

The corollary, obviously, is that "those who defy G-d"
must be those who do return insults and who do react to
being offended by responding in kind to their assailants.

What does the Torah say of the latter people? They will be
destroyed! The inability to restrain oneself and the impul-
siveness to respond defensively is self-destructive. Resentments and hate are to be overcome, not only because they
are morally wrong, but also because they are self-destructive, and they can consume every bit of our energy, as well
as distort our thinking and behavior.

Those who can achieve self-mastery will shine like the
sun at its full strength.

NOTES

May 12, 1991
May 31, 1992
May 19, 1993
May 9, 1994
May 28, 1995
May 17, 1996

From our Prayers

כִּי הַאֻמְנָם יֵשֵׁב אֱלֹקִים עַל הָאָרֶץ . . .

Does G-d dwell on the earth? Even the many heavens cannot contain You, how much less so this house that I have built. But You will hearken to Your servant's prayer that Your servant prays before You this day *(prayer of Solomon on dedication of the Temple, I Kings 8:27-28).*

Inasmuch as G-d is everywhere, why do we need synagogues as designated places for prayer? Why is prayer in a synagogue preferable, as the Talmud claims?

This was essentially Solomon's question. G-d is ubiquitous. Since the expanse of the universe cannot contain Him, then why a special building?

And Solomon answered that just as prayers are "this day," meaning that out of all eternity man can grasp only a small segment of time, so it is with space. We cannot imbue the entire world with holiness. Any attempt to do so would so dilute our efforts that the impact would be imperceptible.

We must recognize our limitations. Just as we cannot deal efficiently with more than one day at a time, so we cannot manage effectively with more than a small segment of space. The house of worship is a circumscribed area which is devoted to prayer and learning, and the concentration of Torah and worship in a small space should enhance the quality of our prayer therein.

From the Sages

He who manifests anger becomes subject to control by all the forces of Gehinnom *(Nedarim 22a).*

I once met a recovering alcoholic who had been treated very unjustly by his employer. "I am full of bitterness and resentment," he said, "but I will go to an AA meeting tonight and try to rid myself of these feelings. You see, if I hang on to resentments, I know I will drink again."

NOTES

I was impressed that this person was aware of how destructive it is to harbor resentments. There are many people who do not realize this, and they retain their anger and grudges. Perhaps this may not lead them to drinking if they are not alcoholic, but it may cause high blood-pressure, migraine headaches, ulcers, and depression.

A wise man said, "Hanging on to resentments is letting someone you don't like live rent-free inside your head."

Perhaps we cannot avoid *becoming* angry. But Solomon was right when he said that letting anger rest within you is foolish. It is not only foolish, but frankly dangerous.

From our Prayers

. . . הַלְלוּיָהּ כִּי טוֹב זַמְּרָה אֱלֹקֵינוּ

Give praise to G-d, for it is good to sing to our G-d. For it is pleasant and beautiful to praise Him *(Psalms 147:1, daily morning service).*

Too often we pray as a matter of routine. Even daily services at the synagogue can become mechanical, and we fail to be moved by prayer.

Unfortunately, there are those tragic occasions on which one is not permitted to pray. In the event of the death, G-d forbid, of a close relative, one is forbidden to pray, even to recite a blessing, until after the burial.

I remember the anguish of that period. If only I had been permitted to say a few chapters of Psalms, and be soothed by David's chants as he accepts and praises the supreme judgment of G-d, as he expresses his anguish, and as he restores hope for those who feel abandoned. Being deprived of the ability to pray was one of the most difficult aspects of those hours of bitterness.

After that experience my attitude toward prayer changed dramatically. I do not pretend that I always pray with the requisite *kavanah* (intensity of meditation), but I have since learned that prayer is a true privilege.

And the Jews camped (at Sinai) facing the mountain *(Exodus 19:2).*

The Rabbi of Karlin remarked, "Where there is an attempt to establish Jewishness, there will be mountains of obstacles."

The Hebrew term for serving G-d, *avodas Hashem*, may also be translated as "the work of G-d."

Observing the Divine commandments is not easy. It was never meant to be easy. Man is to achieve his ultimate reward with hard work. Fulfilling the Divine will is hard work because it consists of self-restraint, subduing one's passions, and overcoming temptation. This was symbolically conveyed at the Revelation at Sinai. The Torah was given with the people confronting the mountain. We must make an effort to ascend to Torah.

The Talmud tells us that Sinai was the smallest of the mountains. This too is significant. While fulfilling the Divine will may require us to climb, and it may be a strenuous climb indeed, it is nevertheless well within our capability. The Torah was not given on a mountain so high that the climb would be beyond the capacity of the average person. We can do the Divine will; we just must make the effort.

IYAR

29

אייר

May 13, 1991
June 1, 1992
May 20, 1993
May 10, 1994
May 29, 1995
May 18, 1996

From the Sages

NOTES
_____
_____
_____
_____
_____
_____
_____
_____
_____

LIVING EACH DAY / 239

Rosh Chodesh
May 25, 1990
May 14, 1991
June 2, 1992
May 21, 1993
May 11, 1994
May 30, 1995
May 19, 1996

From our Prayers

פִּתְחוּ לִי שַׁעֲרֵי צֶדֶק אָבֹא בָם אוֹדֶה קָהּ

Open for me the gates of justice; I will enter them and give praise to G-d *(Psalms 118:19, Hallel, recited on Rosh Chodesh).*

A person may sometimes feel alienated from G-d, as though somehow he was being denied entrance into the Divine presence. At such times it might be well to check: Did one knock on the proper door? Was one prepared to pay the entrance fee?

No, there is no money involved in the admission. All that is necessary for admission into the Divine presence is our appreciation of G-d, expressed in prayer.

The kabbalists state that before coming down to this earthly world, the human soul was in the Divine presence, basking in the indescribable bliss of the Divine radiance. But since this was an unearned pleasure, it lacked in wholesomeness because of the soul's sensitivity in receiving something which it had not earned. The sojourn of the soul on earth, where it can fulfill the Divine will, enables it to earn the privilege of being in the Divine presence.

Our entire life should thus be dedicated to return to the Divine presence, in a way that will be thoroughly pleasing to both man and G-d.

From the Sages

One who visits a sick person relieves him of one sixtieth of his illness *(Nedarim 39b).*

Today the *mitzvah* of *bikur cholim* (visiting the sick) has taken on special significance.

As a result of medical advances, many people live longer. However, some of these people are, G-d forbid, widowed. As a result of our highly industrialized, mobile society, their children may be employed elsewhere and live at great distances from them. These people are retired, and often unoccupied. Problems of advanced age such as arthritis and emphysema make it difficult for them to leave their homes. Many of their friends either are no longer living or are similarly limited. These people are alone and lonely.

A visit to these people is *bikur cholim.* Just spending some time with them to relieve their loneliness and boredom is a great *mitzvah.* There also may be things that one can easily do for them, such as simple errands, accompanying them to a doctor's office, or taking them shopping.

Bikur cholim is a *mitzvah* of inestimable value. It makes everyone a bit healthier.

NOTES

_____
_____
_____
_____
_____
_____
_____
_____

. . . בְּרוּךְ אַתָּה ה' . . . אֲשֶׁר קִדְּשָׁנוּ בְּמִצְוֹתָיו . . . *From*

B lessed are You, L-rd our G-d, King of the *our* universe, Who has hallowed us with His *Prayers* commandments . . . *(the beginning of the blessing prior to performance of a mitzvah).*

May 26, 1990
May 15, 1991
June 3, 1992
May 22, 1993
May 12, 1994
May 31, 1995
May 20, 1996

There are special laws pertaining to sacred objects.

In the days of the Sanctuary in Jerusalem, a person could designate any object he owned as sacred, and it then would be given to the Sanctuary. The object could either be put to use in the Sanctuary, or could be sold for maintenance of the Sanctuary.

Today, objects can be rendered sacred if they are designated for sacred purposes, such as a parchment which has been designated for the writing of a Torah scroll, *tefillin*, or a *mezuzah*.

Objects which are sacred require special handling. They may not be abused. They may not be taken into unclean places. They must be treated with reverence.

Each time we recite a blessing for a *mitzvah*, "Who has hallowed us," we are reminded that we too are sacred. G-d has designated us as sacred, and therefore we dare not abuse ourselves. We must treat ourselves with due respect, and we are not permitted to be in places that are "unclean" and beneath the dignity of a sacred being.

How different our lives would be if we indeed considered ourselves sacred.

Hospitality to wayfarers is greater than receiving the Divine presence *(Shabbos 127a).*

From the Sages

The Chafetz Chaim, even in his very old age, would personally prepare meals for wayfarers who stopped at his home. If they lodged there, he would personally make their beds and attend to their comforts.

Once, a guest — who could not stand seeing the elderly and widely acknowleged Torah sage bother himself with preparing the bed for him — tried to intervene and said, "Please don't do that. I can do it myself."

The Chafetz Chaim looked at the guest in bewilderment. "If you saw me putting on *tefillin* in the morning," he asked, "would you take them away from me and offer to put them on yourself? What difference is there between this *mitzvah* and any other? Preparing meals and lodgings for a guest is a Torah obligation upon me, not upon the guest."

That is an example of Torah Judaism.

NOTES

May 27, 1990
May 16, 1991
June 4, 1992
May 23, 1993
May 13, 1994
June 1, 1995
May 21, 1996

From our Prayers

וְהַעֲרֶב נָא . . . אֶת דִּבְרֵי תוֹרָתְךָ בְּפִינוּ . . .

O G-d, make the words of the Torah sweet in our mouths...and may we, and our children, and our children's children, be knowledgeable of Your name and sincere students of Torah *(daily morning prayers)*.

This is a blessing which is recited every day of the year. In the days preceding Shavuos, it deserves special attention.

Torah knowledge cannot be acquired by the equivalent of a sweepstakes ticket. There are no easy winners. Torah knowledge requires study, effort, persistence, diligence, and sacrifice.

If we pray that our children and their children be knowledgeable of Torah, then we must do something to bring this about. We must begin with ourselves. Whatever our degree of previous Torah study may be, from the most meager to the most advanced, we must continue our personal pursuit of Torah study if we expect our children to value it. We must plan and choose our children's Torah education very carefully. We must take a deep interest in the support of Torah institutions.

We must put our priorities in order. If our children and grandchildren do not see us placing great value on Torah study, they are hardly likely to value it themselves.

From the Scriptures

Go to the people, and sanctify them today and tomorrow *(Exodus 19:10)*.

The three days before receiving the Torah were days of intense spiritual preparation, with abstinence from physical gratifications. Although the restrictions of these special days did not extend beyond the Revelation at Sinai, their effects were to be of long duration.

Periods of intense spirituality and abstinence are of little value if after their termination people return to self-indulgence. There must be a carry-over of spirituality into our everyday lives. Moses was instructed by G-d, "Sanctify them today and *tomorrow*." Help them achieve a sanctity that will endure into the future.

Sometimes we experience moments of heightened spirituality, but they are transient. When such moments occur, we should stop and meditate, and allow the experience to become imprinted. We should preserve these precious moments and make these feelings part of our personality.

NOTES

_____
_____
_____
_____
_____
_____
_____
_____
_____
_____

... וְתֵן בְּלִבֵּנוּ בִּינָה לְהָבִין וּלְהַשְׂכִּיל ... *From*
O merciful Father, have compassion *our*
upon us, and give unto our hearts *Prayers*
understanding, that we may listen, learn,
teach, observe, do, and fulfill the words of
the Torah (*daily morning service*).

The Chafetz Chaim related a parable.

A person once asked a very wealthy man for a loan of a substantial sum of money to enable him to go into business. After a great deal of pleading, the rich man consented, and told the borrower to come to his home that evening for the money. All that evening he waited, but the borrower never came.

The following day, the man again approached him, again pleading for the loan. "I have already agreed to give you the money, and I waited for you all last night. I will be home again tonight, and you may come for it." But again that night, the borrower did not appear.

When the man approached him again the next day, the rich man became angry. "This is foolishness! I have offered you the money and sat there waiting for you to come and get it. If you don't want it, why do you persist in asking for it?"

We ask G-d for the capacity to learn and understand Torah. He will gladly give it to us, but we have to show up for it. To ask for it daily and then not show up where Torah is being taught is absurd.

May 28, 1990
May 17, 1991
June 5, 1992
May 24, 1993
May 14, 1994
June 2, 1995
May 22, 1996

For the ways of G-d are just. The righteous will walk in them, and the sinful will stumble in them (*Hoshea 14:10*).

From the Scriptures

A wealthy man of a community gave a sumptuous feast for all the townsfolk, providing the most delightful delicacies. One guest, who suffered from gastrointestinal disease, fell sick after partaking of the feast, and criticized the host for causing him to be sick.

"How foolish of you," said the host. "Just see how many people enjoyed the feast without any ill effects. Your reaction was not due at all to the food being unhealthy, but to your particular illness."

So it is with the teachings of the Torah. For the person who is spiritually well, the ways of the Torah are healthy and enjoyable. The person who is deprived and spiritually impoverished will find the practice of Torah restrictive and burdensome. But the problem lies within him, and not in the Torah.

NOTES

Erev Shavuos
[Eve of Shavuos]

May 29, 1990
May 18, 1991
June 6, 1992
May 25, 1993
May 15, 1994
June 3, 1995
May 23, 1996

From our Prayers

אֲשֶׁר נָתַן לָנוּ תּוֹרַת אֱמֶת . . .

He has given us a Torah of truth, and has planted eternal life within us (*blessing following reading of the Torah*).

The Talmud states that the prophets were asked why the Israelites were driven from their homeland, but they had no answer until G-d revealed the reason: "For they have forsaken My Torah" (*Jeremiah 9:11*). The Talmud explains that they did not recite the blessings for the Torah.

Why does the Talmud give this interpretation to "they have forsaken My Torah"? The Chafetz Chaim explains that if the Israelites would have forsaken study of the Torah and observance of the *mitzvos*, then the prophets would not have been at loss to give a reason for the exile. The fact was that they *did* study the Torah, but it was an academic study, just as one would pursue any philosophical study. They *did* observe the *mitzvos*, but they did so because they considered them to be social measures or of hygienic value. Torah and *mitzvos* that are not observed primarily because they are the dictates of G-d are of little spiritual value.

It is by reciting the blessing for the Torah that we indicate that our study and observance of the Torah is in deference to the Divine will, and not because they comply with our understanding.

From the Scriptures

There was a burdensome prophecy from G-d to Malachi. "I love you," says G-d to Israel. I asked, "Why do You love us?" "Because Esau is a brother to Jacob. I love Jacob and I despise Esau" (*Malachi 1:1-3*).

Rabbi Levi Yitzchok of Berdichev asked, "Why is this referred to as a 'burdensome prophecy' when G-d is telling of His love for Israel?"

Rabbi Levi Yitzchok answered, "The burden is that Israel did not merit being loved for its virtue, but rather that by comparison to the degeneracy of Esau, Jacob is preferred. If we are preferred only because we are less degenerate than others, that indeed is a heavy burden for the prophet to convey."

Some people take pride that they are better than others. In an age where there is so much corruption and immorality, a person who is halfway decent may consider himself to be a saint, even though his behavior is far beneath his potential.

We must always strive to improve ourselves and to develop our character to its maximum. We must always strive for greater spirituality, and not be content that we are more spiritual than others.

NOTES

_____
_____
_____
_____
_____
_____
_____
_____
_____

The nations inquire of Israel, "Whence and Who is your beloved, that for His sake you endure so much suffering? You would be honored if you would join us, and we would grant your every wish." Israel wisely responds, "If only you knew, you would understand that none of the rewards you can offer compares to the glory of G-d we share" *(Akdamus, chanted prior to reading the Torah on Shavuos).*

... מְנָן וּמָאן הוּא רְחִימֵךְ ... *From our Prayers*

In this beautiful hymn we affirm that G-d is infinite and His majesty is beyond description; He has chosen Israel to reveal His Torah; Israel has suffered because of its refusal to abandon the Torah and assimilate with the nations; and ultimately G-d will redeem Israel, and His glory will be revealed to the entire world.

The reading of the torah on Shavuos relates the Revelation at Sinai, or how it all began. The Akdamus hymn tells what happened afterward, and how it will all be in the end. It is a theme of identity, of pride, and of universal hope.

First Day of Shavuos

[In the Land of Israel Shavuos is only celebrated one day.]

May 30, 1990
May 19, 1991
June 7, 1992
May 26, 1993
May 16, 1994
June 4, 1995
May 24, 1996

The Israelites gathered it (the manna), one gathering more, the other gathering less. When they measured they found that the one who gathered much did not have more, and the one who gathered little did not have less. Each had received according to his particular needs *(Exodus 16:17-18).*

From the Scriptures

The Chafetz Chaim asked someone why he was not devoting more time to prayer and study. The man answered that he had to work extra hard to provide for all his needs.

The Chafetz Chaim told the man about a passenger on a train, who was pushing with great force on the forward wall of the wagon. When he was asked what he was doing, he explained that he was in a great hurry to reach his destination, and he was therefore pushing forward to make the train go faster.

NOTES

"You fool," people said to him. "Do you think that your pushing will get you there any faster? The train will reach its destination at the same time, whether you push or not. All you will do is exhaust yourself."

The Chafetz Chaim said, "Whatever one is destined to earn, he will earn." Of course, one must do something to earn a living, but it is a mistake to think that the intensity of one's effort determines the amount of his earnings.

Second Day of Shavuos
[Yizkor]

May 31, 1990
May 20, 1991
June 8, 1992
May 27, 1993
May 17, 1994
June 5, 1995
May 25, 1996

From our Prayers

קֶדֶם מִפְעָלָיו מֵאָז . . . הָיִיתִי עָמוּד מֵאָז . . . *From ... our*

Before all was created, Torah preceded ... While there were yet no depths, no springs, no mountains or hills ... before the land and its existence, before G-d stretched out the firmament, Torah was there *(Machzor of Shavuos)*.

The Talmud states that Torah preceded creation itself *(Pesachim 54a)*. "G-d looked into the Torah and created the universe according to its design" *(Zohar, Terumah)*.

From the smallest amoeba to the tallest giraffe, from the intricate structure of the atom to the complex movements of the heavenly bodies, there is design in the universe. The ancients could only surmise this. Modern telescopes and electron microscopy have revealed a structure and order in the universe which baffles the human mind. Recent studies have revealed a kind of order even in chaos. The more we learn about the universe, the more evident the design becomes.

The master plan for this intricate system was the Torah. This helps us understand why the Talmud says that a person should always think that his every behavior may alter the state of the universe. The obligation to fulfill the Divine will is more than a personal one. Deviation from the Divine will disrupts the harmony of the universe.

From the Sages

Teshuvah preceded creation *(Pesachim 54a)*.

We generally translate *teshuvah* to mean repentance. The Rabbi of Pshis'cha emphasized the literal translation of *teshuvah*, which is "return." "I must go back to my place, because I do not belong where I am now. I must return to the place that was designated for me in the six days of creation." That is *teshuvah*.

The universe has an order. The heavenly bodies do not deviate from their designated orbits. Plants and animals have the order of their lives in their natural growth and instincts.

NOTES

The human being is unique in that he was given free will and the capacity to make moral choices. In contrast to everything else in creation, man is free to deviate from the proper order in the universe. When he does so, he is out of place, and when one thing in the universe is out of its place, this brings disorder into the entire universe. When humans transgress the Divine will, they upset the harmony of creation.

Teshuvah is more than repentance. It is returning to where one belongs, and it is the restoration of harmony to the universe.

SIVAN

סיון

June 1, 1990
May 21, 1991
June 9, 1992
May 28, 1993
May 18, 1994
June 6, 1995
May 26, 1996

From our Prayers

וְזֹאת הַתּוֹרָה אֲשֶׁר שָׂם מֹשֶׁה . . .

Thisis the Torah which Moses set before the people of Israel (*Deuteronomy 4:44*).

The significance of this verse, and the reason it is included in the prayers, is because of its context in the Torah, according to the Chafetz Chaim.

Immediately preceding this verse, the Torah tells that Moses designated three cities of refuge in Trans-Jordan, where a person who accidentally killed someone could find asylum and protection from those who might seek to avenge the victim's death. These three cities of refuge did not become functional until three similar cities of refuge in Canaan became operative. Of course, since Moses could not enter Canaan, there was really no purpose in his designating those in Trans-Jordan. The whole task could have been left to his successor, Joshua.

What Moses taught us is that when one has the opportunity to do a *mitzvah*, one should do it promptly. One should not allow oneself to be deterred by any arguments.

This, then, is the teaching that Moses set before the people of Israel: When you have the opportunity to do a *mitzvah*, do it promptly.

From the Scriptures

His heart will not fear evil tidings, because his heart is firm with trust in G-d (*Psalms 112:7*).

I have developed a relaxing technique of self-hypnosis, wherein I allow myself to relive some enjoyable and relaxing experiences of the past. Very often I re-experience pleasant times of childhood, enjoyable days of summer vacation.

Recently, while vacationing, I again used my usual technique of relaxation. It occurred to me, however, "Why do I have to go back to the past to find relaxation when my present circumstances are completely stress-free?"

The answer is that whereas my present circumstances indeed may be free of stress, I have no idea how things will go the rest of the day. Any one of many things could still happen to ruin the day. But the enjoyable days of the past that I relive did end enjoyably. The past is certain, but the enjoyment of the present is still an uncertainty.

But if we had the requisite *bitachon*, trust in G-d, then we would not anticipate bad things happening. We would not be apprehensive, and we could relax in the present.

Anxiety is not only a heavy emotional burden, but also a major cause of many physical illnesses. We would be better emotionally and physically if our trust in G-d were more complete, and if we were spiritually healthier.

NOTES

סיון

June 2, 1990
May 22, 1991
June 10, 1992
May 29, 1993
May 19, 1994
June 7, 1995
May 27, 1996

From our Prayers

שָׁמַיִם אוֹמְרִים הַשָּׁמַיִם מְסַפְּרִים כְּבוֹד קֵל . . . *From*

The heavens say, "The heavens relate the Glory of G-d, and the firmament tells of His handiwork." The earth says, "To G-d belongs the land and its fullness, the world and all its inhabitants." *(Perek Shirah).*

Perek Shirah, or the Chapter of Song, relates the praises sung to G-d by all creation, the inanimate as well as all the members of the plant and animal kingdom. It was held in high esteem by the Talmud. Various Talmudic Sages taught that whoever recites *Perek Shirah* in this world will be privileged to sing it in Paradise.

The Midrash relates that when King David composed the Book of Psalms, he said, "O G-d, is there any other creature in the world who has sung as many hymns of glory to You as I have?" At that moment a frog appeared and said, "Do not boast, David, for I, a tiny frog, sing to G-d more often than you do."

What the Midrash is saying is that all nature is a testimony to the glory of the Creator, and that all nature, by its very being, sings praises to the infinite wisdom of G-d. Should man begin to feel conceited because of his great artistic compositions, he is reminded that other forms of nature far surpass him in testifying to the glory of G-d.

From the Scriptures

My son . . . (sinners say), "We will find treasures and fill our homes with loot. Cast your lot with us and we will share our purse with you." My son, do not go in their ways. Withhold your feet from their paths . . . for the bird that sees the net of the trapper thinks that it is all in vain *(Proverbs 1:13-17).*

Never has a better guide to spiritual living been composed than the Book of Proverbs. Every phrase is a treasure house of wisdom.

The bird who sees the birdseed bait has no concept that it is there only to lure him into the trap, and that he will pay with his life. The bird thinks that the seed is there for him to enjoy.

That is how seduction works. People are tempted by the bait, and are completely unaware that yielding to temptation will cost them dearly.

The single most effective protection against spiritual harm is to avoid the companionship of those who seek only self-indulgence. Spirituality can best be attained by associating with those people who pursue spiritual growth.

NOTES

_____
_____
_____
_____
_____
_____
_____
_____
_____

From our Prayers מִי יַעֲלֶה בְהַר ה' . . .

Who shall ascend the mountain of G-d . . .? One with clean hands and a pure heart, who has not borne his soul in vain (Psalms 24:3-4).

Resisting temptation is a great achievement. Indeed, the Talmud states that overcoming temptation and resisting sin, it is considered a *mitzvah* (Kiddushin 39b). But avoiding the negative is not enough. Doing the Divine will consists of "Desist from evil and do good" *(Psalms 34:15)*.

The Chafetz Chaim gave a parable. A man once gave a broker a sum of money to invest for him. After a long period of time had elapsed, he inquired from the broker how his investment was doing. The broker opened his safe and proudly showed the man that his money was there intact. Not a single bill had been touched.

"You fool!" the man exclaimed. "I did not give you the money to put away in a safe and give it back to me. I gave it to you to generate income, and you have done nothing with it."

Who shall deserve to dwell on the mountain of G-d? He who has not borne the Divine soul in vain. When we ultimately return our souls to G-d, we should be able to show what positive achievements we accomplished with it, for otherwise it will have been borne in vain.

June 3, 1990
May 23, 1991
June 11, 1992
May 30, 1993
May 20, 1994
June 8, 1995
May 28, 1996

If you will seek wisdom like silver and search for it like for gold, then you will understand the veneration of G-d and find Divine wisdom (Proverbs 2:4-5).

From the Scriptures

The search for true wisdom can be most frustrating. It is axiomatic that the essence of human wisdom is to recognize how little one knows. True wisdom is Divine wisdom and is as infinite as the Almighty Himself. Hence, the more one knows, the greater becomes one's concept of infinity, and the more one realizes that there is so much more that one does not know.

Solomon suggests searching for wisdom in the same manner that a treasure hunter searches for silver and gold. He does not stop when he does not find the treasure, but continues digging away in the hope that the next shovelful that he unearths will reveal it to him. On the other hand, if he does find gold and silver he does not stop digging, but continues to work to amass even more.

That is how we must strive for wisdom. We should not be discouraged if we do not immediately achieve it, and when we do, we should always continue to search for more.

NOTES
_____
_____
_____
_____
_____
_____
_____
_____
_____
_____

SIVAN

סִיוָן

June 4, 1990
May 24, 1991
June 12, 1992
May 31, 1993
May 21, 1994
June 9, 1995
May 29, 1996

From our Prayers

שָׁלוֹם עֲלֵיכֶם – עֲלֵיכֶם שָׁלוֹם

Shalom aleichem! Peace be unto you. Aleichem shalom! Upon you may there be peace (traditional greetings).

Not all prayers are to be found in the *siddur*. Wishing someone well is really a prayer that G-d grant him that wish, and that is as valid a prayer as any formal part of the liturgy.

The Talmud says, "Do not dismiss lightly the blessing of a common man" (*Berachos 7a*).

One of the purposes of prayer is for man to come into a closer relationship with G-d. Wishing another person well is one way to come closer to G-d. The Baal Shem Tov said that loving another person is the royal road to love of G-d.

The Talmud states, "Would that a person would pray all day" (*Berachos 21a*). We can certainly engage in prayer much of the day: "G-d bless you!" "*Zei gezunt* (Be well)!" "*Gai gezunderheit* (Go in good health!)" "*Mazel tov!* May you have a great deal of *nachas*" (joy in children).

All these and more are prayers. However, one essential of prayer is that it be with *kavanah* (thoughtfulness and meaning). Let our good wishes be sincere and meaningful. We will then be praying much of the day.

From the Scriptures

For you did not call upon Me, O Jacob, that you became weary of Me, O Israel (*Isaiah 43:22*).

If you are not enjoying Judaism, you are not doing it right.

The Maggid of Dubno explained the verse from Isaiah with a parable:

Two merchants were traveling by coach. One was a jeweler, and the other a book dealer. The first had a small case containing his merchandise, and the second had large crates of heavy books.

The porter mixed up the addresses, and unloaded the heavy crate at the inn where the jeweler lodged. Exhausted and dripping with perspiration, he asked the jeweler for his pay.

The jeweler remarked, "You have made a mistake. My merchandise is not the kind whose carrying would cause exhaustion and sweating."

This is the Divine message that the prophet is conveying. "If you have grown weary of My service, O Israel, it is because you have not been calling upon Me with sincerity." Dedicated devotion to G-d does not result in weariness, but in joy and vigor.

NOTES

_____

_____

_____

_____

_____

_____

_____

_____

וְשָׁמְרוּ בְנֵי יִשְׂרָאֵל אֶת הַשַּׁבָּת . . . *From our Prayers* T he children of israel shall keep the Shabbos, to make the Shabbos an eternal covenant throughout their generations. For it is an eternal sign between Me and the children of Israel, that in six days G-d created the heavens and the earth, and He rested on the Seventh day *(Exodus 31:16-17, Shabbos service).*

SIVAN
סיון

June 5, 1990
May 25, 1991
June 13, 1992
June 1, 1993
May 22, 1994
June 10, 1995
May 30, 1996

The Talmud considers observance of the *Shabbos* to be one of the basic *mitzvos*. If one rejects *Shabbos,* it is equivalent to rejection of the entire Torah. The Chafetz Chaim explained this attitude by reference to the above prayer, wherein G-d designates *Shabbos* as a "sign."

The sign above a store indicates who the proprietor is. Even if the owner should leave for a period of time, as long as the sign is up, one can assume that he still owns the store and that he will return. If the sign is taken down, then one concludes that the owner has left permanently.

Even if a person transgresses any other *mitzvah,* as long as *Shabbos* is intact, there is still a relationship betweeen man and G-d. There is an awareness that G-d created the world, and hence there can be a sense of purposefulness and of responsibility that a person is obligated to do the Divine will. If a person rejects the *Shabbos,* the "sign" has been taken down. The person then falls prey to total absorption in the mundane world, with consequent loss of all hope for spirituality.

If a person will bring of you a sacrificial offering to G-d . . . *(Leviticus 1:2).*

From the Scriptures

"What a strange sentence structure," said Rabbi Obadiah Sforno. "It should read, 'If one *of you* will bring a sacrificial offering.'

"The Torah is telling us that the true offering is the personal sacrifice one makes by setting aside his own will in deference to the will of G-d. 'If a person will bring *of you* ,' of yourself, an offering, then it is meritorious. Gifts upon the altar which are not accompanied by sincere devotion and *teshuvah* are of little value."

The personal sacrifices that are called for are not fasting and self-denial. The surrender of one's own will when it conflicts with what we believe to be the will of G-d is the meaning of sacrifice and that is the offering which G-d asks of us.

NOTES

_____
_____
_____
_____
_____
_____
_____
_____
_____

SIVAN

13

סיון

June 6, 1990
May 26, 1991
June 14, 1992
June 2, 1993
May 23, 1994
June 11, 1995
May 31, 1996

From our Prayers

יִרְאַת ה' טְהוֹרָה עוֹמֶדֶת לָעַד
מִשְׁפְּטֵי ה' אֱמֶת, צָדְקוּ יַחְדָּו

When the reverence of G-d is pure, it endures forever. The laws of G-d are true, they are righteous, taken all together *(Psalms 19:10, Shabbos morning service).*

A very fine timepiece that records time with great precision can be thrown off course completely if just one of the tiny parts in its intricate mechanism is removed. The fact that the remainder of the mechanism is intact does nothing to preserve its accuracy.

The Torah, which is the law of G-d, is composed of 613 commandments. These are true, fair, and just. Occasionally those who wish to scoff at Torah will isolate one or several laws for criticism. But the Divine commandments cannot be separated. When any one is separated, the entire mechanism malfunctions.

From the Scriptures

There is an evil that I have seen under the sun, and it is a great human evil: a person whom G-d has granted riches and who lacks for nothing, but does not have the mastery to use it, and strangers consume it. This is vanity and an evil disease *(Ecclesiastes 6:1-2).*

Here Solomon describes the character defect of miserliness. G-d grants a person wealth, but instead of his assets belonging to him, he belongs to them. He becomes a slave of his wealth, having no mastery over it.

The Torah concept is that whatever a person has, whether it is much or little, is what G-d has given him to use wisely. As Maimonides says, virtue is not found in extremes. Squandering one's assets foolishly is irresponsible, but being tight fisted is just as bad.

There is much good that can be done with wealth. One can live respectfully, but need not live in lavish luxury nor in self-indulgence. There are many people that can be helped by judicious allocation of one's wealth.

How tragic it is to see a person unable to enjoy what G-d has given him. This is indeed a "terrible disease."

NOTES

_____
_____
_____
_____
_____
_____
_____
_____
_____

From our Prayers

. . . הַמֵּאִיר לָאָרֶץ וְלַדָּרִים עָלֶיהָ בְּרַחֲמִים

He Who in compassion grants light to the earth and to them that dwell upon it, and in His goodness each day renews the work of the beginning . . . Therefore G-d, in Your abundant compassion, have mercy upon us *(daily morning service)*.

This prayer declares the majesty of G-d in creating the universe and all that is in it, and in sustaining the universe in an ever-ongoing process of renewal. How then does the prayer for mercy follow? Is it not out of context here?

The answer is that what we are pleading for is Divine grace so that we may be able to recognize the fact that G-d indeed continues to sustain and renew the universe every moment of its existence.

It is so easy, even for people who profess to believe that G-d created the universe, to become complacent. "Yes, G-d did create the universe, but that happened in the ancient, prehistoric past. G-d does not have much ongoing interest with the trivial affairs of the world. He is far too lofty and removed from it. The world now operates according to natural laws."

We need special Divine grace to prevent us from being misled into such thinking. We therefore pray for mercy: "Help us to see you everywhere in the universe."

From the Scriptures

Behold! There will come days, says G-d, when the one who plows will meet the one who harvests (i.e., the land will be so fruitful that the end of the harvest will extend to the beginning of the plowing) *(Amos 9:13).*

The Maggid of Dubno explained this with a parable:

A city dweller, who for the first time saw a farmer plant seeds, thought, "That man must be insane. Why is he taking good grain and burying it in the ground?"

Only much later, after he saw the grain grow, did he understand the reason for burying the seeds in the earth.

When we see things happen that appear to us to be destructive, we lack the foresight that would show us that these are seeds from which good will later emerge.

There will be a day, says the prophet, when the Divine beneficence will be evident to all, when the "harvest" will be immediately visible at the time of the "plowing."

Until then we must believe.

NOTES
_____
_____
_____
_____
_____
_____
_____
_____
_____
_____

June 8, 1990
May 28, 1991
June 16, 1992
June 4, 1993
May 25, 1994
June 13, 1995
June 2, 1996

From our Prayers

. . . הַצֵּל מְאַחֲרֵי לִפְרוֹשׁ מִן הַשַּׁבָּת

Spare those who delay taking leave from the Shabbos, that it not be concealed from them in the six days, they that absorb the sanctity of the holy Shabbos, and purify their hearts with truth and faith to serve You *(Friday-evening Zemiros)*.

The above is from the beautiful Friday-evening chant composed by the Rabbi of Karlin, one of the early Chassidic masters. The chant describes the Jew's longing for the *Shabbos,* how it brings a person into closer contact with G-d, and how the soul can savor the sweetness of Divine love.

Even among those who observe *Shabbos* by avoiding forbidden acts there are many who do not fully appreciate the sweetness of *Shabbos.* They are clockwatchers who wait for the moment that *Shabbos* is over so that they can return to their mundane tasks. This betrays their complete failure to grasp the essence of *Shabbos,* that it is an oasis in the desert. Why should one want to leave the fresh fruit and life-sustaining water of an oasis for the dry, barren desert, unless one is actually torn away from it and forced into the desert?

Shabbos is an oasis of total spirituality. It is not only a day when abstinence from daily activities permits time for study and meditation, but is also a day blessed by G-d with holiness and sweetness that nurtures our spirituality. How foolish we would be to wish to leave it!

From the Sages

Let the honor of your friend be as dear to you as your own *(Ethics of the Fathers 2:15).*

Rabbi Shmelke of Nikolsburg came to a city where he was greeted by a throng of his followers. Before meeting the crowd, he asked for a few moments of seclusion.

In the privacy of his seclusion, he was overheard to be saying to himself, "Welcome, great Rabbi. What a great honor to have you here," and such other expressions of praise.

When asked about this practice he said, "When you say praises to yourself, they sound absolutely ridiculous. That is about the same effect on the ego it should have when others say them to you. I just wanted to make sure that my head would not be turned by the welcome I was about to receive."

Rabbi Shmelke interpreted the passage, "Let the honor of your friend be as dear to you as your own," to mean that just as the honor you give yourself does not inflate your ego, neither should the honors accorded to you by others impress you.

NOTES

_____
_____
_____
_____
_____
_____
_____
_____
_____
_____

וְזַכֵּנִי לְשַׁבֵּר וּלְסַלֵּק מֵעָלַי מִדַּת הַגַּאֲוָה . . . *From*

M aster of the universe! Guide us and *our* teach us the truth of Your ways. Grant *Prayers* me correct thinking so that I can be aware of how little I have accomplished and how great are my responsibilities, so that I will be spared from any feelings of vanity (*prayer of Rabbi Nachman of Breslov*).

June 9, 1990
May 29, 1991
June 17, 1992
June 5, 1993
May 26, 1994
June 14, 1995
June 3, 1996

Prior to the death of the Maggid of Mezeritch his disciples asked him whom to choose as their spiritual leader.

The Maggid responded, "If you look for a spiritual leader, test him by asking for advice on how to rid yourself of vanity. Anyone who recommends any technique to achieve this is not qualified to be your leader. The one who says that he cannot give you any method, and that you must pray to G-d to spare you from vanity, he is your true leader."

The Jewish ethical works all consider vanity to be the root of all character defects. People humiliate others only because they think themselves to be better than others. People become angry because they consider themselves to have been slighted, because they were not accorded the respect that they think is their due.

Our intelligence can help us realize how great a character defect vanity is, but only G-d can help us rid ourselves of it. However, we must ask Him to do so in utmost sincerity.

For G-d has told you, O man, what is good, and what it is that G-d asks of you. It is only to do justice, to love compassion, and to walk humbly with G-d (*Michah 6:8*).

From the Scriptures

People may think that fulfilling the Divine will is so difficult. There are so many requirements, so many do's and don't's, that it is a most complex and bewildering task.

The prophet tells us it is not complex at all. Keep it simple. All G-d asks of you is three things. Do justice, be compassionate, and be humble. Once we set ourselves a goal of these three simple things, we can then look for ways to achieve them. If we are sincere in our quest, we will eventually discover that the formula for achieving these goals is the way of life designated by the Torah.

Don't be alarmed that Torah living is so difficult. Keep in mind that it is composed of three essential elements: justice, kindness and humility. All you have to do is to find out what *is* true justice, what constitutes true kindness, and what is true humility.

June 10, 1990
May 30, 1991
June 18, 1992
June 6, 1993
May 27, 1994
June 15, 1995
June 4, 1996

From our Prayers

שֶׁתָּכִין לִבֵּנוּ וּתְכוֹנֵן מַחְשְׁבוֹתֵינוּ . . . . . . *From our Prayers*

May it be Your will, O G-d, that You prepare our minds and make firm our thoughts, and make our prayers fluent *(prayer of Rabbi Elimelech of Lizensk)*.

Although the obligatory prayers must be recited verbally, there is also a need for thought and meditation.

The Talmud relates that the pious people of earlier days would meditate for an hour before prayer and for an hour after prayer *(Berachos 32b)*. The Chassidic masters were known to have sought seclusion in the forests and fields where, alone with nature and away from the disturbing turbulence of civic life, they were able to meditate.

As rich as our vocabulary may be, there are feelings that do not lend themselves to verbal expression. Meditation is not restricted by words, and we can allow ourselves to feel, with the knowledge that G-d is aware of and understands our feelings.

Sincere meditation not only provides an additional dimension for an emotional relationship with G-d, but also allows us to become aware of our own feelings. Too often our ignorance of our own feelings results in our being unfamiliar with them, and sometimes frankly frightened of them.

From the Scriptures

I rejoice with Your commandments, just as one who has found a great treasure *(Psalms 119:162)*.

The Baal Shem Tov commented on this verse that a person who discovers an enormous treasure — one that is much greater than he can possibly carry away — although he is certainly happy about the riches he acquired, is nevertheless also somewhat saddened by the fact that he cannot have it all, and must leave some behind.

So it is with *mitzvos*, says the Baal Shem Tov. Although we rejoice with the performance of *mitzvos*, we must realize how many there are that we have not yet fulfilled, and how many we will be leaving behind undone.

It is told that prior to his death, the Gaon of Vilna said, "How precious this world is. For just a small sum of money one can acquire a *mitzvah*: to give to the poor, to acquire *tzitzis*, etc. In the eternal world there are no *mitzvos* to be acquired at any price."

How wise we would be if we properly utilized the precious time we spend on earth.

NOTES

_____
_____
_____
_____
_____
_____
_____
_____
_____

... הַחוֹלֶה אֶת וִירַפֵּא ... שֶׁבֵּרַדְ מִי *From* **May He who blessed our forefathers ... *our*** speedily send a complete healing from *Prayers* heaven, a healing of the spirit and a healing of the body. Amen *(prayer for the sick)*.

SIVAN

18

סיון

June 11, 1990
May 31, 1991
June 19, 1992
June 7, 1993
May 28, 1994
June 16, 1995
June 5, 1996

Although the person for whom we pray is afflicted with a physical illness, our prayer also asks for "healing of the spirit." Moreover, healing of the spirit is mentioned *before* healing of the body, although the latter condition precipitated the prayer.

Long, long before anyone thought in terms of psychosomatics, the Sages of the Talmud knew the crucial role of the spirit in physical health. The Talmud cites the verses of Proverbs, "Good tidings strengthens the bones" *(16:24)*, "A depressed spirit will make bones wither" *(17:22)*, to prove that a person's emotional attitude directly affects the body.

This is the reason why *bikur cholim*, visiting a sick person and doing whatever we can to improve his spirits, is counted among those *mitzvos* whose reward is given in this world without diminishing the reward in the eternal world.

As we recite the prayer for the sick, we are reminded of our responsibility to them. Even if medical treatment is the domain of the physician, we can make significant contributions to the healing process if we contribute to an uplifting of the patient's spirit.

And I said unto G-d, "I do not know how to speak, because I am too young." G-d said, "Do not say, 'I am too young,' for you will carry My message to whomever I send you" *(Jeremiah 1:6-7).*

From the Scriptures

Jeremiah was commanded to carry a harsh warning to the Israelites. Their behavior was self-destructive. Persisting in their errant ways would result in their losing everything. Jeremiah sought to avoid this mission. He did not wish to be the bearer of bad tidings. But G-d gave him no option.

When someone we love indulges in self-destructive behavior, we may wish to ignore it and not take the necessary, albeit painful, steps to try and prevent an impending disaster.

In dealing with alcoholics who appear hopelessly trapped in their self-destructive behavior, there is an approach called "tough love." If we truly love a person, we will not hesitate to do what is necessary to save him.

This is true wherever we observe self-destructive behavior. Parenting calls for discipline along with love. Many children have been permitted to ruin their lives as a result of parents failing to institute "tough love."

NOTES

June 12, 1990
June 1, 1991
June 20, 1992
June 8, 1993
May 29, 1994
June 17, 1995
June 6, 1996

From our Prayers

עֲנֵנִי ה' כִּי טוֹב חַסְדֶּךָ . . .

Answer me, O G-d, in the goodness of Your mercy . . . And do not conceal Your countenance from me** *(Psalms 69:17-18)*.

I have often wondered what an infant thinks when its mother — whom it has always depended on for security — holds it tightly while the doctor administers the painful injection to immunize him against serious diseases. The infant undoubtedly remembers this procedure from one time to another, as is evident by his crying as soon as he sees the doctor in the white coat. What does the infant think of its mother, who seems to have joined forces with the aggressor to hurt him?

Whatever it is that the baby thinks while it is struggling, once the painful injection has been given, the baby clings to its mother for dear life — the same mother who just a moment ago assisted the doctor in inflicting pain.

It is evident that the basic trust the infant has in the mother is not eroded by the painful episode, even though at that very moment the baby sees the mother as conspiring to assist the assailant.

It is so much easier for the infant because the mother's immediate presence is so evident. What we lack in our relationship to G-d is the awareness of the immediate presence of G-d.

"Do not conceal Your countenance from me. Help me to see that You are there. My distress will be so much easier to bear."

From the Scriptures

G-d said to me, "You are my child. Just today I gave birth to you" *(Psalms 2:7)*.

The Maggid of Mezeritch told Rabbi Zusia that we should consider ourselves infants in three ways.

(1) An infant is always happy. You rarely see a baby depressed.

(2) An infant never sits idle. A baby is always in motion, always searching for new things, always doing something. The world is an exciting place for an infant. So many new discoveries to make! As we grow older, we tend to lose the excitement of our childhood.

(3) An infant cries for whatever it wants, and cries for something trivial just as for something of importance. We too must learn to pray to G-d with sincere tears for whatever it is that we lack.

NOTES

_____
_____
_____
_____
_____
_____
_____
_____
_____
_____

O **אַיֵּה כָּל נִפְלְאוֹתָיו הַגְּדוֹלוֹת וְהַנּוֹרָאוֹת** *From where are Your great and mighty our wonders that our ancestors related to Prayers us? . . . Each new day is harsher than the* day that preceded it, and I am so weary of carrying the burdens of exile *(Selichos).*

SIVAN

סיון

June 13, 1990
June 2, 1991
June 21, 1992
June 9, 1993
May 30, 1994
June 18, 1995
June 7, 1996

For more than 300 years, those martyred during the pogroms of *tach vetat* (1648-9) have been memorialized on this day. Jewish history is unfortunately replete with such national tragedies. In every age, Jews have asked, "Why, O G-d, why?" In vain have people tried to provide answers. There is no logical answer that can explain our unparalleled suffering.

But Jews are obstinate in their faith. The survivors of these terrible episodes preserved the memories of these calamities with special prayers and days of fasting.

In some prayers, as in the one above, we hear the complaints of pious people. Why does G-d not intervene? These prayers were composed by our Sages, by men of great faith. Are not the faithful supposed to accept the Divine decree in silence?

It is obvious from the above prayer that faith does not preclude complaining. In fact, one must have faith in order to complain. You cannot complain to someone whose existence you doubt.

And G-d said to Abraham, "Know for certain that your children will be strangers in a foreign land" *(Genesis 15:13).*

From the Scriptures

The Rabbi of Sochochov noted that the prophecy of the exile followed G-d's promise that Abraham would have children, and that they would inherit the Promised Land. Abraham then asked, "How can I be certain that I will bequeath it to them?"

Abraham had been raised among idolaters. His discovery of the one true G-d was a refreshing insight, achieved in sincere searching. To him every day was new and exciting as his knowledge of G-d deepened.

"But what will happen to my children?" asked Abraham. "They will inhabit a well-established faith. They will take awareness of G-d for granted. How can I bequeath to them the excitement and enthusiasm of learning about G-d?"

G-d's response was therefore, "Have no fear. Your children will be exiled. They will struggle to maintain their faith among people who deny G-d. Being a Jew will never be taken for granted."

It is our struggle for Judaism that keeps it alive and fresh.

NOTES
_____
_____
_____
_____
_____
_____
_____
_____
_____

June 14, 1990
June 3, 1991
June 22, 1992
June 10, 1993
May 31, 1994
June 19, 1995
June 8, 1996

From our Prayers

בָּרוּךְ אַתָּה . . . אֲשֶׁר קִדְּשָׁנוּ בְּמִצְוֹתָיו . . . From

Blessed are you, L-rd our G-d, King of the universe, Who has sanctified us with His commandments . . . Blessed are You, O G-d, King of the universe . . . Who has created . . .

The above are examples of all the *berachos* (blessings). The structure of each *brachah* is noteworthy, in that it begins in the second person, "Blessed are *You*" and promptly switches to the third person, "Who has," and not "You have." Why the change?

There are two aspects of man's relationship to G-d. The first is a very personal one. We speak directly to G-d without any intermediary. We are to remember that we stand before Him, and always maintain the appropriate attitude of reverence. He is not removed from us, and we can place our requests directly before Him.

But although He is imminent to us in His presence, we must remember how infinitely distant we are from an understanding of G-d. His wisdom is far beyond our grasp. We defer to the Divine wisdom without examining it, and we accept His will for us with absolute subjugation.

The structure of the *brachah* thus reminds us of both aspects. G-d is close to us in contact, but distant from us in terms of our grasp of His essence.

From the Sages

If one pursues honor, it will elude him, but if one flees from honor, it will pursue him *(Eruvin 13b).*

We understand this to mean that the person who seeks glory exposes his false pride, and therefore his pursuit is self-defeating, whereas the humble person will be appreciated and recognized for his modesty. But this Talmudic passage also seems to have a flavor of reward and punishment, asserting that if one tries to avoid honor, he will be rewarded by having honors heaped on him.

One of the Chassidic masters asked, "What kind of reward is it to be honored, if one sincerely dislikes being honored?"

NOTES

The master answered, "It is not a reward at all. It is his just deserts for giving honor any substance and value whatever. For the truly humble person, public recognition should simply not have any significance whatever. It should be so meaningless to him that he does not accord it the attention of even avoiding it."

How true. False pride can be manifested as much by avoiding honor as by pursuing it.

From our Prayers

... אִלּוּ פִינוּ מָלֵא שִׁירָה כַּיָּם

Though our mouths were as filled with song as the sea, and our tongues with joy outpouring as the swell of its waves, and our lips with praise as the expanse of heaven, we would still be unable to adequately thank You, O G-d . . . therefore the limbs which You have apportioned for us, the spirit which You have created into us, and the tongue which You have put into our mouths, shall all bless, praise, glorify, and exalt Your name (Shabbos morning prayer).

June 15, 1990
June 4, 1991
June 23, 1992
June 11, 1993
June 1, 1994
June 20, 1995
June 9, 1996

Is this not somewhat contradictory? We begin by declaring how grossly inadequate we are to praise G-d, and close by saying, "Therefore we *will* praise You with our capacities."

The answer is that we say that it is with "the spirit which *You* have created into us, and the tongue which *You* have put in our mouths" that we shall praise, glorify, and exalt G-d.

Granted, we are indeed limited. The majesty of G-d requires far greater praise than we are capable of providing. But these are the tools He has given us, and if we use them to their fullest, we have done all that we can.

A person is never held accountable for anything which is beyond his capacity. But we are never dispensed from fully realizing the potential that we do have.

Keep your distance from falsehood (Exodus 23:7).

From the Scriptures

It is not enough to avoid lying. The Torah demands that we "keep our distance" from falsehood.

For many of the 613 *mitzvos* of the Torah, there are Rabbinic laws that were established as protective measures, to put distance between ourselves and the forbidden act, and to prevent us from inadvertently transgressing a Biblical prohibition. But when it comes to falsehood, the Torah itself requires that we take protective measures.

If we do something which we might later have to conceal, if we behave in a manner that we might subsequently have to lie about, we have already transgressed the *Biblical* commandment, although we have not yet lied. We have transgressed because we did not *distance ourselves* from falsehood.

This should serve as a guide to everything we do. If it cannot pass the test of truthfulness, and it is something that we may have to lie about in the future, we should not do it now.

NOTES

_____
_____
_____
_____
_____
_____
_____
_____
_____

June 16, 1990
June 5, 1991
June 24, 1992
June 12, 1993
June 2, 1994
June 21, 1995
June 10, 1996

From our Prayers

בְּרֹגֶז רַחֵם תִּזְכּוֹר . . .

Remember Your mercy, even in wrath, O G-d, Who came forth from Teiman, O Holy One, Who came forth from the mountains of Paran (Habbakuk 3:2-3).

The Midrash states that before G-d gave the Torah to Israel, He offered it to other nations, who rejected it. G-d came to Sinai after offering the Torah to the Ishmaelites in Teiman, and to the Edomites in Paran. But only the Israelites accepted the Torah and acknowledged G-d as Master of the universe. By virtue of this, we pray for mercy.

A parable: A king once went hunting alone, and was lost in the forest. He wandered for several days with no food. A recluse who lived in the forest found him, provided him with food, and led him out of the forest. The king then rewarded the man by appointing him to a high office.

Years later, the former recluse became involved in a palace intrigue. He was found guilty of treason and was condemned to death. When asked if he had a last wish, he requested to appear before the king clad in his clothes as a recluse. When the king saw him so clad, he was reminded how this man had saved his life, and commuted his sentence.

Thus, says Habbakuk, even if we have incurred the wrath of G-d, we remind Him of how the nations rejected Him and clung to their idols, and that only the Israelites acknowledged Him. For this alone, we deserve Divine mercy.

From the Scriptures

Everything that G-d made was for its purpose, even the wicked for the day of retribution (Proverbs 16:4).

The question of why G-d allows evil to occur is hardly new. Solomon addressed this question in *Proverbs*.

It is our belief that man was created to exercise his freedom of will, the unique characteristic that distinguishes man from other forms of life. Free will implies an option to do good or evil. Clearly, if every sinner was promptly struck down by lightning, no one would dare sin. This would not be a moral choice, but an avoidance of pain.

For moral good to exist, there must be the option of evil, and the punitive consequences of evil cannot come immediately.

So when we see things that we think to be unjust, we must remember that in a truly "just" world, one without evil, man's behavior would be compulsory rather than free, and man's ability to make himself spiritual would be non-existent, because spirituality requires true freedom of choice.

NOTES
_____
_____
_____
_____
_____
_____
_____
_____
_____

*C*reate a new heart for me, O G-d, and renew a proper spirit within me. Do not cast me away from before You, and do not remove your Holy Spirit from me *(Psalms 51:12-13).* לֵב טָהוֹר בְּרָא לִי אֱלֹקִים . . . *From our Prayers*

June 17, 1990
June 6, 1991
June 25, 1992
June 13, 1993
June 3, 1994
June 22, 1995
June 11, 1996

A woman who had repeated relapses into alcoholism phoned me, very obviously intoxicated. However, when I offered her hospitalization and treatment, she rejected them.

"If you are not ready for help now," I said, "you will be one day. I'm not giving up on you."

"Please don't ever give up on me, Doctor," she said. "Don't ever give up." Before long she entered treatment on her own, and has since done very well.

Regardless of how far we may have strayed from the way of G-d, there is always hope of return. We pray that we not be abandoned, that G-d not give up on us.

The above prayer was said by David after his liaison with Bathsheba. The word "create" that David chose means to make something out of nothing, which only G-d can do. What David was saying is, "If I have anything within me which can be renewed, help me rehabilitate. If I am so far gone that I have nothing, then You, O G-d, can create a new spirit within me. Just never abandon me."

There is never, never any reason for us to despair of ourselves and of our salvation.

Calculate what you may lose by performing a mitzvah as opposed to its reward, and calculate what you may gain by committing a sin as opposed to its cost *(Ethics of the Fathers 2:1).* *From the Sages*

We live in a culture that lives by credit and is based on the philosophy, "Get what you want now, and pay later." The ultimate cost of this life style may be exorbitant.

Torah requires us to calculate, at least in regard to our spiritual lives. How much do we stand to gain from working on *Shabbos?* How much spirituality are we sacrificing by not having a day that is sacred and dedicated to prayer, study, and meditation? How much do we gain by taking time out for daily prayer? Is that not worth the few minutes we take from our business affairs?

We might not make so many unwise decisions if only we stopped to think. Our problem is that we often do not bother to make decisions, but act rather out of habit.

Calculate. Think. Make decisions.

SIVAN

סיון

June 18, 1991
June 7, 1991
June 26, 1992
June 14, 1993
June 4, 1994
June 23, 1995
June 12, 1996

From our Prayers

שְׁמַע יִשְׂרָאֵל ה' אֱלֹקֵינוּ ה' אֶחָד

Hear, O Israel, the L-rd our G-d, is one *(recited three times each day; Deut. 6:4).*

Shema Yisrael — declaring our belief in the oneness of G-d — the most sacred prayer in the Jewish liturgy.

On the eve of the eighth day of a male infant's life, when he is to enter the covenant of circumcision, children gather at the side of the crib and read the *Shema*, welcoming the child into the family of Israel.

It is with these six simple words that Jewish men and women throughout the ages have gone to the stake and to the gas chambers, giving their lives for *Kiddush Hashem*, the sanctification of G-d. Declaring that renunciation of their Judaism would be a fate much worse than death.

Thousands of miles may separate one Jew from another. Thousands of years separate the modern Jew from the ancient Jew. Yet there is no separation, because the *Shema Yisrael* binds us all together.

Twice daily in our prayers, and at night when we return our *neshamah* (soul) to G-d, we bind ourselves to each other across both time and space, and thus we bind ourselves to G-d.

From the Sages

If one walks along the way and, upon seeing a beautiful tree, interrupts his learning to exclaim, "How beautiful is that tree!" he has forfeited his life *(Ethics of the Fathers 3:9).*

What heinous crime has a person committed if he pauses to admire the beauty of nature?

The answer is in the phrase "interrupts his learning." Appreciation of the beauty of nature should stimulate a person to a greater admiration for G-d.

When a person is shown the miracles of the modern computer, he marvels at its ability to complete complicated calculations in fractions of a second. Yet when he sees a leaf, he gives it little thought.

Just place that leaf under a powerful microscope and observe its intricate structure. Note the layers of cells, the thousands of tiny canals that distribute water and nourishment to all the cells. Analyze the complex chemical processes that go on in the leaf every moment, and the precise and intricate enzyme systems governing many phases of the operation of the plant.

Yes, failure to recognize G-d in nature is indeed a grievous sin.

NOTES

_____
_____
_____
_____
_____
_____
_____
_____
_____
_____

From our Prayers טַעֲמוּ וּרְאוּ כִּי טוֹב ה' . .

Taste and you shall see that G-d is good. Fortunate is the person who trusts in Him *(Psalms 34:9, Shabbos morning service).*

There are some people who are chronically dissatisfied. They feel that everyone is getting more out of life than they are. Life appears drab to them, without excitement. They feel they have somehow been cheated.

In desperation they may turn to alcohol or drugs to fill the void, or they may do radical things to try and get the excitement and attention they think they are missing.

The truth is that reality is good, but they have not learned how to taste it. Some people appear to set up a blockade against feeling things, perhaps because they do not know how to deal with their feelings and they are frightened of them. However, they hold reality at fault for being insipid.

A person who has a sincere trust in the benevolence of G-d is much less likely to be frightened. The security of the knowledge that G-d protects him allows him to taste and partake of the world instead of withdrawing from it. In times when he is indeed in distress, he does not become bitter and angry at the world, because he knows that G-d is always nearby, sharing in his distress, and supporting him through his ordeals.

June 19, 1990
June 8, 1991
June 27, 1992
June 15, 1993
June 5, 1994
June 24, 1995
June 13, 1996

From the Sages

Ten of Rabbi Yochanan's sons died in his lifetime. He used to carry a tooth of the tenth son and, when he saw someone in deep grief, he would say, "This is the tooth of my tenth deceased child" *(Berachos 5b).*

It is hollow consolation to tell people who are in distress that there are others who are worse off than they. Someone else's misery does not at all relieve mine.

Rabbi Yochanan was saying that a person should not allow adversity to paralyze him. We were all created with a mission to accomplish in our lives. For reasons known only to G-d, some people are given easier conditions in life, and some are subjected to harsh circumstances. The task that we must achieve in this earthly existence must be worked at regardless of our circumstances.

Rabbi Yochanan was too wise to try to comfort someone by relating his own tragedy. What he was really saying was, "In spite of losing ten children, I go on with my work, and so must you."

Adversity can rob us of all ambition. We must strengthen ourselves to overcome its paralytic pressures.

NOTES

_____
_____
_____
_____
_____
_____
_____
_____
_____

SIVAN

סיון

June 20, 1990
June 9, 1991
June 28, 1992
June 16, 1993
June 6, 1994
June 25, 1995
June 14, 1996

From our Prayers

זוֹכֵר הַבְּרִית וְנֶאֱמָן בִּבְרִיתוֹ וְקַיָּם בְּמַאֲמָרוֹ

He remembers the covenant, is trustworthy to keep His covenant, and is reliable for His word *(blessing upon seeing the rainbow).*

A blessing is recited when one sees a rainbow in the sky. As stated in Genesis, following the great deluge G-d promised that He would never again destroy all mankind. He designated the rainbow as an assurance that regardless of how degenerate the world may become, G-d will allow it to survive.

Our faith in humanity often falters. An assembly of the nations of the world applauds a ruthless dictator, a known cannibal; a civilized world allows an unspeakable holocaust to occur, and after the inhuman atrocities are revealed to all, a civilized country gives asylum to a Mengele, as evil a demon as ever walked on earth; a nation elects as its chief of state a known participant in the Nazi atrocities, and the leader of a major religion gives his tacit approval by granting this criminal an audience.

Does such a world deserve to survive? Would it be at all out of order if G-d wiped out mankind and allowed it to try again? Each time we see the rainbow we are reminded that G-d knew full well how corrupt and degenerate the world could become, yet for reasons known only to Him, He allows its survival.

G-d never loses faith in humanity. Neither should we.

From the Scriptures

If you would see the donkey of your enemy lying under his burden, do not allow yourself to desert him, but forsake everything else and hasten to his aid *(Exodus 23:5).*

Why does the Torah instruct us what to do when conditions of hatred prevail? Inasmuch as we should *eradicate* hatred from our hearts, why give instructions on how to behave in the presence of it?

The answer is that the Torah is not referring to personal animosity, but to a situation in which a person despises another person's evil behavior, and keeps his distance from him for fear that the association with an evil person might be harmful to his own spiritual welfare.

Even under such circumstances, says the Torah, be careful that condemning the evil behavior of another person does not progress to personal animosity. Hence, even if it is not wise to keep his company, you must nevertheless assist him at a time of need *(Tosafos Pesachim 113b).*

NOTES

_____
_____
_____
_____
_____
_____
_____
_____
_____
_____

. . . צִדְקָתְךָ צֶדֶק לְעוֹלָם וְתוֹרָתְךָ אֱמֶת *From*
The righteousness You have taught us is *our*
eternal justice, and Your Torah is truth. *Prayers*
Your merciful justice reaches unto high
heaven. Your righteousness is like the
mighty mountains and Your judgments are
profound like the great deep *(Shabbos
afternoon service).*

SIVAN

סִיוָן

June 21, 1990
June 10, 1991
June 29, 1992
June 17, 1993
June 7, 1994
June 26, 1995
June 15, 1996

Some commentaries on the *Siddur* state that these three verses are recited following the *Shabbos* afternoon service because that was the time of death of three great luminaries: Moses, Joseph, and David.

These verses are in acceptance of the absolute righteousness of Divine justice. Moses was chastened because, according to the Midrash, he asked to live eternally. Joseph taunted his brothers because, his great piety notwithstanding, he fell prey to the vanity of his royal status. David had sought to delay the time of his death until after *Shabbos*, but G-d told him that he had no right to encroach even for a moment on the destined reign of his son Solomon.

Every person is accountable to G-d, and great people are held responsible to an even greater degree.

As we prepare to part with the *Shabbos* and return to the work week, we are reminded of these important principles. If we are in a position of authority, we must be careful not only to not abuse our power, but also that it does not cause us to become vain. We must accept our mortality, and not live as though we were going to be here forever. And finally, that which is destined to be will be, and we must realize that there are limits to how much we can direct our destiny.

G-d has no liking for scoundrels, therefore that which you promise you should pay. It is better not to promise than to promise and not deliver. Do not allow your mouth to bring sin upon your person *(Ecclesiastes 5:3-5).*

From the Scriptures

NOTES

_____

_____

_____

_____

To some people, words come easily. Sometimes they make promises with a good intention, but extend themselves beyond their capacity to perform.

When we are unable to deliver on a promise, we tend to act defensively. We may avoid the person to whom we promised or fabricate stories to try to justify our dereliction.

Solomon's words are sound advice. Do not make any commitment if there is any question of your ability to fulfill it.

Erev
Rosh Chodesh
[Eve of the
New Month]
June 22, 1990
June 11, 1991
June 30, 1992
June 18, 1993
June 8, 1994
June 27, 1995
June 16, 1996

From
our
Prayers

כְּמוֹ שֶׁכָּבַשׁ אַבְרָהָם אָבִינוּ אֶת רַחֲמָיו . . .

Just as Abraham suppressed his compassion to do Your will with a complete heart, so may Your compassion suppress Your wrath with us, and treat us with mercy *(daily morning service)*.

The readiness of the patriarch Abraham to offer his son as a sacrifice is often cited in the liturgy.

The greatness of Abraham is not in his willingness to part with what was dearest to him, but in absolute obedience to the Divine will.

Abraham could have argued forcefully that the Divine command to sacrifice his son must have been an error, or at least that he had misunderstood it. Had not G-d promised him that Isaac would be the father of a new nation? This promise would have been nullified had Isaac been sacrificed. Certainly G-d does not renege on a promise; hence the command to sacrifice Isaac could not possibly be valid.

The greatness of Abraham was that he did not stop to deliberate on the Divine word. His faith in G-d was absolute. The Divine command was to be obeyed without processing it logically to determine whether it was in conflict with a previous Divine promise.

Turning our lives over completely to the will of G-d means just that. Absolute obedience, with no questions asked.

From
the Sages

The Torah says, "You must have reverence for G-d" *(Deuteronomy 6:13).* **This also subsumes reverence for Torah scholars** *(Bava Kamma 41b).*

The Maggid of Dubno explained with a parable.

A blind man was leaving the country. He came to the border with his guide, and produced his exit visa. Upon examining his papers, the official said, "We see authorization here only for you to leave the country. Where is the exit visa for your guide?"

"It is contained in mine," the blind man said. "It is obvious to everyone that I have no way of traveling without someone to guide me. An exit visa given to me obviously implies that I can take someone else along."

So it is with reverence for G-d. With improper guides and teachers, how could we possibly know anything about G-dliness? If we do not revere and respect the Torah scholars who can teach us about G-d, how would we ever get to revere Him?

Reverence for G-d therefore implies reverence for those who can teach us about G-d.

NOTES
_____
_____
_____
_____
_____
_____
_____
_____
_____
_____

אָנָּא ה׳ כִּי אֲנִי עַבְדֶּךָ . . . פִּתַּחְתָּ לְמוֹסֵרָי *From*
I thank you, O G-d, that I am your servant. *our*
Yes, your servant, the son of Your *Prayers*
handmaid. You have loosened my bonds
(Psalms 116:16, Hallel).

This verse expresses two important concepts. Firstly, we acknowledge our gratitude to our forebears for conveying to us the teachings of Torah that enable us to fulfill our mission in life. Secondly, contrary to popular opinion, Torah is not restrictive. Indeed, Torah provides for the possibility of true freedom.

There is no enslavement that is as absolute as that of a person who is under the domination of his passions and internal drives. Unless a person disciplines himself and develops self-mastery, he becomes a pawn at the mercy of his lust, greed, and hunger. Just as an addict is subject to the unrelenting dictatorship of alcohol and drugs, so does the undisciplined individual lose all freedom of choice.

Torah teaches restraint, discipline, and self-mastery, thereby actually "loosening the bonds," and enables the person to exercise true freedom of choice.

First Day of
Rosh Chodesh
Tammuz
June 23, 1990
June 12, 1991
July 1, 1992
June 19, 1993
June 9, 1994
June 28, 1995
June 17, 1996

A person who does not use his intelligence to avoid that which is harmful to his soul is lower than an animal or beast, for the latter instinctively protect themselves and will flee from anything that they perceive as dangerous *(Path of the Just, Chapter 1).*

From
the Sages

Animals do not indulge in excesses. In their natural habitat, they are neither obese nor addicted. Why is indulgence to excess restricted to humans?

The answer is that each biological drive has its end point at which it is satisfied. Man, in addition to biological drives, also has a craving for a spirituality, a need for closeness to G-d. This is indeed an infinite craving, which can never be fully satisfied.

But when a person does not recognize this need and does not identify his need for spirituality, he may try to satisfy this undefined need by those methods that have provided him with some pleasure. He will therefore eat, drink, or indulge in physical pleasures in a futile attempt to satisfy spiritual cravings. Since none of these methods can fill the spiritual void, he futilely continues to indulge, achieving nothing but frustration.

For a person to be happy, his spiritual needs must be recognized and appropriately addressed.

NOTES
_____
_____
_____
_____
_____
_____
_____
_____
_____

Second Day of Rosh Chodesh

June 24, 1990
June 13, 1991
July 2, 1992
June 20, 1993
June 10, 1994
June 29, 1995
June 18, 1996

From our Prayers

מְקִימִי מֵעָפָר דָּל מֵאַשְׁפֹּת יָרִים אֶבְיוֹן

He raises out of the dust him who has sunk low, and lifts the needy up from the dung hill *(Psalms 113:7, Hallel, recited on Rosh Chodesh)*.

The Rabbi of Gur interpreted this verse as follows: He elevates those who have sunk spiritually, so that their needs become more noble.

How foolish we are that we often are not aware of our true needs. Watching small children play, we will see a child become angry because another child has a toy or a piece of candy that he wants. What appears to us to be an inconsequential trifle may be very important to that child. If the child somehow gets the coveted object, he may lose interest in it after a few moments and throw it away.

We often act in a similar fashion. When we desire something, it may appear to us to be of monumental importance. Once we have it, it may lose its appeal.

We need to pray to G-d, along with the Psalmist, to help us know what it is that we truly need.

From the Sages

When the fetus is in the mother's womb, an angel teaches him the entire Torah. When the time arrives for him to enter the world, an angel touches him on his lips, and he then forgets all that he has learned *(Niddah 30b)*.

The question is obvious. What purpose is there in the infant being taught the entire Torah if he will be made to forget it?

One commentary says that if you fold a strip of paper and then straighten it out, the crease of the fold remains permanently, and it is then so much easier to fold the paper at the site of the crease. Another commentary explains that the infant forgets the Torah he learned in the way we forget many things, which actually are stored deep in the recesses of our unconscious mind, and may be recalled spontaneously many years later, or can appear in dreams, or can be elicited by hypnosis.

The infant's learning of the Torah is thus not in vain. According to the first interpretation, subsequent learning of Torah is greatly facilitated, and according to the second interpretation, all we must do in our efforts to learn Torah is to uncover what we already know.

Not only were we given access to the Divine wisdom, but it is actually instilled within us. How foolish we would be not to seek it.

NOTES

_____
_____
_____
_____
_____
_____
_____
_____

בּוֹרֵא מְאוֹרֵי הָאֵשׁ . . .

From our Prayers

Blessed are you, L-rd our G-d, King of the universe, who created the flames of the fire *(Havdalah service at the close of Shabbos).*

The Talmud says that the blessing thanking G-d for the gift of fire is to be recited on *Shabbos* night, because that is when Adam was given fire for the first time.

Fire is representative of forces that can be constructive or destructive. When used wisely, fire produces light and warmth and the energy that enables smelting, welding, cooking, and a multitude of processes that can enrich man's life. When fire is not used wisely and cautiously, it can be devastatingly destructive.

Modern man has unleashed heretofore undreamt-of quantities of energy, but is now faced with the awesome threat of annihilation of all life by careless or malevolent use of nuclear power.

Adam was not given fire until he first experienced a *Shabbos,* a day of prayer, a day of meditation and spiritual development. It is only when man is spiritual that the destructive potentials in the powerful forces he commands can be restrained.

June 25, 1990
June 14, 1991
July 3, 1992
June 21, 1993
June 11, 1994
June 30, 1995
June 19, 1996

From the Scriptures

Do not take a bribe, for a bribe will blind the eyes of the wise and distort the words of the righteous *(Deuteronomy 16:19).*

The Rabbi of Berdichev once sat in judgment on a case in his rabbinical court. In the midst of the proceedings, he abruptly disqualified himself.

On the following Friday afternoon, when the Rabbi put on his kaftan for *Shabbos,* he discovered an envelope with money which one of the litigants had put in his pocket in an attempt to bribe him.

"I could not understand at the time what had happened," said the Rabbi. "I suddenly found myself persistently favoring the arguments of one of the litigants, and I felt I was no longer an impartial judge. I did not know why until I discovered the attempted bribe. This shows us how far reaching the effects of a bribe can be, that it can affect the judge's impartiality *even if he is unaware of the bribe!*"

We, too, often must make judgments in our own lives. Essentially, we are judges. If we allow ourselves to be influenced by ulterior motives rather than by an impartial search for truth, are we not guilty of accepting a bribe?

NOTES

_____
_____
_____
_____
_____
_____
_____
_____
_____

TAMMUZ

תמוז

June 26, 1990
June 15, 1991
July 4, 1992
June 22, 1993
June 12, 1994
July 1, 1995
June 20, 1996

From our Prayers

נִפְּלָה נָּא בְיַד ה' כִּי רַבִּים רַחֲמָיו
וּבְיַד אָדָם אַל אֶפְּלָה

And David said to Gad, ". . . Let us throw ourselves into the hands of G-d, for His mercies are abundant, but let us not fall into the hands of mortals" (II Samuel 24:14, morning service).

This prayer is recited in a posture of bowing and leaning one's head on the forearm in supplication, as a symbol of total effacement before G-d.

Jewish liturgy permits complete kneeling in prayer only on Rosh Hashanah and Yom Kippur. However, three times in the *Amidah*, which is recited three times daily, there is genuflection and deep bowing in reverence before G-d.

These various postures are symbolic, but since attitudes may be more forcefully impressed by actions than by words, the genuflection and bowing are important in intensifying a feeling of humility and of absolute subjugation of the self before G-d.

It is noteworthy that one of the genuflections and bowing accompanies the prayer of gratitude in the *Amidah*. Gratitude and humility are interdependent. One cannot exist without the other.

From the Sages

If one studies Torah during the night, the Almighty shows him special compassion during the day (Chagigah 12b).

The Rabbi of Zidochow was a child prodigy. One time one of the older scholars asked him how he would reconcile the above quote of the Talmud with the stark fact that so many fine scholars who studied Torah all night long nevertheless exist in abject poverty. Where is the special Divine compassion?

The child promptly answered, "Even though one lives in abject poverty, he continues to study every night, in spite of his day having been so difficult. That in itself is the special compassion, that you are given the strength and stamina to persist in doing that which you believe to be right."

Why a person's living circumstances are often so hard is beyond our human understanding. That we are able to survive and go on with life even in the face of adversity, that is a special Divine gift.

NOTES

_____
_____
_____
_____
_____
_____
_____
_____
_____

... בְּכָל עֵת יִהְיוּ בְגָדֶיךָ לְבָנִים ... *From*
Almighty G-d of all spirits, Master of all *our*
worlds, give me strength to serve You, to *Prayers*
revere You, and to study Your Torah, so
that I may fulfill what is written in the
Scriptures, "At all times shall your garments be white, and there be no dearth of
oil on your head" *(Ecclesiastes 9:8).* And may
I be a suitable vessel to contain the spirit
that You have instilled in me *(prayer in
Shaarei Tzion).*

June 27, 1990
June 16, 1991
July 5, 1992
June 23, 1993
June 13, 1994
July 2, 1995
June 21, 1996

The Rabbi of Kotzk explained the above Scriptural quote
as follows. If a person were wearing white garments and
carrying a container of oil on his head, he would take great
caution to measure each step carefully, because an
ever-so-slight deviation would cause the oil to spill and stain
his garments.

That is the sense of responsibility whereby we must live.
We value freedom so greatly that we may lose sight of the
fact that while we are indeed free to choose, we are held
accountable for whatever we do. Freedom to act does not
mean the right to do whatever one pleases.

Accountability for one's actions is an essential for
spirituality. One of the meanings of spirituality is the
attainment of mastery over one's self. The interpretation of
the Rabbi of Kotzk provides us with a good model. Think of
yourself as dressed in white, carrying a container of oil on
your head. Let all your actions be as carefully considered as
your walking would be under such circumstances.

Thus shall you bless the children of Israel *(Numbers
6:23).* **This means, by raising of your hands** *(Sotah 35a).*

*From
the Sages*

A poor man asked a certain *tzaddik* for help in raising a
dowry for his daughter. "I will grant you the rewards of
various *mitzvos* that I have done," said the *tzaddik.*

The man related this to another *tzaddik* who reprimanded
the first one. "When a person comes to you for help with a
pressing need for funds, blessings alone are insufficient.
Give him tangible help. Go to your friends who are people
of means and gather the money to relieve the person's
plight."

The words of the Priestly Blessing are indeed very
precious. But the Talmud reminds us that verbal blessings
may not be enough. We must lift our hands and provide
tangible assistance as well as good wishes.

NOTES

_____
_____
_____
_____
_____
_____
_____
_____
_____

June 28, 1990
June 17, 1991
July 6, 1992
June 24, 1993
June 14, 1994
July 3, 1995
June 22, 1996

From our Prayers

יְהִי רָצוֹן שֶׁתְּהֵא עוֹלָה כַּוָּנוֹת אָמֵן שֶׁלִי . . .

Master of the universe! You know that I am but a mortal, and that I cannot achieve the requisite kavanah (concentration and meditation). When I respond, "Amen," please accept my meager "Amen" as though it were with the full kavanah of those who are more learned and pious than I *(Or Tzaddikim)*.

The Talmud accords great importance to responding "Amen" upon hearing the praise of G-d. Indeed, the one who responds "Amen" has a greater *mitzvah* than the one who actually recites the blessing.

The word "Amen" is an affirmation of what has been said. The response "Amen" thus means, "I, too, affirm the truth of what has been said."

Even in the service of G-d, we are not immune to interference of self-interests. It is possible that a person may wish to have the distinction of being the most pious. Sincere service of G-d exists when we rejoice in the glorification of G-d, even though it comes about through others rather than ourselves.

As commendable as the Divine service is, we should not try to outdo one another as when we are motivated by our own aggrandizement. Hence, when one simply answers "Amen," and joyfully affirms the praise of G-d that he has heard from another person, this constitutes the highest level of Divine service.

From the Scriptures

For there is no action, no account, no knowledge, and no wisdom in Gehinnom *(Ecclesiastes 9:10).*

NOTES

It does not take great wisdom or effort to bring oneself down to the depths. However, it takes a great deal of effort, calculation, knowledge, and wisdom to keep oneself out of the depths.

The Rabbi of Rizhin was once asked for a rule-of-thumb to guide one through life. He answered, "How does a tightrope walker manage to maintain his balance? When he feels himself pulled towards one side, he leans toward the other side."

Your natural inclinations are the forces you must overcome. As a general rule, when you feel yourself drawn to do something, lean toward the other side, even if you overcompensate a bit. That way, you are likely to be safe.

From our Prayers

... שֶׁתַּרְגִּילֵנוּ בְּתוֹרָתֶךָ ... הַמַּעֲבִיר שֵׁנָה ...

He Who removes sleep from my eyes and slumber from my eyelids. And may it be Your will to make us familiar with Your teachings and to cause us to adhere to Your commandments (daily morning service).

June 29, 1990
June 18, 1991
July 7, 1992
June 25, 1993
June 15, 1994
July 4, 1995
June 23, 1996

This, the last of the series of blessings on arising, would appear to be an expression of gratitude for awakening from sleep. However, since it is preceded by many other blessings, some which explicitly refer to awakening, such as "Blessed are You, O G-d, Who opens the eyes of the blind," it is obvious that this is not the blessing for awakening.

We know too well that it is possible for a person's eyes to be physically open, looking at the world of reality, and yet misperceiving it as though one were still asleep, with all the distortions that can occur in dreams. Even our colloquial expression of "having a rude awakening" when reality finally jolts one out of the world of make-believe indicates our propensity to a kind of "sleepwalking" or dream state while awake.

How can we avoid the pitfall of the dream-like distortion of reality? By being familiar with Torah teachings and adhering to the Divine commandments. True Torah observance, with its emphasis on character development and trust in G-d, can remove the "sleep" from our open eyes.

From the Scriptures

Every man's holy things shall be his own. Only that which a man gives to the priest belongs to him (Numbers 5:10).

Many commentaries have interpreted this verse to mean that only that which you give away truly belongs to you.

History has amply demonstrated that people do not have absolute title to their possessions. Whether through war, economic upheaval, confiscation, or plundering, many wealthy people have become impoverished. However, that which they have given to charity and to worthy causes in their day of affluence can never be taken from them.

When I became involved in the treatment of alcoholics, I heard people say that if you want to keep your sobriety, you must respond when others need help to become sober. The maxim is, "You only get to keep sobriety if you give it away."

This maxim applies not only to sobriety, but also to knowledge, happiness, and wealth.

Greed and miserliness blind us to the truth and prevent us from gaining the irrevocable and undisputed ownership of anything that we have, if only we give it away.

NOTES

_____
_____
_____
_____
_____
_____
_____
_____
_____

June 30, 1990
June 19, 1991
July 8, 1992
June 26, 1993
June 16, 1994
July 5, 1995
June 24, 1996

From our Prayers

אִישׁ תִּשְׁבִּי תַּצִּילֵנוּ מִפִּי אֲרָיוֹת . . .

Elijah the Tishbi, may he rescue us from the lions' mouth. May he herald good news for us. May he gladden children together with parents on the departure of the Shabbos *(Zemiros for the close of Shabbos)*.

In modern times, various social trends and forces have brought about rifts within the family. Instead of the family being a functioning unit, the emphasis on everyone "doing his own thing" has led to unprecedented gaps between children and parents. Even the traditionally closely knit Jewish family has not been spared.

Some social psychologists have fanned the fires of divisiveness by implying that family cohesiveness stifles the individual's initiative and impedes self-fulfillment. They fail to realize that the individual is not a "self" any more than any single organ of the body is a "self." The heart, lungs, kidney, liver and all other organs are dependent on one another, and only together, as a unit, can they function. Similarly, the functioning individual is not the "self," or to put it another way, the "self" is the family unit.

An observant family, at least on the *Shabbos*, has all family members together at the *Shabbos* table. We must pray hard to maintain this family cohesiveness when *Shabbos* departs and we are thrust into the midst of modern life, whose forces tend to pull children and parents away from one another.

From the Sages

It is impossible for any reasonable person to conclude that the purpose of man's creation is to fulfill himself in this earthly world *(Path of the Just, Chapter 1)*.

Anyone seeing a child dressed in a coat whose sleeves are far too long and which drags on the floor behind him will conclude that the child has put on his father's clothes. They are obviously too large to have been designed for the child.

Similarly, says the Steipler Gaon, when one sees the enormity of man's mental capacity, and his ability to grasp spiritual concepts, it is absurd to think these were created simply to enhance man's earthly existence. Adaptation to mundane living is served much better by the instinctual capacities of lower forms of life than by the far-reaching intellect of man.

That there is something far greater than man can thus be observed from our analysis of man's composition. "And from my flesh, I can see G-d" *(Job 19:26)*.

NOTES

_____
_____
_____
_____
_____
_____
_____
_____

מִזְמוֹר שִׁיר חֲנֻכַּת הַבַּיִת לְדָוִד . . . *From*

A song of dedication of the house, to *our*
David . . . O G-d . . . You kept me alive *Prayers*
(Psalms 30:1-4, daily morning service).

תמוז

July 1, 1990
June 20, 1991
July 9, 1992
June 27, 1993
June 17, 1994
July 6, 1995
June 25, 1996

This psalm is puzzling. Its opening line refers to the dedication of the Temple, built not by David, but by his son, Solomon, after David's death. Furthermore, the psalm refers to gratitude for being cured of a serious illness, rather than consecration of the temple. Also, why was this psalm chosen by the Sages as the opening prayer of the daily service?

When the prophet told David that not he but his son Solomon would build the Temple, David began to plan and store materials for the Temple. Then David fell seriously ill and feared that he would not live to transmit his ideas to Solomon. When he recovered and was able to do so, he was grateful not merely for his physical recovery, but because he was able to help bring about the reality of the holy Temple.

To David, the Temple was now a *fait accompli*. In his imagination, he saw the Temple and all its splendor, with the services of the priests, the songs of the Levites, and the gathering of Jews from all corners of the world.

David teaches us how to enjoy the future. When we aspire to do the Divine will, we may justly take pleasure in things even before they become reality. David also teaches us that our personal recoveries are not only personal triumphs, but renewed opportunities to serve G-d.

It is clear now why the Sages chose this psalm as the opening prayer of the daily service. Its message of hope, joy, and devotion to G-d is unparalleled.

And it was when the priests exited from the holy temple, the Divine cloud filled the building, and the priests could not perform the service. Then Solomon said, "G-d said His presence would be in the dark cloud" *(I Kings 8:10-12).*

From the Scriptures

NOTES

Rabbi Meir Shapiro interprets these words as a prophecy.

Solomon foresaw that one day the Temple would go up in flames and the priests would be driven from it. In reference to those dark days, Solomon said, "G-d's presence will be felt even in the darkness of exile and oppression."

Judea's period of glory was short lived. But the greatness of Judaism and the beauty of the Divine teachings are transmitted and perpetuated through thousands of years of exile. The Divine presence never left us, and has sustained us through inquisitions, pogroms, and the holocaust.

G-d said that His presence would be felt in the darkness.

July 2, 1990
June 21, 1991
July 10, 1992
June 28, 1993
June 18, 1994
July 7, 1995
June 26, 1996

From our Prayers

כִּי לֹא תַחְפֹּץ זֶבַח וְאֶתֵּנָה עוֹלָה לֹא תִרְצֶה . . .

For You do not demand that I bring sacrifices, and You do not desire burnt offerings. The proper offering to G-d is the broken spirit of a contrite heart, which You, O G-d, will never reject *(Psalms 51:18-19)*.

Temple offerings were not an end in themselves, but only a means to arouse contrition in a penitent person.

When the Psalmist talks of the desirability of a broken spirit, he refers to the spirit of arrogance and defiance that lead man to place his own will above G-d's, and consider his own knowledge and wisdom as superior to the Torah. It is this spirit of vanity that must be broken, for contrition can occur only with humility.

Just as vanity is the root of all sin, humility is the root of all virtue. Indeed, the Talmud states that a person who brought an offering to the Temple had the merit of only that particular offering. However, one with a contrite heart had the merits of countless offerings *(Sotah 5b)*.

Our greatest offering is to humble ourselves before G-d.

From the Sages

The vestment of the jeweled breastplate was given to Aaron as a reward for his rejoicing when Moses returned to Egypt *(Shabbos 139a).*

Aaron was three years older than Moses, and was the more fluent of the two. Yet when Moses was commissioned by G-d to become the leader of the Jewish people, there was not a trace of envy in Aaron's heart. The Torah testifies that Aaron was genuinely glad for Moses' assignment of greatness.

It is no small feat to genuinely rejoice in another person's success. Many people have, at the very least, a tinge of envy, and sometimes far more than that.

One of the character traits the Talmud praises is called "a beneficent eye" *(Ethics of the Fathers 2:13).* This is cited as one of the outstanding features of the patriarch Abraham's character. "A beneficent eye" means taking pleasure in another person's good fortune, based on the profound faith that whatever is destined to be mine will be mine. No one can encroach on what was preordained for me.

A beneficent eye also indicates a true sense of kinship and love for another person, and is not only commendable as an interpersonal trait, but also gives one a degree of serenity that is otherwise unattainable.

NOTES

_____
_____
_____
_____
_____
_____
_____
_____
_____
_____

... בְּרָכוֹת וְהוֹדָאוֹת לְשִׁמְךָ הַגָּדוֹל ... *From our Prayers*

We gratefully avow to You, Who are our G-d and G-d of our fathers, our Creator ... blessings and thanks to Your great and holy name for keeping us alive and preserving us *(prayer during the reader's repetition of the Amidah).*

The repetition of the *Amidah* by the reader was instituted as a proxy for those people who were unable to recite the prayers. The reader thus served as their representative or spokesperson.

All one's requests for personal needs could be delivered by a spokesperson, but expression of gratitude had to be done personally. Hence, even illiterate members of the congregation had to learn and join in with a prayer of gratitude.

There is so much we can learn from our prayers! Not only is it important for a person to feel and express gratitude, but it must also be done personally, and not through an agent.

Many people find it easier to send "thank you" notes than to call a person and say "thank you" directly. As charming as a note can be, it still lacks the flavor of a direct and personal contact. Why should we allow the expression of our gratitude to be less personal when it can be more personal?

The next time you wish to thank someone, do it simply and directly.

July 3, 1990
June 22, 1991
July 11, 1992
June 29, 1993
June 19, 1994
July 8, 1995
June 27, 1996

A lazy person hides his hand in the dish, without ever returning it to his mouth *(Proverbs 19:24).*

From the Scriptures

The commentaries interpret this verse as referring to a behavior that must be as old as mankind itself: beginning something and abandoning it before bringing it to its conclusion.

Whether it be a *mitzvah* or a secular act, we often are seized by enthusiasm to begin something, only to abandon it midway. Sometimes it is because the thrill of the novelty wears off, and at other times because one may be afraid of bearing the responsibility that accompanies a completed project.

We often bite off more than we can chew, and the enormity of an undertaking may cause us to abandon it. We should avoid getting carried away by unrealistic enthusiasm, and plan carefully and realistically what we feel we can actually accomplish.

NOTES

_____
_____
_____
_____
_____
_____
_____
_____
_____
_____

July 4, 1990
June 23, 1991
July 12, 1992
June 30, 1993
June 20, 1994
July 9, 1995
June 28, 1996

From our Prayers

וַיְדַבֵּר אֵלַי זֶה הַשֻּׁלְחָן אֲשֶׁר לִפְנֵי ה' . . .

And He said to me, "This is the table before G-d" (Ezekiel 41:22). I am hereby prepared to fulfill the mitzvah of grace after meals, as it is written, "and you shall eat and be satisfied and give thanks to G-d" (Grace after Meals).

The first verse cited is from the plan of the holy Temple, and the "table" referred to is the Altar of Divine service.

The Sages tell us that a person's table can be the equivalent of an altar. If one shares his food with the hungry, and if one eats in order to sustain life and health so that one may fulfill the Divine will, and if one remembers to give thanks to G-d for what he has been given, then the table is indeed an altar, for one has used it in the fulfillment of the Divine will.

However, if one eats only in self-indulgence, does not share with others, and is not grateful to G-d, then the table is nothing but a feeding trough, for one has not elevated his eating above that of the animal level.

It is not etiquette that makes a person's eating refined. A daintily set table can be a feeding trough, and a very simple table can be an altar.

From the Sages

Torah is the nutrient of the soul (Tanya, chapter 4).

Medical science tells us that the body requires certain nutrients, referred to as essential vitamins and minerals, without which it cannot maintain a healthy function.

If one is deficient in, say, vitamin C, he will develop a deficiency disease which cannot be treated with large doses of vitamin A, B, or D. Only providing the specific vitamin C will satisfy the body's need.

The neshamah requires Torah as its specific nutrient. Lack of Torah will result in a state of discontent. Attempting to relieve this discontent by accumulating wealth, by indulgence in food, drink and other physical pleasures is futile. Only the specific nutrient of Torah will satisfy the needs of the neshamah.

Is it not strange that animals do not have diseases of excesses? Alcoholism, drug addiction, and eating disorders are uniquely human diseases. This is because animals gratify their physical desires with appropriate objects and reach a point of satiety. It is when humans are unaware that they are lacking in spirituality, and they try to gratify their spiritual cravings by indulgence in physical pleasures, that diseases of excesses result.

NOTES

_____
_____
_____
_____
_____
_____
_____
_____
_____

שֶׁעָשָׂה לִי נֵס בְּמָקוֹם הַזֶּה . . . *From*
Blessed are You, King of the universe, *our*
Who has performed a miracle for me at *Prayers*
this place *(blessing recited at the site of a personal miracle).*

July 5, 1990
June 24, 1991
July 13, 1992
July 1, 1993
June 21, 1994
July 10, 1995
June 29, 1996

When a person escapes from a precarious situation, he is required to offer thanks to G-d. Any time he returns to the site of his escape from danger, he is supposed to recall the Divine grace. This is not only a personal obligation, but one which carries over to one's descendants, who are required to offer thanks to G-d, "Who performed a miracle for my father at this place."

Reciting these blessings is not only the proper thing to do in acknowledgment of G-d's kindness to us, but it should also make us aware of G-d's constant vigilance over us. There are countless miracles that occur to us, but we are unaware of their miraculous character because they seem to us to be natural phenomena.

The fact that we are preserved by miracles should reinforce our sense of purpose and mission. G-d does not perform miracles in vain. We are being sustained because G-d has a purpose for us.

Already today, G-d has performed miracles for me. What is it that He expects of me today?

Be rather a tail among lions, than a head among foxes *(Ethics of the Fathers 4:20).*

From the Sages

People who are bothered by feelings of inferiority and inadequacy may tend to enhance their self-esteem by associating with people who are inferior to them. They can then consider themselves to be superior to these people, and may even achieve a position of leadership among them.

The Talmud cautions us against this. It is a spurious attempt to obtain self-esteem this way. We do not grow by associating with inferiors. Quite the contrary, we are apt to deteriorate to their levels. Such deterioration will only aggravate our feelings of unworthiness, and lead us to more desperate drives to support our low self-esteem, thus resulting in a vicious cycle of deterioration.

"Be a tail among lions." Associate with those who are clearly superior to you. Emulate them and learn from them. You will thereby grow in stature, and as you do so, you will constantly be looking for other superior people to emulate. This will become a self-reinforcing cycle, but one of personality growth rather than personality deterioration.

NOTES

_____
_____
_____
_____
_____
_____
_____

TAMMUZ

תמוז

July 6, 1990
June 25, 1991
July 14, 1992
July 2, 1993
June 22, 1994
July 11, 1995
June 30, 1996

From our Prayers

. . . אֲדוֹן הַנִּפְלָאוֹת . . . הַבּוֹחֵר בְּשִׁירֵי זִמְרָה

Blessed are You, O G-d and King, great in hymns of praise, G-d of thanksgiving, Master of wonders . . . Who takes pleasure in songs of praise *(daily morning service)*.

Music has always occupied an important place in Jewish liturgy. The harp of David, with which he accompanied his beautiful psalms, used to hang above his head, and he would be aroused to worship when the midnight breeze strummed a melody in its strings. In the Temple, the Levites underwent unparalleled training to participate in the choir, and the music of the Temple was legendary in its beauty.

Music reaches a level of feeling that words cannot reach. There are emotions of joy and exaltation as well as feelings of longing and pining that can be expressed only through music.

Music also has a binding and unifying function, both in time and space. Jews the world over may share in the same refrain, and the somber melodies of *Kol Nidrei* span the centuries and unite the contemporary Jew with the victims of the Inquisition who composed the solemn chant.

No wonder G-d takes pleasure in songs of praise. They bring His children closer to Him and to one another.

From the Scriptures

And you shall love your G-d *(Deuteronomy 6:5)*. **And you shall love your fellow man like yourself** *(Leviticus 19:18)*.

One of the obstacles to love of another person is our perception of his defects, particularly those behaviors that may affect us adversely.

There are two things we should bear in mind when judging the behavior of another person. Firstly, even if his behavior is defective, why are we so lenient in relation to our own defects and so harsh with others? We all have our imperfections and moments of weakness, yet we tend to justify these, or if we recognize our mistakes, we may forgive ourselves and resolve not to repeat them again. Why do we not accord others similar consideration?

Secondly, we love G-d even though we have experienced adversity, and even if our prayers to Him were not answered. We should learn from this that love for another must not always be predicated on his doing what we like.

If we combine our attitude toward ourselves with our attitude toward G-d, we can also develop love for another person.

NOTES

_____
_____
_____
_____
_____
_____
_____
_____
_____

... אַהֲבַת עוֹלָם בֵּית יִשְׂרָאֵל עַמְּךָ אָהָבְתָ *From our Prayers*

With eternal love You have loved Your people, the house of Israel. You have taught us Torah and mitzvos, laws and judgments *(daily evening prayer)*.

July 7, 1990
June 26, 1991
July 15, 1992
July 3, 1993
June 23, 1994
July 12, 1995
July 1, 1996

A parent or grandparent who wishes to indulge an infant will often buy him a little toy. The child may squeal with glee and happiness, but the joy with the toy is apt to be very transient. The child often loses interest in the toy within a few days. On the other hand, if the parent or grandparent invests money in a fund which will continue to grow over the years, so that when the child needs an education he is well provided for, the child has a lasting gift.

In the latter case the infant has no appreciation of what was done for him. The wise parent and grandparent knows that only after many years will the child be able to appreciate the gift.

G-d knows how great are the rewards for *mitzvos*. To give us earthly goods, which are so transient and are ultimately limited by a person's brief sojourn on earth, would be grossly unjust. Of what value can a mundane gift have when compared to something that is eternal?

G-d loves us with true love, and therefore provides us with just rewards in an existence that is infinite.

If not for My covenant of day and night, I would not have made the rules of heaven and earth *(Jeremiah 33:25).*

From the Scriptures

The "covenant of day and night," says the Talmud, refers to the Torah of which it is said, "And you shall think of Torah day and night" *(Joshua 1:8).*

The rules of Torah are as immutable as the laws of nature. It is a law of nature that fire burns. If one puts his hand into a flame and sustains a burn, it is not that he is "punished" for putting his hand into the flame. Rather he suffered the natural consequences of his act.

The laws of Torah are similar to the laws of nature. If one suffers harmful consequences as a result of violating the laws of Torah, it is not that G-d punishes him in His wrath, any more than G-d punishes the person who puts his hand in fire.

"It is the wickedness itself that kills an evil person" *(Psalms 34:22).* Violation of righteousness has its own harmful consequences. We would do well to observe the teachings of Torah, even if only for the purely selfish motivation of survival.

NOTES

_____

_____

_____

_____

_____

_____

_____

TAMMUZ

תמוז

July 8, 1990
June 27, 1991
July 16, 1992
July 4, 1993
June 24, 1994
July 13, 1995
July 2, 1996

From our Prayers

... הַמֵּנִיחַ לְעַמּוֹ בְּיוֹם שַׁבַּת קָדְשׁוֹ ...

The Shield of our Fathers ... Who gives rest to His people on His holy Shabbos day because He has found them worthy of His favor to grant rest ... to the people which draws blissful delight from this memorial to the work of creation *(Friday night service).*

This prayer is an abridged version of the Friday night *Amidah,* and is repeated by the reader.

During the weekdays, the reader does not repeat the *Amidah* of the evening prayer. The Friday night repetition was instituted to extend the services so that any latecomers will have an opportunity to complete their prayer and not be left alone in the synagogue. During weekdays, this function is accomplished by an additional extended prayer (Blessed is G-d unto eternity, Amen, Amen).

This is a beautiful example of how prayer should draw people to one another. The Talmud states that if two people enter a synagogue together, the one who finished praying first must wait for his comrade, lest his prayer be rejected.

Devotion to G-d without *"menschlichkeit"* or the decency and consideration for other people is of little value.

From the Scriptures

And G-d said to Moses, "Hew for yourself (Psal lecha) two tablets of stone" *(Exodus 34:1).*

Do not make for yourself a hewn image (lecha pesel) *(Exodus 20:4).*

The Rabbi of Gur called attention to the use of the same word — *pesel* or *psal* — referring to something hewn, in such polar opposite contexts, one relating to idolatry, while the other relates to the formation of the tablets for the ten commandments.

He explained that the same term can refer to two opposites, but the key to the meaning depends on where the word *lecha* (yourself) appears. If the word *lecha* is placed first, or in other words, when you give primacy to the self, making gratification of your own needs the goal of your life, then your behavior is idolatrous. Idolatry is nothing other than manipulating a godhead to gratify one's desires.

If the word *lecha* is placed last, or in other words, if one gives little importance to the gratification of one's desires, then one is engaged in the fulfillment of the Divine will, and in bringing the spirituality of the ten commandments into this earthly world.

NOTES

_____
_____
_____
_____
_____
_____
_____
_____
_____
_____

From כִּי אַתָּה שׁוֹמֵעַ תְּפִלַּת כָּל פֶּה . . .
For You mercifully hear the prayers of *our*
every mouth ... Blessed are You, O *Prayers*
G-d, Who hears prayers (*daily Amidah*).

July 9, 1990
June 28, 1991
July 17, 1992
July 5, 1993
June 25, 1994
July 14, 1995
July 3, 1996

One of the Chassidic masters commented, "G-d hears all prayers, even if the words only emanate from the mouth and not from the heart."

What a strange notion! Does the prophet not castigate those who worship G-d only with their lips, without involvement of their hearts (*Isaiah 29:13*)? What kind of devotion is it if the prayer does not emanate from the very depths of one's being?

What the rabbi meant was if one thinks about the quality of one's prayer and realizes, "I have only spoken the words with my lips, but my heart was not in it," and recognizes that his prayer was lacking devotion, and consequently resolves to henceforth pray with more fervor, that is meritorious. The virtue of this resolution to improve the quality of one's prayer merits the prayer being answered.

On the other hand, if one thinks, "How profoundly I prayed with intense devotion today!" and prides himself in it, then his prayer diminishes in value.

Prayer should stimulate us to come closer to G-d. This can be accomplished only when we realize how far from Him we are, because only then will we put forth the requisite effort to draw closer.

Abundant waters cannot extinguish the love (for G-d), and rivers cannot sweep it away. Even if a person were to give all his wealth to acquire this love, people would mock him (*Song of Songs 8:7*).

From the Scriptures

The Maggid of Dubno was critical of those who built ornate synagogues but were derelict in regular attendance. He gave the following parable:

A young boy showed his friends a shiny, new wallet he had bought for two dollars. An envious boy tried to buy the identical wallet for himself. However, he had only one dollar. He pleaded with the proprietor to sell him the wallet for less.

"Isn't that rather foolish of you?" the proprietor asked. "If you spend all your money on the wallet, then of what use is the wallet to you, since you have nothing to put in it?"

That is what Solomon means when he says that if a person spends all that he has for the love of G-d, people will mock him. If you show your love for G-d by spending on a lavish structure but not putting anything into it in terms of frequent worship, of what good is it?

NOTES

_____
_____
_____
_____
_____
_____
_____
_____

TAMMUZ

תמוז

**Fast of
Shivah Asar
B'Tammuz**
*[When 17 Tammuz
falls on the
Sabbath the fast is
observed on Sunday.]*

July 10, 1990
June 29, 1991
July 18, 1992
July 6, 1993
June 26, 1994
July 15, 1995
July 4, 1996

*From
the Sages*

NOTES

_____
_____
_____
_____
_____
_____
_____
_____
_____
_____

. . . כִּי בְּשִׁבְעָה עָשָׂר בְּתַמּוּז נִשְׁתַּבְּרוּ הַלּוּחוֹת

*From
our
Prayers*
We have come before You, Creator of all spirits. Because of our sins we are heavy with sighs. Evil decrees abound, and our wailings are many, for on the seventeenth day of Tammuz the tablets (of the ten commandments) were broken *(Selichos)*.

The Talmud and the ethical works cite the worship of the golden calf *(Exodus 32:1-6)* as the major transgression of the Israelites.

Although this sin occurred on the seventeenth day of Tammuz, it is not the sin itself which is cited as the cause for our sufferings, but rather Moses' reaction to the sin, his breaking the tablets of the law.

The Torah states that the first tablets given to Moses were engraved by G-d himself. "The tablets were the work of G-d, and the inscription was the Divine inscription" *(Exodus 32:16)*. The inscription on the tablets was miraculous, because it penetrated the stone and could be read from either side.

The original tablets were directed by Divine revelation. Man could look at the tablets and have a clear understanding of what the Divine will was. Regardless of the vantage point, the Divine message was evident, without confusion, and without the possibility of distortion.

When we lost the first tablets, we lost this clarity of perception of the Divine will. Our struggle for spirituality is now so much more difficult. We therefore grieve for the irreparable loss of the manifest Divine will.

On the seventeenth day of Tammuz, Menashe, King of Judah, erected an idol in the Sanctuary *(Taanis 26b).*

No other king in Israel is so thoroughly condemned as Menashe. Bringing an idol into the Sanctuary was the epitome of defiance of G-d.

In later years, after he was taken captive to Assyria, Menashe repented. The Talmud states that the angels pleaded with G-d not to grant Menashe forgiveness because his sin was so grave. The Divine response was, "If I deny anyone forgiveness, those who would repent may think that their sins, too, are grave, and they will be discouraged from *teshuvah* (repentance)."

It is therefore a Divine dictum, "Nothing stands in the way of sincere *teshuvah*."

From our Prayers

פְּזַרְנוּ בְּלִי מְצוֹא רְוָחָה . . . *From*

We have been scattered without finding *our* respite, therefore our anguish has been *Prayers* great. O Mighty One, see how our souls have been humbled, and convert the seventeenth day of Tammuz to joy and gladness *(Selichos)*.

July 11, 1990
June 30, 1991
July 19, 1992
July 7, 1993
June 27, 1994
July 16, 1995
July 5, 1996

Many commentaries have asked why it is that our prayers for the Redemption have gone unanswered for so many centuries. The answer most frequently given is that our prayers for redemption are essentially motivated by a desire for freedom from oppression, for political freedom, and for relief from our physical distress.

Physical comfort and political freedom are not, however, the primary goals of Redemption. The latter will usher in an era of great spirituality, when man will be closer to G-d.

If we fail to pray for spiritual redemption, it is because we are unaware of the extent of our spiritual impoverishment. One does not pray for something he does not feel he needs.

"O Mighty One, see how our *souls* have been humbled." If we appreciate that our prime concern should not be the deprivation of our bodies, but the lack of spiritual achievement of the soul, and we pray sincerely for our spiritual redemption, then we can anticipate that we will merit redemption, and that the three weeks of mourning will be converted to a period of jubilation.

From the Sages

Every generation in whose time the Sanctuary was not rebuilt is as guilty as the generation in whose time it was destroyed *(Jerusalem Talmud, Yoma 1:1)*.

Every year from the seventeenth day of Tammuz through the ninth day of Av we observe a period of mourning for the Sanctuary which was destroyed thousands of years ago. Granted that this was indeed a calamity at the time, why do we perpetually mourn an ancient event?

The answer is that we are not mourning an event of the past. We grieve for the loss of the Divine presence and the spiritual illumination that could have been ours this very day. The Holy of Holies that was destroyed two thousand years ago is not the reason for our mourning. We grieve for the Holy of Holies that could be built today, but is still absent.

Simple sadness and grief accomplish nothing. This period of the Jewish calendar should remind us that we can achieve spirituality today, and that if we fail to do so, it is the result of our own dereliction.

NOTES

TAMMUZ

תמוז

July 12, 1990
July 1, 1991
July 20, 1992
July 8, 1993
June 28, 1994
July 17, 1995
July 6, 1996

*From
our
Prayers*

בְּאַהֲבָה . . . וַתִּתֶּן לָנוּ
[שַׁבָּתוֹת לִמְנוּחָה וּ] מוֹעֲדִים לְשִׂמְחָה

And in Your love . . . You have given us Shabbosos for serenity and festivals for joy *(Amidah of the Festivals).*

What is the relevance of the Festival prayers to be quoted this time of the year?

Some commentaries note that the prayer does not refer to *Shabbosos of* serenity and Festivals *of* joy, but *for* serenity and *for* joy. In other words, *Shabbos* and the Festivals should provide us with a supply of serenity and joy upon which we can draw during the week and during the entire year.

If one travels through a desert, one takes along an adequate supply of food and water, because one knows that these are not available in the desert. Similarly, since we know that there are periods of the year which are not conducive to joy, we must store away joy on the festivals, and establish a reserve upon which we can draw all year.

A fuller understanding of the festivals would enable us to better withstand periods of stress, and an appropriate observance of the spirit as well as the technicalities of *Shabbos* would provide serenity for the entire week.

During this period of the three weeks of mourning, the messages of the redemption of Passover, the giving of the Torah of Shavuos, and the Divine protection of the clouds of glory of Succos should ameliorate our grief.

*From the
Scriptures*

Ask your father and he will relate it to you. Ask your elders and they will explain it to you *(Deuteronomy 32:7).*

In *Path of the Just,* Rabbi Moshe Chaim Luzatto compares the world to a complicated maze, where there is no indication which path leads to the goal. One may try a path which leads to a dead end, retrace his steps, and mark that path as one not to be tried again. In this manner, path after path can be eliminated until the correct path is found.

This is an exhausting method. We may not have enough time and energy to try until successful.

If, however, there are those who have successfully traversed the maze, and can direct us to the correct path so that we can avoid the costly trial and error method, we would be most foolish to reject their counsel and try on our own.

"Ask your elders and they will instruct you." Youth has enthusiasm and vigor, but should avail itself of the wisdom of experience.

NOTES

שִׁירוּ לָנוּ מִשִּׁיר צִיּוֹן אֵיךְ נָשִׁיר . . . *From*

Our captors asked of us to sing for them *our* the songs of Zion. How can we sing the *Prayers* songs of G-d on a foreign land? *(Psalms 137:3-4, recited before Grace after Meals).*

July 13, 1990
July 2, 1991
July 21, 1992
July 9, 1993
June 29, 1994
July 18, 1995
July 7, 1996

What is the relationship of a psalm that refers to mourning the fall of Zion to Grace after Meals?

The Talmud states that in the absence of the Altar of the Holy Temple, a person's table replaces the Altar *(Berachos 55a)*. That is to say, that when one eats with the intent that healthy nutrition will give one the strength to better fulfill the Divine will, and when one considers the needy and helps provide food for them, this accomplishes the same purpose as the service in the Sanctuary.

We recite the psalm referring to the destruction of Jerusalem to remind us that in the absence of our intensive source of spirituality, we must increase our efforts at achieving spirituality. Eating is a prime example of how the very same act can be either mundane or spiritual. If we indulge and seek only self-gratification, we do not exercise our unique human traits, for animals also eat to satisfy their appetites. Man can be above that. His eating can be goal directed toward enabling him to achieve his mission on earth, and eating can be a spiritual act.

Words that emanate from the heart enter into the *From* **heart of another** *(Midrash).* *the Sages*

Why is it that some people reject admonishment, even when it is given with the utmost sincerity?

The Maggid of Dubno explained with a parable. A village blacksmith had an apprentice whose job it was to fan the fire to increase the size of the flame. On a visit to a large city, the apprentice observed the local blacksmith using a bellows. He bought a bellows and brought it back to his master with great joy. "We now have a machine that produces a very large flame without anyone having to fan it!" he said. He then proceeded to pump the bellows, but to his dismay no fire was forthcoming.

NOTES

"I can't understand it," the apprentice said. "I saw with my own eyes that the bellows made a large flame."

"You fool," the blacksmith said. "The bellows produces a flame only when there is a spark. In absence of a spark, you can pump all day and no flame will appear."

Sincere admonishment is like a bellows. If a person has a spark of spirituality, it will enlarge it. But if a person is totally devoid of spirituality, even sincere admonishment will not affect him.

July 14, 1990
July 3, 1991
July 22, 1992
July 10, 1993
June 30, 1994
July 19, 1995
July 8, 1996

From our Prayers

הַקְשִׁיבָה לְקוֹל שַׁוְעִי מַלְכִּי וֵאלֹקָי . . .

Hear the voice of my prayer, O my King and my G-d, for it is to You that I pray *(Psalms 5:3).*

According to the Jerusalem Talmud, G-d says, "Let them not pray to the angel Michael or to Gabriel. Let them pray to Me, and I will answer them promptly" *(Berachos 9:1).*

Why, then, do so many of our prayers appear to go unanswered, even though we pray directly to G-d?

A person is indeed required to take certain actions, such as to work for a living or to avail himself of medical treatment when sick. But he should believe that it is G-d that provides for him, and that it is G-d that heals him. Man is required to "go through the motions," as it were, but the immediate source of his sustenance and healing is G-d.

Angels are not the only intermediaries whose help we are not permitted to seek. Man should relate directly to G-d for all his needs. If man thinks that it is his work that is earning for him, that he can control his fate and earn more money by more work, he is essentially trusting in an intermediary rather than in G-d.

Perhaps we pray *verbally* directly to G-d, but our actions too often consist of the use of various "intermediaries." A sincere trust and faith in G-d and G-d alone will indeed merit prompt reward.

From the Sages

Moses' expression of humility was even greater than that of Abraham, for Abraham said, "I am but dust," whereas Moses said, "What are we at all?" *(Chullin 89a).*

The ethical works are replete with the importance of self-effacement in the Divine presence. One who realizes that he stands in the presence of G-d should not even feel his own presence.

Self-consciousness is a symptom that something is not right. A healthy person is usually not aware of the existence of his ears, eyes, or throat. It is only when they are affected by some disease which produces pain that he becomes aware of their existence.

A spiritually healthy person is similarly not aware of his own existence. He does not think of himself. He is not self-conscious.

Self-consciousness occurs only when the self is somehow diseased. The sick self is constantly aware of its existence.

Self-effacement before G-d eliminates self-consciousness, and thus restores spiritual health.

NOTES

_____
_____
_____
_____
_____
_____
_____
_____
_____

Praise G-d, O my soul. I will praise G-d while I live. I will sing to G-d while I exist *(Psalms 146:1,2, daily morning service)*.

הַלְלוּיָהּ הַלְלִי נַפְשִׁי אֶת ה' . . . *From our Prayers*

When we feel alive and are pleased with the way our lives are progressing, prayer comes quite easily. It is not difficult to express gratitude when we feel we are productive and are appreciated.

There are unfortunately times when we are less than euphoric about life. Circumstances may be such that we find life to be burdensome, and we hardly consider ourselves to be living. At best, we can say that we exist. At such moments it is difficult to sing praises to G-d, because our logical thought sees no reason for being grateful.

Where logic ends, faith begins. We must be aware that unless there were a Divine purpose to our lives, we would not be here. We may have to seek out that purpose, but it is certainly there.

The Psalmist says, "I will praise G-d when I feel alive, and I will sing to Him even though all I feel is that I am merely existing." Our faith should carry us over the periods of distress and confusion.

July 15, 1990
July 4, 1991
July 23, 1992
July 11, 1993
July 1, 1994
July 20, 1995
July 9, 1996

My soul thirsts for You, my flesh pines for You, as one in a desolate land without water *(Psalms 63:2).*

From the Scriptures

Hunger and thirst are what make food tasty and water refreshing. If one is not hungry, even the most delicious food may not be tempting.

Spirituality is precious. If we meditate on the values of life, we can easily see the folly of indulgence in physical pleasures and earthly pursuits. Yet this intellectual understanding often does not motivate us, and we still are drawn to mundane preoccupations while our spirituality remains neglected.

The problem is that we are hungry and thirsty for food and drink, but our "appetite" for spirituality may be lacking.

What can one do if one lacks an appetite for spirituality? Well, what does one do if one lacks an appetite for food? One consults a doctor to find out what is wrong. That is what one must do when there is no hunger for spirituality. One should consult the appropriate "doctor" of spirituality, the wise and competent teachers of spirituality who can help. They do exist. We will find them if we look for them.

NOTES
_____
_____
_____
_____
_____
_____
_____
_____
_____
_____

July 16, 1990
July 5, 1991
July 24, 1992
July 12, 1993
July 2, 1994
July 21, 1995
July 10, 1996

From our Prayers

יְהִי רָצוֹן . . . וְלֹא אֶכָּשֵׁל בִּדְבַר הֲלָכָה
וְיִשְׂמְחוּ בִי חֲבֵרַי

O G-d, grant that I may not err in halachah causing my colleagues to **mock me** *(prayer of Rabbi Nechunia, Berachos 28b).*

The Talmud relates that when Rabbi Nechunia entered the study hall, he would recite the above prayer. The commentaries remark that his concern about making an error in judgment was not so much that he might come to a wrong conclusion, for that is only human and is tolerable. What Rabbi Nechunia feared was that his colleagues might mock him for his mistake, and that they would be held accountable for this. He would then, however indirectly, have been the cause for their transgression!

The Torah says, "do not put a stumbling block in the path of the blind" *(Leviticus 19:14),* which the Talmud interprets to mean that you should not cause another person to transgress.

The Torah holds us responsible not only for our own actions, but for the spiritual welfare of others. We must be cautious to avoid doing things that may result in the spiritual regression of other people.

From the Sages

Rabbi Mendel of Kotzk said, "My mission on earth is to recognize the void — inside and outside — and to fill it."

Many people would react by saying, "What an order! I can't go through with this! How can this be expected of any human being?"

Perhaps the reason some people avoid searching for their mission in life is precisely because the enormity of the challenge — to recognize the external and internal void and fill it — is so overwhelming that they defensively avoid its recognition.

It is clear, however, that what the Rabbi of Kotzk meant is that each person must do his or her share to fill the void. All that can be expected of us is to do what is within our capacity to do.

If the challenge appears too great, do not be discouraged. Our goal is spiritual growth, not spiritual perfection. Do all that you can, and G-d will assist you in achieving the remainder.

NOTES

_____
_____
_____
_____
_____
_____
_____
_____

יִרְאוּ אֶת ה' קְדֹשָׁיו כִּי אֵין מַחְסוֹר לִירֵאָיו . . . *From*

Venerate G-d, you His holy ones, for *our*
there is no deprivation for those who *Prayers*
revere Him. The mighty may want and go
hungry, but those who seek G-d will not
lack for any good *(Psalms 34:10-11, Shabbos
morning service, and Grace after Meals).*

July 17, 1990
July 6, 1991
July 25, 1992
July 13, 1993
July 3, 1994
July 22, 1995
July 11, 1996

How can one say that the pious are never deprived? We
so often see that some saintly people live in poverty,
whereas others prosper although they are not in the least
spiritual.

The Sages essentially answered the question when they
stated, "Who is a wealthy person? One who is satisfied with
what he has" *(Ethics of the Fathers 4:1).* The wise Solomon
says, "The sleep of the worker is pleasant, whether he eats
little or much, but satiety of the wealthy man does not
permit him to sleep" *(Ecclesiastes 5:11).* Of what value is
wealth if one lives in constant fear of losing it?

The truly pious may not be people of means, but they do
not feel deprived. They trust that G-d will provide them with
their needs, and if they lack something, they do not crave it.
They are certain that if it were to their advantage to have it,
G-d would provide it for them. They are not consumed by
the envy that so often destroys people of lesser faith.

The mighty may want and go hungry because they are
never satisfied, but those who seek G-d will not lack for any
good.

And you gird your loins, and speak to them all that
I instruct you. Do not fear them, lest you be
shattered before them *(Jeremiah 1:17).*

From the
Scriptures

There is nothing so destructive as fear and anxiety. The
Torah states that those that are afraid to go to war should
return home, lest they cause their comrades to lose
courage *(Deuteronomy 20:8).* Fear is not only self-perpetu-
ating, but is also contagious.

Many emotional disorders have their origin in fear and
anxiety. Many people who have become victims of
alcoholism or other chemical addictions have turned to
these substances to alleviate the distress of anxiety.

Firm, unfaltering faith in G-d is a powerful antidote
against anxiety. A helpless infant who feels cradled in the
powerful, protective arms of a loving parent knows no fear.

"Fortunate is he who trusts in G-d and places his security
with G-d" *(Jeremiah 17:7).*

NOTES
_____
_____
_____
_____
_____
_____
_____
_____

TAMMUT

תמוז

July 18, 1990
July 7, 1991
July 26, 1992
July 14, 1993
July 4, 1994
July 23, 1995
July 12, 1996

From our Prayers

זַכֵּנִי לַעֲסוֹק בְּמַשָּׂא וּמַתָּן בֶּאֱמוּנָה . . .

Master of the universe, have mercy upon us, and help us to be honest in our business affairs, that we do not utter any falsehood for whatever profit, and that we may live up to all the laws of the Torah, not to deceive anyone either in money or in words, but that we always be truthful *(prayer of Rabbi Nachman of Breslov).*

Since man has freedom of will to make moral decisions and choices, how can one ask G-d to intervene and prevent us from doing wrong?

There are two answers to this question. First, the fact that we were given the freedom does not mean that we have to keep it. Just as we have the right to use it, we also have the right to return it to G-d. When one turns his life over to the will of G-d, that is essentially what one is doing. A wise child, knowing that his parents are trustworthy and more knowledgeable, would choose to surrender his freedom of choice and be guided by his parents' dictates.

The second point is that even if we retain the freedom to make moral choices, it helps us to keep things in proper perspective if we pray, as Rabbi Nachman did, for Divine strength to be honest and truthful. This prayer increases our alertness to the deceptive lure of profit, and helps us bear in mind that there are powerful distorting forces in personal gain. Even if free will means that G-d will not act to keep us honest, asking Him to do so should strengthen our own resolve to do so.

From the Sages

To give a gift to an honorable person is really to receive something *(Kiddushin 5b).*

This passage from the Talmud is more than a moral value statement. The Talmud states that in a transaction wherein one must receive consideration for the contract to be legally binding, giving something can be equivalent to receiving.

A gift given with pure motivation — as an expression of appreciation or out of esteem for another person or because we wish to make a person happier — enhances the giver.

When we hold another person in high esteem, our self-esteem increases. When we degrade another person, we degrade all humanity, and our self-esteem lessens.

Whether a gift is a tangible gift, a considerate act, or even just a kind word, the giver benefits at least as much as the recipient, if not more.

NOTES

_____
_____
_____
_____
_____
_____
_____
_____
_____
_____

בָּרוּךְ ה' אֱלֹקֵי יִשְׂרָאֵל מִן הָעוֹלָם ... *From*

Blessed be G-d, the G-d of Israel, from *our*
this world to the coming world, and all *Prayers*
the nation responded, "Amen, give praise
to G-d" *(I Chronicles 16:36, daily morning service).*

TAMMUZ

26

תמוז

July 19, 1990
July 8, 1991
July 27, 1992
July 15, 1993
July 5, 1994
July 24, 1995
July 13, 1996

When the Rabbi of Lubavitch was arrested in Russia for violating the ban against promulgating Torah, the officer who took him prisoner at gunpoint remarked that he did not seem at all frightened when he aimed his gun at him.

The Rabbi remarked, "Fear of death occurs only when a person has only one world, but many gods. However, when the reverse is true, when one has only one G-d, and two worlds, death is not frightening."

As much as we wish to cling to life and are motivated by self-survival, the knowledge that this world is not our entire existence, and indeed, is only a preparatory stage for the afterlife in the eternal world, removes much of the fear of death.

The absence of this anxiety can allow us to function much more efficiently and with a greater degree of serenity. Belief in this earthly world as a "portico before the palace" (*Ethics of the Fathers 4:21*) not only gives meaning to our lives, but also removes much of the anxiety that can impair our functioning.

(The angel, in informing Samson's mother that she would have a son, said,) "Now you must be cautious. Do not drink wine or any intoxicating beverage, and do not eat anything unclean, for this lad shall be dedicated to G-d from the womb" *(Judges 13:4-5).*

From the Scriptures

If we wish our children to become spiritual people, at what point do we begin to train them in that direction?

The answer is in the quote from the Scriptures. Spiritual training begins in the womb.

From the scientific aspect, the facts are not all in. It has been established that maternal use of alcohol, even in small amounts, can impair fetal development. It is not clear yet whether there are other effects that parental behavior may have on the unborn child. However, it is certain that effective role-modeling and imprinting certainly occur very early in a child's life.

NOTES

If we wish our children to have spiritual values, we cannot expect this to come about solely by schooling, regardless of how carefully we choose where they learn. Parents must provide an example, and do so very early in a child's life, preferably even prior to his birth.

July 20, 1990
July 9, 1991
July 28, 1992
July 16, 1993
July 6, 1994
July 25, 1995
July 14, 1996

From ...
our
Prayers

אַתָּה אֶחָד וְשִׁמְךָ אֶחָד וּמִי כְּעַמְּךָ יִשְׂרָאֵל

You are One and Your name is One, and who is like Your nation Israel, one people in the land *(Shabbos afternoon Amidah).*

The *neshamah* (soul) is a part of G-d himself. G-d is uniquely One and indivisible.

Since we are all in possession of a Divine *neshamah*, we are in fact all one, indivisibly fused with each other and with G-d.

Why, then, is there so much divisiveness among us? Because whereas our souls unite us, our physical bodies separate us. We are distinct only in our physical beings.

To the degree that we emphasize our physical selves, to that degree we stress that which divides us. To the degree that we give priority to our *neshamah* and enhance our spiritual lives, to that degree we come closer to one another as well as to G-d.

During the work week we engage in those activities which pertain primarily to our physical selves. On *Shabbos* we have time for reflection and meditation. We can study, pray, and associate with friends in a more spiritual manner. After we enhance our spiritual lives through prayer and Torah study, we can then appreciate that through our spiritual lives we can indeed become one with G-d, and one with each other.

From the
Scriptures

Would that I had the wings of a dove, and could fly to a distant place and rest there *(Psalms 55:7-8).*

Everyone needs some time for solitude, for uninterrupted reflection.

People of great spirituality would spend many hours and even days away from the hectic tumult of urban life in undisturbed meditation, to be able to think without distraction.

But moments of solitude should be just that, brief periods of time for serious reflection. They must not become an escape from life nor a monastic existence. The Talmud says that a person should not retreat into isolation, but should remain in contact with others *(Kesubos 17a).*

Spirituality is enhanced when we take out time to think clearly, but we must then return from our solitude and apply the results of our thinking to everyday life.

NOTES

_____
_____
_____
_____
_____
_____
_____
_____

From our Prayers אָדָם בִּיקָר וְלֹא יָבִין נִמְשַׁל כַּבְּהֵמוֹת נִדְמוּ

The person who does not understand his own glory is likened to a brute animal *(Psalms 49:21, recited at the home of a mourner).*

July 21, 1990
July 10, 1991
July 29, 1992
July 17, 1993
July 7, 1994
July 26, 1995
July 15, 1996

One of the greatest tragedies is a life that has been lived in ignorance of one's potentials.

Imagine a person who believes himself to be destitute and who scrapes together or begs for a meager subsistence for his family, but who does not know that he is the sole legitimate heir of a distant relative who has willed him an immense fortune. The deprivation and suffering are so much more tragic because they are unnecessary. The family has the means to live in comfort and luxury, but since they are unaware of what they have, they suffer in poverty.

This is the tragedy of a person who does not maximize his potential because he is unaware of it.

"It is better to go to the house of mourning than to the house of celebration, for when a person's life comes to an end, people will search their own hearts" *(Ecclesiastes 7:2).*

A person who had great capacities may have been ignorant of them, and conducted his life as though he were of inferior mettle. We should take this to heart and learn.

And you shall write them (the selected verses of the Torah) on the doorposts of your homes and your gates (i.e., the *mezuzah*), in order that your days will be extended *(Deuteronomy 11:20-21).*

From the Scriptures

The Talmud states that observance of the *mitzvah* of *mezuzah* is rewarded with longevity.

The Jerusalem Talmud relates that Artaban, a wealthy Roman, sent Rabbi Yehudah the Prince a gift of a very precious diamond. Rabbi Yehudah reciprocated by sending him a *mezuzah*.

Artaban was astonished. "I sent you a precious diamond, and you send me a piece of parchment!"

Rabbi Yehudah replied, "The gift you sent me is one that I will have to guard. The gift I sent you is something that will guard and protect you."

Rabbi Yehudah's response has a broad application. We pursue acquisition of earthly possessions which we must care for and guard, but we often neglect pursuit of spiritual acquisitions, which protect us and safeguard our *menschlichkeit*.

Just a bit of careful, honest thinking will put things in proper perspective.

TAMMUZ

תמוז

Erev
Rosh Chodesh
[Eve of the
New Month]
July 22, 1990
July 11, 1991
July 30, 1992
July 18, 1993
July 8, 1994
July 27, 1995
July 16, 1996

*From
our
Prayers*

תַּמְשִׁילֵהוּ בְּמַעֲשֵׂי יָדֶךָ ...

You have given man dominion over Your handiwork ... over sheep and cattle and beasts of the field, over birds of the sky and fish of the sea *(Psalms 8:7-9).*

One of the most forceful exhortations in the Torah is that in *Deuteronomy 8:11-18,* where Moses cautions the Israelites that after they inherit the Promised Land, build great cities and prosper, they may think, "It is my strength and my might that has acquired all this fortune." Moses reminds them of the Divine deliverance from bondage, and of the many miracles that enabled their survival for forty years in the fierce wilderness. "Remember, it is G-d that gives you the capacity to gain wealth."

It is so easy for a person to forget that he is totally dependent upon G-d and to attribute his success to his own cunning and sagacity. Lack of awareness of one's dependence on G-d jeopardizes faith and trust, and may ultimately lead to a rejection of G-d.

Even in spiritual matters, we should be aware that only a Power greater than ourselves can save us from spiritual destruction. As the Talmud says, "If not for the assistance of G-d, man could never subdue his evil inclination" *(Kiddushin 30b).* We must make the utmost effort to overcome temptation because that is our responsibility, but without the help of G-d we could not possibly succeed.

*From the
Scriptures*

I passed a field of a lazy person, and it was all covered with thorns and leaves, and the stone fence was shattered ... A bit of sleep here, a bit of slumber there, a bit of lying with folded hands, and poverty comes marching *(Proverbs 24:30-34).*

In *Path of the Just* (chapters 6-9), Rabbi Moshe Chaim Luzatto shows how a lack of diligence can insidiously undermine a person. There seems to be no sin in just delaying things a bit, relaxing for the present, with every good intention of doing what one is obligated to do just a little bit later. However, since rest is the natural state of the body, and unless effort is exerted to overcome the inertia, lethargy will actually increase, because laziness feeds on itself.

Many centuries earlier, Hillel said, "And if not now, when?" *(Ethics of the Fathers 1:14).* The introduction to *Path of the Just* states: "The character traits required *for* Torah observance are every bit as important as the actual observance of the Torah's dictates."

NOTES

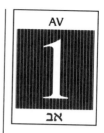

From our Prayers

חַדֵּשׁ עָלֵינוּ . . . לְטוֹבָה וְלִבְרָכָה לְשָׂשׂוֹן וּלְשִׂמְחָה לִישׁוּעָה וּלְנֶחָמָה

Inaugurate for us this month for good and for blessing, for joy and for gladness, for salvation and for consolation *(Mussaf service for Rosh Chodesh)*.

This prayer has special significance for this day. The mourning of the Three Weeks (17 Tammuz through 9 Av) increases in intensity on this, the first of the "Nine Days." There are various restrictions that minimize activities that generate joy during this month in which Jerusalem was twice overrun and both Temples were destroyed.

Judaism, however, is a lifestyle of joy and gladness, themes which pervade the Scriptures, the Talmud, and all the ethical works. When Judaism advocates mourning rituals, their function is to dissipate the paralysis of grief that results from the awareness of our enormous spiritual losses. As with the mourning rituals following a personal loss, the rituals for the nation's losses serve both to remind us of the magnitude of our losses and to help us find strength to rise above them and continue with the constructive achievements of life.

The Talmud says, "As the month of Av enters, we diminish with joy" *(Taanis 26b)*. One of the Chassidic masters commented, "One must learn how to diminish the grief of the period with the joy of the anticipated Redemption."

Rosh Chodesh
July 23, 1990
July 12, 1991
July 31, 1992
July 19, 1993
July 9, 1994
July 28, 1995
July 17, 1996

From the Sages

The prayer, "I thank You for restoring my soul to me," can be said promptly upon awakening, even before one has washed one's hands *(commentaries on the Siddur)*.

No other prayer is permitted to be said until a person is in a state of cleanliness. Why is this prayer an exception?

"Because," said Rabbi Yosef Yitzchak of Lubavitch, "one should know that gratitude is of supreme importance. The sense of gratitude for being alive and being able to do the Divine will is so vital, that the Sages waived the mandatory precondition of cleanliness that applies to other prayers.

"Furthermore, this symbolically conveys to us that regardless of how depraved (unclean) a person may consider himself to be, he is nevertheless held accountable to recognize the kindness bestowed upon him, and to express his gratitude."

NOTES

AV

אב

July 24, 1990
July 13, 1991
Aug. 1, 1992
July 20, 1993
July 10, 1994
July 29, 1995
July 18, 1996

From our Prayers

בּוֹנֵה יְרוּשָׁלַיִם ה' נִדְחֵי יִשְׂרָאֵל יְכַנֵּס . . .

G-d, the builder of Jerusalem, gathers the dispersed of Israel. He who is a Healer to the broken-hearted will relieve their sadness *(daily morning service, Psalms 147:2-3).*

Rabbi Bunim of Pshis'cha asked, "Is it not a virtue to be humble and broken-hearted, as the Psalmist says, 'G-d is close to the broken-hearted and the humble' *(Psalms 34:19)?* Why then should He heal the broken-hearted, and thereby remove their virtue?"

Rabbi Bunim answered, "There is a difference between being humble and broken-hearted as opposed to being sad. The Scriptural reference to "broken-hearted" is to a person's awareness that he has not yet done enough, and this brings about a sense of humility which stimulates him to greater achievement, to fulfill his mission on earth.

"But sometimes this awareness of how little one has achieved may spill over into sadness and dejection. These latter feelings are destructive, because they lead to despair and inactivity.

"G-d heals the broken-hearted by relieving their sadness and their feelings of hopelessness that may be generated by their dejection. With their dejection gone, the healthy humility will stimulate them to achievement."

From the Scriptures

I gave them silver in abundance and gold, which they used for idolatry *(Hoshea 2:10).*

Idolatry is a concept whereby man creates his own gods to serve him, rather than man being a servant to G-d. When man's interests are all self-serving, he is essentially idolatrous.

Rabbi Uri of Strelisk was intensely spiritual. Earthly things had no significance for him. His fierce devotion to G-d earned him the appellation, "The Fiery One," in Chassidic lore.

Rabbi Uri's followers were all poor. One time the Rabbi's wife asked him, "Why do you not pray to G-d on behalf of your devotees, that He bless them with greater earnings?"

The following morning after services, Rabbi Uri had his wife observe as he announced to his followers, "Who ever wishes wealth, let him come forward now, and I will bless him with abundant wealth." Not a single soul budged.

"You see," Rabbi Uri said to his wife, "Not one of them is interested in wealth. Why should I pray to G-d to give them something that they do not want?"

To one who possesses true spirituality, earthly riches are of little importance.

NOTES

_____
_____
_____
_____
_____
_____
_____
_____
_____
_____

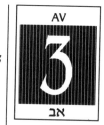
From our Prayers אֵין כֵּאלֹקֵינוּ אֵין כַּאדוֹנֵינוּ אֵין כְּמַלְכֵּנוּ . . .

There is none like our G-d, none like our Master, none like our King, none like our Savior. For who is like our G-d, who is like our Master, who is like our King, who is like our Savior? *(daily morning service).*

July 25, 1990
July 14, 1991
Aug. 2, 1992
July 21, 1993
July 11, 1994
July 30, 1995
July 19, 1996

The sequence appears to be reversed. Should it not read, "Who is like our G-d?" etc., and then the response would be "There is none like our G-d," etc.?

The reason for the sequence is that we must accept the existence of G-d as an act of faith before we set our minds toward searching into the essence of divinity.

Judaism has never discouraged inquiry into divinity. Rabbi Saadiah Gaon, Rabbi Bachya, Maimonides, and many of the kabbalists were avid students of religious philosophy. However, it is one thing to grope for an understanding of a G-d that one believes to exist, and it is another thing to try and develop a belief in G-d on the basis of logical induction.

If there was a way to prove beyond all doubt that G-d exists, there would be no place for the *mitzvah* of belief in G-d. Faith is necessary only when something cannot be demonstrated. Our belief in G-d is based on an unbroken chain of transmission from parent to child since the Revelation at Sinai. With the belief secure, we are then at liberty to seek to probe the greatness of G-d.

Open your hand to the poor person, and lend him sufficient funds for all his needs *(Deuteronomy 15:8).*

From the Scriptures

The *tzaddik* of Sanz, renowned for his *tzedakah* (charity), borrowed a large sum of money shortly before sunset on the eve of Succos. He delivered it to a needy person just prior to the festival, when there was no longer any possibility of purchasing anything for the festival.

The *tzaddik's* followers were bewildered, especially since the *tzaddik* had previously provided the needy man with sufficient money for the holiday expenses.

The *tzaddik* explained, "The Torah requires us to provide the poor with *all* their needs. The joy of the festivals is an essential need. Even if this man has adequate food for the holiday, how could he possibly have rejoiced knowing that at the close of the holiday he must face his many creditors? Now he will be able to rejoice without worry."

Too often our charitable acts are limited to a single check to an agency. The *tzaddik* of Sanz teaches us that charity involves a profound empathy and an understanding of others' needs.

July 26, 1990
July 15, 1991
Aug. 3, 1992
July 22, 1993
July 12, 1994
July 31, 1995
July 20, 1996

From our Prayers

רִבּוֹנוֹ שֶׁל עוֹלָם הֲרֵינִי מוֹחֵל
לְכָל מִי שֶׁהִכְעִיס וְהִקְנִיט אוֹתִי . . .

Master of the universe! I forgive anyone who has angered or provoked me, or who has aggressed against my person, my belongings, or my honor, intentionally or unintentionally . . . And may no one be made to suffer because of me *(prayer on retiring)*.

If we truly live one day at a time, then each day is an independent unit. We return our souls to G-d at night, and we are given a new existence the following morning.

We readily understand that a person in his last moments in life may well forgive his enemies, for what good can it possibly do to hold on to a grudge after death? As we bring the previous day to a close, and realize that tomorrow will be a fresh start, we should understand that there is no purpose in carrying over the resentments of a previous existence to a new existence.

G-d relates to us in the manner that we relate to others. If we bring closure to the past day and start the next day without a carry-over of resentments toward those who offended us, G-d too will consider us as newly born, unencumbered by the sins of our past.

From the Sages

If one kindles a flame, and another adds wood, and the flame spreads and destroys property, the one who added the wood is liable for the damage, because without fuel the flame would have been extinguished *(Bava Kamma 59b)*.

When adults intervene to separate children who are fighting it is customary to hear the youngsters shout, "He started it!" When, as grown-ups, we observe other grown-ups fight or see nations at battle, we hear the same juvenile claim, "He started it!" The argument is often about who was the instigator, as though it were a very valid conclusion that the instigator is always at fault.

The law of the Talmud regarding damage by fire has an important moral implication. The instigator is not necessarily always liable. The responsibility for the damage lies with whoever provided the fuel.

Solomon said, "A soft answer turns away wrath" *(Proverbs 15:1)*. Before we indict someone for his anger, we should examine our own role in provoking and fanning it.

NOTES

_____
_____
_____
_____
_____
_____
_____
_____
_____

From our Prayers

יְמֵי שְׁנוֹתֵינוּ בָהֶם שִׁבְעִים שָׁנָה . . . *From*
Our years may be seventy, and if with *our*
strength, eighty . . . For it is cut off with *Prayers*
swiftness, and we fly away . . . Teach us to
number our days, then we shall bring with
us a heart of wisdom (*Shabbos morning*
service, Psalms 90:10,12).

It is noteworthy that the two most significant events in
Judaism are characterized by "numbering the days." Prior to
Shavuos, on which we celebrate receiving the Torah at Sinai,
the event that made us a nation, we count the seven weeks
of the *Omer*. Prior to Tishah B'av, on which we remember
the destruction of our homeland and the Temple, we again
number the days, counting three weeks of mourning.

The Psalmist says that numbering days leads to wisdom.
In anticipation of receiving the Torah we have to live one day
at a time, and gradually bring about the changes in ourselves
to make us worthy of, and prepared to, receive the Torah.
When we commemorate the national tragedy and we have
to accept the reality that we cannot change the past, we need
to deal with this too one day at a time. We need to number
the days to develop the serenity that will enable us to survive
adversity, and the courage to do those things that will return
to us our glory of old.

Today we have counted just over two of the three weeks
of mourning, and five of the nine days of grieving for our
national loss. Numbering our days also helps us realize that
in only four more days the mourning period will be over, and
we then can begin to rebuild with joy.

July 27, 1990
July 16, 1991
Aug. 4, 1992
July 23, 1993
July 13, 1994
Aug. 1, 1995
July 21, 1996

Silence is a protective fence for wisdom (*Ethics of*
the Fathers 3:17).

From the Sages

If silence is only a protective fence for wisdom, what does
wisdom itself consist of ?

Wisdom consists of the ability to communicate even in
silence. There are, unfortunately, incidents when people
suffer tragic losses. Many people avoid the bereaved person
because they are ill at ease in the mourner's presence. What
can one say to a grieving parent who has, G-d forbid, lost a
child to illness or accident? Because people feel awkward
about having nothing to say, they tend to stay away.

The stricken person needs the tiny bit of solace that he can
derive from others empathizing with him. There is no need
to say anything. Do not avoid a suffering person just because
you feel you have nothing to say. Your being there is a
communication that you care.

NOTES

AV

6

אב

July 28, 1990
July 17, 1991
Aug. 5, 1992
July 24, 1993
July 14, 1994
Aug. 2, 1995
July 22, 1996

From our Prayers

פַּלְגֵי מַיִם תֵּרַד עֵינִי . . .

My eyes will stream with tears, and I will summon to weeping and gird with sackcloth to lament the Torah, the Scriptures, the Mishnah, and the Aggadah (the homiletical portion of the Torah), which are more precious than gold. Where is the Torah and where are the disciples who studied it? (Lamentations of Tishah B'Av).

People who live in an environment that is free from oppression and provides opportunity, who have comfortable homes and pleasant furnishings, may wonder, "Why should we mourn the fall of Jerusalem that occurred some two thousand years ago? We have long since accommodated to life outside the ancient homeland. We are comfortable where we are."

It is not necessarily the loss of physical comforts that we mourn. Many peoples throughout history have sustained national loses, but none of them have set aside an annual period of three weeks of mourning.

Our grief is for our spiritual losses. Every center of Torah study that was destroyed represented a source of spiritual wealth. Every scholar that was lost was a teacher of Torah values. When we are deprived of teachers of Torah and centers of Torah learning, we become more vulnerable to secular influences.

In this period of the Jewish year, we must resolve to strengthen our efforts to achieve the spirituality which pursuit of Torah study provides.

From the Scriptures

The punishment of your iniquity is complete, O daughter of Zion. He will no longer send you into exile (Lamentations 4:22).

For whatever faults we had, for whatever sins we have committed, we have been sufficiently chastened. If we have offended G-d with our vanity, we have learned humility. The calamities that have befallen our people have taught us humility.

We have reached our rock bottom. A person who has hit bottom often perceives with greater clarity the beauty of what he once had and has now lost. He yearns with greater intensity to return to that level.

The prophet tells us, "The punishment of your iniquity is complete." We are deserving of redemption and we are more than ready for the return of the Divine presence among us.

NOTES

_____

_____

_____

_____

_____

_____

_____

_____

_____

... **כַּסְפֵּךְ הָיָה לְסִיגִים סָבְאֵךְ מָהוּל בַּמָּיִם** *From*

Your silver is adulterated with base *our*
metals, your wine is diluted with water. *Prayers*
Your leaders are wayward . . . all favoring
graft, pursuing profit. They do not judge
for the orphan, and the complaint of the
widow does not come before them . . . Zion
will be redeemed with justice and her
returnees by charity *(Isaiah 1:22-27, Haftarah*
for the Shabbos preceding Tishah B'Av).

July 29, 1990
July 18, 1991
Aug. 6, 1992
July 25, 1993
July 15, 1994
Aug. 3, 1995
July 23, 1996

As we mourn the fall of Jerusalem and Israel, we must remind ourselves of how this came about. Only by eliminating the causes of our exile will we be able to emerge from it.

The prophet tells us that G-d turned away from us because of corruption. Even if there was no overt theft, there were dishonest practices which were rationalized as acceptable because "everyone is doing it." Popular practice became the standard for right and wrong. The leaders whose function it was to exhort us to rigorous honesty were themselves corrupted by motives of personal gain.

Torah demands rigorous honesty in dealing with one's fellow man. This is one area where there is no leniency. Furthermore, absolute justice requires not only avoidance of illicit gain, but also caring for the needy and being considerate of those who are less fortunate.

"Zion will be redeemed with justice, and her returnees by charity."

All Israel's people are sighing, searching for a morsel of bread. They trade their prized possession for food to survive. See, O G-d, how gluttonous I have become!" *(Lamentations 1:11).*

From the Scriptures

Why does the prophet consider it gluttony when one struggles for food to survive?

The Maggid of Dubno explained with a parable: A wealthy man lost his fortune and became so poor that he was forced to beg. After he collected enough for his basic needs, he continued begging to buy delicacies. When confronted about this he said, "What difference does it make? Once I have stooped to begging, I might as well get what I like."

The prophet chastises us, "You neglect Torah and spiritual pursuits because you say you must engage in earning money to provide for your essential needs. But why, then, do you spend so much time to acquire luxuries that are not essential to life?"

NOTES

_____
_____
_____
_____
_____
_____
_____
_____
_____

July 30, 1990
July 19, 1991
Aug. 7, 1992
July 26, 1993
July 16, 1994
Aug. 4, 1995
July 24, 1996

From our Prayers

אֵשׁ תּוּקַד בְּקִרְבִּי . . . בְּצֵאתִי מִמִּצְרָיִם . . . *From*

A fire of joy is kindled within me as I think of the time I departed Egypt.

But I raise my voice in lamentations as I recall when I departed Jerusalem (*Lamentations of Tishah B'Av*).

In everyone's life there is rain and shine. Why is it that we generally retain the memories of our sufferings, and do not equally preserve memories of joyful experiences?

Of course, as a psychiatrist, I can hardly expect patients to relate their pleasant experiences. They come for help with emotional problems, which they believe to be the result of painful experiences. This selectivity is determined by the patient's judgment of what the psychiatrist needs to hear.

But why do we do this when talking to our friends? Do we not more often tell our friends about our troubles than we share our joys with them? Could it be that we are projecting, and that we assume that this is the attitude of others because we ourselves would rather hear about others' distress rather than their joys?

This is a harsh accusation, but let us pause and think. Hearing of someone else's good fortune tends to arouse envy, an uncomfortable feeling. Hearing of their distress may make us grateful that we have been luckier than they, a good feeling.

Perhaps if we rid ourselves of envy and developed empathy, so that we would rejoice with others' joys and suffer along with their distresses, our selectivity of memories would improve.

From the Sages

When praying the Amidah one should face towards Jerusalem and the site of the Temple (*Orach Chaim 94:2*).

On Tishah B'Av, one of the Chassidic masters was crying and grieving so relentlessly and intensely that his followers feared for his life. They decided that they must do something to interrupt their master's mourning.

One of the disciples approached him. "Master," he said, "So you are grieving that the Holy Temple was destroyed. Please listen to me. We may have lost the building, but the plot of land is still there."

The master ceased his crying, and a faint smile appeared on his face.

Three times a day we face Jerusalem. The plot of land where the Temple stood binds all Jews to one another in prayer. Not all was lost.

NOTES

בְּלֵיל זֶה . . . גָּזַר עַל אָבוֹת בִּפְרוֹעַ פְּרָעוֹת . . . *From* **O**n this night . . . G-d brought sentence *our* upon the forefathers, and many suffer- *Prayers* ings occurred on this day *(Lamentations of Tishah B'Av).*

Fast of Tishah B'Av [When 9 Av falls on the Sabbath the fast is observed on Sunday.]

July 31, 1990
July 20, 1991
Aug. 8, 1992
July 27, 1993
July 17, 1994
Aug. 5, 1995
July 25, 1996

The Talmud states that on the ninth day of Av the spies sent by Moses to Canaan returned with a discouraging report. The Israelites wept all that night, thereby revealing their lack of trust in G-d, even after having witnessed the many miracles of the Exodus and the Revelation at Sinai. On the ninth day of Av, G-d decreed that the generation of the Exodus would perish in the desert, and this day was designated as one of punishment for future generations *(Sotah 35a).*

Why do we have to pay for the mistakes of our forebears? The Talmud answers this in explaining the verse, "He visits the sins of the parents on their children" *(Exodus 34:7).* When parents make mistakes, and children refuse to learn from them and repeat the same mistakes, they are held even more liable than the parents *(Sanhedrin 27b).*

As fallible humans, we are entitled to make mistakes. As rational people, we should not repeat mistakes others have made.

Our forefathers were denied the Promised Land because they lacked faith in G-d. When their descendants lost faith in G-d, they were driven from the land. If we develop true faith in G-d, we are certain to be returned to the land.

The Temple was actually destroyed on the tenth day of Av. The fast day, however, is on the ninth day, when it was set afire. It is the beginning of the destruction that is most severe *(Taanis 29a).*

From the Sages

The designation of the ninth day of Av rather than the tenth day as commemorating the loss of the Temple teaches us that it is the onset of a destructive process that is most significant.

This principle applies to human behavior as well. Character defects, once they take root, are difficult to extirpate. The time to deal with them most effectively is at their incipience.

We must be on the alert for early signs of deviance, and take forceful steps to nip it in the bud before it becomes engrained in our personality. This applies to ourselves as well as to our children. We should have someone in a supervisory capacity for ourselves who can alert us when the first indications of decline appear.

NOTES

Aug. 1, 1990
July 21, 1991
Aug. 9, 1992
July 28, 1993
July 18, 1994
Aug. 6, 1995
July 26, 1996

*From
our
Prayers*

הֲשִׁיבֵנוּ ה' אֵלֶיךָ וְנָשׁוּבָה . . .

Return us to You, O G-d, so that we may be restored; renew our days as of old. For You have utterly rejected us, and have been very angry with us. Return us to You, O G-d, so that we may be restored; renew our days as of old *(Lamentations 5:21-22).*

On what grounds do we ask G-d to favor us and restore us to our former glory?

The essence of Judaism is to know that Divine providence governs the universe. Things do not happen by chance. There is a master plan for everything.

Part of the master plan is that we maintain a close relationship with G-d and turn our lives over to His will. If we deviate from G-d and distance ourselves from Him, the master plan then calls for His turning away from us, and leaving us at the mercy of the vicissitudes of time and place.

If we recognize that all that has befallen us is indeed due to our having severed our relationship with G-d, and hence precipitated His rejection of us, this very recognition constitutes the requisite *teshuvah*. By virtue of this we can then ask for the return of the Divine favor.

*From the
Scriptures*

O my enemies, do not rejoice over me, for after my fall I have arisen, for when I dwell in darkness, G-d shines His light upon me *(Michah 7:8).*

Following the period of mourning, this prophetic message is vital.

The Midrash comments on this passage, "Had I not fallen, I would have not arisen. Had I not been subject to darkness, I could have not seen the light." It is often the fall that stimulates us to growth.

One of the most treacherous dangers to spirituality is plodding along in the daily routine without taking inventory of our lives or analyzing our actions. It is only when a crisis interrupts our routine and forcefully calls our attention to our laxity in spirituality that we take cognizance.

In treating alcoholism, I tell patients what I truly believe: The crisis of alcoholism may be the greatest stimulus to rebuilding one's personality. People whose lives are uninterrupted by crisis may live their entire life span without giving serious thought to the meaning of their lives.

As an individual as well as a nation, a fall is often the key to a rise, and the awareness of the darkness of our lives is often the beginning of the path to the Divine illumination.

NOTES

_____
_____
_____
_____
_____
_____
_____
_____
_____

From our Prayers

C ast your burden upon G-d and He will provide for you. For He does not allow the righteous to fall *(Psalms 55:23).* הַשְׁלֵךְ עַל ה' יְהָבְךָ וְהוּא יְכַלְכְּלֶךָ . . .

Aug. 2, 1990
July 22, 1991
Aug. 10, 1992
July 29, 1993
July 19, 1994
Aug. 7, 1995
July 27, 1996

If we had a correct perception of how the world functions, our lives might be altogether different.

Humans were given free will in the sphere of morality. This is one area where man is totally responsible for what he does. In every other area of life, what transpires is controlled by G-d.

The appropriate division of labor, then, should be that man occupy himself with moral decisions, and leave everything else to G-d. Is it not strange that so many people do just the reverse, and try to change the unchangeable things in the world while resigning themselves to a spiritual status which could lend itself to a favorable change?

The Psalmist tells us, "Cast your burden upon G-d." Let go of your burdens and let G-d manage them. Put your efforts into achieving righteousness, for that is within your sphere of control.

We should pray for the wisdom to be able to distinguish those things which we can change from those which we must turn over to G-d.

Each warrior could aim at a target of a hairsbreadth and not miss it *(Judges 20:16).*

From the Scriptures

The significance of this passage is that the Hebrew word for "missing the target," *chet*, is the word that also means "sin."

This conveys an important concept. To sin is to miss the target.

We were not put on earth to amuse ourselves. Each of us has a mission, a goal to achieve. To sin is to miss the goal.

NOTES

Imagine yourself embarking on a trip to a particular city where you must complete a major business transaction. The plane goes off course, and you end off far from where you needed to be. Not only have you lost a profitable transaction, but the time, effort, and the expense of the trip were all in vain.

If we sin, we fail to arrive at the target and our lives will have been in vain. Thus, sin is its own punishment, as Ben Azai says, "The consequence of sin is sin" *(Ethics of the Fathers 4:2).*

Aug. 3, 1990
July 23, 1991
Aug. 11, 1992
July 30, 1993
July 20, 1994
Aug. 8, 1995
July 28, 1996

From our Prayers

עֹז וְהָדָר לְבוּשָׁהּ וַתִּשְׂחַק לְיוֹם אַחֲרוֹן . . .

Strength and majesty are her garments and she rejoices until the last day. She opens her mouth with wisdom, and a lesson of kindness is on her tongue *(Proverbs 31:25-26, chanted at Friday night Kiddush).*

We pray for long life, yet so often we see elderly people to whom life appears to be burdensome.

Time is relative. When we are young, active, and busy, the days and weeks seem to pass with the speed of light. When we are old, each day may drag like an eternity.

It is unfortunate that too often in the more active phase of our lives we forget that some day in the future so much of our lives will be spent recalling the past. If we live now so that when the present becomes the distant past we can look back upon it with pride, then we too can "rejoice until the last day."

Solomon gives the formula for this achievement: Speak with wisdom and practice kindness. Reflecting upon a life of wisdom and kindness will indeed make our later years happier. And if we live in such a manner that reflection upon the past will be pleasant, our present is also certain to be happier.

From the Sages

How can we reconcile the verse, "The earth and its fullness belong to G-d" *(Psalms 24:1)* **with the verse, "The earth He gave to man"** *(Psalms 115:16)?* **The first verse refers to the status before one says a berachah (blessing), and the second is after one has said a berachah** *(Berachos 35a).*

"What is the essence of a *berachah*?" asked Rabbi Tzadok of Lublin. "It is an acknowledgment that everything belongs to G-d, and that we have only what He gives us."

This is one of the many interesting contrasts. If we are aware that everything belongs to G-d, then whatever He gives us becomes ours to own. If we think we can attain something completely on our own, then even what we have is not truly ours.

Similarly, if we recognize that we are in fact powerless over our destinies, and we turn our lives over to the will of G-d, then He grants us the power to achieve our goals. If we believe that we are powerful on our own without the assistance of G-d, then we soon learn how powerless we really are.

NOTES

_____
_____
_____
_____
_____
_____
_____
_____
_____

עַל הַצַּדִּיקִים וְעַל הַחֲסִידִים *From*
וְעַל זִקְנֵי עַמְּךָ בֵּית יִשְׂרָאֵל . . . *our*

O n the righteous, the devout, and the *Prayers*
elders of Israel . . . may Your compassion be aroused, and grant them abundant reward, and place our share with them
(daily Amidah).

Why do we have to pray that G-d reward the righteous? Is it not self-evident that G-d will give the righteous their due?

Rabbi Moshe Leib of Sasov explained that this prayer is to remind us that there are virtuous people who are so selfless that they never pray for their own needs. We therefore intercede for them.

How refreshing it is to know that our Sages had to formulate this prayer because there actually are people on this earth who do not think at all of their own needs and are concerned only with the needs and wants of others. Since this prayer has been preserved today, we have every right to believe that even today such wonderful people exist.

The Sages tell us that in each generation there are at least thirty-six truly righteous people. In an age where there is so much self-centeredness and self-indulgence, it is refreshing to know this. But more important, if this degree of selflessness is attainable even today, why should we all not aspire to it? "Place our share with them," says the prayer, "that we may become like them."

Oppressing someone verbally may be a greater sin than stealing his money (Bava Metzia 58b).

From the Sages

NOTES

There are things that we tend to dismiss as insignificant, such as making a cutting remark to someone, or causing him to be embarrassed in the presence of others. Such insults generally cause a person to feel deeply hurt and depressed. If we deprive someone of his composure, is it any less grave a sin than depriving him of his belongings?

If we take someone's money, our conscience may so torment us that we are likely to make restitution, but we are less likely to feel obligated to ask someone's forgiveness for something we said to him or about him. Without making amends toward that person, the sin remains unforgiven.

It would serve us well if we reviewed the events of each day, to see whether there may be someone to whom we should make amends.

Aug. 5, 1990
July 25, 1991
Aug. 13, 1992
Aug. 1, 1993
July 22, 1994
Aug. 10, 1995
July 30, 1996

From our Prayers

תּוֹרָה צִוָּה לָנוּ מֹשֶׁה מוֹרָשָׁה קְהִלַּת יַעֲקֹב

Moses instructed Torah to us; it is an inheritance to the community of Jacob *(Deuteronomy 33:4).*

Many *siddurim* include this verse with the first sentence of the *Shema* as the first prayers that a child is taught upon learning to speak. In what way is this verse a prayer?

Prayer is more than asking G-d for the various things we want. Prayer is also praise of G-d. The Hebrew word for prayer, *tefillah*, connotes additional meanings. *Tefillah* can mean to decide or to judge, it can mean to make distinction, and can also mean to bind together.

Actually, all these functions of prayer can also be achieved through the study of Torah. Indeed, the Talmud states that Rabbi Shimon and his colleagues, who did not interrupt their study of Torah for any worldly cause, were exempt from prayer.

This Talmudic statement may provide the answer to our question. If we interrupt our Torah study for even the briefest moment to engage in earthly activities, we are in danger of losing the effects of Torah on our lives. Prayer, therefore, is the means by which we can maintain the closeness to G-d which Torah provides, even when we interrupt the study of Torah to attend to our earthly needs.

From the Sages

At the celebration of the water libation at the Temple, the elders would say, "Fortunate are we that in our old age we are not embarrassed by the behavior of our younger days" *(Succah 53a).*

Would it not be a wonderful guide for good living if we would reflect before doing something, "Is this something I may later regret having done?"

Has it ever happened that a person in the last days of his life said, "I regret not having spent more time at the office"? On the other hand, how many people have said, "I was so foolish. I should have spent more time with my wife and children"?

While it is true that a person should live one day at a time, this means that we should do today only what we are capable of doing today, and not assume worries about things that we can do nothing about today. However, it is not a violation of living "one day at a time" to put away money in a pension fund so that one can have a reasonable income in later years of life.

Just as we put away money for our old age, we should also invest in behavior that will provide memories that can enrich our old age.

NOTES

_____
_____
_____
_____
_____
_____
_____
_____
_____

. . . אֲשֶׁר בָּרָא שָׂשׂוֹן וְשִׂמְחָה חָתָן וְכַלָּה . . . *From*

Blessed are You, O G-d, King of the *our* universe, Who has created joy and *Prayers* gladness, bridegroom and bride; mirth, glad song, pleasure, delight; love, brother-hood, peace, and companionship *(Blessing at the marriage ceremony).*

The Talmud cites the fifteenth day of Av as one of the most festive days of the Jewish calendar. On this day, all young maidens of marriageable age would *borrow* clothes and join in dancing. The theme of the day was announced to all young men. "Do not give consideration to physical beauty which is so superficial and transient. Pay attention to family background and to character, for it is written, 'Appearances are deceiving, and beauty is vain. A woman who is G-d-fearing, she is to be praised' " *(Proverbs 31:30).*

Aug. 6, 1990
July 26, 1991
Aug. 14, 1992
Aug. 2, 1993
July 23, 1994
Aug. 11, 1995
July 31, 1996

The important feature which the Talmud emphasizes is that *all* the young women had to wear borrowed clothes in order not to embarrass any girl who did not have fine garments of her own. This was an event marked by equality and consideration for others.

In this spirit, the marriage blessing mentions the goals for a young couple: mirth, glad song, pleasure, and delight. The ways to reach these goals are: love, brotherhood, peace, and companionship. A lasting and happy relationship can only result when equality and consideration predominate.

A person should always study the Torah, even if he lacks the proper motives, because the study of Torah will eventually bring about the proper motives *(Arachin 16b).*

From the Sages

When we know what is the right thing to do, we should do it, even if we lack the ideal feeling, intent, or motivation.

This is not at all being hypocritical. Hypocrisy is doing something which one is convinced is wrong, yet one does it to impress people, or for some other ulterior motive.

However, there are things we know to be right, but have resistances to doing for various reasons. We can overcome these resistances by practicing the particular behavior until we are able to do it with the proper feeling.

In this sense we say, "If you do not feel like smiling and appearing pleasant, do so anyway. If you do not feel grati-tude for something you should, express your gratitude anyway. If you do not feel like praying, pray anyway."

Spirituality requires practice. You are not being hypocrit-ical when you practice something.

NOTES

_____
_____
_____
_____
_____
_____
_____
_____

AV

16

אב

Aug. 7, 1990
July 27, 1991
Aug. 15, 1992
Aug. 3, 1993
July 24, 1994
Aug. 12, 1995
Aug. 1, 1996

From our Prayers

וְיָדַעְתָּ הַיּוֹם וַהֲשֵׁבֹתָ אֶל לְבָבֶךָ . . .

You shall know this day and reflect in your heart that Hashem is G-d, in the heavens above and on the earth below, there is none else (*closing prayer of daily services, Deuteronomy 4:39*).

When Rabbi Yehoshua Leib Diskin was a young boy, his father attempted to explain to him that the concept expressed in the *Shema* that G-d is one does not only refute a plurality of gods, but also asserts that G-d is the only being in existence. Everything else in the universe which seems to have an independent existence is nothing more than a cloak beneath which there is the Divine presence.

Rabbi Yehoshua Leib interrupted his father. "But I already know that, Father," the child said.

"Why do you say you know that?" the father asked.

"Because we know that two things cannot occupy the same space at one time. And since we say in the *Kedushah*, 'The world is full of His glory,' then since G-d is everywhere in the universe, there cannot be anything else," the child said.

A concept that great philosophers of religion struggled to understand was clear and simple to the uncluttered mind of a brilliant child.

We can now read the above prayer to mean, "In the heavens above and on the earth below, nothing exists except G-d."

From the Scriptures

These are the words that Moses spoke to all of Israel (*Deuteronomy 1:1*).

The Rabbi of Lelov said that, "Every person felt that Moses' words were intended only for him, and for no one else." The Rabbi of Kosov said, "Whenever I speak to a group of people, I have no intention for anyone in particular. But if anyone feels my words were directed toward him, then it was really him for whom they were intended."

We no longer have the privilege of prophets who convey to us messages from G-d. Today, G-d speaks to us through various people. When we hear a person speak about character defects and the need for spiritual development and growth, and we feel that his words were intended for us, we may be sure that they were indeed so. Somewhere deep down we have an awareness of what it is that we are lacking spiritually. When someone strikes a chord that calls our attention to our spiritual needs, that message was indeed intended for us.

NOTES

_____

_____

_____

_____

_____

_____

_____

_____

שִׁיר הַמַּעֲלוֹת אֵלֶיךָ נָשָׂאתִי אֶת עֵינַי *From*
הַיֹּשְׁבִי בַּשָּׁמָיִם *our*

S ong of Ascents. To You, I lift my eyes to *Prayers*
the One Who resides in the heavens
(Shabbos morning service, Psalms 123:1).

Aug. 8, 1990
July 28, 1991
Aug. 16, 1992
Aug. 4, 1993
July 25, 1994
Aug. 13, 1995
Aug. 2, 1996

Rabbi Yaakov Yosef of Polnoah used to interpret the verse, "In the heavens above and on the earth below" (see prayer 16 Av) to mean that when one thinks of where he stands in heavenly matters, in achievement of spirituality, one should always "look above," i.e., one should look up to those who have achieved greater spirituality and aspire to reach their status. However, where earthly matters are concerned, such as physical comfort and belongings, one should always "look below" and realize that regardless of how deprived one thinks himself to be, he is more fortunate that those who have less than he.

What a wonderful formula! Is it not tragic that so often we do just the reverse? We often seem to be quite content with our spiritual achievements, but constantly expend energy to improve our physical welfare.

"To You, I lift my eyes, to the One Who resides in the heavens." If we look upwards spiritually, we will see how far we have to go, and renew our efforts to grow spiritually.

And all the nation answered in unison, "All that G-d commands we will do" *(Exodus 24:7).*

From the Scriptures

There are 613 *mitzvos* in the Torah. Some are restricted to *Kohanim* (priests), some are dependent on particular circumstances which may not apply to all people, such as redemption of a first-born son, and some apply only in the Holy Land, and not to people who live elsewhere. How then can anyone fulfill *all* that G-d commanded, since some *mitzvos* cannot be fulfilled by everyone?

Rabbi Meir Simcha answered, "When one fulfills the *mitzvah* of putting on *tefillin* on one's arm, it is not the arm that is credited with the *mitzvah*, but the person as a whole. When Jews are all bound to one another as one unit, any *mitzvah* that one does is credited to the unit as a whole. The Israelite is credited with a *mitzvah* performed by a *Kohen*, the person who did not have a son as his first-born shares the redemption *mitzvah* with one who did, and those who live outside the Holy Land share the *mitzvos* of those who live in it.

No one can achieve wholeness alone. We are all dependent on each other.

Aug. 9, 1990
July 29, 1991
Aug. 17, 1992
Aug. 5, 1993
July 26, 1994
Aug. 14, 1995
Aug. 3, 1996

From our Prayers

עָלֵינוּ לְשַׁבֵּחַ לַאֲדוֹן הַכֹּל . . .

It is upon us to give praise to the Master of all, to accord greatness to the Creator, that He did not allow us to remain idolatrous, for we bow and humble ourselves before the King of Kings *(closing prayer of daily service)*.

In the commentaries on the *siddur* it is noted that this beautiful prayer was composed by Joshua at the conquest of Jericho. In the Hebrew, the first letters of each phrase form an acrostic of Joshua's name. However, the sequence of the letters is reversed, and Joshua's name is not immediately recognizable in the acrostic. Joshua, because of his profound humility, did not wish to boast of his authorship of the prayer, hence the concealed acrostic.

But if Joshua shunned prominence, why did he bother to put his name into the prayer at all? Why not leave it totally anonymous?

Joshua's love for G-d was so intense that he wanted to achieve some identity with prayer and worship. He wished to become an integral part of Judaism, not merely as a historical figure, but as one who would never be separated from prayer and worship. He physically put himself into a prayer, to be part of prayer forever.

When we finish our prayers and close our prayer books after services, we go about our daily affairs and leave a gap between our prayer and the rest of the day. We would do well to learn from Joshua.

From the Scriptures

Judges and enforcement officers shall you give unto yourselves *(Deuteronomy 16:18)*.

"Unto *yourself*," said Rabbi Yaakov Yosef of Polnoah, "means that you ought to hold yourself to the same rigorous standards that you apply to other people."

Rabbi Yaakov Yosef obviously knew human nature very well. We are often quick to condemn others for the same behavior for which we can find many justifications when we do it ourselves. In *halachah* there is a principle that if you wish to demand a degree of strictness greater than that required by the law, you may demand it of yourself, but not of others.

There are many references in Jewish writings to the principle that we must be more demanding of ourselves than we are of others. This is one area where just the reverse so often prevails. We tend to justify our own behavior, but rarely that of others.

NOTES
_____
_____
_____
_____
_____
_____
_____
_____
_____

מִזְמוֹר לְתוֹדָה הָרִיעוּ לַה' כָּל הָאָרֶץ *From* · · · A Song of Gratitude. All the land, shout *our* unto G-d. Serve G-d with joy, come *Prayers* before Him in song *(daily morning service, Psalms 100:1-2).*

Aug. 10, 1990
July 30, 1991
Aug. 18, 1992
Aug. 6, 1993
July 27, 1994
Aug. 15, 1995
Aug. 4, 1996

This psalm corresponds to the offerings of thanksgiving that were brought upon the Altar in the time of the Temple.

It is noteworthy that whereas all other grain offerings had to be of *matzah*, the thanksgiving offering included both *matzah* and leavened bread.

Matzah symbolizes haste. *Matzah* must be prepared and baked quickly before it has a chance to rise. In contrast, bread requires time to rise, and represents delay and temporizing.

What does this have to do with gratitude? Some people who are beneficiaries of a favor may not respond immediately with an expression of gratitude. When they do finally get around to it, there may be so much resentment for their not having shown their appreciation earlier that their gratitude is not accepted.

We often talk about the need to *express* gratitude. There is also something to say about being able to *accept* gratitude properly. The unique inclusion of leavened bread in the thanksgiving offering conveys the concept that even after long delay and procrastination, gratitude should be accepted gracefully.

Remember what Amalek did to you on your way out of the bondage of Egypt *(Deuteronomy 25:17).* **One must recite this passage every day in order that the attack of Amalek not be forgotten** *(Megillah 18a).*

From the Sages

"Amalek" says Chidah, "is the personification of the *yeitzer hara* (man's evil inclination). The latter is a relentless enemy, constantly seeking to entrap man into defying the Divine will. Daily remembrance that the *yeitzer hara* is insidious, conniving and plotting our destruction, is necessary to keep us on our guard against his nefarious machinations."

In my work with recovering alcoholics, I hear them say, "We must remember that our enemy is alcohol, cunning, baffling, and powerful." The only defense against this enemy is to maintain a constant state of vigilance.

NOTES

People who have had an alcohol problem know from their past experience that if they lower their guard against their "enemy" even momentarily, they will relapse. We would do well to learn from them and keep our guard up against the *yeitzer hara*, an enemy that never ceases to plot our destruction.

Aug. 11, 1990
July 31, 1991
Aug. 19, 1992
Aug. 7, 1993
July 28, 1994
Aug. 16, 1995
Aug. 5, 1996

From our Prayers

בְּבֵית אֱלֹקִים נְהַלֵּךְ בְּרָגֶשׁ . . .

For together we had joined in sweet council, and to the House of G-d we would walk in throngs *(Selichos, Psalms 55:15).*

The latter verse can also be read, "To the House of G-d we will go with great emotion."

The *tzaddik* of Sanz used to put on his *tallis* and *tefillin* in his home, and then go to the synagogue to pray.

One day when he was about halfway to the synagogue, he stopped, went back home, and without pause, immediately started back to the synagogue. His followers who accompanied him could not restrain themselves, and asked why he had turned back home for no apparent purpose.

"Every *mitzvah*," the *tzaddik* said, "must be done with proper *kavanah* (concentration and meditation). The act of going to the synagogue to pray is a *mitzvah* in itself, just as prayer is. On the way to the synagogue, my mind had been preoccupied with other thoughts, and I did not concentrate on performing the *mitzvah* of going to *shul*. I therefore went back to repeat the *mitzvah* with the proper *kavanah*."

Many of us would be content if we had the proper *kavanah* during prayer itself. The *tzaddik* of Sanz teaches us that preparation for a *mitzvah* also requires thought and concentration, for here, too, we are doing the Divine will, and this should not be done thoughtlessly.

From the Sages

And you shall serve G-d with all your heart. What service is performed by the heart? This refers to prayer *(Taanis 2a).*

A follower of the Rabbi of Kotzk once complained that he had difficulty concentrating on prayer because of severe headaches.

"Headaches!" exclaimed the Rabbi. "What does the head have to do with prayer? Prayer must come from the heart, not from the head!"

There are many psychological problems that occur because of improper perception of emotions. Some people, who may not be willing to deal with issues of intense emotion, may try to intellectualize and think things through. They often become entangled in intellectual exercises which lead nowhere. They may indeed develop a headache as a result of futile head work.

We should know how to feel emotions and how to deal with them. "Understanding" emotions is usually of little value. Neither is it important that we understand or intellectualize our relationship with G-d. We should *feel* it.

NOTES

_____
_____
_____
_____
_____
_____
_____
_____
_____

וּבָאתִי לְבֵיתְךָ לְהַפִּיל תְּחִנָּתִי לְפָנֶיךָ . . . *From*

And I have come to Your house to place *our* my supplication before You, that You *Prayers* remove my weariness. And I will testify that You created all that exists in six days *(prayer before Friday night Kiddush).*

Aug. 12, 1990

Aug. 1, 1991

Aug. 20, 1992

Aug. 8, 1993

July 29, 1994

Aug. 17, 1995

Aug. 6, 1996

Although it is possible for a person to recite prayers privately in his home, the Talmud places great emphasis on communal prayer.

In solo prayer it is easy for an individual to become preoccupied with his own needs. In communal prayer we are not only aware of each other, those immediately present, but we are more likely to pray for Divine blessings for all humanity. We are also likely to be stimulated by the prayers of others, and this helps remove the "weariness" that can occur when prayer is but a rote performance.

When we assert our belief in the majesty of G-d and the principles of faith in the company of others, we reinforce one another's faith, and gain strength in our own convictions. This facilitates our struggles against those forces that tend to detract from our spirituality and that tend to pull us into the pursuit of mundane desires.

The Talmud states that the prayer of the multitude is never rejected. If you are one who does not go to the synagogue to pray, begin doing so. If you are in the practice of going to *shul*, by all means continue to do so. Keep coming back. It works!

(Naomi said to Orpah and Ruth,) "I am so embittered for you, because the hand of G-d has been harsh with me" *(Ruth 1:13).* — *From the Scriptures*

This interpretation of the verse was offered by the *Gaon* of Vilna. In good times, many people can empathize with those who are in distress. However, if they have their own suffering, they may be so preoccupied with their own misery that they do not empathize with others.

The Scripture tells us that although Naomi was grieving over the deaths of her husband and her two sons, she was nevertheless able to feel the distress of her daughters-in-law and share in their grief.

"Although the hand of G-d has struck me," Naomi said, "I can feel the pain of your suffering."

Compassion for others is something we must maintain at all times, even when we think we can use all our pity for ourselves.

NOTES

_____

_____

_____

_____

_____

_____

_____

_____

_____

Aug. 13, 1990
Aug. 2, 1991
Aug. 21, 1992
Aug. 9, 1993
July 30, 1994
Aug. 18, 1995
Aug. 7, 1996

From ‏דִּין הָאֱמֶת . . . שֶׁהֶחֱיָנוּ . . . לַזְּמַן הַזֶּה‎
our **B**lessed are You, L-rd our G-d, King of the
Prayers universe, Who is the true Judge *(Blessing
upon hearing tragic news)* . . . **Who has kept
us alive, sustained us and brought us to
this day** *(Blessing upon hearing good news).*

The above blessings are polar opposites. The first is said
when, G-d forbid, a loved one dies, and it is an acceptance
of the Divine judgment. The second is said on festive occasions, or when one has experienced unusually good fortune.

Seemingly, these two blessings can never be said at one
time. Tragedy and good fortune are mutually exclusive. But
the Talmud says otherwise. If a father dies and leaves his son
a large estate, the son is required to say both blessings. In
his grief he must accept the Divine wisdom and judgment,
but he must also acknowledge the feeling of good fortune at
acquiring the wealth of the inheritance.

Our Sages understood human nature. A person does feel
joy when he acquires wealth. This feeling occurs regardless
of how the acquisition came about. Many people, consciously or unconsciously, try to deny the feeling of joy
because they feel that it is wrong to be happy about wealth
acquired through their father's death. However, denial of
reality and repression of feeling cannot have good results.

The Sages say that we can genuinely grieve the loss of a
parent, and yet feel good about the acquisition of wealth.

Conflicting feelings do coexist. One should not deny
them, but learn how to live with them.

From the
Scriptures

**One who loves discipline loves wisdom, but he
who despises admonishment is a fool** *(Proverbs 12:1).*

The Psalmist expressed the same idea in *Psalms 92:12*:
"My ears listen when my adversaries rise up against me."

Too often our friends will only tell us things about
ourselves we like to hear. They are apt not to call attention
to our shortcomings for fear of losing our friendship. Indeed,
if we are chastised by friends, we may avoid their company
because it is unpleasant to listen to criticism.

Those who do not like us are certain not to withhold any
critical comment. Granted, much of what is said in hostility
is untrue, yet if there is a kernel of truth in uncomplimentary
remarks, it is worth listening to.

The wise person will seek out constructive criticism and
will encourage his friends to apprise him of any character
defects they may notice. The fool who shuns admonishment
becomes more foolish as his defects intensify.

NOTES

_____
_____
_____
_____
_____
_____
_____
_____
_____

AV

אב

Aug. 14, 1990
Aug. 3, 1991
Aug. 22, 1992
Aug. 10, 1993
July 31, 1994
Aug. 19, 1995
Aug. 8, 1996

וְקָרְבֵנוּ מַלְכֵּנוּ לַעֲבוֹדָתֶךָ From our Prayers

Draw us near to do Your work (daily Amidah).

There is something to be accomplished in the universe which only man can accomplish. This is clearly beyond human understanding, and known only to the unfathomable Divine wisdom, but the creation of man was because there was something which G-d wanted man to accomplish. This has to be accomplished by man and not G-d Himself, by man and not by heavenly angels.

Whatever this mission is, it is the work of G-d, that which He commanded man to do. When we observe the Divine dictates, it is not just that we are worshiping and serving G-d, but we are actually doing His work. We are, as it were, agents of G-d.

It is both an awesome responsibility and a privilege of the highest order to be an agent of G-d. This is an assignment we should bear with joy and reverence.

From the Scriptures

"And I said to my master, what if the maiden does not wish to come with me?" (Genesis 24:39, Eliezer's narration of his assignment to fetch Rivkah to be Isaac's wife).

Rashi notes that the Hebrew word אֻלַי, which means "what if," is written in this verse minus a *vav*, and can be read as אֵלַי, which means "for me." He interprets this to mean that Eliezer was admitting that he had secretly hoped that Rivkah would refuse to come with him, and he would then be able to take Isaac as a husband for his own daughter.

The Rabbi of Kotzk asked, "Why, then, is the word not written minus a *vav* in the original dialogue between Abraham and Eliezer in verse 5?" The Rabbi answered, "Before Rivkah consented, Eliezer himself was not aware of his self-interest in the matter. His awareness came only after Rivkah consented to marry Isaac, and when the feasibility of his personal wish was eliminated, his previous unconscious wish came to his awareness."

This is a profound insight, and also somewhat frightening. We may be unaware of our true motives, and we may make important decisions based on unconscious motives, decisions which we might not make if we were aware of their origin.

How can we avoid being misled by unconscious motivations? Our only defense is to pray for Divine guidance for truth, and to bare our hearts to competent teachers and trusted friends who can help us uncover the true motives for our decisions.

NOTES

Aug. 15, 1990
Aug. 4, 1991
Aug. 23, 1992
Aug. 11, 1993
Aug. 1, 1994
Aug. 20, 1995
Aug. 9, 1996

From our Prayers

אַתָּה קִדַּשְׁתָּ אֶת יוֹם הַשְּׁבִיעִי לִשְׁמֶךָ
תַּכְלִית מַעֲשֵׂה שָׁמַיִם וָאָרֶץ

You have sanctified the seventh day to Your name. It is the purpose of the creation of heaven and earth *(Friday night Amidah).*

During the week, the first of the blessings after the opening paragraph of the *Amidah* is the prayer for wisdom. It is therefore logical to assume that the above prayer, which is the first prayer of the *Shabbos Amidah*, corresponds to the prayer for wisdom that we say during the week.

The weekly prayers are our pleas, and the *Shabbos* prayer is the response to them. Thus, the answer to the quest for wisdom is to understand the essence of *Shabbos*.

Shabbos is the goal and purpose of creation. It is a day dedicated to G-d, meaning that it is a day on which man can separate himself from his earthly preoccupations and come closer to G-d through prayer, meditation, and Torah study.

We can do many unwise things if we do not understand what our existence is all about. We can pursue earthly pleasures and possessions, even to the ruination of our bodies and spirits. Once we understand that we exist to come closer to G-d, we are in possession of true wisdom. We ask for wisdom, and we receive the *Shabbos*.

From the Scriptures

Jacob worked seven years for Rachel's hand in marriage, but it seemed to him like single days because of his intense love for her *(Genesis 29:20).*

How are we to understand this? Is is not true that when a person is separated from someone he loves, each day appears to be an eternity, rather than the reverse?

But note, the Torah does not say it was "like a few days," but "like single days." This means that Jacob was able to survive the long seven years of separation because he took them "one day at a time."

Looking at a deprivation of seven long years would be completely intolerable. But Jacob took this deprivation one day at a time. Each day he dealt with his deprivation of only that day, and that was indeed manageable.

Many difficulties in life are made easier if we do not try to carry more of the burden than we must at any one time. Just deal with today's burden today. Leave tomorrow's burden for tomorrow, because except for worrying about it in futility, there is nothing you can do about tomorrow's burdens today.

NOTES

_____
_____
_____
_____
_____
_____
_____
_____
_____
_____

B lessed are You, L-rd our G-d, King of the universe, Who gave us a Torah of truth, and implanted eternal life within us. Blessed is G-d, Giver of the Torah *(Blessing after reading the Torah).*

. . . נָתַן לָנוּ תּוֹרַת אֱמֶת וְחַיֵּי עוֹלָם . . .

From our Prayers

What do we mean when we say that the Torah is G-d-given?

The Midrash says that when G-d instructed the Israelites to build a Sanctuary, it was like a king who married off his only daughter. "I cannot keep you for myself, because you must go with your husband," he said, "but neither can I separate from you. I therefore beg of you, build me a small hut near your home, so that I can be close to you."

G-d could not keep the Torah from Israel for whom it was intended, but neither would He part with it. He therefore said, "Build me a Sanctuary, a small hut, where I can be near the Torah and Israel."

"G-d-given" Torah thus means that G-d gave himself to us, along with the Torah.

Aug. 16, 1990
Aug. 5, 1991
Aug. 24, 1992
Aug. 12, 1993
Aug. 2, 1994
Aug. 21, 1995
Aug. 10, 1996

There are three precious gifts that G-d gave Israel: the Torah, the Holy Land, and Paradise. However, these gifts could be acquired only through pain and suffering *(Berachos 5a).*

From the Sages

It is understandable that when a person suffers pain, he is bitter, resentful, and may even rebel against G-d. Our Sages tell us, however, that pain and suffering is the only way that certain special gifts can be obtained.

When Jacob had mourned the loss of his son Joseph and questioned the Divine justice, G-d said, "I am manipulating things to make his son viceroy of Egypt, yet he complains!" *(Midrash).*

Why it is essential that special gifts be acquired only through suffering is beyond our capacity to understand. Moses himself asked G-d to explain this mystery, and G-d responded that this is something that even Moses could not understand as long as he was living, limited as he was by residing within his physical body. Only after the soul separated from the body would it be allowed to understand the Divine mystery.

When we experience suffering, the words of Talmud should provide some consolation. Although we cannot understand it, our suffering is ultimately for some good. It is often through suffering that we achieve our greatest growth.

NOTES

_____
_____
_____
_____
_____
_____
_____
_____

Aug. 17, 1990
Aug. 6, 1991
Aug. 25, 1992
Aug. 13, 1993
Aug. 3, 1994
Aug. 22, 1995
Aug. 11, 1996

From our Prayers

הִנֵּה כְעֵינֵי עֲבָדִים אֶל יַד אֲדוֹנֵיהֶם
כְּעֵינֵי שִׁפְחָה אֶל יַד גְּבִרְתָּהּ . . .

Just as the eyes of servants are lifted up to their master, and as the eyes of a maid are toward her mistress, so are our eyes lifted to G-d until He favors us *(Shabbos prayer, Psalms 123:2).*

Indeed, we pray and ask G-d for our various needs. But all we can do is ask, and we must realize that the decisions rest with G-d. Prayer is asking G-d for something, not *demanding* it. Furthermore, how and in what way G-d chooses to give us our needs is purely His decision, not ours.

One of the great Chassidic masters was importuned by one of his followers to bless him that he have ample money to marry off his daughter. The Rabbi advised him to buy a certain number in the sweepstake. When the Rabbi's blessing bore no fruit, he was despondent. "G-d no longer accepts my prayers," he said. A colleague then pointed out that everyday we say in the morning service, "Who among all creation can tell You how and what to do?"

"If you wish to bless someone with wealth, that is fine. But don't tell G-d how he is supposed to carry out your blessings."

Our attitude should be like that of the servants to a master. We should ask, but we do not give orders.

From the Sages

Give me companionship or give me death *(Taanis 23a).*

There are few feelings that are so intolerable as loneliness. Yet, too often loneliness is actually self-inflicted.

Some people shun the company of others out of a fear that others will not like them. They avoid people in order to avoid the anticipated rejection. This is invariably due to the fact that they do not like themselves, and they reason that others will not like them either.

This feeling is in turn due to a person's distorted self-image. So often we underestimate ourselves, and we fail to see our gifts and talents.

Awareness that we are good people is not false pride or conceit. We are all in possession of a Divine soul. We are all capable of being liked and loved, and we should not allow ourselves to be deluded to the contrary.

NOTES

_____
_____
_____
_____
_____
_____
_____
_____
_____

וְאַל תְּבִיאֵנוּ לֹא לִידֵי חֵטְא . . . *From*
Lead us not into sin, transgression, iniq- *our*
uity, temptation, or disgrace . . . compel *Prayers*
our evil inclination that it may submit to
You *(daily morning service).*

How can we ask that the *yeitzer hara* (the evil inclination)
should become submissive to G-d, when it was created for
the specific purpose of tempting man to sin?

A Chassidic master explained that man would not have
as much difficulty in resisting sin if only he were aware that
his act was indeed wrong. The problem is that man is often
deluded, and rationalizes that what he is doing is not sinful.

The Divine assignment to the *yeitzer hara* was to urge
man to sin, but not to delude him that a sinful act is
virtuous. When a person rationalizes that a wrong act is
right, that is the work of the *yeitzer hara*, which distorts his
thinking and perception. The *yeitzer hara* has thus over-
stepped his limits, because he deludes mankind.

That is why we pray, "Compel the *yeitzer hara* to submit
to You." Let him confine himself to urging us to sin,
because then we can resist him. It is when he deludes us
that wrong is right that we are helpless.

Aug. 18, 1990
Aug. 7, 1991
Aug. 26, 1992
Aug. 14, 1993
Aug. 4, 1994
Aug. 23, 1995
Aug. 12, 1996

G-d created the world with the letter ה so that *From*
anyone who wishes to exit "through the opening of *the Sages*
the ה" has the freedom to do so *(Menachos 29b).*

Why is it that animals will instinctively avoid harm while
humans can behave in a manner that is self-destructive?

It is because man does not perceive what is harmful the
way an animal does. Man has the capacity to deny, to
rationalize, to project, and to distort his perception of
reality.

The letter ה is the Hebrew question mark. G-d created
the world in such a manner that man should be able to
question His existence and also question the validity of the
word of G-d. G-d did this so that man would be free to
make moral choices. In a world where good and evil were
visible and unmistakable certainties, there would be no
possibility of free moral choice.

Man was given the possibility of questioning and the
capacity to deny. This is what is meant by the opening of
the letter ה.

We must be aware that our minds can play tricks on us
and lead us to deny reality. Intensive prayer and submitting
ourselves to the guidance of our elders is our only
salvation.

NOTES

_____
_____
_____
_____
_____
_____
_____
_____
_____

Aug. 19, 1990
Aug. 8, 1991
Aug. 27, 1992
Aug. 15, 1993
Aug. 5, 1994
Aug. 24, 1995
Aug. 13, 1996

From our Prayers

. . . הָאָב הָרַחֲמָן הַמְהֻלָּל בְּפֶה עַמּוֹ

Blessed are You, L-rd our G-d, King of the universe, the merciful Father, Who is praised by the mouths of His people, whose praise and glory is proclaimed by the tongues of His pious ones and servants *(daily morning service).*

Since G-d is the Searcher of all hearts and knows our innermost thoughts, why is it essential that we verbalize our prayers? Why is silent meditation not sufficient?

The answer is that man must worship G-d with all his faculties, as the Psalmist says, "All my bones shall proclaim, O G-d, Who is like unto You" *(Psalms 35:10).* If one has a melodious voice, one should sing to G-d. If one was endowed with grace and agility, one should dance before G-d.

Man was endowed with the capacity to speak as well as to think. If he does not utilize the gift of speech in the service of G-d, he is derelict in his worship.

"Therefore, the limbs which You have apportioned us, the spirit and soul which You have breathed into us, and the tongues which You have put into our mouths, shall all praise, glorify, and exalt Your name" *(Shabbos morning service).* All our energies are to participate in Divine worship.

From the Sages

The human soul resembles G-d in five ways: (1) The soul fills the entire person, just as G-d fills the entire universe. (2) The soul is invisible just as is G-d. (3) The soul nurtures the body, just as G-d nurtures the universe. (4) The soul is pure just as is G-d. (5) The soul is concealed within the body, just as G-d is concealed in the universe *(Berachos 10a).*

NOTES

_____
_____
_____
_____
_____
_____
_____
_____
_____
_____

Rabbi Simchah Zisl states that the difficulty in achieving spirituality is because it pertains to the development of the soul. Just as a person is naturally more involved with those who are close to him than with strangers, so a person occupies himself more with his physical self with which he is familiar than with his soul which is invisible, concealed, and unknown to him.

If we are interested in spiritual growth, our first task must be to become more familiar with our own soul. What is it? What are its needs? What nourishes it and what harms it?

Sincere self-searching and praying to G-d to open our eyes that we may become aware of our souls is the first step towards spiritual growth.

רִבּוֹנוֹ שֶׁל עוֹלָם לוּלֵי חָטָאנוּ וּפָשַׁעְנוּ **From**
לֹא הָיִינוּ בּוֹשִׁים . . . **our**

Master of the universe! If not that we **Prayers**
have sinned, we would not be ashamed
. . . may it be Your will to forgive us for our
sins *(prayer on the day preceding Rosh Chodesh).*

This prayer warrants an entire book as commentary.

Elsewhere (30 Shevat) it was pointed out that shame and
guilt are very distinct. Guilt is a painful feeling that follows
the realization that one has done something wrong. Shame
is a feeling that one is somehow not good.

Often a person who feels shame does not know why he
feels that way about himself. The origins of shame are
frequently in mistaken impressions that occur early in life,
which result in the child seeing himself as somehow being
inherently bad.

Guilt can be removed by resolving not to repeat the wrong
act, by making amends, and by praying for forgiveness.
Shame is much more resistant. If I feel that I am essentially
no good, independent of my actions, what is there that I can
do? Healthy guilt is constructive, because it can lead to
corrective action. Shame leads only to depression and
despair.

The prayer says this so beautifully. "I am not ashamed of
myself. I am ashamed of what I *did* that was wrong.
Therefore, I can ask forgiveness, and once again can be free
and at peace with myself."

Erev
Rosh Chodesh
[Eve of the
New Month]

Aug. 20, 1990

Aug. 9, 1991

Aug. 28, 1992

Aug. 16, 1993

Aug. 6, 1994

Aug. 25, 1995

Aug. 14, 1996

**For I have seen all the wrongdoing as well as
proper actions, but when the latter are motivated by
envy, they are also void and empty** *(Ecclesiastes 4:4).*

From the
Scriptures

Envy is not only a destructive character defect, but also
one that is patently useless. A person can be envious of
someone else even though he knows he can never achieve
or attain what the other person has. Of what use then is
envy? It prevents a person from enjoying what he has, and
brings nothing but heartache.

While some emotions are contemptible, they may at least
have some rationale. Envy is totally devoid of any rationale.
Yet a person may ruminate over envy, accomplishing
nothing other than generating bitterness, resentment, and
thereby allowing himself to become victim to both physical
and emotional illnesses.

How right the wise Solomon was. "A person with a
bountiful eye is indeed blessed" *(Proverbs 22:9).*

NOTES

AV

אב

First Day of
Rosh Chodesh
Elul
Aug. 21, 1990
Aug. 10, 1991
Aug. 29, 1992
Aug. 17, 1993
Aug. 7, 1994
Aug. 26, 1995
Aug. 15, 1996

From our Prayers

אוֹדְךָ כִּי עֲנִיתָנִי וַתְּהִי לִי לִישׁוּעָה
אֶבֶן מָאֲסוּ הַבּוֹנִים הָיְתָה לְרֹאשׁ פִּנָּה . . .

I give thanks to You, even when You cause me to suffer, for You have been my salvation. The stone that the builders despised became the cornerstone. This can be only from G-d, and is wondrous to our eyes. This is the day that G-d has made, we will rejoice and be glad with it *(Hallel, Psalms 118:21-24).*

In these four verses, David sums up the Jewish attitude toward human suffering.

"This can be only from G-d, and it is wondrous to our eyes." The wisdom of G-d is unfathomable, and we cannot expect to understand it. G-d has been our salvation, and if He allows us to suffer before coming to our aid, it is not for lack of His interest in us, but because that suffering is somehow essential for our betterment. Therefore, "I give thanks, even for the suffering, for it has contributed to my growth."

David was not free of torment for a single day of his seventy years. He saw himself as "the stone the builders despised," and although he was despised and rejected in his youth, he became the cornerstone of Israel.

David did not wallow in self-pity. The suffering had meaning for him. "This is the day that G-d has made, and I can rejoice and be glad." Since he was never free of distress, this can only mean that David had learned how to be glad even with his intense suffering.

From the Sages

Tithe, in order that you may retain your wealth *(Taanis 9a).*

The Sages compare *tzedakah* (charity) to a preservative that one puts into grain to prevent it from spoiling in storage. One who refuses to spend money to buy the preservative is indeed foolish, because he is apt to lose his entire crop. It is a small expenditure that will prevent a major loss.

Tzedakah is a preservative. If we selfishly try to keep everything we have to ourselves, we may end up with nothing.

This is as true of physical wealth as it is of spiritual wealth. You only get to keep it if you give it away.

תִּקְעוּ בַחֹדֶשׁ שׁוֹפָר בַּכֶּסֶה לְיוֹם חַגֵּנוּ *From*
כִּי חֹק לְיִשְׂרָאֵל הוּא מִשְׁפָּט לֵאלֹקֵי יַעֲקֹב *our*

Sound the shofar on the new moon, on *Prayers*
the day the moon is veiled, which leads
to our festival. For there is a statute in
Israel, and the G-d of Jacob sits in judgment *(Song of the day for Thursday; Psalms
81:4-5).*

**Second Day of
Rosh Chodesh**

Aug. 22, 1990

Aug. 11, 1991

Aug. 30, 1992

Aug. 18, 1993

Aug. 8, 1994

Aug. 27, 1995

Aug. 16, 1996

On this day of the year, we begin sounding the *shofar*
each morning, to arouse us to the forthcoming Rosh
Hashanah, Yom Kippur, and Succos.

The *shofar* is a call to *teshuvah* (repentance). The month
of Elul is particularly propitious for renewal and rededica-
tion. We must take a moral inventory, for the days of
accountability are approaching. Life is not a free-for-all.
There are statutes by which we must live, and the G-d of
Jacob sits in judgment.

Teshuvah is hard work. Self-examination is not comfortable, and changing those habits which we discover to be
objectionable requires persistence and diligence.

"Sound the *shofar* . . . which leads to our festival." The
days of awe are followed by Succos, the festival of joy. All
the effort expended in self-examination and in ridding
ourselves of our character defects will ultimately be
rewarded by the attainment of true joy.

**The Hebrew letters of the word Elul form an
acrostic of the verse** אֲנִי לְדוֹדִי וְדוֹדִי לִי, **"I am devoted**
to my Beloved (G-d), and He is devoted to me" *(Song
of Songs 6:3).*

*From
the Sages*

The *neshamah,* the human soul, is identified with
Divinity. Spirituality, man, and G-d are one. It is only the
barriers that are erected when man succumbs to temptation leading him away from G-d that separate man from
G-d.

As we intensify our *teshuvah* in the month of Elul, we
progressively remove these barriers, and we can once again
enjoy the pristine spiritual state of being one with G-d.

Judaism calls for intensification of prayer, Torah study,
meditation, and acts of benevolence in the month of Elul.
We must overcome the inertia that may have developed
during the year, and make the painstaking efforts necessary
for *teshuvah*.

The task may be a difficult one, but the rewards are more
than adequate. We become one with G-d.

Aug. 23, 1990
Aug. 12, 1991
Aug. 31, 1992
Aug. 19, 1993
Aug. 9, 1994
Aug. 28, 1995
Aug. 17, 1996

From our Prayers

לְדָוִד ה' אוֹרִי וְיִשְׁעִי מִמִּי אִירָא
ה' מָעוֹז חַיַּי מִמִּי אֶפְחָד

A Psalm of David. With G-d as my illumination and my salvation, whom need I fear? With G-d as the strength of my life, before whom need I tremble? *(daily service during month of Elul, Psalms 27:1).*

The Midrash comments on the above verse, "G-d is my illumination on Rosh Hashanah, and my salvation on Yom Kippur."

The Talmud states that sins are committed only out of folly, when a person has taken leave of his senses *(Sotah 3a)*. No rational person would do something which is harmful to him. The person who sins invariably has a distorted perception and cannot see that what he is doing is destructive. The transient physical gratification that the sin provides blinds the person to the true facts. Sin is nothing other than the darkness of ignorance.

When a person's eyes are open to truth and he sees the harm inherent in sin, then he will no longer succumb to temptation. To be properly enlightened is therefore the key to avoidance of all sin, and is the key to *teshuvah* which will bring about the forgiveness of Yom Kippur.

Illumination achieved by meditation on Rosh Hashanah will therefore lead to the salvation on Yom Kippur.

From the Sages

Moses was like the sun, Joshua like the moon *(Bava Basra 75a).*

Illumination can be provided in one of two ways. One can be a source of light, or one can reflect light from elsewhere, like a mirror.

Moses' light was original. Whereas Joshua did not lack for originality, his major contribution was that he reflected the light of Moses, and thereby became one of Israel's greatest leaders.

"The soul of man is the lamp of G-d" *(Proverbs 20:27).* Everyone has the responsibility of shedding light upon the world. Some people may generate light, while others can illuminate the world by reflecting light.

In order to reflect light, one must keep close to a source that generates light. The most highly polished mirror cannot reflect any light if it is kept in the dark.

If we associate ourselves with those who are spiritual, we ourselves will shine, and we will help spread their light.

NOTES
_____
_____
_____
_____
_____
_____
_____
_____
_____

From our Prayers . . . מָחִיתִי כָעָב פְּשָׁעֶיךָ וְכֶעָנָן חַטֹּאתֶיךָ
שׁוּבָה אֵלַי כִּי גְאַלְתִּיךָ

Erase our sins and iniquities as You said, "I have erased your sins as a dispersed thick fog, and your iniquities like a cloud. Return to Me, for I have redeemed you" (Selichos, Isaiah 44:22).

Although Divine forgiveness is always forthcoming, the month of Elul is particularly propitious for forgiveness.

The forgiveness of G-d is different than that of the human being. People who forgive someone who offended them may nevertheless retain residues of resentment. They can overlook the offense, but generally cannot completely extirpate its memory.

Divine forgiveness is otherwise. Just as when a cloud disappears and a fog clears, there is no sign of their having existed at all, so it is with G-d's forgiveness. When there is proper *teshuvah*, G-d totally erases and undoes the act, making it as though it had never happened.

Too often people ruminate over their mistakes, and they create their own purgatory. "No need for this," says the prophet. "G-d's forgiveness provides absolute redemption. Whatever the sin may have been, G-d removes it completely. You are free of the burden. You have been redeemed. Now get on with your life."

They are drunk, albeit not with wine. They stagger, but not from ale (Isaiah 29:9).

From the Scriptures

Involvement in the treatment of alcoholism has given me a better understanding of the prophet's admonishment. It is typical for the alcoholic to behave destructively and not recognize what his problem is. He attributes all his misery and failures to other people, and is unable to see that his drinking is his undoing. He rejects all help, insisting that he can manage everything by himself, although it is obvious to everyone that he cannot manage anything. The inability to give up the alcohol dominates and dictates all his actions.

The prophet tells us that when we sin, we are similar to the alcoholic, even though we may be stone sober. We adamantly refuse to change our ways, and turn a deaf ear to any criticism.

Too often the alcoholic's self-deception is shattered only by some catastrophic event that shocks him into reality. We need not wait for this. If we open our minds to the teachings of Torah, we can restore ourselves to healthy living without the trauma of a personal cataclysm.

Aug. 24, 1990
Aug. 13, 1991
Sept. 1, 1992
Aug. 20, 1993
Aug. 10, 1994
Aug. 29, 1995
Aug. 18, 1996

NOTES

Aug. 25, 1990
Aug. 14, 1991
Sept. 2, 1992
Aug. 21, 1993
Aug. 11, 1994
Aug. 30, 1995
Aug. 19, 1996

From our Prayers

וּבָא לְצִיּוֹן גּוֹאֵל וּלְשָׁבֵי פֶשַׁע בְּיַעֲקֹב נְאֻם ה׳

A Redeemer shall come to Zion, to those of Jacob who returned from their defection, thus spoke G-d *(daily morning prayer, Isaiah 59:20).*

Sins are catagorized as (1) unintentional, (2) intentional transgressions that are due to temptation, and (3) acts of rebelliousness and defiance.

Logically it would seem that forgiveness should apply only to the first two, where either negligence or the inability to overcome temptation resulted in sin. But an act of defection, where one knowingly and intentionally defied G-d without having any gratification from the sin, why should he be forgiven? What defense can a person give for himself?

When there is no logical plea that can offset the sin of defiance, then G-d considers our observance of those of his laws that are beyond our understanding, and cleanses us with His justice *(Rosh Hashanah liturgy).*

Some of the Divine *mitzvos* lend themselves to our understanding, but there are others that are totally beyond our grasp. Why should one not be permitted to wear a mixture of linen and wool? How does application of the ashes of a sacrificed animal remove contamination?

G-d relates toward man as man relates toward G-d. If we observe those Divine decrees that are beyond our logic, then G-d responds by forgiving *all* our sins, even when there is no logical basis for forgiveness.

From the Sages

There is a popular aphorism, "When a burglar crawls under a fence, he prays to G-d that he should not be caught" *(Ein Yaakov, Berachos 63a).*

The Talmud shows how our logic is subject to distortion. It is possible for a person who is in the process of stealing to pray to G-d that he succeed and not be caught!

Should it not be obvious that one cannot pray to G-d for help in committing sin? Yes, it is obvious to everyone, except to the thief who feels himself to be in danger. At that point he does not see the absurdity of his prayer for success.

Such a contradiction may not be frequent, but more subtle incompatibilities occur frequently. Logical thinking is very fallible when there is strong self-interest. The only way to avoid such illogical thinking is to share our thoughts and plans with another person, a teacher, or a trusted friend. His more objective perspective can allow us to make a more correct judgment, so that we can be made aware of irrational thinking when it occurs.

NOTES
_____
_____
_____
_____
_____
_____
_____
_____
_____
_____

From אָבִינוּ מַלְכֵּנוּ חָנֵּנוּ וַעֲנֵנוּ

Our Father, our King, be gracious to us **our**
and answer us (daily morning service). **Prayers**

When Rabbi Menachem Mendel (the *Tzemach Tzedek*)
was a small child, his grandfather, Rabbi Shneur Zalman,
held him on his lap and asked the child, "Where is *Zeide*
(grandfather)?"

The child touched the grandfather's nose. "No," the
Rabbi said, "that is *Zeide's* nose. But where is *Zeide*?"

The child touched the grandfather's beard. "No, that is
Zeide's beard. But where is *Zeide*?"

The child descended, ran to the next room and shouted,
"*Zeide!*" and Rabbi Shneur Zalman went into the room.

Gleefully the child pointed, "There is *Zeide!*"

The message is a powerful one. *Zeide* is the one who
responds when called.

We know that G-d is our Father. He responds.

Aug. 26, 1990
Aug. 15, 1991
Sept. 3, 1992
Aug. 22, 1993
Aug. 12, 1994
Aug. 31, 1995
Aug. 20, 1996

**You have made man just a bit less than the
heavenly angels, and have adorned him with honor**
(Psalms 8:6).

*From the
Scriptures*

The word "*Elohim*" in this verse is generally translated
"angels," although its more common usage is to refer to
G-d as being all-powerful.

Rabbi Simcha Zisl gives this verse a somewhat different
interpretation. He states that the glory and honor of the
human being lies in his freedom of choice. Inorganic matter
and vegetation have no will at all. Animals are driven by
instinct, and have no free will. The glory and honor of man
is that he is a free agent, free to choose between good and
evil.

Although G-d is all-powerful, He has relinquished control
of human behavior. "All is in the hands of G-d except for
man's veneration of G-d" (Berachos 33b).

When it comes to man's choice between moral good and
evil, the power lies with man, not with G-d.

Rabbi Simchaa Zisl translates the verse, "By giving man
the freedom of choice, You have lessened Your omnipotence."

It may be frightening to realize that in matters of morality,
man is powerful and G-d, in a manner of speaking, has
abdicated His power.

The wise person will return this gift to G-d. It is too potent
a force to remain within human hands. "Here is the
freedom of choice You have given me. I return it to You, and
surrender totally to Your will."

NOTES

_____

_____

_____

_____

_____

_____

_____

_____

Aug. 27, 1990
Aug. 16, 1991
Sept. 4, 1992
Aug. 23, 1993
Aug. 13, 1994
Sept. 1, 1995
Aug. 21, 1996

From our Prayers

וְאָשׁוּב אֵלֶיךָ בִּתְשׁוּבָה שְׁלֵמָה . . .

I will return unto You with a complete repentance . . . and I say that if I have done wrong, I will not repeat it. Create in me a new heart, O G-d, and make fast a new spirit within me *(prayer of Rabbeinu Bachya).*

A man with twenty-seven years of sobriety said, "The man I *was* drank, and the man I *was* will drink again. If I am sober now, it is because I am no longer the man who took the first drink."

This philosophy is also relevant to sin or to any wrong a person does. It is unusual for a person to do something that is completely out of character. An observant person is not likely to eat pork, because that particular sin is totally alien to him. If he transgresses by speaking or listening to *lashon hara* (gossip), it is because this transgression is not totally alien to him.

For *teshuvah* to be complete, it is not enough that one regrets having done wrong. One must analyze, "How is it that I came to commit such an act?" One must improve one's character to the point where the possibility of doing such an act is eliminated, when one will be no more vulnerable to listening or speaking *lashon hara* than an observant person is to eating pork.

"Create in me a new heart." *Teshuvah* consists of becoming a totally new person, one who is no longer capable of committing those acts that one regrets doing.

From the Sages

He who says, "I need nothing else except Torah," does not have Torah either *(Yevamos 109b).*

Rabbi Tzadok HaKohen interprets this to mean that a person who thinks that he does not need prayer and Divine guidance because he is completely fulfilled by the study of Torah is deceiving himself. Without Divine assistance man is totally lost.

NOTES

One of the Sages of the Talmud said, "I always prayed in the place where I studied Torah" *(Berachos 8a).* Another said, "I always read Torah in the place where I prayed" *(Megillah 29a).* This teaches us that even with a total absorption in Torah, which G-d provides as an antidote to temptation, a person is still dependent on a power higher than himself to avoid the pitfalls in life.

We must consistently seek, through sincere prayer and meditation, to be shown the Divine will and to be strengthened to fulfill it.

Those whose sow in tears shall reap in joy. Though he who bears the measure of seed goes on his way weeping, he shall surely come home with exultation, bearing his sheaves *(Psalms 126:5-6, recited before Grace after Meals)*.

Aug. 28, 1990
Aug. 17, 1991
Sept. 5, 1992
Aug. 24, 1993
Aug. 14, 1994
Sept. 2, 1995
Aug. 22, 1996

One of the Chassidic masters read this verse to say, "There are those who sow in tears and in joy." Tears and joy are not mutually exclusive.

The Baal Shem Tov once received a complaint about a cantor who sang the *Al Chet* (Confession on Yom Kippur) with a very cheerful, lively tune. The townsfolk thought it was most irreverent to chant the confession with a joyous melody, because it deserved a very solemn melody.

The Baal Shem Tov summoned the cantor and asked him to explain this unusual behavior. The cantor replied, "If I were a janitor in the palace of the king, and was assigned to remove all the accumulated rubbish, thereby beautifying the palace for the king, should I not exult in my duty?"

G-d dwells in each of us. Each of us is a palace for the Divine presence. When we confess our sins and repent, we remove all that is objectionable within us and cleanse ourselves. We are thus beautifying the palace so G-d can dwell therein. Is that not adequate reason for a joyous melody?

Remembering our sins can be painful, and we may weep about our offenses against G-d. But we can also rejoice with our *teshuvah*. Tears and joy can coexist.

He who gives life will also provide sustenance *(Taanis 8b)*.

From the Sages

A man driving a horse and wagon passed a pedestrian who was carrying a heavy sack on his shoulders and offered him a ride. The foot-weary traveler gratefully accepted the offer. A few moments later, the driver turned around and noticed that the passenger was still carrying a heavy sack on his shoulders "Why don't you put the load down?" he asked.

The passenger replied, "Is it not enough that I have imposed upon you to take me in your wagon? I do not wish to add even more to your load."

"How foolish," the driver said. "Once you are on the wagon, it makes no difference whatever whether you carry the load or put it down. Either way, I am carrying it."

Since G-d provides us with life, is it not foolish that we should insist on carrying our sustenance by ourselves? Either way it is He Who provides for us. Why exert ourselves more than we are required to?

ELUL

8

אלול

Aug. 29, 1990
Aug. 18, 1991
Sept. 6, 1992
Aug. 25, 1993
Aug. 15, 1994
Sept. 3, 1995
Aug. 23, 1996

From our Prayers

שִׁירָה חֲדָשָׁה שִׁבְּחוּ גְאוּלִים . . .

With a new song the redeemed lauded Your name at the shore of the sea. In unison they praised and acknowledged Your sovereignty saying, "G-d shall reign forever" *(daily morning service)*.

The concept of "a new song" is found elsewhere in the liturgy. "Sing to G-d a new song, His praise is among the pious" *(Psalms 149:1)*, and "Sing to G-d a new song for He has done wondrous deeds" *(Psalms 98:1)*. What is the significance of "a new song"?

The Talmud says, "when one makes his prayer a routine task, that prayer is not a supplication." To pray only out of rote, without sincere feeling and devotion to G-d, is to miss the entire essence of prayer *(Berachos 28b)*.

If we pray out of routine, then today's prayer is not at all new. It is yesterday's, last week's, last month's, or last year's. If we pray with true devotion and awareness of the majesty of G-d and our utter dependence upon Him, then our prayer can be new.

Elsewhere we have cited the concept of "prayer before prayer" (5 Teves) and the meditation that should precede prayer (3 Shevat). Adequate preparation before prayer will increase our insights into the greatness of G-d and our gratitude to Him. Each day's prayer should therefore be fresh and stimulating.

From the Scriptures

And you shall remember the whole way in which G-d led you for forty years in the desert, in order to deprive you (of ready sources of food and water) and to test you whether you will keep His commandments or not *(Deuteronomy 8:2)*.

When we are in distress, we often cry out, "Why, G-d, O why are you doing this to me?"

NOTES

Do we need any clearer statement than that given by Moses? G-d puts us to the test, that we may manifest our faith and strengthen our faith and trust in Him.

True, Moses spoke these words *after* a forty-year ordeal, when the Israelites were on the verge of entering the Promised Land.

G-d is not angry with us when we cry out in our distress. The Talmud says that a person is not held accountable for what he says when he is suffering *(Bava Basra 16b)*. But when the suffering has passed, he must be able to reflect and accept the superior wisdom of G-d as being just.

אוֹדֶה לָקֵל לֵבָב חוֹקֵר בְּרָן יַחַד כּוֹכְבֵי בֹקֶר *From*

I thank G-d, the Searcher of all hearts, and *our*
praise Him together with the stars of the *Prayers*
dawn *(introduction to the morning service).*

Aug. 30, 1990
Aug. 19, 1991
Sept. 7, 1992
Aug. 26, 1993
Aug. 16, 1994
Sept. 4, 1995
Aug. 24, 1996

The Rabbi of Rizhin strongly disapproved of those who were lax in praying the morning service within the time specified in *halachah*. Someone remarked that some *tzaddikim* were known to meditate for hours before prayer, and that they therefore exceeded the specified time.

The Rabbi of Rizhin responded, "There was once a man whose wife regularly served him grits for supper. One evening he returned from work and found that his supper was not ready. 'Ah,' he thought, 'Tonight she is making something special for me!' An hour later there was still no supper on the table, and he then concluded, 'My wife must be preparing a roast, and that is why there is such a long delay.' To his surprise, the long delay ended with the serving of the usual grits. 'What!' he exclaimed. 'For this I had to wait so long? You could have served me grits immediately.' "

The Rabbi of Rizhin concluded, "Those *tzaddikim* who spend hours meditating, doing *teshuvah*, and elevating themselves to a more lofty level of spirituality, provide G-d with a prayer that is worth waiting for. But those who serve Him the same prayer menu as always, they have no right to delay." (See 10 Elul for the sequel to this.)

If a person has relapsed into sin after teshuvah, *From*
even if this occurs repeatedly, he can still do *the Sages*
teshuvah, but his subsequent teshuvah must be
more thorough than the previous teshuvah *(Orchos*
Tzaddikim, chapter on teshuvah).

Relapse after *teshuvah* should be taken as an indication that the *teshuvah* was incomplete. Thorough *teshuvah* usually precludes relapse.

Without competent help it is extremely difficult to analyze our previous *teshuvah* and to determine in what way it was defective. We may have failed to grasp the gravity of the wrong we have committed. We may have failed to make amends to people we offended, and no *teshuvah* is complete without appropriate amends. We may have failed to seek out what character defects led us to commit transgressions, and we may have failed to correct these defects.

Again, a spiritual counselor and a trusted friend can be of inestimable value in helping us recognize the inadequacies in our *teshuvah*. Fervent prayer is essential for Divine guidance that we may see the truth.

NOTES

_____
_____
_____
_____
_____
_____
_____
_____

Aug. 31, 1990
Aug. 20, 1991
Sept. 8, 1992
Aug. 27, 1993
Aug. 17, 1994
Sept. 5, 1995
Aug. 25, 1996

From our Prayers

יוֹנָתִי בְּחַגְוֵי הַסֶּלַע בְּסֵתֶר הַמַּדְרֵגָה . . .

My beloved is in the crevices of the rock, in the depth of the terraces. Let Me see your countenance, let Me hear your voice, for your voice is sweet and your appearance is beautiful *(Song of Songs 2:14)*.

The followers of the Rabbi of Rizhin, on their way home, stopped at an inn to refresh themselves, and reviewed the teachings they had heard from the master. They repeated his admonishment about delaying the morning prayer, and the parable about the wife who served her husband grits after a long delay. One of the guests at the inn who overheard the conversation said, "I am not so sure that your Rabbi is right. If the husband truly loves his wife, he would certainly overlook the delay, even if all she served him was grits."

On their next trip to Rizhin, the chassidim told the Rabbi of this man's comment. The Rabbi was ecstatic with joy. "That man was none other than the prophet Elijah, who intervened to defend and support the virtue of those who are tardy with their prayers.

"Yes," said the Rabbi, "G-d so wishes to hear our prayers that He will listen to them at all times. But that does not give you license to deviate from the halachic specifications for the time of prayer."

From the Scriptures

Jacob said, "In truth, there is the presence of G-d in this place, and I did not know" *(Genesis 28:16)*.

One of the followers of Rabbi Shmuel of Lubavitch came to the Rabbi for a private audience.

"What do you do before prayer?" the Rabbi asked.

"I meditate about the majesty of G-d," the man answered.

"And what do you do during prayer?" the Rabbi asked.

"Then, too, I think about the greatness of G-d," the man answered.

"And what about during the *Shema*?" the Rabbi asked.

"Of course I think about the unity of G-d," the man answered.

"Well, if you are constantly absorbed in thinking about G-d, when do you have time for self-examination?" the Rabbi asked.

Our forefather, Jacob, took himself to task. "I was so absorbed in the contemplation of G-d that I did not know myself. I have been derelict in self-examination."

Meditation about G-d is certainly important, but we must be careful that we do not exploit this to escape our duty to examine ourselves.

NOTES

From our Prayers

הִתְהַלְלוּ בְּשֵׁם קָדְשׁוֹ יִשְׂמַח לֵב מְבַקְשֵׁי ה' . . .

Seek your glory in His holy name. Those that seek G-d, their hearts shall rejoice. Seek G-d and His strength, seek His countenance continually (*I Chronicles 16:10-11*).

Sept. 1, 1990
Aug. 21, 1991
Sept. 9, 1992
Aug. 28, 1993
Aug. 18, 1994
Sept. 6, 1995
Aug. 26, 1996

It is important to note that the prayer does not say that those who *find* G-d should rejoice, but rather those who *seek* G-d. Indeed, the second verse underscores this, "Seek His countenance *continually*."

Often we become frustrated with our lack of understanding of G-d. We try our utmost to know Him, and pray for Him to bring us closer to Him. The wise Solomon stated it well. "I thought I would be wiser (in the knowledge of G-d), but it is beyond me. It is as distant as it ever was" (*Ecclesiastes 7:23-24*). All of his efforts seemed not to have advanced him in the knowledge of G-d.

The reason for the illusion that one has not made any progress is that G-d is infinite, and it makes little difference if one advances a millimeter toward infinity or a thousand kilometers. The end is never in sight.

However, this very realization, the recognition of the infinity of G-d, is an important achievement. If a person's search has led him to the correct conclusion that there is no end because G-d is infinite, then the search has certainly been most productive, and he has ample reason to rejoice in his discovery of the truth.

From the Sages

One who gives a gift to another person must inform him of it (*Shabbos 10b*).

In giving alms, anonymity of the donor is preferable. This is because one should try to avoid embarrassing the recipient of the charity, who feels crushed by his dependency on the graces of others. This does not apply to a gift.

A gift should elicit gratitude from the recipient to the giver. Giving an anonymous gift deprives the recipient of an opportunity to express his gratitude, and one has no right to do this.

Gratitude is a central theme of Judaism. "The ox knows its master, and the donkey knows who feeds him, but My people do not know Me" (*Isaiah 1:3*). This is one of the sharpest prophetic reprimands.

Learning how to be grateful is so important that no opportunity to develop this trait should be lost.

NOTES

_____

_____

_____

_____

_____

_____

_____

_____

Sept. 2, 1990
Aug. 22, 1991
Sept. 10, 1992
Aug. 29, 1993
Aug. 19, 1994
Sept. 7, 1995
Aug. 27, 1996

From our Prayers

וְלִמַּדְתֶּם אֹתָם אֶת בְּנֵיכֶם לְדַבֵּר בָּם . . .

And you shall teach them (the words of Torah) to your children, that they speak of them, when you sit in your house, when you walk on the road, when you rise, and when you retire *(the Shema, Deuteronomy 11:19)*.

We may sometimes have the narrow view that Torah is taught only in lectures and in classrooms. Not so. Torah is a way of living, and everything the Jew does should be within the framework of Torah.

The chief of the Polish gendarmes said to the Rabbi of Bobov, "When my workday is done, I take off my cap, and I am free of duty." The Rabbi of Bobov responded, "I never remove my cap (*yarmulke*), and so I am never free of my duty."

A person who truly observes the Torah speaks with the decency that Torah requires, relates with other people with the sensitivity and courtesy that Torah mandates, transacts business according to Torah standards, and is guided in his every move by Torah. He thereby teaches Torah to his children by his every action.

The Rabbi of Rimanov made this point when he said, "I walked miles to see how the master ties his shoes." What he was saying was that with his master, the Maggid of Mezeritch, no action, even the most insignificant, was performed without a Torah intent.

Yes, you teach your children by how you behave in your home, on the road, by how you arise, and by how you retire.

From the Scriptures

All the ways of a person are just in his own eyes. Only G-d can set straight one's heart *(Proverbs 21:2)*.

NOTES

_____
_____
_____
_____
_____
_____
_____
_____
_____
_____

We often observe other people doing things that we know to be wrong, yet it is evident that they are convinced that what they are doing is correct. If this happens to others, are we not also vulnerable to making similar misjudgments?

Being one's own final arbiter of right and wrong is hazardous. It is human nature to see one's actions as right. We cannot judge our own actions accurately.

Only G-d can set our hearts straight and keep us from becoming victims of self-deception. We must pray fervently for this Divine guidance.

שֶׁתְּחַדֵּשׁ עָלֵינוּ שָׁנָה טוֹבָה וּמְתוּקָה ... *From*

May it be Your will, L-rd our G-d, that *our*
You inaugurate for us a good and sweet *Prayers*
year *(prayer on the eve of Rosh Hashanah).*

Sept. 3, 1990
Aug. 23, 1991
Sept. 11, 1992
Aug. 30, 1993
Aug. 20, 1994
Sept. 8, 1995
Aug. 28, 1996

This prayer is traditionally said on Rosh Hashanah eve when eating an apple dipped in honey, which is symbolic of the sweetness for which we pray.

Why the symbolism of honey?

In the prayer we ask for a "good and sweet" year. To ask for simply a "good" year is not enough because we know that many things which are distressful to us are actually blessings in disguise, hence "good" may also be painful. Therefore, we specify "good and sweet," a kind of good that we can easily appreciate.

"Good" can be understood intellectually, but "sweet" is a sense experience which even a little child can appreciate. We ask G-d for uncomplicated and unsophisticated goodness, the sweet kind of good that can be appreciated by all, rather than that which is understood only by people of profound faith. "Give us simple good, sweet as honey."

G-d relates to us as we relate to Him. If we accept His word with simple, unquestioning faith, then He will respond with simple, uncomplicated good. If we complicate faith, accepting only that which we can grasp intellectually, then G-d may give us the kind of "good" that requires great intellectual effort to accept.

It is not good for a righteous person to punish *(Proverbs 17:26).*

From the Scriptures

When Rabbi Levi Yitzchok of Berdichev was Rabbi in the town of Ritzval, he suffered bitter persecution from a group of adversaries. One time when he was out of town, they put his wife and small children onto a dung wagon and drove them out of the city.

Rabbi Levi Yitzchok's colleagues, shocked by this atrocious behavior, gathered in Zhitomer with the *tzaddik* Rabbi Wolf, and asked him to bring down the wrath of G-d on those who committed this heinous act.

Rabbi Wolf said, "You are too late. Rabbi Levi Yitzchok is standing with his book of Psalms at the holy ark, praying fervently that no evil befall these people on his behalf."

We may feel that revenge is sweet. Like any other temptation, revenge gives us a momentary "high," and is followed by spiritual torment.

Each night we pray, "Let no person be punished on my account." We should live what we pray.

NOTES

_____
_____
_____
_____
_____
_____
_____
_____
_____

Sept. 4, 1990
Aug. 24, 1991
Sept. 12, 1992
Aug. 31, 1993
Aug. 21, 1994
Sept. 9, 1995
Aug. 29, 1996

From our Prayers

אָדָם יְסוֹדוֹ מֵעָפָר וְסוֹפוֹ לֶעָפָר . . .

Man's origin is dust, and he returns unto dust. With his soul he provides for his bread (Rosh Hashanah liturgy).

An elderly man was praying these solemn words, and flooding his prayer book with tears.

"Why are you crying?" a young man asked.

"Why, the tragedy of life is described in this prayer," he said. "What is man's destiny other than to return unto dust?"

"I see nothing tragic in this," the young man said. "If man's origin were gold and turned into dust, *that* would be tragic. but if he begins as dust and returns to dust, and in between he has the opportunity to say *Lechaim*, why that is pure profit!"

Jesting aside, if one invests a sum of money, and the sum of money is returned plus a profit, that should be considered a successful investment.

Even if life's experiences are harsh, we should never consider our lives as failures. We began as dust, and we will return to dust. And in between we have the opportunity to accomplish valuable *mitzvos*. That is certainly not a bad deal.

From the Sages

G-d said, "Bring a sin offering for Me, for having decreased the brightness of the moon" (Chullin 60b).

Does G-d need to be forgiven?

Rabbi Elimelech of Lizensk was asked by a disciple how one should pray for forgiveness. He told him to observe the behavior of a certain innkeeper before Yom Kippur.

The disciple took lodging at the inn and observed the proprietor for several days, but could see nothing relevant to his quest.

On the night before Yom Kippur, he saw the innkeeper open two large ledgers. From the first book he read off a list of all the sins he had committed throughout the past year. When he was finished, he opened the second book and proceeded to recite all the bad things that had occurred to him during the past year.

When he finished reading both books, he lifted his eyes to heaven and said, "Dear G-d, it is true I have sinned against You. But You have done many distressful things to me, too.

"However, we are now beginning a new year. Let us wipe the slate clean. I will forgive You, and You forgive me."

If we can forgive others — even when we cannot understand why they acted as they did — we can deserve to be forgiven ourselves.

NOTES

_____
_____
_____
_____
_____
_____
_____
_____
_____
_____

סְלַח נָא לַעֲוֹן הָעָם הַזֶּה כְּגֹדֶל חַסְדֶּךָ וְכַאֲשֶׁר *From*
נָשָׂאתָה לָעָם הַזֶּה מִמִּצְרַיִם וְעַד הֵנָּה *our*

Forgive the sins of this nation in Your *Prayers*
infinite mercy, just as You have forgiven
them from the time of Egypt until the
present day *(Selichos, Numbers 14:19)*.

Sept. 5, 1990
Aug. 25, 1991
Sept. 13, 1992
Sept. 1, 1993
Aug. 22, 1994
Sept. 10, 1995
Aug. 30, 1996

Although these words were said by Moses, they have
been retained throughout Jewish history. We assert that G-d
has forgiven our sins from our very beginnings until the
present. Why should we be any different? If we do *teshuvah*,
G-d is certain to forgive us as well.

Many people have difficulty in accepting forgiveness.
They ruminate over their past mistakes, wallowing in guilt
and self-flagellation. Even though they have sincerely
regretted their wrongs and resolved not to repeat them, they
allow the past to haunt them day and night.

Why is it so difficult to accept Divine forgiveness? After all,
G-d has told us that if we do proper *teshuvah* He will
completely erase our sins. If they do not exist before Him,
why do we hold on to them?

Perhaps we do not have an adequate understanding of
forgiveness. If we would truly forgive those who have
offended us, let go of our resentments and grudges, and
dismiss the incidents as though they had never occurred, we
could understand how G-d can forgive us, and we could put
our past behind us.

We need to practice true forgiveness toward others, and
then we will learn how to accept Divine forgiveness and be
able to forgive ourselves.

Do not place yourself with the wicked, to be an
unrighteous witness *(Exodus 23:1)*.

From the
Scriptures

NOTES

Rabbi Moshe Leib of Sasov said that anyone who speaks
evil of another person is compelled to bear witness against
him on judgment day, and repeat his words of condemnation.

The *halachah* is that witnesses are thoroughly examined
by the court to determine their integrity and reliability.

"Imagine having to appear as a witness before the
heavenly tribunal. You must then subject yourselves to a
meticulous scrutiny."

Before making critical comments about another person,
we would do well to consider whether we wish to bear
testimony against them before the heavenly tribunal, and
leave ourselves open to a fastidious scrutiny.

Sept. 6, 1990
Aug. 26, 1991
Sept. 14, 1992
Sept. 2, 1993
Aug. 23, 1994
Sept. 11, 1995
Aug. 31, 1996

From our Prayers

. . . סְלַח לָנוּ מְחַל לָנוּ כַּפֶּר לָנוּ

Our G-d and G-d of our fathers, forgive us, pardon us, accept our atonement, for we are Your people and You are our G-d . . . we are full of sin, but You are full of compassion *(Yom Kippur service).*

When we do appropriate *teshuvah*, make amends to those whom we offended, sincerely resolve not to repeat our sins, and try to remove those character defects that led to our doing wrong, then we should be confident that G-d has accepted our *teshuvah* and grants us a complete pardon.

If we have any residual doubt about the absoluteness of Divine pardon, the comment of Rabbi Levi Yitzchok of Berdichev on the above prayer may help.

"True, I am full of sin," said Rabbi Levi Yitzchok, "but You, G-d, are full of compassion. Assume that I am *full* of sin and that every bit of me is saturated with sin. But how big is Levi Yitzchok anyway? How much sin can this small body contain even when it is full of sin? But You, G-d, You are *full* of compassion, and You are infinite! So great! So vast! Yours is an endless, limitless compassion! Surely this enormous compassion can pardon this limited and finite sinful person."

We must do what is necessary to achieve Divine forgiveness, but let us not doubt the absoluteness of His pardon.

From the Sages

There are four types of temperament. One who is easy to provoke and easy to pacify . . . hard to provoke and hard to pacify . . . hard to provoke and easy to pacify . . . easy to provoke and hard to pacify *(Ethics of the Fathers 5:14).*

Why does the Talmud not describe the most virtuous person as one who cannot be provoked to anger at all?

Our Sages understood human nature. With the exception of a select few, total absence of anger when severely provoked is more apt to be pathological repression than a noble virtue. The most that can be asked of the average person is that he not be so sensitive that he is easily aroused to anger, and that when he does become angry, to quickly rid himself of his resentment and allow himself to be appeased.

Man, by his own efforts, cannot totally extirpate anger, because it is a normal human response to unjust treatment by others. If we recognize anger to be a character defect, and do our utmost to overcome it, then we can pray to G-d to remove *all* anger from us. This is a Divine prerogative, and if G-d wishes, he may free us of the emotion of anger. Man alone cannot accomplish this.

NOTES

_____
_____
_____
_____
_____
_____
_____
_____
_____
_____

O **... וְרוֹצֶה אַתָּה בִּתְשׁוּבַת רְשָׁעִים ...** *From*
Merciful G-d of forgiveness, You desire *our*
the return of those who have strayed, *Prayers*
and You do not desire their destruction ...
For it is said, "This is the word of G-d, 'Do
you think I prefer the death of a sinner?
What I desire is that he repent his errant
ways and live' " *(Yom Kippur service).*

Sept. 7, 1990
Aug. 27, 1991
Sept. 15, 1992
Sept. 3, 1993
Aug. 24, 1994
Sept. 12, 1995
Sept. 1, 1996

The physician cautions the diabetic not to eat sweets and
save his health. He cautions the alcoholic to abstain from
alcohol because it will utterly destroy him. If the patient
chooses to ignore the doctor's instructions, the doctor may
shake his head sadly, thinking, "If that is what he wishes to
do with his life, that is his business." Although certainly
interested in the patient's health, the doctor cannot take to
heart the patient's decision to disregard his instructions.

If the patient presents himself with the ruinous consequences of his indulgence, it is likely that the doctor may say,
"Go elsewhere for help. I cannot treat you if you do not listen
to me." Even if he decides to help the patient, he frequently
cannot undo the harm that has already been done.

How different is the Divine Healer. He instructs us on
what to avoid that is harmful to us. When we sin, He
anxiously awaits our relinquishing our destructive behavior.
When we repent, He never rejects us. Furthermore, he
totally eradicates the wrong we have done.

**Rabbi Judah the Prince wept. "A person can
acquire his eternal world in just a brief period of
time"** *(Avodah Zarah 17a).*

*From
the Sages*

This remark was elicited by the episode of Elazar Ben
Doradia, a person who lived a totally dissolute and depraved
life. Late in his life, he had a momentary flash of insight into
his depravity, and in his remorse, he wept so bitterly over the
wasteful and shameful life he had led that he died of a broken
heart while crying. A voice from heaven then pronounced,
"Rabbi Elazar Ben Doradia has merited Paradise."

NOTES

Rabbi Judah wept. Why did a soul like Elazar have to
wallow so long in the mud of depravity? He could have come
to the realization of truth and virtue so much earlier and
could have contributed so much to mankind.

How does such a person merit to be called "Rabbi"? Rabbi
means "teacher," and Elazar Ben Doradia teaches us a great
deal. It is never too late to repent, to make corrections in
one's life. One may indeed merit Paradise even in the final
moment of life. But how tragic is it to waste a life.

Sept. 8, 1990
Aug. 28, 1991
Sept. 16, 1992
Sept. 4, 1993
Aug. 25, 1994
Sept. 13, 1995
Sept. 2, 1996

From ...
our
Prayers

אָבִינוּ מַלְבֵּנוּ סְלַח וּמְחַל לְכָל עֲוֹנוֹתֵינוּ

Our Father, our King, forgive and pardon our sins ... in Your compassion erase the indebtedness of our sins ... inscribe us in the Book of Good Life *(Avinu Malkeinu prayer recited during the Ten Days of Penitence).*

A merchant who suffered a severe business reversal came to his wholesaler and said, "Look, I cannot possibly pay what I owe you. If you will give me another shipment of goods on credit, I can try to turn a profit, and there is at least a reasonable chance that I can repay what I owe. If you choose to deny me further credit, I can well understand your position, but you must realize that there will never be any possibility of your getting your money."

This is essentially our plea to G-d. True, we have sinned. But if You grant us life and health, we will correct our ways and do what is necessary to improve ourselves and compensate for our dereliction.

The supplier of the merchandise is likely to say, "Very well, I will extend your credit. But please examine carefully your business practices so that you can avoid the mistakes that resulted in your previous failure."

That is exactly what G-d's response is to us.

From the
Scriptures

We remember the fish that we ate in Egypt gratis, and the squash, melons, leeks, onion, and garlic *(Numbers 11:5).*

How peculiar human nature can be. These words were spoken by the people who had been delivered from bondage, who slaved under the ruthless drive of cruel taskmasters, and who saw their infant children drowned in the Nile. Now, although provided with ample nutrition in the form of the manna from Heaven, they are nostalgic for the "good times" in Egypt!

It is almost beyond belief that our cravings may so affect us as to virtually deprive us of our senses. We may accept unspeakable tortures to gratify a craving. It is indeed absurd, but not completely beyond belief. I have repeatedly observed this phenomenon in the alcoholic or addict, who will endure anything to gratify his craving.

The Torah tells us this to teach us the treachery of our cravings. They can lead to self-destruction. Partaking of the pleasures of the world to the degree necessary to sustain life is appropriate, but if we allow ourselves to indulge, we risk disaster.

NOTES

_____
_____
_____
_____
_____
_____
_____
_____
_____

From our Prayers

. . . וְהָיָה בַּיּוֹם הַהוּא יִתָּקַע בְּשׁוֹפָר גָּדוֹל

And it shall be on that day, a great shofar will be sounded, and those who have been lost in Assyria and cast away in the land of Egypt will come and bow down to G-d on the sacred mountain in Jerusalem *(Rosh Hashanah Amidah, Isaiah 27:13).*

Sept. 9, 1990
Aug. 29, 1991
Sept. 17, 1992
Sept. 5, 1993
Aug. 26, 1994
Sept. 14, 1995
Sept. 3, 1996

Today, as during all of Elul, the *shofar* is sounded at the morning service.

Many interpretations have been given for the *mitzvah* of sounding the *shofar*. One of these, as the above prayer indicates, is that the *shofar* represents the gathering of all Israel at the Redemption, when the clarion call of the *shofar* will reunite Jews from all corners of the earth.

Another significance of the *shofar* is that it is a simple sound without words. Much of our communication is verbal and consequently subject to intellectual distortion. The *shofar* provides a wordless sound, which penetrates into our emotions. It is a sound of arousal, and because it is non-verbal, it can arouse different feelings in different people.

One person may be aroused to self-examination. "What am I doing with my life? What do I have to show at the end of the day, the week, the month, the year?" Another may awaken to reality. "Abandon the fantasy of the world as you would like it to be, and learn to live with the world as it is."

The *shofar* calls to all of us. As we approach the beginning of a new year, we should not turn a deaf ear to its sound.

Minimize your involvement in business, and maximize your involvement in the study of Torah. Be humble with everyone. If you are idle from Torah, you will formulate many reasons to prolong the idleness *(Ethics of the Fathers 4:12).*

From the Sages

When we are too lazy or otherwise wish to avoid doing something, we are never at a loss for rationalizations or excuses to explain away our indolence.

Spirituality is the nutrient of the *neshamah* (soul). Without spirituality, the *neshamah* perishes.

If a person is deprived of food and water, he will die of starvation even if there are legitimate reasons why he could not get the necessary food and water.

We can come up with many reasons why we do not have enough time to devote to Torah and prayer. We must realize that the deprivation of spirituality, for whatever reason, will result in spiritual deterioration, even if the rationalizations seem to have merit.

NOTES

_____
_____
_____
_____
_____
_____
_____
_____
_____

Sept. 10, 1990
Aug. 30, 1991
Sept. 18, 1992
Sept. 6, 1993
Aug. 27, 1994
Sept. 15, 1995
Sept. 4, 1996

From our Prayers

הוֹשַׁע ה' אֶת עַמְּךָ אֶת שְׁאֵרִית יִשְׂרָאֵל . . .
O G-d, save Your people, the remnant of Israel. Even at a time when they stray from You, may all their needs be before You. Blessed are You, O G-d, who hearkens to prayer *(abridged Amidah, Berachos 28b).*

This brief prayer was composed to be said in place of the regular *Amidah* if one is in a perilous situation and cannot take time out for the usual prayer.

It is noteworthy that the content of the prayer to be said at a time of great personal danger stresses two things. (1) One does not pray only for one's own safety, but for that of the entire nation, and (2) one invokes the Divine compassion even upon those who have deviated from the Divine commandments.

Even if as an individual I may not be deserving of Divine grace, I can nevertheless merit such grace if I am one with the entire nation. Furthermore, if my own behavior has not been virtuous, I can merit salvation by praying for others who may not be deserving. The Talmud says, "One who is in personal need, and overlooks his own needs to pray for others, is answered promptly" *(Bava Kamma 92a).*

From the Sages

Judge your friend justly *(Leviticus 19:15).* **This means that you must always give another person the benefit of the doubt and judge him favorably** *(Shevuos 30a).*

Rabbi Alexander Ziskind states that judging someone favorably is a prerequisite for the fundamental *mitzvah,* "Love your neighbor as yourself." He points out that when we allow ourselves to feel negatively about another person, it is most difficult to overcome such feelings and love him.

Rabbi Alexander Ziskind states that in judging another person's behavior we should consider even the most unlikely and absurd possibilities in order to judge him favorably. The person may have been acting under duress, or there may have been circumstances of a life and death nature that led to his actions. Even if it turns out that the favorable considerations were totally wrong, says the Rabbi, we have nevertheless fulfilled the *mitzvah* of judging another person favorably.

Furthermore, by going to extremes to judge another person favorably, we evoke a similar response from G-d, and He judges us favorably too.

NOTES

_____
_____
_____
_____
_____
_____
_____
_____
_____

From our Prayers

יָרֵאתִי בִּפְצוֹתִי שִׂיחַ לְהַשְׁחִיל . . . From I fear to open my lips to speak as I arise to pray before the Awesome One. I am so poor in good deeds, therefore I tremble, I am so lacking in wisdom, how can I possibly pray *(Rosh Hashanah liturgy)*.

The Scriptures and the Talmud often stress the importance of "fear of G-d." Moses says, "What does G-d ask of you but to fear Him and to go in His ways" *(Deuteronomy 10:12)*. David says, "The beginning of wisdom is the fear of G-d, and the understanding of what is good is given to those who practice His commandments" *(Psalms 111:10)*. The Sages say, "Only if one's fear of sin precedes his knowledge will his knowledge endure" *(Ethics of the Fathers 3:11)*.

Some people have difficulty with the concept of "fear of G-d." Why should we think of G-d as being threatening?

The idea of "fear of G-d" representing a threat is a very juvenile one. If we examine the above quotes, we can see that there are two concepts in "fear of G-d."

The first is the fear of sin. We must understand that defying G-d's will is as lethal to a person as the most toxic poison. But while there is little danger that a person would ingest poison, the temptations of the human being and his vulnerability to indulge in physical pleasures should indeed cause us to fear that we may transgress the will of G-d.

The second is a concept of awe. A person who observes a natural phenomenon, such as the Grand Canyon or a giant waterfall, or who contemplates the vastness of the universe with billions of stars extending over an expanse of billions of light years, is overcome with the feeling of awe that can be literally breathtaking. Contemplation of the infinity of G-d should arouse a feeling of awe of His majesty.

From the Sages

As one leaves the House of Prayer, one should not walk with large paces *(Berachos 5b)*.

If we truly appreciated the spiritual aspect of our lives, we would certainly spend more time in prayer and less time in worldly affairs.

Unfortunately, we live a life style in which most of our day is devoted to earthly pursuits. The least we can do is to indicate our displeasure with this state of affairs. We should wish to be able to spend more time in communion with G-d.

When we leave the House of Prayer, we should walk slowly, to remind ourselves that we are being torn away against our true will, as it were, from where we should long to be.

Sept. 11, 1990
Aug. 31, 1991
Sept. 19, 1992
Sept. 7, 1993
Aug. 28, 1994
Sept. 16, 1995
Sept. 5, 1996

NOTES

Sept. 12, 1990
Sept. 1, 1991
Sept. 20, 1992
Sept. 8, 1993
Aug. 29, 1994
Sept. 17, 1995
Sept. 6, 1996

From our Prayers

מִי קֵל כָּמוֹךָ נֹשֵׂא עָוֹן וְעֹבֵר עַל פֶּשַׁע . . .

Who is like unto You, O G-d, who forgives sin and pardons transgression? . . . You will cast all our sins into the depths of the sea. And all the sins of Your people Israel You will cast in a place where they will not be recalled nor counted, nor will they even be thought of unto eternity *(Tashlich prayer on Rosh Hashanah; Michah 7:18-19).*

This prayer is said at the shore of a lake or river, and a popular misconception has developed that we divest ourselves of our sins by throwing bread crumbs into the water.

Sins cannot be disposed of so easily. The only way to rid ourselves of our sins is by appropriate *teshuvah*: sincere regret, remorse, and a firm resolution never to repeat the wrong acts.

The symbolism of the *tashlich* is in the prayer. Once we have done what is necessary to achieve forgiveness, our sins will be cast away so that they are never recalled nor counted, nor thought of again.

From the Scriptures

And Abraham grew old, well along in days, and G-d blessed Abraham with everything *(Genesis 24:1).*

When our days are rich with content, we can bring them along with us. Days that are empty, devoid of good deeds, cannot be brought along. One cannot collect vacuum. A hundred zeroes and one zero are equal.

It would appear that the appropriate expression for growing old would be "well along in *years*," rather than in days. Apparently a year is much too great a unit to handle. If one tries to manage an entire year, he may find himself with nothing. As the Talmud says, "If you grasp too much, you have nothing at all" *(Rosh Hashanah 4b).* The manageable unit is the day: "Each day's subject in its day" *(I Kings 8:59).*

If we live one day at a time, we can bring all our days with us and achieve the Divine blessing: "And G-d blessed Abraham with everything."

NOTES

_____
_____
_____
_____
_____
_____
_____
_____
_____
_____

אֲרֶשֶׁת שְׂפָתֵינוּ יֶעֱרַב לְפָנֶיךָ קֵל רָם וְנִשָּׂא . . . *From our Prayers*

May the expression of our lips be sweet before You, almighty and exalted King, who understands, listens, sees, and hearkens to the sound of the shofar (Rosh Hashanah liturgy).

Sept. 13, 1990
Sept. 2, 1991
Sept. 21, 1992
Sept. 9, 1993
Aug. 30, 1994
Sept. 18, 1995
Sept. 7, 1996

Rabbi Levi Yitzchok of Berdichev observed a man who was reciting his prayers very rapidly, mumbling the words in an unintelligible manner.

The Rabbi approached the man, and mumbled some nonsense syllables. "I'm sorry, Rabbi," the man said, "but I cannot understand what you are saying."

"Then why did you mumble your prayers unintelligibly?" the Rabbi asked. "You should say your prayers distinctly so that each word can be understood."

The man responded, "When you hear an infant crying or saying nonsensical syllables, you may not understand what he wants, but his parents are sensitive to his sounds, and understand what each sound means. G-d is my Father. He understands my mumbling."

Rabbi Levi Yitzchok was thrilled. He had acquired a new plea to defend people's behavior.

This is the blessing bestowed by Moses, the G-dly man, upon the children of Israel (Deuteronomy 33:1).

From the Scriptures

Rabbi Meir of Premishlan noted that this verse in Hebrew can also be read, "Moses, the G-dly man, was *with* the children of Israel." Despite his lofty spiritual achievements, Moses never lost contact with all the children of Israel, and was never too preoccupied with heavenly issues to attend to the needs of even the least of the people.

Rabbi Dov Ber of Lubavitch lived in an apartment below his father, Rabbi Shneur Zalman. Once he was so absorbed in his studies that he did not hear his baby crying. Rabbi Shneur Zalman, who heard the baby's cry from upstairs, came down and took care of the infant, and then chastised his son.

NOTES

"One should never be so absorbed, even in devotion to G-d, so as not to hear the cry of another person."

If that is so, even with spiritual devotion, how much more so with earthly pursuits! We should never become so absorbed with what we are doing that we become deaf to the needs of others.

Sept. 14, 1990
Sept. 3, 1991
Sept. 22, 1992
Sept. 10, 1993
Aug. 31, 1994
Sept. 19, 1995
Sept. 8, 1996

From our Prayers

. . . וַיֹּאמֶר כֹּל אֲשֶׁר נְשָׁמָה בְאַפּוֹ . . .

Our G-d and G-d of our fathers, reign over the entire universe in Your Glory . . . Let every living thing declare, "The G-d of Israel is G-d, and His sovereignty is over all" *(Rosh Hashanah liturgy)*.

The Midrash relates a Divine command: "Recite before Me verses referring to Divine sovereignty, so that you will accept My sovereignty over you."

How can one achieve an acceptance of the sovereignty of G-d? The human mind is so limited in its scope, it cannot possibly conceptualize the Divine majesty.

Rabbi Simchaa Zisl Ziv quotes a Midrash that an individual will be asked on his Day of Judgment, "Did you accept the sovereignty of G-d over yourself each morning and evening?" and "Did you relate to your fellow man with the royal reverence due him?"

Rabbi Simchah Zisl points out that respect for a human being and reverence towards G-d are inseparable. The Talmud is replete with admonishment relating to disrespect for another person. "Better a person should cast himself into a fiery furnace than embarrass someone publicly" *(Berachos 47b)*. Man was created in the likeness of G-d.

The Midrash states that on the Day of Judgment we will be held accountable for not according our fellow human "royal consideration." We are to respect the *majesty* of every human being. Nothing less will do.

Behaving respectfully toward other people is essential for accepting Divine sovereignty.

From the Sages

Let all your deeds be for the sake of heaven *(Ethics of the Fathers 2:17)*.

The Rabbi of Kotzk said, "Even that which you do for the sake of heaven should be for the sake of heaven."

One might think that fulfillment of *mitzvos* is the highest achievement. The Rabbi of Kotzk requires that even *mitzvos* be done for the greater glory of G-d, and not for personal reward of any kind. In *Path of the Just*, Rabbi Moshe Chaim Luzatto emphasizes purity of devotion to the Divine will as one of the essentials of a Torah personality.

Rabbi Zusia said, "If I could trade places, so that I would be the Patriarch Abraham and he would be Zusia, I would not do so. Of course, I would stand to profit enormously, but what would G-d gain thereby? He would still have only one Abraham and one Zusia."

NOTES

_____
_____
_____
_____
_____
_____
_____
_____
_____

עַל חֵטְא שֶׁחָטָאנוּ לְפָנֶיךָ בְּקַלּוּת רֹאשׁ ... *From* **our** **Prayers**

Forgive us for the sins we committed before You by frivolity, and for the sins we committed before You with obstinacy *(Confession of Yom Kippur)*.

Sept. 15, 1990
Sept. 4, 1991
Sept. 23, 1992
Sept. 11, 1993
Sept. 1, 1994
Sept. 20, 1995
Sept. 9, 1996

Some sins are rather easy to confess. We made a mistake, or were deceived, or fell into the trap of temptation. But there are some sins we did because our philosophy of life led us to think that this was the right thing to do. Recognition of such sins would require us to admit that our entire philosophy of life was erroneous. This can be a most difficult admission. Some people would rigorously defend their actions so as not to have to admit that their whole attitude toward life until now was wrong.

The Jerusalem Talmud *(Yoma 8:9)* requires that a penitent person admit, "I was incorrect in my thinking, and my path in life was faulty."

This type of confession can evoke resistance. Refusal to admit that one's *weltanschaung* was wrong can lead to frivolity, to scoffing and mocking, and to defensively dismissing anything that challenges one's previous position as being undeserving of consideration.

To attain forgiveness we must overcome our obstinacy and the frivolous attitude it may produce.

The angels asked of G-d, "As a just G-d, how can You show favoritism toward Israel?" G-d responded, "I instructed them, 'You shall eat and be satiated and give thanks to G-d' (Deuteronomy 8:10), yet they say grace even after eating a morsel which does not satiate them. Do they not merit favor?" *(Berachos 20b)*.

From the Sages

Although the letter of the law requires expression of gratitude only after our needs have been fully met, the Sages taught us that we must be grateful for everything we receive, even if it is much less than we requested.

The sensitivity of expressing gratitude for whatever was done for us, even when our needs are largely unmet, is a character trait so dear to G-d that by its virtue He is willing to overlook many of our transgressions.

Why is this so important a trait? Because learning to be grateful for everything is a character refinement that will ultimately lead to avoidance of all improper behavior. Hence, this is the essence of *teshuvah*.

NOTES
———————
———————
———————
———————
———————
———————
———————
———————
———————

ELUL

26

אלול

Sept. 16, 1990
Sept. 5, 1991
Sept. 24, 1992
Sept. 12, 1993
Sept. 2, 1994
Sept. 21, 1995
Sept. 10, 1996

From our Prayers

כִּי עַל רַחֲמֶיךָ הָרַבִּים אָנוּ בְּטוּחִים . . .

For in Your great mercies we trust, and on Your righteousness we rely, and for Your forgiveness we hope *(Selichos)*.

The Midrash states that when people stand before judgment, they are generally very solemn and subdued. They eat sparsely because their worry and anxiety about what awaits them depresses their appetite. Their mood is one of dejection.

Not so on Rosh Hashanah. We wear our finest garments and prepare a festive holiday meal. Although our demeanor is serene, we celebrate with joy, secure in the knowledge that an all-merciful G-d will judge us favorably.

A visitor to the Chassidic master, the Seer of Lublin, who observed that following services on Rosh Hashanah Eve the worshipers joined hands in dancing, was shocked at this apparent violation of the solemnity of the day. The Seer explained that their joy was due to their utmost trust that G-d has already inscribed them into the Book of Life.

An unfaltering faith in the infinite benevolence of G-d is a virtue that merits a favorable judgment.

From the Sages

One who loves his wife as he loves himself, and who respects her even more than he respects himself, of him it is said, "And you shall know that there is peace in your home" *(Job 5:24, Yevamos 62b)*.

The alarming incidence of broken marriages in our society can be attributed largely to a perverted concept of love. People profess to love another person, but in reality they love only themselves, and they see the other person as one who is providing for their needs. The type of love that keeps a marriage together is true love for the other person rather than self-love.

How can we distinguish between the two types of love? Simply by observing whether one will consistently set aside one's own desires in deference to the needs of the other person. Self-love will be frustrated if one repeatedly sacrifices one's own comforts. True love will thrive and flourish on this.

Our Sages have given us the correct formula for a happy and peaceful home. Let each spouse respect the other *more* than himself or herself.

NOTES

_____
_____
_____
_____
_____
_____
_____
_____

From our Prayers

רִבּוֹנוֹ שֶׁל עוֹלָם מַלֵּא מִשְׁאֲלוֹת לִבִּי . . . From

M aster of the universe! Grant the requests of my heart . . . fulfill for us the
Scripture, "And the spirit of G-d will rest
upon you, a spirit of wisdom, understanding, counsel, and strength" (Festival prayer
before removing the Torah from the Ark).

Sept. 17, 1990
Sept. 6, 1991
Sept. 25, 1992
Sept. 13, 1993
Sept. 3, 1994
Sept. 22, 1995
Sept. 11, 1996

It appears that we are asking here for ruach hakodesh, or
Divine inspiration, similar to that which imbued the
prophets.

Many people often wish they had prophetic foresight, to
be able to foresee the consequences of their actions. But do
we fully utilize the foresight we already have?

There are many things whose consequences we do
know. Past experience has taught us that some things we
do will cause us to feel badly afterwards. Yet, like the
alcoholic, who knows he will suffer greatly for his
indulgence yet goes on to drink, we repeat our behavior
anyway.

"Who is wise? He who can see the consequences of his
behavior" (Tamid 32a). Perhaps we should demonstrate
how constructively we use the capacity that we already
have to foresee events before asking G-d for more.

From the Scriptures

You shall not kill; you shall not commit adultery;
you shall not steal; you shall not bear false witness
against your neighbor; you shall not desire that
which belongs to your neighbor (Exodus 20:13-14).

How can one be commanded not to desire something?
Desire is an emotion which occurs spontaneously, and
would appear to be beyond a person's control.

The answer is that the commandment against desiring
something which is not yours comes after four other
commandments which prohibit actions whereby you
would acquire the property of others.

Although desire may not be under conscious control, it is
a fact that a person will not desire something which he is
absolutely certain he can never attain. A firm commitment
never to take that which belongs to others will preclude
occurrence of the desire.

We may read the commandments this way: "If you will
not kill, commit adultery, steal, or testify falsely, then you
will not desire that which is not legitimately yours."

Sept. 18, 1990
Sept. 7, 1991
Sept. 26, 1992
Sept. 14, 1993
Sept. 4, 1994
Sept. 23, 1995
Sept. 12, 1996

From our Prayers

תִּכְלֶה שָׁנָה וְקִלְלוֹתֶיהָ . . .
תָּחֵל שָׁנָה וּבִרְכוֹתֶיהָ

Let the misfortunes of the past year come to an end . . . Let the new year begin with blessings (*prayer prior to Rosh Hashanah Eve*).

One of the most moving experiences in my life was listening to my father's repetition of the *Amidah* on the afternoon before Rosh Hashanah.

This was the last *Amidah* of the year. According to *halachah*, one day of a year can sometimes be considered a whole year (*Rosh Hashanah 10a*), and a portion of a day can be considered a whole day (*Pesachim 4a*). Combining these two, it is possible that in just a portion of one day one can redeem an entire year.

This was the spirit that prevailed in my father's repetition of the *Amidah*. Every verse was saturated with heart-rending tears. "Return us, Our Father, to Your Torah . . . Forgive us, our Father, for we have sinned . . . Bless for us, O G-d, this year . . . " This year? There were only a few moments left to this year! But the feeling was that in these few precious moments, the entire past could be redeemed.

The last few days of the bygone year present us with a unique opportunity. With the proper *teshuvah*, resolve and dedication, we can redeem the whole year. We can then truly say, "Let the misfortunes of the past year be gone, and let the new year begin with blessings."

From the Scriptures

(When the populace heard the reading of the Torah, they wept in remorse. Nechemiah and Ezra said to them,) **"Eat, drink and send portions to the needy, for this day is sacred unto G-d. Do not be sad, for the joy of G-d is your strength"** (*Nechemiah 8:10*).

NOTES

If we recognize our character defects and sincerely resolve to correct them, and if we look after the needs of the less fortunate, then we need not approach the awesome Days of Judgment with trepidation.

G-d rejoices when His children do His will. When we sincerely dedicate ourselves to His will and help bring the full joy of the festivals to the needy, then we bring joy to G-d. By merit of this virtue, we can be certain of a favorable judgment and the Divine blessings for the coming year.

לְשָׁנָה טוֹבָה תִּכָּתֵב וְתֵחָתֵם *From*

May you be inscribed and sealed for a *our*
good year *(greeting on Rosh Hashanah Eve).* *Prayers*

As we said earlier (11 Sivan), greetings can be prayers.
When we wish someone good, we are essentially praying
that G-d bless him with all that is good.

During the course of the year, when we are preoccupied
with our business affairs and social interactions, we may
become very competitive and believe that we can gain
profit or prestige by asserting ourselves even when we
encroach on others.

On Rosh Hashanah Eve, when we stand in judgment
before G-d, the truth may dawn upon us that it is not our
assertion that will bring us either riches or fame, and only
that which G-d decrees will come to pass. We may then
relinquish our competitiveness, and relate to our fellow
men with greater compassion and kindness. Our greetings
can then be sincere and can constitute a prayer.

**The fear of G-d prolongs days, while the years of
the wicked are too short** *(Proverbs 10:27).*

The theme of this book, "living each day," has stressed
the importance of living one day at a time.

Rabbi Samson Raphael Hirsch comments on the above
verse, "The G-d-fearing man lives in terms of days,
whereas the lawless person lives in terms of years; yet even
years are not sufficient to bring him the fulfillment of his
schemes. The G-d-fearing man's endeavor, his faithful
compliance with the Divine commandments, can be
successfully accomplished on each and every day. Each day
that has been lived through in faithful observance of the
Torah is a gain, a profit for him. Having accomplished this,
he can have it entered on the life-calendar of his sojourn
upon earth; he has not lived in vain. He counts days, not
years.

"The lawless person, however, sees the value of his life
only in external acquisitions. Such acquisitions, though,
reach their full value under the rays of the earthly sun, and
need years for their development. Mere days, therefore, are
meaningless to the lawless man; he can count only years.
But even years are not sufficient to bring him fulfillment of
his forever-increasing wishes."

Let us begin a new year living each day in faithful
observance of the Divine will.

May G-d bless you with a healthy, prosperous, and truly
joyous new year.

ELUL

29

אלול

Erev
Rosh Hashanah
*[Eve of
Rosh Hashanah]*

Sept. 19, 1990
Sept. 8, 1991
Sept. 27, 1992
Sept. 15, 1993
Sept. 5, 1994
Sept. 24, 1995
Sept. 13, 1996

*From the
Scriptures*

NOTES

ספר בראשית
Bereishis / Genesis

בראשית

Bereishis

Awareness of Purpose

בְּרֵאשִׁית בָּרָא אֱלֹקִים אֵת הַשָּׁמַיִם וְאֵת הָאָרֶץ — *In the beginning, G-d created the heavens and the earth* (Genesis 1:1).

In the kaballah there is an interesting syllogism. Since the attributes of G-d are not acquired, they are not external to Him but are one and the same with Him. Since Torah is the wisdom of G-d, and His wisdom is not something separate from Him, the person who embraces Torah embraces G-d Himself. Furthermore, since G-d is perfect unity and hence indivisible, one who embraces part of G-d is embracing all of Him. Hence, one who embraces the first letter of the Torah has embraced all of G-d.

Let us see how the first letter of the Torah can represent all of G-dliness.

The Torah begins with the word בְּרֵאשִׁית, *Bereishis*. The prefix ב usually means "in" and the word רֵאשִׁית means "beginning" or "first". Thus, בְּרֵאשִׁית means "in the beginning" or "at first". The Midrash points out that the prefix ב may also mean "for" or "for the sake of". The first verse of Genesis thus reads "*for* the sake of the first, the world was created." The Midrash then continues to list the various things that the Torah refers to as *reishis* or *firsts,* for whose sake the universe was brought into being, e.g., Torah, Israel.

The salient point here is that the first letter ב, *for,* teaches that the world was created for a purpose. The ultimate purpose is known only to G-d, and we can know only that which was revealed to us.

The concept of a purposeful creation is pivotal in living a Torah-true life. Just as the universe in its entirety has a purpose, so does everything in the universe have a purpose. Each individual has a purpose. My existence is not an accident. I have to accomplish something with my existence. Being is not haphazard or meaningless.

The conviction that one has a purpose is important because it means that a person must search to find that purpose so that he may fulfill his obligation. Even beyond that, the concept of having a purpose should influence and direct one's attitude toward life. The idea of freedom which is so dear to every thinking person should not be misconstrued to mean that one can do whatever he wishes. There is a difference between being a free man and one without responsibility. The first is a virtue, while the latter is the most derogatory term found in Torah, אִישׁ בְּלִיַּעַל, a vulgar person, without responsibility.

Humans have many emotions and many impulses that influence their behavior. A person who is without a sense of responsibility seeks only to gratify whatever drives he has. To the degree that a person lives with a sense of purpose, to that degree his behavior is directed by a responsibility to achieve that purpose rather than to gratify his wishes.

Love, hate, anger, pride, thirst for knowledge, envy, greed, humility, desire to please others, self-preservation — these and various other feelings that are part of the human makeup — how do we deal with them? The concept of *tikun hamidos,* correcting, improving, and adjusting our personality traits, is all contingent on having a sense of purpose and obligation. All *midos* (traits) are potentials, raw materials out of which we are to fashion something. This often requires restraint and self-discipline, both of which can cause discomfort when we deny ourselves free expression of all our biological drives.

What is the motivating force that will give us the determination to withstand the discomfort inherent in *tikun hamidos?* It is the concept of purposes. It is the ב of *Bereishis,* the realization that the universe is for something and that each of us is for something. For every emotion, for every impulse, for every trait, we must ask ourselves, ''How does this contribute to the fulfillment of the purpose of my existence?'' Whatever does not fit into this scheme must be discarded.

Torah teaches us *tikun hamidos* in the examples of the lives of *tzaddikim,* in both the written and the oral Torah, and in the great ethical works. To incorporate these teachings is to reject being without responsibility, and to surrender ourselves to the will of G-d.

The entire Torah is thus an extension and an elaboration of the first letter, the ב of *Bereishis.*

Awareness and Responsibility

נח

Noach

כִּי מָלְאָה הָאָרֶץ חָמָס מִפְּנֵיהֶם וְהִנְנִי מַשְׁחִיתָם אֶת הָאָרֶץ . . . — *for the earth is filled with theft . . . and I shall destroy them from the earth (Genesis 6:13).*

Only twice in the Torah do we find the Heavenly destruction of an entire population: the Deluge, and Sodom and Gomorrah. As deviant and as sinful as various people or cultures may have been, only in these two incidents were they considered completely incorrigible and totally beyond any hope of change. Where there is even the faintest possibility of change, there is no destruction. ''For I do not wish the death of a sinner, is the word of G-d, rather that he repent his ways and live'' *(Ezekiel 18:32).* Destruction of an entire population occurred only when its condition was such that it ruled out any possibility of correction.

What was it about these two populations that rendered them so utterly hopeless?

The Midrash states that although the generation of the Deluge was morally corrupt, their doom was sealed only because of theft. The Midrash goes on to explain that this was a unique kind of theft, because they practiced a thievery of less than a *prutah* (the smallest coin), less than the amount that could legally be considered theft, and which was consequently not remediable by appeal to law.

The people of Sodom and Gomorrah had a somewhat similar behavior. Instead of finding a technical loophole to put them beyond the reach of the law, they simply changed the laws to comply with their behavior, and by altering the laws to accommodate their self-indulgence, they legalized every evil.

The common denominator of both populations was that they convinced themselves that their actions were not wrong. The generation of the Deluge accomplished this by circumventing the law, and the Sodomites by altering the law. Both therefore believed that they had not violated any law, and where there is no awareness of wrongdoing, there is no possibility of *teshuvah,* of correcting one's actions.

Sin *per se* does not warrant the ultimate of punishments, because there can be an awareness that one has sinned and abandonment of one's errant ways. It is only when one deceives himself that wrong is right that there is no possibility of change. ''For this I shall judge you harshly, for saying 'I have not sinned' '' *(Jeremiah 2:35).*

Within all of us there is a powerful tendency to rationalize our behavior. The *yeitzer hara* (evil inclination) is shrewd, and provides us with an abundance of logical-sounding arguments to justify what we are doing. A person can become quite degenerate without being aware of his deviance.

As we read the history of our people as recorded in the Scriptures, we are struck with the prevalence of the decadence of *midos* (character traits), and the repeated exhortation by the prophets to do justice, to protect the rights of the poor, the widows, and the orphans. Our sensitivities are offended by the rampant corruption. How could this have come about?

The answer is found in the Scriptures. There were *nevi'ei sheker*, false prophets, who distorted the word of G-d to satisfy the greed of those in positions of authority, seeking to appease them for their own nefarious motives. Although there were many true prophets, people heard what they wanted to hear, and turned deaf ears to those who told them what they needed to hear.

In every age we are vulnerable to the influences of *nevi'ei sheker*, whether these be persons who, under the guise of being spiritual leaders, actually divert people from spirituality by sanctioning self-indulgence, or whether these are internal rationalizations that tell us that what we are doing is right.

It is most difficult to step outside oneself and be objective. Our emotions can thoroughly distort a self-analysis. The only salvation can come from true teachers, true leaders, and true friends, who are not motivated by a quest for popularity or a wish to ingratiate themselves. These would be people who would not hesitate to call us to task when our actions require a reprimand, who would not be deterred by the risk of losing our favor. Such individuals can arouse us to the truth about ourselves, and enable us to see aspects of our behavior that are wrong, and traits that need correction or improvement.

There are such individuals who can help us, but only if we let them.

Spirituality vs. Idolatry

לֶךְ לְךָ
Lech Lecha

וַיֹּאמֶר אֱלֹקִים אֶל אַבְרָהָם וְאַתָּה אֶת בְּרִיתִי תִשְׁמֹר אַתָּה וְזַרְעֲךָ אַחֲרֶיךָ לְדֹרֹתָם — *G-d said to Abraham, "You shall keep My covenant, you and your offspring for all their generations" (Genesis 17:9).*

In this portion of the Torah our ancestor, the patriarch Abraham, enters the scene of world history. The Midrash states that in an era when idolatry was rampant, and in the very midst of an idolatrous society and family, Abraham's reasoning led him to the belief in the one true G-d. Is it possible that in the ten generations preceding Abraham there was not even one person with sufficient intellect to be capable of reasoning to the truth and to reject the patent fallacy of idolatry?

In addition to being the first monotheist, the patriarch Abraham was also renowned for his perfection of *chesed* (kindness). Indeed, Abraham is the personification of *chesed*. For him, being of help to others was not only a matter of responding to their needs. Abraham had a personal need to do *chesed*, and if he was not able to be of service to others, he was distressed. Abraham is the one who sat outside his tent in the most intense heat of the day, scanning the horizon for travelers whom he might be able to invite to partake of his hospitality.

The occurrence of these two features in the same individual is not a coincidence.

The practice of idolatry requires a bit of analysis. Are we to believe that myriads of people were so utterly stupid as to believe that a piece of wood that they fashioned into an image with their own hands was a god that had power to grant their requests?

The concept of idolatry is not that simple. What happened was that people realized that humans needed to be guided and governed by some code of conduct, but they were insistent that whatever authority they accept upon themselves should not encroach upon their personal desires. They therefore developed a system of religion which they could manipulate to accommodate their needs. A man-made god served this purpose very well, because if conditions were such that the prevailing religion interfered too much with their lives, it was a minor task to fashion a new idol through which they could establish more accommodating rules. They were indeed capable of reasoning to the truth just as Abraham did, but realization of the truth would have made them subject to the sovereignty of the true G-d, and this would have impinged on their comfort. Their self-centeredness and self-indulgence thus blinded them to the truth, much as anyone's judgment is distorted by personal interests. People believed in idols because this is what they wanted to believe and, as so often happens, emotion overruled intellect.

The truth could therefore be evident only to a person whose character was one of *chesed,* who looked to be of service to others rather than to indulge himself. *Chesed* and *emunah* (faith) have a parallel relationship. To the degree that one possesses *chesed,* to that degree he can accept G-d as his sovereign, and subject himself to the will of G-d. Abraham's selflessness was so absolute that he became a "bearer" of the Divine presence. The Midrash refers to Abraham as a *merkavah lashechinah,* a "chariot" for the Divine presence. Just as a chariot has no spontaneous motion and goes only where the driver directs it, so was Abraham's surrender of his will to G-d so complete that he did nothing except that which was the will of G-d.

We tend to think of *chesed* as one of the *midos* we must cultivate in order to be able to appropriately fulfill those *mitzvos* that require benevolent deeds toward other people. As we now see, *chesed* extends beyond that, for if we are lacking in *chesed* we are also lacking in subjugating ourselves to the will of G-d.

One does not have to worship statues or graven images in order to be an idolater. If a person is motivated primarily by what will satisfy his personal desires, he is practicing the essence of idolatry. One can even be technically observant of many *mitzvos,* but to the degree that self-indulgence is one's goal in life, to that degree one is guilty of idolatry.

"Hear me, those who pursue justice and seek G-d. Look to the rock from which you were hewn, and to the source from which you were derived. Look to your father Abraham . . ." *(Isaiah 51:1-2).*

Three times a day we begin our prayer with "G-d of Abraham." This is not merely an expression of reverence for the founder of our nation. Perfection of the *midos* exemplified by the patriarch is fundamental to Judaism.

Equanimity

וירא

Vayeira

וַיַּשְׁכֵּם אַבְרָהָם בַּבֹּקֶר — *And Abraham arose early in the morning (Genesis 22:3).*

The outstanding event in this week's Torah reading is the *akeidah,* the readiness of the patriarch Abraham to bring his beloved son Isaac as a sacrificial offering because he understood this to be the will of G-d. In many of our prayers we recall this absolute devotion of our ancestor to G-d, and ask that we be blessed by virtue of his devotion.

While no one detracts from the greatness of Abraham's devotion, some commentaries have noted that Jewish history is unfortunately replete with incidents of sacrifice and martyrdom. And whereas Abraham's trial was only a test and was not permitted to progress to completion, there were so many incidents of martyrdom that did go on to completion. The story of Hannah who witnessed her seven sons killed because of their refusal to join in pagan worship would seem to surpass even that of Abraham. Why then is so much attention given to the patriarch?

One of the commentaries points out a tiny detail in the saga of the akeidah that is often overlooked. "And Abraham arose early in the morning . . . " If he awoke, then obviously he slept during the night. That is what distinguishes Abraham. Knowing that in the morning he was going to sacrifice his beloved son did not disturb his sleep. He faced this challenge with equanimity. Indeed, the uniqueness of Abraham was that what appears to us to be the ultimate challenge was to him no challenge at all.

The Talmud states that a person is required to praise G-d for the bad things that happen to him just as for the good things (Berachos 54a). It further requires that this praise be with simchah. Rashi (ibid. 60b) is careful to point out that in this case simchah does not mean joy, but "with a perfect heart", or in other words, with acceptance that whatever G-d does is just, even though it may be very distressing and appear to us to be most unjust.

For most of us, who are at least somewhat interested in gratifying our physical and emotional needs, equanimity is not easily achieved. We welcome pleasant things, and we are upset when our wishes are denied or frustrated. Personal losses, whether they are of close relationships or material assets, cause us to be depressed. Physical pain causes us suffering. We may think it beyond possibility for a person to have the same reaction toward adversity as he does when his fondest wishes are fulfilled.

But this is because we have ourselves as reference points, and we judge things according to how pleasant or unpleasant they are to us. If our only desire would be to fulfill the will of G-d, then how things affect us would be irrelevant. That which fulfills the will of G-d becomes desirable, and that which does not is undesirable. How things affect us personally does not enter into the equation.

For Abraham there was only one reason for existence: to do the will of G-d. If it was the will of G-d for him to have a son, so be it. If it was the will of G-d that he not have a son, so be it.

For us, the knowledge that when we arise in the morning we will have to put on tefillin (phylacteries) does not disturb our sleep. To Abraham, fulfilling the Divine will by offering his son as a sacrifice was of the same character and magnitude.

What does this say to us? Are we expected to achieve a self-effacement as complete as that of Abraham? Hardly. The Talmud does indeed state that a person should aspire that his actions reach those of his ancestors, but to "reach" does not mean to "equal." Yet, while we may not be able to achieve their greatness, there should at least be some point of contact between our ancestors and ourselves.

Our lives tend to be turbulent. We are subject to extremes of emotion. We may be exuberant over our successes and overwhelmed with despair when we suffer reversals. To whatever degree we can achieve self-effacement and replace our own will with the will of G-d, to that degree we can achieve equanimity, a more serene and tranquil attitude toward life, which at once gives us the courage to achieve, while allowing us to accept those things we cannot change.

Sensitivity to Others

וְהָיָה הַנַּעֲרָה אֲשֶׁר אֹמַר אֵלֶיהָ הַטִּי נָא כַדֵּךְ וְאֶשְׁתֶּה וְאָמְרָה שְׁתֵה וְגַם גְּמַלֶּיךָ אַשְׁקֶה אֹתָהּ הֹכַחְתָּ לְעַבְדְּךָ לְיִצְחָק — *It will be that the maiden to whom I say, "Please pour from your jug that I may drink," and she replies, "Drink and I shall also water your camels," she is the one You will have designated for Your servant Isaac (Genesis 24:14).*

Many important laws in Judaism, some pertaining to life and death judgments, are derived in the Talmud from analysis of the syntax of a verse in the Bible. Some are derived from a hardly noticeable nuance in word structure, perhaps an extra vowel or the omission of a vowel. Yet in Genesis the Torah goes to great length to relate biographical incidents of the patriarchs and matriarchs, none of which yield any new laws whatever.

In this portion of the Torah, Abraham's servant, Eliezer, devises a plan for choosing a wife for Isaac. He will ask the maidens to water his camels, and the young woman who will offer to fetch water to quench his thirst as well will be the one that G-d has designated as the mate for Isaac. After describing Eliezer's plan in detail, the entire soliloquy is repeated when Eliezer meets with Rivkah's family.

The Torah thus makes it abundantly clear that the events in the lives of the patriarchs are at least as important as the technical details of the *mitzvos*. This is because the lives of the patriarchs are lessons in *midos,* and teach us how to develop our characters, for the latter is a prerequisite for Torah observance. Torah knowledge and character refinement are mutually interdependent (*Ethics of the Fathers 3:21*).

Since the Torah devotes so much space to it, the episode of Eliezer must be of unusual significance.

The message is simple and obvious. The woman who is to share in assuming the responsibilities of Abraham and Sarah and who is to be the mother of the Jewish nation must be a person of *chesed*, with an exquisite sensitivity to the needs of others. She must be a person who will not only respond to a request for help, but will anticipate a person's unspoken needs and respond to them.

Rabbi Moshe Leib of Sasov said that he learned what it means to love another person when he overheard a dialogue between two drinkers. One man was proclaiming his love for his comrade, but the other rejected his assertion. When the first man, amidst an abundant flow of tears, continued to protest his love, the second man put him to the test.

"If you truly love me," he said, "then you must be able to tell me what my needs and wants are."

Rabbi Moshe Leib said, "If you truly love another person, you will be sensitive to what his needs and wants are, even if he has not verbalized them."

This was Eliezer's test for the one who was to be the matriarch of Israel. "Will she understand and respond to my needs without my asking?"

The Torah does not demand of us that which is beyond our capacities. If we are required to develop such sensitivity, then it is well within our means to do so.

If we are remiss in this respect, it is probably because we are too occupied with the pursuit of our own desires. And while there is no requirement that we deny our legitimate desires — indeed, asceticism is discouraged except for the select few who have achieved an advanced degree of spirituality — self-indulgence, to the extent that we are not sensitive to the needs of others, is wrong.

In our prayers we ask of G-d, "Please answer us even before we call upon you." We are taught that G-d relates to us מִדָּה כְּנֶגֶד מִדָּה, in the same fashion that we relate to others. If we wish to merit His anticipating our needs and providing for them even before we experience the lack and before we pray for their fulfillment, then we must adopt this pattern ourselves. We must take to heart the needs of our fellow men and help them in a manner that will obviate their need to humble themselves before us and ask our assistance.

This is *chesed* at its finest.

Contingent vs. Non-Contingent Love

תולדות
Toldos

וַיֶּאֱהַב יִצְחָק אֶת עֵשָׂו כִּי צַיִד בְּפִיו וְרִבְקָה אֹהֶבֶת אֶת יַעֲקֹב — *Isaac loved Esau for he fed him game; but Rebecca loves Jacob (Genesis 25:28).*

In this week's portion of the Torah we are introduced to Jacob and Esau, the two sons of Isaac and Rebecca. Jacob is described as a sincere person, devoted to scholarship, and Esau as a "man of the field," interested only in pursuit of earthly desires.

The Torah tells us that Isaac favored Esau because he hunted food for him, whereas Rebecca loved Jacob. However, no reason is given for Rebecca's preference.

The Shelah takes note of this omission, and also calls attention to a significant grammatical construct. Accurately translated, the verse reads, "Isaac *loved* (past tense) Esau," but "Rebecca *loves* (present tense) Jacob" (25:28). Why the change in tenses?

The Shelah refers to *Ethics of the Fathers (5:19),* "Love which is dependent on anything disappears when the thing (on which it was dependent) is gone." Isaac loved Esau because he provided him with food. Such love is transitory, and can easily become a thing of the past, hence the use of the past tense. Rebecca's love for Jacob was not contingent on anything he did for her, but was a love of Jacob for what he *was.* This type of love endures, hence the use of the present tense.

We tend to use the word love in a rather flippant manner. Many times it is used to refer to love of another person, when the true state of affairs is that the subject really loves *himself,* and the other person is "loved" only because he or she gratifies one's desires.

True love for another person, and self-love where the other person is only a medium for self-gratification, are poles apart. As the Shelah points out, the former is apt to be transitory, and only the latter, the non-contingent love, is of lasting duration.

In a subsequent portion of the Torah we read of Jacob's love for Rachel, and although he had to wait for seven years to marry her, "it seemed to him as but a few days, because of his love for her" *(Genesis 29:20).*

Isn't this a rather strange statement? Is it not rather that when one is in love each day of separation seems to be an eternity? What sense is the assertion that because of Jacob's great love for Rachel, seven years seemed to him as a few days?

The Rabbi of Apt provided the answer. To people who primarily love themselves and who crave the companionship of another person for their own gratification, each day of deprivation is indeed an eternity. But the Torah is very precise when it speaks of "Jacob's love for *her,*" because Jacob loved Rachel rather than himself. Jacob appreciated and admired Rachel for whom she was rather than for what she would provide for him. This was a non-contingent love, a spiritual love.

If we are unable to grasp how a separation of seven years can be like a few days, perhaps it is because we lack a frame of reference. Perhaps we have never experienced a non-contingent love, one that is completely other-directed.

The word "love" is used in the Torah to refer to the ideal relationship between man and G-d *(Deuteronomy 6:5)*. The test for this type of love, says the Talmud, is the willingness to sacrifice one's very life for G-d.

If we wish to analyze the character of our love, we must reflect, "How much are we willing to sacrifice for those we profess to love?" What would happen if circumstances were such that the sacrifices we had to make for the loved one's welfare far outweighed any possible gratification from the relationship? Would that love still prevail?

We live in a culture in which the word "love" has been so cheapened that it has lost its meaning. Torah tells us what true love is.

Requirements for Spirituality

וְהִנֵּה סֻלָּם מֻצָּב אַרְצָה וְרֹאשׁוֹ מַגִּיעַ הַשָּׁמָיְמָה — *There was a ladder whose foot was on the ground, and whose head extended into the heavens (Genesis 28:12).*

ויצא
Vayeitzei

When people are confronted with the demands that Torah makes of them in regard to refinement of character, they sometimes respond with the remark that these demands are unrealistic and beyond the average person's capacity. Accounts of the spiritual achievements of great men and women are dismissed with, "That was possible in the olden days", as though the Chafetz Chaim lived hundreds of years ago, instead of in the twentieth century, and as though there were no truly spiritual people living today.

The lives and experiences of the patriarchs were meant to serve as models for us. Our forefather Jacob had a dream: "There was a ladder whose foot was on the ground, and whose head extended into the heavens." The dream of the patriarch tells us that although our physical beings may be anchored to the earthly world, this does not preclude our minds from reaching the heavenly heights.

If we fail to aspire to spirituality, it is not because we lack the capacity to achieve it. We may be unaware of our capabilities, since it is not at all uncommon for people to grossly underestimate themselves. There may even be a convenience in such underestimation, since this allows us to resign ourselves to a lesser status. Spiritual achievement takes a great deal of effort and may call for giving up various pleasures. Considering oneself to be deficient in spirituality may give rise to very uncomfortable guilt feelings. It is so much easier to assume that one lacks the capacity for spirituality, and this relieves one of the obligation to try.

The fact is that spirituality is well within everyone's means, but it requires some self-sacrifice. Self-indulgence and spirituality are mutually exclusive. Pursuit of wealth, of lavish living conditions, of diamonds, of costly furs, and of luxurious automobiles is incompatible with spirituality.

Jacob dreamt of a ladder whose foot was on the earth but whose head extended into the heavens. If one is absorbed in earthly pursuits, then one's head as well as one's feet is anchored to the ground.

After his vision Jacob said, "If G-d will be with me and give me bread to eat and a garment to wear . . . then G-d will be my G-d" *(Genesis 28:20)*. If we are satisfied when our basic physical needs are met, we can reach G-dliness. If we seek more than our basic needs and pursue self-indulgence, we cannot hope to achieve spirituality.

The choice is between spiritual versus mundane pursuits, and it is ours to make.

Changing Character Traits

וישלח
Vayishlach

וַיִּקַּח מִן הַבָּא בְיָדוֹ מִנְחָה לְעֵשָׂו אָחִיו — *Then he took from his possessions, a gift to his brother Esau* (Genesis 32:14).

On his way homeward, Jacob learns that his brother, Esau, his sworn enemy, is marching toward him with an army of four hundred men. Jacob prepares an elaborate gift in the hope of appeasing his brother, and sends a procession of herds of livestock to him.

Ramban states that although Jacob prayed to G-d to be saved from his brother's wrath, he knew that one should not rely on Divine miracles, but try to use any natural means available to save oneself, hence the elaborate gift.

Rabbi Yerucham Levovitz asks, "Why did Jacob's salvation call for a supernatural miracle and Divine intervention? Is it not a natural phenomenon that two brothers, who have had their differences, meet after an extended period of separation and decide to let bygones be bygones? Why could Jacob not expect that his brother might forgive him?"

Rabbi Yerucham answers, "This teaches us that changing one's personality is indeed a miraculous feat. Esau hated Jacob with a passion. For Jacob to rely on a change in his brother's personality would be equivalent to expecting a supernatural miracle."

Rabbi Yerucham expands on this theme. Changing one's personality traits is so difficult that it generally cannot be achieved by unaided human effort. Character traits may be so deeply ingrained that they cannot be extirpated even with concerted effort, and their elimination may require an act of Divine intervention.

This concept was also stated by the Rabbi of Rizhin, who once asked one of his followers, "What is it that you are trying to accomplish?"

"I am trying to break some of my objectionable traits," the man answered.

"All your efforts are for naught," the Rabbi said. "You will break your neck more easily than you will break a character trait. If you wish to change your personality, study Torah and implement it in your daily living, and pray to G-d to remove your undesirable traits. You cannot do it by yourself."

People may try various techniques to change their personalities. Rabbi Yerucham states that all such efforts are doomed to failure. Only G-d can remove our character defects, if we ask him to. Our part of the job is to sincerely dedicate ourselves to fulfilling the will of G-d as it is expressed in the Torah.

This is the meaning of the Talmudic assertion that G-d says, "I have created a *yeitzer hara* (evil inclination), and I have created Torah as its antidote" *(Bava Basra 16a)*. Torah is the only antidote to undesirable character traits.

For Torah to transform one's personality, the study of Torah in the abstract does not suffice. It must be studied with the intent to live up to what it teaches, and it must be implemented in daily living. The study must involve the ethical as well as the formal halachic aspects. Then and only then can we expect favorable changes in our personalities to occur.

Leisure

וַיֵּשֶׁב יַעֲקֹב (בִּקֵּשׁ יַעֲקֹב לֵישֵׁב בְּשַׁלְוָה קָפַץ עָלָיו רָגְזוֹ שֶׁל יוֹסֵף – רש"י)
— *Jacob lived (Genesis 37:1) (Jacob wished to live in peace, when the travails of Joseph came upon him — Rashi).*

In *Ethics of the Fathers (2:2)* we read, "It is best that the study of Torah be combined with earning a livelihood, because exhausting oneself in pursuit of both will eliminate sin."

For reasons known only to the Divine wisdom, man was created with a propensity for sin, and with numerous drives, desires, and appetites whose gratification constitutes sin. It is the Divine plan that man triumph over these impulses. To accomplish this formidable feat, man was given the Torah. The Torah also commands man to earn his livelihood. "By the sweat of your brow shall you eat your bread."

This combination of the study of Torah and working for one's livelihood was summed up in the passage, "Man was created to toil" *(Job 5:5)*. This, then, is the assignment of man in this world: to study Torah and provide for himself and those dependent on him.

No mention is made of leisure. Rest and relaxation, to the degree that they are essential for optimum physical and mental well-being, are similar to food and water as vital needs for survival. Beyond that, leisure, especially as a goal, has no place.

The Rabbi of Kotzk said that the reason a person should not sin is not only because it is forbidden. One should not be able to sin because one should not have free time to sin.

If a person accepts his existence in the world as a mission and takes his assignment seriously, then he works diligently at accomplishing that assignment. There is no time at which he is free from pursuit of that assignment. When he is not at work, he is studying Torah, performing *mitzvos*, or getting the necessary rest for his health. He has no leisure time, no time for sin. Not committing sin is not enough. One must be so engaged in the exhausting pursuit of one's mission that the possibility of sin is eliminated.

"Jacob was a wholesome person, who dwelt in the tents of learning" *(Genesis 28:27)*. Jacob would certainly have continued this into his old age, but as the progenitor of the Jewish nation he had to set an example for his children. He sought peace and leisure in his old age, but the travails of Joseph were visited upon him. There is no place for the concept of leisure in Judaism.

We are subject to the impact of the philosophy of life that prevails in the society in which we live. In Western civilization, leisure has become a desirable goal. An entire industry of entertainment and amusement has arisen to help people deal with this goal so that they do not lose their minds out of boredom.

Torah excludes leisure as a desirable goal for man.

Keeping a Confidence

וְהוֹרַדְתֶּם אֶת שֵׂיבָתִי בְּיָגוֹן שְׁאֹלָה — *You will have lowered my old age in sorrow into the grave (Genesis 42:38).*

What does it mean to be trustworthy? If someone tells you something in confidence and you have an overwhelming urge to tell someone else this piece of information, how successful are you in resisting this urge? If we look at what has been happening in contemporary government, with highly confidential information finding its way through various "leaks," it appears that keeping a confidence may be a rare quality indeed.

Throughout the Torah, each time G-d speaks to Moses, we read, "G-d spoke to Moses, *to say* (*leimor*)," and the Talmud tells us that this was necessary in order to permit Moses to convey the Divine message to the Israelites. In other words, it is not necessary to place a restriction on information to indicate that it is not to be repeated. On the contrary, everything one is told must be considered absolutely confidential and one is forbidden to repeat it to another unless one is given express permission to do so.

In this portion of the Torah the saga of Joseph is continued, and we read of Jacob's intense suffering and his unmitigated grief over the loss of his favorite son whom he assumed to be dead. In last week's portion we hear Jacob's anguish, "I know that I will go down to the grave still grieving over my son" *(Genesis 37:35)*.

On the verse, "His father wept for *him*" (ibid.), the Midrash states that this refers not to Joseph's father but to Jacob's father, Isaac. Isaac wept because he witnessed the heart-rending grief and suffering of Jacob. But, says the Midrash, Isaac did not weep for Joseph, because he knew through his prophetic vision that Joseph was indeed alive! "How dare I reveal this information to Jacob," Isaac said. "He too has prophetic vision, and if G-d chooses to conceal from him that Joseph is alive, what right do I have to reveal it?"

Think for a moment. Imagine the scene. Jacob rends his garments in his grief. Far beyond the usual *shivah* (seven days of mourning), Jacob refuses to accept any consolation. Isaac sees his son in deep grief, broken in spirit, resigning himself that he will never have a single moment of happiness for the rest of his life, and yet he keeps silent! With just a few words he could have relieved this horrible anguish. "No need to grieve, my son. Your dear child, Joseph, is alive and well. I know this, because it was revealed to me in prophecy."

But Isaac keeps his silence. He weeps along with Jacob because he shares in Jacob's pain, although not in his grief. He bears this pain for years, to the end of his days, but does not reveal what he knows. "If G-d chooses to conceal it, I have no right to reveal it."

The patriarchs were great men, people of lofty spirituality, but they were not superhuman. We are told about their lives because they were meant to serve as models for us to emulate.

How often do we allow our tongues to wag needlessly? How often do we violate a trust by revealing, in one way or another, something that was told to us in confidence? And remember, the halachic requirement to keep a confidence applies to everything one has been told unless one has been given express permission to repeat it. All communication, unless explicitly classified otherwise, is privileged communication.

How much there is to learn from our patriarchs!

An Option to Forgiveness

ויגש

Vayigash

כִּי עַבְדְּךָ עָרַב אֶת הַנַּעַר מֵעִם אָבִי . . . יֵשֶׁב נָא עַבְדְּךָ תַּחַת הַנַּעַר עֶבֶד לַאדֹנִי

— *For your servant took responsibility for the lady from my father . . . please let your servant remain instead of the lad as a slave unto my master (Exodus 44:32-33).*

How important is self-esteem?

Let us look at the events of this portion of the Torah. Joseph has been sold into captivity by his brothers, eventually becomes viceroy of Egypt, and by warehousing grain, saves Egypt from the famine he had predicted. His brothers come from famine-stricken Canaan to purchase grain, and he provokes them by accusing them of being spies. He maneuvers their bringing his brother Benjamin to Egypt, and — after showing frank favoritism to Benjamin — sends them on their way, but not before planting his silver goblet in Benjamin's bag. When they are searched, Benjamin is accused of thievery. Joseph then proposes to keep Benjamin prisoner, but his brothers intercede and offer to remain in Benjamin's place. At this point Joseph reveals his identity.

Why all the drama? Is it for sheer revenge, which the Torah explicitly forbids *(Leviticus 19:18)?*

An even more nagging question: After becoming viceroy, why does Joseph not send a message to his grief-stricken father to let him know that he is alive and well? How does he allow his aged father to suffer needlessly for years, when he has the means to relieve his suffering?

Forgiveness is a virtue. It is expected of us that we forgive someone who has offended us when he apologizes. But forgiveness is not an unmixed blessing. The person who forgives is the magnanimous one, and the person who has been forgiven remains humiliated, and may continue to live with tormenting guilt.

There is another option. Rather than simply forgive, provide the offender with an opportunity *to redeem himself*. Let him feel that he has grown, that he has eliminated the character defect that led to his misdeed, and that he merits being forgiven. Give him the opportunity to once again hold his head high with the self-esteem of one who has learned from his mistakes and has grown in stature, rather than being a humiliated, albeit forgiven, sinner.

Joseph could easily have forgiven his brothers. He was not seeking revenge. But graciously forgiving them would have made him magnanimous and them groveling penitents. Instead he ingeniously maneuvered it so that they were in a position where they would be tempted to repeat their offense against him. Benjamin had now taken Joseph's place as their father's favorite. The brothers' readiness to sacrifice their lives in order to return Benjamin to their father indicated that they had overcome their envy, and that they had eliminated the character defect of jealousy. They would now be not merely forgiven, but also proud of their growth, and their self-esteem would be preserved.

All this would not have been possible had Joseph notified his father of his whereabouts. This would have denied his brothers the opportunity to redeem themselves, and would have forever eliminated their regaining self-esteem.

How important is self-esteem? Important enough that Joseph allowed his aged father to suffer years of grief until he would be able to provide his brothers the opportunity to essentially undo their sin against him by redeeming themselves in a similar situation.

If you are ever tempted to say or do something that would so affect another person as to depress his self-esteem, stop and think a moment. Think about how Joseph was willing to let his beloved father suffer years of anguish in order to preserve his brothers' self-esteem.

Character Refinement by Faith

ויחי

Vayechi

הֲתַחַת אֱלֹקִים אָנִי וְאַתֶּם חֲשַׁבְתֶּם עָלַי רָעָה אֱלֹקִים חֲשָׁבָה לְטֹבָה — *Am I in the place of G-d? You intended to harm me, but it was G-d's intention that your actions turn out favorably* (Genesis 50:21-22).

Earlier *(Vayishlach)* we mentioned that changes in one's character are difficult — if not impossible — to bring about solely by one's efforts, even when such efforts are intense. The method whereby undesirable character traits can be completely eliminated is by Torah observance and prayer. It is much like the futility of being in a dark room and trying to drive the darkness out the window. But if you just light a candle, the darkness will disappear on its own. If one is diligent in Torah and prayer, undesirable character traits will leave on their own.

In today's portion, Joseph's brothers, following their father's death, are concerned that now Joseph will take revenge for their having sold him into slavery. They fall before his feet, pleading for forgiveness, even fabricating a death-bed request from their father in their behalf.

Joseph responds by assuring them that he had no intention of seeking revenge. "Am I in the place of G-d?" he asks. "You intended to harm me, but it was G-d's intention that your actions turn out favorably for me."

Note that Joseph does not say, "I forgive you." Rather, he points out how powerless he is to take revenge, hence he has no intention of doing so. "Is it not obvious," he asks, "that we cannot determine the outcome of our actions? What sense does it make for me to try to punish you? If it is the Divine will that you be spared from punishment, then all my efforts to inflict punishment upon you will be in vain, just as your efforts to harm me were all in vain."

Joseph does not profess to be a saint who will set aside his deep resentments and be magnanimous in forgiveness. Rather, he dismisses seeking revenge as a useless act, because he considers resentments to be futile feelings. That which G-d intends will come to be regardless of our efforts to bring it about or to prevent it.

That is the ideal approach to rid ourselves of undesirable traits. We must realize that we do not control the world, and that G-d does. The verse, "You *shall* not take revenge" *(Leviticus 19:18)* can also be correctly translated, "You *cannot* take revenge." It is simply out of our hands to make things happen.

A person does not have the urge to do the impossible and does not need to struggle to overcome such an urge. For example, while it might be very convenient to fly like a bird, no one has the urge to flap his arms and soar in the air, and one does not have to struggle to restrain himself from yielding to such an urge. Its very impossibility eliminates it without any effort on our part.

That is how undesirable traits should be eliminated — envy, greed, lust, vanity, and all the others. We need only know for a fact that what is intended to be will be, and that which we are not intended to have we cannot acquire and retain, regardless of how much effort we exert.

Many principles of correct behavior were given by Moses and the prophets. Habakkuk reduced them all to one simple principle, "The righteous shall live by faith" *(Habakkuk 2:4)*. With proper faith in G-d, everything will fall into proper place.

ספר שמות
Shemos / Exodus

Empathy

וַיְהִי בַּיָּמִים הָהֵם וַיִּגְדַּל מֹשֶׁה וַיֵּצֵא אֶל אֶחָיו וַיַּרְא בְּסִבְלֹתָם — *And it was in those days when Moses grew up and went out amongst his brethren and saw their travail (Exodus 2:11).*

It is generally accepted that empathizing with a person who is in distress is a commendable trait, and many people believe that they are indeed empathic. If they hear of someone who is suffering, they genuinely feel sorry for that person and may think that if there were any practical way of being of assistance to that person they would gladly do so.

Rabbi Yerucham Levovitz challenges this widely accepted assertion of being empathic. He sees this as a superficial feeling which generally yields little, and indeed is misleading, because a person may consider himself to be empathic when in reality he is quite far from that.

To explain his position, Rabbi Yerucham draws upon a comment from the Midrash which Rashi quotes in this week's portion of the Torah: "And it was in those days when Moses grew up and went out amongst his brethren and saw their travail," upon which Rashi comments, "He put his eyes and his heart into suffering with them." Merely observing their distress and feeling sorry for them was not sufficient. That is not true empathy. Moses threw his entire being into understanding the depth of their distress, to know every tiny detail of it, just as one puts his entire being into something which is of vital importance.

But it does not stop there. The Midrash goes on to say that Moses put his shoulder under the load and shared the heavy burden with all of his brethren. This was not so much to help them, says Rabbi Yerucham, because how much actual help could he provide for such a multitude? Rather, he shared in their hard labor so that he could truly understand and actually feel the back pain, the muscular strain, the shortness of breath, the total body exhaustion, and the crushing of the spirit. Then and only then could he be truly empathic.

To share in another's burden is an essential for the acquisition of Torah, as is clearly stated in *Ethics of the Fathers (6:6)*. Rabbi Yerucham states that this trait is fundamental not only for all *mitzvos* between man and man, but also for those between man and G-d. Since true empathy and sharing another's burden is an essential for Torah, one cannot be Torah observant if one is derelict in this trait. Ritual piety without sharing another's burden is not Torah observance.

The Talmud spares no one, even the greatest of the great. When the sage Rabbi Gamliel, the prince of Israel, visited the great scholar Rabbi Joshua who made his meager living as a blacksmith, and saw that the walls of his sparse dwelling were covered with soot, he remarked, "It is evident from your walls that you are a blacksmith." Rabbi Joshua responded, "Woe unto a nation if you are its leader, since you are not aware of the difficulties under which scholars live" (Berachos 28a).

The natural feeling is for a person to isolate himself from others who are suffering. We do not wish our meals to be spoiled by the awareness that there are people who suffer starvation. But Torah observance is not designed to provide one with maximum comfort. Torah requires us to investigate the depth of other people's distress and, as Moses did, feel along with those who suffer.

That is true empathy.

Unnecessary Resignation

וארא

Vaeira

וְהוֹצֵאתִי אֶתְכֶם מִתַּחַת סִבְלֹת מִצְרָיִם — *I will deliver you from under the burdens (sivlus) of Egypt (Exodus 6:6).*

One of the most difficult challenges that Moses faced was the adaptation that many Israelites had made to slavery. Many accepted their fate, and made peace with being slaves. Many who refused freedom actually perished in Egypt during the three days of darkness. Even among those who followed Moses there were some who rebelled against him in the desert and opted for returning to Egypt, accepting the role of slaves as long as "we had a pot of meat and could eat bread to our satiety" (Exodus 16:3).

"I will deliver you from under the burdens (sivlus) of Egypt." Although sivlus is usually translated to mean "burdens", Rabbi Yitzchok Meir of Gur points out that sivlus also means "tolerance", and what G-d said was, "I will deliver you from the tolerance you have developed toward being enslaved."

There is a folk saying, "The worm that infests the horseradish thinks, 'There is no sweeter place in the world to be.'" Foolish insect! Why do you choose to make your home in the pungent and bitter horseradish, when there are so many sweet and delicious vegetables available to you? But the worm has never tasted anything else. All he knows is the horseradish, and to him that appears to be the best there is.

I watch people living at a hectic pace, making giant strides toward the development of heart disease and high-blood pressure, while others anesthetize themselves regularly with huge quantities of alcohol, and still others pursue illusory goals which lose their charm once they have been attained. They seem to me very much like the worm infesting the horseradish. Can't they realize that there is a better way to live?

I have even seen some who have tried to live a Torah life, but seem to have missed the point, because they are lacking in simchah, in the joy of observing the Torah. From the emphasis the Torah puts on simchah, even to the point of attributing all evils that happen to a person "because you did not serve G-d with simchah" (Deuteronomy 28:47), it is clear that if one is not thoroughly enjoying Judaism, there is something wrong with the way he is living a Jewish life.

There are many faulty adjustments to life, and our problem often is that we resign ourselves to them, and we think that this is the only way life can be. We resign ourselves unnecessarily to misery.

This was the great challenge that Moses faced, and why G-d had to assure him that He would not only deliver the Israelites from enslavement, but also from the tolerance and acceptance of slavehood.

We do not have to live in unhappiness, and we do not have to resign ourselves to misery. There is a way of living that can provide true happiness, even under adverse circumstances. The words of the Torah are eternal truth: "The ways of the

Torah are pleasant, and all its paths are peace" *(Proverbs 3:17)*.

There is one feature that is essential to the happiness of Torah living, and that is that Torah must be accepted and lived in its entirety, with a total dedication to the will of G-d, without any deviation to doing our own will.

That is the characteristic of Torah. In order for it to work it must be whole. Piecemeal Torah will not work.

The Talmud compares Torah to a medical prescription. "If it is pure *(zakah)*, it is a life-sustaining medicine. If it is impure, then it can be poisonous" *(Yuma 72b)*. Just as tampering with the ingredients of a prescription can make it harmful, so can tampering with Torah reverse its effects. Adulteration of Torah, as when one tries to get Torah to comply with one's personal wishes, can be most dangerous.

There is a life of *simchah* in Torah, but to achieve it we must reject any other life style to which we may have become accustomed and to which we may have developed tolerance.

Learning from Experience

בא

Bo

. . . כִּי אִם מָאֵן אַתָּה לְשַׁלֵחַ אֶת עַמִּי הִנְנִי מֵבִיא . . . — *For if you refuse to send out my people, behold, I bring (upon you) . . . (Exodus 10:4)*.

The account of the Exodus is not merely a historical narration. Everything in Torah is a teaching, a universal and eternal lesson, to be applied in every age and in every place. The story of the ten plagues and Pharaoh's reaction to them may seem irrelevant to us in our daily lives, but it is in fact most relevant.

How is it that after each plague Pharaoh promised to yield to Moses' request and allow the Israelites to leave for three days of worship in the desert, but no sooner is the pressure of the plague removed than Pharaoh becomes recalcitrant and reneges on his promise? When Moses subsequently warns him of additional oncoming plagues, Pharaoh remains unimpressed until the predicted disaster occurs, and then again promises, only to recant again when the pressure is off. This repeats itself ten times! Was Pharaoh so stupid that he was unable to learn from experience?

I did not fully understand Pharaoh until I became involved in the treatment of alcoholics, and witnessed a rather similar phenomenon occuring with great regularity. The alcoholic suffers some grave consequence as a result of his drinking, and is in great distress and sometimes even near death. His reaction is invariably, "That's it! I've had it with alcohol. Never again will I drink. No, never!" It is common experience that within several weeks, if not just a few days, he is back to drinking. People will warn him of how dangerous alcohol is for him, and remind him of the disastrous consequences he had suffered from his drinking. It is all to no avail. He drinks again.

What seems so illogical in the case of both Pharaoh and the alcoholic is not really all that unique. Many people fail to learn from experience. When the prophet Isaiah used the metaphor, "You are drunk, albeit not with wine" *(29:9)*, he was not using the expression loosely. Our Biblical history demonstrates how time and again we have strayed from Torah observance and each time sustained grave consequences, yet we so quickly forgot and returned to our errant ways.

What is true of our people historically is often true of many individuals even today. Too often we just do not learn from experience.

What is it in the alcoholic that renders him refractory to learning from experience? It is probably because he does not wish to change his life style and does not want to give up whatever sensation it is that alcohol provides. What was it that rendered Pharaoh incapable of accepting the testimony of his senses? Probably the refusal to admit that he was wrong. Self-centered feelings such as these prevent people from learning from painful experiences and thereby avoiding repetition of mistakes.

What is it then that prevents us from learning from experience? Probably some self-centered feeling or idea that we refuse to surrender.

Since it is our self-centeredness that renders us oblivious to the obvious, what can we do to overcome this? One of the most effective ways is to avail ourselves of a trusted teacher and guide, someone who is unaffected by our emotional distortions, and who can help us see reality more clearly and learn from our experiences.

"Make unto yourself a teacher" *(Ethics of the Fathers 1:16)* is an invaluable piece of advice.

בשלח
Beshalach
Togetherness

וְהִנֵּה מִצְרַיִם נֹסֵעַ אַחֲרֵיהֶם — *Behold, Egypt was pursuing them (Exodus 14:10).*

Immediately preceding and during the Six-Day War, when Israel faced the danger of extinction by hundreds of millions of its hostile neighbors, something unusual occurred. Jews of various political persuasions, and of diverse ethnicity and religious orientation, all united in a firm bond of brotherhood. For a brief period of time all factionalization disappeared. Who knows if it was not this unique unity that merited the miraculous triumph. This was a period of togetherness that generated great pride.

In today's portion of the Torah we read how Pharaoh and his army pursued the newly emancipated Israelites. The verse reads, "Behold, Egypt was pursuing them," and Rashi, commenting on the text's use of the singular form of the verb "pursuing", explains its use, "because they were of one mind, like one person."

A similar syntax is found in relation to the Israelites' camping at Mount Sinai, and here too the word "camped" is in the singular (19:2). Again Rashi explains the use of the singular, "because they were like one person, of one mind."

The Avnei Nezer notes that Rashi reverses the order. In the first instance he says that the Egyptians were "of one mind, like one person," but in regard to the Israelites, they were "like one person, of one mind." He explains that uniting against a common enemy in the fight for survival is not unusual. This occurs not only among all peoples but also among lower forms of life, where the herd unites against a predator. It is the being "of one mind", the shared impulse for survival that binds the group and makes them as one, hence "of one mind, and *therefore* of one person."

With Israel, says the Avnei Nezer, it is otherwise. Israel at Sinai united ideologically to receive the Torah. There was no enemy threatening its survival, no one to defend against. Israel is "as one person, and *therefore* of one mind."

Would that this were always true. Yes, we united during the Six-Day War, but as the Avnei Nezer explains, this was similar to the herd instinct. Where is the unique togetherness that bound our ancestors at Sinai? Where is the realization that we are one people? Where is the awareness that "Israel, the Torah, and G-d are one" and that what binds us together far outweighs our differences? Why do we allow pettiness to separate us? Why can we not rise above those ego drives that are ultimately responsible for our divisiveness?

The Baal Shem Tov said, "I wish I had the love for the greatest *tzaddik* that G-d has for the worst *rasha* (sinner)." Even with his incomparable love, devotion, and willingness to sacrifice himself for others, the Baal Shem Tov felt that he was nevertheless deficient in his love for others. What, then, are we to say when we allow trivia to divide us and when we permit self-interests to destroy our unity?

We must begin somewhere. Let us examine ourselves honestly, and begin working today toward the goal of true unity.

Prerequisite for Torah

יֵרֵד ה' לְעֵינֵי כָל הָעָם עַל הַר סִינַי

— G-d will descend — before the entire nation — upon Mount Sinai (Exodus 19:11).

The receiving of the Torah at Sinai, which is the outstanding event in this week's portion, required three preparatory days. However, except for the requirements of abstinence and cleansing of the garments, no specifics are given of what comprised these three preparatory days.

Rabbi Yerucham quotes the Talmud, "If there is no *derech eretz* (decency, proper behavior) there can be no Torah" (*Ethics of the Fathers 3:17)*, and also "*derech eretz* precedes Torah" (*Vayikra Rabbah 9:3)*. He states that the three preparatory days were for concentration on *midos*, on developing those character traits that would make a person suitable to receive the Torah.

Rabbi Yerucham further explains how it was possible that the patriarchs, Abraham, Isaac, and Jacob, were able to observe the Torah even before it was revealed. He states that they had so refined their *midos* and had developed such spirituality that their thinking led them logically to all the *mitzvos* of the Torah.

We can now understand why we say in the *Haggadah*, "If G-d had brought us to Sinai and had not given us the Torah, that would have sufficed." What good would it have been to have been at Sinai without receiving the Torah? However, if the three preparatory days enabled the Israelites to achieve a state of *midos* similar to that of the patriarchs, then they would have been able to apply logic to derive all six hundred and thirteen *mitzvos*.

Essential to the development of *midos* is the understanding of the choice of Sinai as the site for the giving of the Torah. The Talmud states that Sinai is the smallest of all the mountains in the desert, and this is to teach us that Torah can exist only in the presence of humility. Vanity is the antithesis of Torah.

There may be many reasons why Torah is repelled by vanity, but one of them is certainly that vanity precludes the development of good *midos*. Preoccupation with oneself, considering oneself superior to others, demanding recognition from others, and indulging oneself, are all natural consequences of vanity. The development of proper *midos* can occur only when one understands, "I was not put into this world to indulge myself. I was put here to accomplish a mission. If not to do the will of G-d, there is no reason for my existence. My personal wants, whatever they may be, are totally irrelevant. I need only to be able to live and function optimally so that I may be able to accomplish my assignment."

Without this conviction and without the self-effacement of total subjugation to the will of G-d, neither study of Torah nor ritual observance has any meaning.

Why does Torah not specifically instruct us on all *midos,* and give *midos* the status of *mitzvos*? The Talmud states that G-d searched for a vessel that could contain the Torah. *Midos* could not be *mitzvos* because they constitute the vessel which contains the *mitzvos*.

If anyone believes that he can study Torah and fulfill *mitzvos* without working on refinement of his character, he is grossly in error. Without a proper vessel to contain Torah and *mitzvos*, they cannot be achieved and maintained.

Spiritual Sensitivity

משפטים

Mishpatim

. . . כִּי תִקְנֶה עֶבֶד עִבְרִי — *If you will purchase an eved ivri . . .* *(Exodus 16:2).*

An *eved ivri*, or indentured servant, is one who is sold into servitude for a maximum six-year term in order to make restitution for a theft he committed. If, after the six years, the servant refuses to take his freedom, he is put through a ritual wherein his ear lobe is pierced.

Rashi *(21:6)* explains that "The ear that heard G-d say 'You shall not steal' and yet this person violated this Divine commandment, deserves to be pierced."

"But," argues Sfas Emes, "it was not the ear that did the stealing. Why not punish the hands that actually committed the crime?"

Sfas Emes answers that had the ear been receptive to the Divine commandment, the hands would not have stolen. It was due to the fact that the ear had absorbed so many improper sounds that it rendered itself insensitive to the word of G-d, and therefore it becomes the site for punishment.

The message of Sfas Emes is crucial. King David began the Psalms with "Fortunate is the person who did not go in the ways of the wicked, nor stand in the path of the sinful, nor sit among the scoffers." If we associate with people who are transgressors, we cannot escape being affected.

People who are exposed to high-noise levels use ear plugs to insulate their ears against the sounds, for otherwise they will become deaf. Just as there can be physical deafness if the ear is exposed to noxious noises, so there can be spiritual deafness when the ear is exposed to improper sounds. The ear that hears *lashon hara* (gossip), scoffing, indecent words and stories can develop a type of deafness that renders it insensitive to Torah and spiritual messages.

This is of particular importance when we live in a society that has, under the guise of freedom of speech, permitted a flood of decadence in all the mass media. It is a mistake to assume that anyone is immune to the noxious effects of these ideas, and that if we learn Torah ethics and teachings, we can allow ourselves to be exposed to these influences without concern. It is a mistake to think that we can listen to gossip and yet remain unaffected in our character traits. We may render ourselves insensitive to the teachings of Torah.

Loss of function of any part of the body is partially disabling, but loss of any of the senses can be totally disabling. Loss of hearing and loss of vision severely constrict a person's perception and his contact with his environment.

Transgression of any of the *mitzvos* is a serious offense, but nothing causes so widespread a degeneracy as the lack of perception of spirituality. For how can one repent if he cannot hear the admonishment? How can one correct his errant ways if he cannot hear when he is alerted to them? How can one profess to be doing acts of kindness if his senses are dulled, and if he is functionally deaf to the needs of others?

If we take caution to wear protective lenses to prevent damage to our eyes from the bright rays of the sun, and if we wear protective ear coverings to shield our sensitive hearing mechanisms from possible harmful sounds, then we should give at least equal importance to our spiritual receptors by avoiding their exposure to improper stimuli.

Standards of Values

וְיִקְחוּ לִי תְּרוּמָה . . . וְעָשׂוּ לִי מִקְדָּשׁ וְשָׁכַנְתִּי בְּתוֹכָם — *Let them take an offering . . . and make for Me a Sanctuary, and I will dwell within them* (Exodus 25:2,8).

When the Israelites responded to Moses with, "Everything that G-d says we will do and we will hear," G-d then said to Moses, "Let them take an offering . . . and let them build for Me a Sanctuary" *(Tana D'vei Eliyahu).*

The Sanctuary symbolized the Divine presence among the people of Israel. "They shall make for Me a Sanctuary, and I will dwell within them." It does not say, "I will dwell within *it*," but "within *them*," meaning within each and every individual *(Midrash).*

How does one merit the Divine Presence? By setting one's own self aside in deference to the will of G-d and to the teachings of G-d.

Concepts such as decency, justice, mercy, and benevolence are espoused by every culture. Yet, many heinous crimes and atrocities have been committed under the guise of "justice and benevolence." This happens when people establish themselves as the arbiters of *midos* (character traits). The Torah-observant person sets his own will and opinion aside. "We will fulfill the dictates of G-d without measuring them against our personal criteria of *midos*."

Rabbi Chaim Shmulevitz cites the Talmud which relates that Rabbi Gamliel invited seven scholars to a special session, but found that eight scholars had come. "Who is here that was not invited?" he asked. Shmuel HaKattan said, "It is I," and left.

The Talmud goes on to say that it was not Shmuel who had been uninvited. Shmuel only acted so to protect the person who had entered without permission. The Talmud says the Shmuel's noble action was similar to that of Rabbi Chiya, who had learned this tactic from Rabbi Meir, who in turn had emulated Shmuel HaKattan, who in turn had emulated another scholar; and so on all the way back to Moses, who was the first to manifest this technique of taking the blame on himself to shield the dignity of another person.

Rabbi Chaim asks why it was necessary for the Talmud to seek a source for Rabbi Chiya's action. Was this not logically a noble thing to do, to implicate himself in order to allow someone else a graceful way out of his mistake?

Rabbi Chaim says that this teaches us that one should not rely on one's own sense of what is proper and what is noble. We are far too vulnerable to being misled by personal interests, and we are capable even of committing atrocities under the mistaken impression that we are doing something noble. If one wishes to act nobly, one must learn *midos* from Torah and from Torah authorities.

Another important point that Rabbi Chaim emphasizes is that Rabbi Meir did not derive his lesson from Joshua or Moses, but from Shmuel HaKattan, who was his contemporary. We must be careful not to leap too far ahead of ourselves and overreach. Our own immediate contact is not with Joshua or Moses, but with the authentic spiritual guides of our own day.

This is the effective formula for developing appropriate character traits. First, we must eliminate self-interest and surrender our will to the Divine truth. Second, we must accept the teachings of Torah in regard to character traits as well as the instructions on *mitzvos*.

Brazenness

תצוה
Tetzaveh

'וְהָיָה עַל מֵצַח אַהֲרֹן . . . לְרָצוֹן לָהֶם לִפְנֵי ה — And it (the golden frontlet) shall be on Aaron (the High Priest's) forehead . . . to achieve favor for them (the people of Israel) before G-d (Exodus 28:38).*

According to the Midrash, all the vestments of the High Priest were to achieve forgiveness for various sins of the Israelites. The function of the golden frontlet was to attain forgiveness for the sin of brazenness.

Forgiveness is not attained vicariously. Forgiveness is attained only with genuine *teshuvah* (repentance). The function of the vestments was to stimulate people to *teshuvah*.

Brazenness is a grievous character defect, so serious that the Talmud states that a person who manifests it is assigned to hell *(Ethics of the Fathers, 5:20)*. Although there is no explicit prohibition in the Torah in regard to brazenness, it is one of the personality traits of which a person must divest from himself in order to achieve the requisite *derech eretz* (decency) that is a prerequisite for Torah.

Brazenness prevents a person from admitting his faults and leads to repetition of mistakes. Our confession on Yom Kippur begins with the statement, "We are not so brazen as to say that we have not sinned." Brazenness is a barrier to the reverence of elders which is necessary to achieve learning. Brazenness is incompatible with *chesed* (kindness) and *tzedakah* (charity), as the Scripture states, "The poor person pleads for compassion, and the rich person responds brazenly" *(Proverbs 18:23)*. Even if a person studies Torah and observes many *mitzvos*, these can be undone by the character defect of brazenness.

From where does brazenness originate? The golden frontlet was worn next to the turban, and the turban in turn, being the uppermost garment of the High Priest, was to stimulate to *teshuvah* and elicit forgiveness for *gaavah* (vanity). This juxtaposition of the frontlet to forgive for brazenness, to the turban, which is to forgive for vanity, indicates that brazenness is a natural consequence of vanity. Arrogance arises when one considers oneself superior to others, when one lacks humility, the source of all noble *midos*.

Just as every trait has its proper application, brazenness does have a very limited positive function. Brazenness is commendable when one finds oneself in a corrupt environment, in a society which sanctions immorality and degeneracy. At such times a person must have the *chutzpah* to stand up for truth, morality, and decency. One must be able to defy one's corrupt environment and not be dragged into conformity.

The golden frontlet was imprinted with the words *kodesh laHashem* (sacred unto G-d). It is only when there is no personal interest involved, no defending of one's offended ego, only when one's attitude and activities are fully and purely dedicated to the glory of G-d, that one may use *chutzpah* constructively.

With this sole exception, brazenness has no place in the character of the spiritual person. It is a violation of both modesty and humility, two fundamental traits of *derech eretz*, without which a person cannot be considered to be Torah observant.

The Hazard of Confusion

עֲשֵׂה לָנוּ אֱלֹהִים אֲשֶׁר יֵלְכוּ לְפָנֵינוּ — *Make for us a god to go before us* (Exodus 32:1).

In the past several decades we have witnessed the phenomenon of cultism. Young people somehow gravitate toward a small faction, often following a charismatic leader. They become alienated from their parents and all their previous associations and they develop a fanatical loyalty to their group. They are often exploited financially and the formative years of their lives are dissipated. In some tragic cases, as with the Jonestown massacre, mass destruction occurs.

What is it that drives young people into these cults? It is nothing other than *confusion*. Not knowing who one is, where one is going, and what one is supposed to do with one's life may be so intolerable that one grasps at anything that seems to provide an answer.

In today's portion of the Torah we read of the worship of the golden calf. How this incident could have occurred is virtually beyond comprehension. Just days earlier the people had witnessed the revelation of the glory of G-d at Sinai, and had proclaimed in unison, "*Naaseh-venishma*, we will obey and we will listen" (24:7). They had heard the Divine voice saying, "You shall not have any gods before Me" and "Do not make any graven images for worship" (20:3-4). How could they abruptly turn around and worship a golden calf? Is this not the height of absurdity?

Rabbi Chaim Shmulevitz explains that the Israelites were caught off guard due to a momentary period of confusion and depression. Since the beginning of the deliverance from Egypt, they had been under the constant and firm leadership of Moses. His unfaltering guidance and his direct communication of the Divine will to the Israelites provided them with certainty and with stability.

But now Moses had been absent for forty days. Could a human being possibly survive forty days without food or water? Moses did not return at the precise time they understood him to have said. Perhaps he had perished of hunger on the peak of Sinai. At this moment of vulnerability, the Midrash says, Satan conjured up an image of Moses being dead and his bier being carried by the heavenly angels.

The shock of this moment was overwhelming. Moses dead! No one to tell us what to do! Stranded in a barren desert without a leader! Grave confusion and pandemonium broke out. Coupled with the depression over the assumed death of Moses, the Israelites became vulnerable to cultism. All logic was suspended. Worship a cow! Exalt an animal to the status of a divinity.

The message of the saga of the golden calf is that we must ever be on the alert for the moments of confusion and depression that are apt to occur in our lives. People of great intelligence and firm convictions can be vulnerable to the grave errors and poor judgments at such times.

The mistake of the Israelites is that when they thought they had lost their leader, they did not turn to a new leader with a request for guidance. Rather, they confronted Aaron with a demand rather than with a request: "Make for us a god to go before us" (32:1).

You do not order a leader what to do. You ask, and then you obey.

We must remember this in those moments when we feel ourselves lost in doubt, bewilderment, and despair. We must remember to turn to our leader to ask for guidance.

Enthusiasm for Mitzvos

וְהַנְּשִׂיאִם הֵבִיאוּ — *And the leaders brought* (Exodus 35:27).

The basic work on Jewish ethics, *Mesillas Yeshorim (Path of the Just)* by Rabbi Moshe Chaim Luzatto, is an elaboration on the Talmudic passage by Rabbi Pinchas ben Yair, wherein he lists ten steps or *midos* (traits) that are essential to fulfilling one's duties to observe the Divine Will. The first two of these ten steps are watchfulness and diligence or zeal. Being the first two, they are obviously the most fundamental, the foundation upon which all the others rest.

In today's portion of the Torah we read of the various donations of materials that the Israelites made to provide for the construction of the Sanctuary in the desert. The leaders of the Twelve tribes donated the precious gems for the breastplate of the High Priest (35:27). Rashi notes that the Hebrew word for leaders is lacking a vowel, and that this omission designates that there was a flaw in their gift.

What was the flaw of the leaders? They said, "Let all the people make their respective donations, and whatever is lacking, we will then provide."

Why was this considered a flaw? Was this not a reasonable and worthy consideration, to underwrite and undertake to fulfill whatever would be lacking? Yes, says Rabbeinu Bachya, but if one has the opportunity to be first in performance of a *mitzvah* and delays doing so for whatever reason, that indicates a lack of diligence and zeal, and for that the leaders were chastised.

The patriarch Abraham is praised for his diligence. In responding to the Divine commandment to sacrifice his beloved son Isaac, the Torah states that "Abraham arose early in the morning" (Genesis 22:3). Would it not have been understandable for Abraham to spend the last few hours in closeness with his son, before parting from him for the remainder of his life on earth? Of course it would have been reasonable, and it would perhaps not have detracted from Abraham's devotion to G-d.

But Abraham awoke early to perform a *mitzvah*. There was no delay, regardless of how well it may have been justified.

In the ethical work *Orchos Tzaddikim (Ways of the Righteous*, author unknown), it is explained that diligence and zeal come from a total commitment. Abraham's devotion to G-d was so absolute that there was no room for any other emotion. Even the intense love for his son was effaced in view of the Divine commandment.

Total commitment is a phenomenon of concentration. We can observe its analogues in the martial arts such as karate, wherein concentrating all one's energy in a single group of muscles can produce an enormous force. Another example is a laser beam, where concentration of light into a single wave length results in a powerful and far-reaching force of energy.

Diligence is an indication of total commitment. One can be the first at services in the synagogue or one of the late comers. One can be first to respond to a community need or one who eventually participates. One can quickly respond to a request for *tzedakah* (charity) or contribute at a later point. All these actions are indeed meritorious whenever they are done, but the degree of diligence and enthusiasm reflects the quality of one's commitment.

The leaders of the Twelve Tribes were unquestionably great men. Their intentions were noble. Nevertheless, the Torah calls them to account for lacking in diligence and zeal.

We would do well to examine our own behavior. It is not enough that we do what we are supposed to do. How enthusiastic and diligent are we in our actions?

ספר ויקרא
Vayikra / Leviticus

Humility

אֵיִּקְרָ — *And He called (Leviticus 1:1)*
   When small children begin to study Torah, they traditionally begin
with this portion.

   The first word of this volume of Torah, *vayikra*, is written with a diminutive א.
Children seem to associate the tiny א with their own small size.

   But why is the א written diminutively? Rashi says that without the א, the word
would read *vayikar*, which would have meant that the Divine vision came to Moses
abruptly, without preparation, just as it is said of the Divine vision that occurred to
the evil Balaam *(Numbers 23:4)*. With the א, the word is *vayikra*, an expression
ofendearment, wherein G-d called to Moses and invited him into the Divine
presence with love and dignity.

   Since Moses wrote down the Torah as G-d dictated to him, he was in a dilemma
with the word *vayikra*. In his profound humility, Moses did not wish to boast that
G-d had accorded him special honor and distinction. Moses would have preferred
to omit the א, and let people read *vayikar*. However, since he could not disobey the
Divine dictate he compromised by writing a diminutive one that might not be so
noticeable.

   Some people think that humility means that one should not be aware of one's
own skills and capacities. They would have it that the wise man should consider
himself stupid, the scholar consider himself ignorant, and the accomplished
musician consider himself tone deaf. However, this would not be humility, but
self-deception.

   Did Moses know that G-d loved him? Of course he did. Was Moses aware that
he had achieved a level of spirituality unequaled by any other human being? Of
course he was. Did he know that he was the greatest of prophets for all time to
come? Of course he did.

   But this self-awareness did not cause Moses to be vain or arrogant. The Torah
testifies that Moses was "the most humble of all men on earth" *(Numbers 12:3)*.
Moses was ready to lay down his life for every individual. When the rebellion of
Korach broke out, the great leader did not sit in his headquarters and order his
adversaries destroyed, but went personally to each and every one of them, pleading
with them to end their rebellion and save their lives. "It is not Aaron and myself
whom you are defying, for what are we, after all?"

   Moses taught us humility by example. He knew his greatness, but it did not turn
his head.

   And so we have the diminutive א that instructs us that even when one's greatness
is evident and undeniable, one does not have to boast about it.

   We refer to Moses as "Moshe Rabbeinu," our teacher. But he can only be our
teacher if we will learn from him.

Dangers of Miserliness

צו

Tzav

צַו אֶת אַהֲרֹן וְאֶת בָּנָיו לֵאמֹר זֹאת תּוֹרַת הָעֹלָה — *Command Aaron and his sons, saying, "This is the law of the burnt offering"* (Leviticus 6:2).

Today's portion of the Torah begins with a Divine command to Moses to emphatically instruct the High Priest, Aaron, and his children to be precise in observance of the ritual of the daily burnt offering. Rashi states that this extra emphasis was necessary because the burnt offering was totally wasted as food, unlike other offerings which could be eaten by the priests.

This calls for some explanation. The amount of meat available for consumption by the priests must have been enormous. All first-born male livestock were sacrificed and eaten by the priests. On each of the Three Festivals, pilgrimage to Jerusalem was mandatory, and every family had to bring an animal offering which was shared by the priests. Then there were sin offerings, eaten only by the priests, and countless voluntary offerings in which the priests shared. Furthermore, the time for consumption of sacrificial meat was twenty-four to thirty-six hours at the most, so that much meat must have been in danger of being left over and disposed. Of what significance then would the daily burnt offering be that it required special instructions for diligence in its observance, lest the priests be lax because they derive no benefit from it?

How clearly the Torah understood the irrational nature of human emotion. A person who has a character trait of miserliness, who has lost control over his possessions so that they are master over him rather than the reverse, may be derelict in a service from which he derives no personal benefit.

Frugality is not the same as being stingy. The patriarch Jacob, who had built up enormous assets, made a separate trip to retrieve small cups (*Rashi, Genesis* 32:25). But when it came to buying off Esau's share in the family burial place in Hebron, Jacob piled up his entire wealth to attain his right to Machpela (*Shemos Rabbah* 31:17). Jacob was indeed frugal, but frugality means to be master over one's assets and not dissipate them. When necessary, Jacob could dispose of all his assets for a worthy purpose.

Rashi states that the extra emphasis on the burnt offering was both for immediate and future generations (*Leviticus* 6:2). "Immediate" refers to the High Priest, Aaron. He too had to be urged and cautioned not to be derelict in a service which was of no tangible benefit to him.

Is this even thinkable? Is the High Priest Aaron, the greatest High Priest in Jewish history, one who shared Divine communication with Moses, to be suspect that he would be lax in the Divine service because he would not get a piece of meat from it? Is this not the height of absurdity?

Apparently not. The Torah knows human nature better than we do. In spite of being the greatest scholar and leader, one who is in every other way totally devoted to G-d, a person may retain a streak of miserliness within himself. The Torah teaches us that no one is immune. Miserliness or stinginess is a character defect which can affect the great and mighty as well as the average person.

How thorough we must be in examining ourselves for character defects. Regardless of who or what we are, we are vulnerable humans and subject to the most irrational traits. Only by sincere prayer for removal of our character defects, and by availing ourselves of a spiritual counselor to help us with our character improvement, can we eliminate this pitfall.

Artificially Enhanced Spirituality

וַיַּקְרִיבוּ לִפְנֵי ה' אֵשׁ זָרָה — *And they brought an alien flame before God (Leviticus 10:1).*

In this portion of the Torah we read of the death of Nadav and Avihu, the two eldest sons of the High Priest Aaron, which occurred when they introduced an alien flame onto the Altar in the Sanctuary (10:1). Rashi comments, "Their sin was that they entered the Sanctuary after having imbibed wine."

Rashi's comment is striking, primarily because the text really needs no explanation. The text states very clearly that the transgression of Nadav and Avihu was that they made an impermissible modification of the service in the Sanctuary. Why does Rashi comment at all, and why does he give an explanation contradicting the one in the text?

Perhaps some recent trends can shed light on Rashi's comment. In the past several decades, there have been those that have advocated the use of various mind-altering chemicals as "mind-expanders." They claim that by using these chemicals one gets a perception of reality that is "more real than real." According to them, the normal human mind is restricted and cannot perceive correctly. This distorted logic results in the conclusion that only after the function of the brain cells has been altered by these chemicals can one perceive the world correctly.

How strange that they do not advocate chemicals that alter the senses of hearing, touch, vision, smell, and taste, which are the media by which we perceive the world around us. They have selected only thought and feeling as somehow being too restricted normally until "released" or "expanded" by drugs.

Their argument is not at all new. The first sin of mankind was when the serpent deluded man to believe that eating of the forbidden fruit would expand his wisdom. Man is very vulnerable to the idea that he can expand his thinking capacity by means of substances.

This vulnerability to delusion does not occur only with simpletons. Nadav and Avihu were great men, perhaps greater than even Moses and Aaron, as the Talmud implies. Yet they too fell prey to this delusion.

But Nadav and Avihu may have believed that the spiritual experience of entering the Divine presence in the Sanctuary could be intensified if they altered their state of mind, if they freed themselves of the usual tensions and pressures by imbibing wine. Their motive appears to have been sincere.

The Torah tells us that a spiritual experience via an altered state of mind is "an alien flame." It is an artificial chemical which is alien to spirituality, and rather than enhancing the soul, it actually constricts and destroys it. It is most significant that the Talmud says of Nadav and Avihu that their bodies were unaffected by the flame that killed them, which penetrated directly to their souls (*Sanhedrin* 52a).

Adam and Eve, Nadav and Avihu. Both pairs mistakenly thought to come close to G-d through artificial means. Both paid dearly for their error. It seems that the only thing that man has learned from history is that man fails to learn from history.

Rashi is not at all contradicting the text, but merely explaining what the exact nature of the "alien flame" was.

Spirituality can be achieved through hard work and dedication, by subduing one's natural inclinations in favor of the Divine will. There is no easy or instant method.

Unanticipated Isolation

בְּדָד יֵשֵׁב מִחוּץ לַמַּחֲנֶה מוֹשָׁבוֹ — *He must dwell in solitude, his place being outside of the encampment* (Leviticus 13:46).

Is there any reason to repeat what has already been said hundreds of times? Reams have been written about the gravity of *lashon hara* (gossip, slander), and it appears that there is little left to be said.

Perhaps just one comment is in order. The Talmud says that the affliction of the *metzora* (a kind of skin condition thought by some to be leprosy) is a consequence of transgressing the sin of *lashon hara*.

In this portion of the Torah we are told that the *metzora* must remove himself from the community. "He must dwell in solitude, his place being outside of the encampment" (13:46).

Some people believe that when they carry tales or spread juicy gossip, they endear themselves to others. They feel that others enjoy engaging them in conversation, because they always have so many interesting stories to tell about other people, and who is not curious to become privy to other people's secrets? It is so easy to gather a circle of listeners when one has gossip to offer. There is no need to ever be alone.

This conclusion has just a tiny fragment of truth because, initially at least, a gossiper will indeed find that he has a large audience. There is no denying that there are people who thrive on gossip. The smut tabloids remain in business because they have many customers.

But let us think a moment. Any person with a modicum of intelligence will not make close friends with a gossiper. If he carries tales about others to you, what is to stop him from carrying tales about you to others? No intelligent person will confide in a gossiper, and one will be very hesitant to invite him home to associate with his family or invite him to dinner or other intimate gatherings. The gossiper is a dangerous person. He may be interesting to listen to, but you dare not befriend him.

Intelligent people will therefore keep their distance from a gossiper, and soon he will have little or no audience. Anyone who does keep his company is probably as empty headed as the gossiper himself. While the gossiper initially may have an interested audience, he will eventually end up alone, or if not alone, in association only with those whose companionship is no better than solitude.

The fate of the *metzora* is the fate of the person who indulges in *lashon hara*. He becomes excommunicated either physically, emotionally, or both.

Like alcohol, drugs, or so many other things which involve an initial pleasant experience only to result in ultimate self-destruction, the carrier of *lashon hara*, too, will pay a dear price for the temporary gratification that spreading gossip provides for him. Our Sages say that *lashon hara* seriously harms not only the one who listens to it and the one who is slandered, but the gossiper himself as well.

Sanctity Versus Indulgence

Acharei-Kedoshim

כְּמַעֲשֵׂה אֶרֶץ מִצְרַיִם אֲשֶׁר יְשַׁבְתֶּם בָּהּ לֹא תַעֲשׂוּ וּכְמַעֲשֵׂה אֶרֶץ כְּנַעַן אֲשֶׁר אֲנִי מֵבִיא אֶתְכֶם שָׁמָּה לֹא תַעֲשׂוּ — *Do* not *follow the actions of the people of Egypt in whose land you dwelt, nor the actions of the dwellers of the land of Canaan into which I bring you* (Leviticus 18:3).

This exhortation is rather vague. We have many specific commandments which forbid certain acts and behaviors. Once these are eliminated, what is it that we are not to do that is done by other nations?

Ramban comments on the verse, "You shall be saintly to G-d" (16:1), that it is possible for a person to observe all specifics of Torah restrictions, yet be a vulgar person who pursues all physical pleasures that are not expressedly forbidden. To be saintly, says Ramban, is to partake of the physical world only to the degree necessary to live, but not to indulge, even when it is technically permissible.

In recent years we have witnessed a rather new phenomenon in Jewish living. Almost anything is available under "strict kosher supervision." No sooner does a new type of wine or cheese appear on the shelves than it is followed by a similar product under kosher supervision. All condiments and delicacies are now available as kosher. In foods there is no longer anything that is unavailable to the Jewish palate, except for pork, and even here artificial kosher "bacon" is available.

The secular world has its popular rock'n'roll stars, and similar performers have emerged whose long *tzitzis* shake with their gyrations. Hair styles in wigs exceed in variety those of natural hair. Clothes that are technically compliant with "*tzenius*" (modesty) can be most provocative.

What has happened is that we have not heeded the Torah exhortation cited above, and that we have emulated the actions of other peoples. There is really no need to have all delicacies available in kosher form. We could survive perfectly well in their absence. Some Jewish affairs, with an excess of all kinds of delicacies, have taken on the character of the Roman orgy. They are technically kosher, but in spirit they are non-Jewish. They are an emulation of the practice of the nations among whom we live, an emulation which the Torah has specifically forbidden.

Ramban says that a person can be technically strictly observant, yet be vulgar in self-indulgence. How prophetic his words were, written more than seven hundred years ago, yet accurately describing some contemporary Jewish life!

Whereas everything that is non-kosher is noxious to spirituality, it does not follow that everything that *is* kosher enhances spirituality. Self-restraint is an essential for spirituality.

Rabbi Shneur Zalman said it succinctly: "What is forbidden is not permissible, and much that is permissible is not essential."

Commitment and Responsibility

אמור

Emor

וְלֹא יְחַלְּלוּ אֶת קָדְשֵׁי בְּנֵי יִשְׂרָאֵל — *They shall not defile that which is sacred to the children of Israel* (Leviticus 22:15).

The Talmud bases an interesting *halachah* on this verse. If a sacrificial offering is brought upon the Altar under the mistaken assumption that it was an offering of a different classification, it is rendered unfit. However, if it was brought under the mistaken assumption that it was not a sacred offering at all, it remains

LIVING EACH DAY / 385

acceptable. The Talmud established the rule, "That which is sacred can disqualify something else sacred, but that which is secular cannot disqualify something sacred" (Zevachim 3b).

This Talmudic principle led one of the Torah commentaries to conclude, "One who has a status of sanctity can have an impact on the sacred, whereas the actions of one who lacks a status of sanctity is relatively insignificant."

There are times when humility can backfire. A person may not think much of himself, but if others see him as an authority, he must take great caution with his words and deeds. The prophet Samuel chastised King Saul for misguided humility. "If you are humble in your own eyes, remember that you are the leader of the people of Israel" (I Samuel 15:17). A person has an obligation to behave responsibly according to the status he assumes in the eyes of observers.

People who are considered to have achieved a level of spirituality serve as role models for others, whether they like it or not. If they do anything improper, observers are apt to reach one of two conclusions: (1) There is nothing improper about this particular behavior since it was performed by a spiritual person who would do no wrong; or (2) spiritual people are hypocrites who profess to be spiritual while they are in fact no different from anyone else. The former conclusion sanctions improper behavior, and the latter casts unjust aspersions on genuinely spiritual people.

The finer one's garments are, the more caution one must take that they not become soiled. The more spiritual we become, the more caution we must exert that we behave as is expected of spiritual people.

We therefore must have a true self-awareness. While spiritual growth increases one's humility and one's awareness of how relatively little one has achieved, one must nevertheless consider what one represents to observers.

People who are Torah scholars and are manifestly pious have great responsibility for their behavior. Any untruth, deception, inconsideration, rudeness, or other indecency will reflect not only on their own person, but on the group whom they are thought to represent. Such action constitutes nothing less than a desecration of G-d's name.

With a primitive or blunt instrument one may not be able to accomplish much, but neither can its misuse be as devastating as that of a powerful instrument, whose potential for harm is directly proportional to its potential for good.

We can achieve much as we grow in spirituality, but we must be cognizant of the responsibility inherent in spiritual growth.

Perfection of Chesed

בהר

Behar

אֶת כַּסְפְּךָ לֹא תִתֵּן לוֹ בְּנֶשֶׁךְ וּבְמַרְבִּית לֹא תִתֵּן אָכְלֶךָ — *Do not give your money in usury, and for increase do not give your food* (Leviticus 25:37).

According to Torah law, all interest is usury. The prohibition against taking interest is one of the most formidable in the Torah. The Midrash states that on Judgment Day, any sins that a person committed will be submitted for debate between accusing and defending angels, but for the sin of taking interest, there is no deliberation and condemnation is immediate.

Rabbi Chaim Shmulevitz states that the principle behind the prohibition of interest is that the latter constitutes a personal gain acquired while performing *chesed* (an act of benevolence), in this case, lending someone money. An act of kindness should be done altruistically, and receiving any return for an act of kindness detracts from it and essentially destroys the concept of *chesed*.

One of the most important acts of *chesed* is that of attending to the burial of the dead. This is referred to as *chesed shel emes*, or a true act of benevolence, because obviously there can be no anticipation of the beneficiary returning the favor. It is therefore a pure *chesed*.

Since the overriding concern is that the person in need should receive the help he requires, the Talmud states that all acts of *chesed* are rewarded, even if one does them for ulterior motives. However, our goal should be to achieve the highest level of *chesed*, that which brings one no personal gain whatever.

The Talmud states that the purpose of creation was to make possible the performance of *chesed*. This gives *chesed* its supreme importance. *Chesed* is the reason for all existence.

Simple survival in this world requires that we do many things for ourselves. Habit has a way of influencing behavior so that things we do that are not for survival purposes also become tainted with self-interest.

While we are not saints and do not claim to have achieved perfection, we should nevertheless have perfection as the goal toward which we strive. The perfection of *chesed* is doing things to help others without anticipating anything in return.

The Deception of Underestimation

בחקתי

וְזָכַרְתִּי אֶת בְּרִיתִי יַעֲקוֹב וְאַף אֶת בְּרִיתִי יִצְחָק וְאַף אֶת בְּרִיתִי אַבְרָהָם
. . . — *I shall remember My covenant with Jacob and also My covenant with Isaac and also My covenant with Abraham (Leviticus 26:42).*

Bechukosai

A young man with a severe alcohol and drug problem was admitted to the hospital for treatment. He asked whether he could have a brain-wave test as part of his examination and explained that he was worried that his use of alcohol and drugs might have caused brain damage. I assured him that he had no reason to suspect brain damage.

The following day he asked whether he could have psychological tests performed to determine whether he had sustained brain damage. Again I reassured him that he had no cause for worry. The next day he inquired about a brain scan, again concerned about having brain damage. This time, however, he refused to accept my reassurance. I then had a lengthy interview with this man, during which it became evident that he was not only *afraid* he had brain damage, but that he actually *wanted* to have brain damage! Why? Because then he could say, "Do not expect anything of me. Just let me continue with my use of alcohol and drugs. I am beyond help, because I am brain damaged." Having brain damage would relieve him of all responsibility of getting well.

Some people may be motivated, albeit unconsciously, to underestimate themselves and minimize their capacities. Awareness of their true potential would obligate them to perform to the extent of their capabilities. Deluding oneself that one is very limited and cannot accomplish much allows one to drift into laziness and inaction without much guilt.

In today's portion of the Torah, we read of the very serious consequences that will follow abandonment of the Torah. Then G-d says, "I shall remember My covenant with Jacob . . . and with Isaac . . . and with Abraham". What is the relevance of this statement in the context of the admonishment?

Shelah explains that a person is held accountable commensurate with his capacities. Our actions will be judged against a very high standard. We are the descendants of the patriarchs. We had forebears who were saintly people, thoroughly spiritual, and completely committed to the Divine will. With such lineage, the demands on us will be far greater than if we derived from people who were less spiritual.

The *yeitzer hara* never relents. If he cannot undermine our spirituality by one technique, he will try another. He is apt to delude us with misguided humility in order to gain his ends. "What makes you think that your study of Torah is of any value? You lack the depth of understanding necessary for Torah study. You do not have sufficient basic knowledge to understand religious philosophy." Or, "Who do you think you are to be punctilious in observance of *mitzvos*? You act as though you are a *tzaddik*, when in fact you are a degenerate."

The *yeitzer hara's* task is facilitated by our natural inclination to laziness and comfort. To combat the *yeitzer hara* we must become aware of our enormous capacities. Every person has potential that approaches that of the angels (*Psalms* 8:6). We must maximize this potential, and not allow ourselves to be deluded that we are incapable of reaching the heights of spiritual achievement.

ספר במדבר
Bamidbar / Numbers

Requisites for Torah

במדבר
Bamidbar

וַיְדַבֵּר ה' אֶל מֹשֶׁה בְּמִדְבַּר סִינַי — *And G-d spoke to Moses in the desert (Numbers 1:1).*

This portion of the Torah, *Bamidbar* (in the desert), invariably coincides with the week of Shavuos, the festival which commemorates the giving of the Torah at Sinai. This supports the Talmudic assertion that Torah can be attained only by a person who renders himself similar to the desert (*Nedarim 55b*). The desert symbolizes physical desolation, a place that is devoid of physical comforts.

This point is again mentioned in *Ethics of the Fathers* (6:4): "This is the way of Torah, to eat bread with salt, to drink water by measure, to sleep on the ground, and live a life of hardship." Torah and luxurious living appear to be incompatible. Indeed, the Talmud says that from the time of Moses there was not one wealthy person who excelled in Torah until Rabbi Yehudah HaNassi, and this phenomenon did not repeat itself for more than two hundred years, until Rav Ashi (*Gittin 59a*). Although these outstanding Torah scholars were extremely wealthy, they were not in the least indulgent. Prior to his death, Rabbi Yehudah HaNassi raised his hands to heaven and said, "Master of the universe! It is known and revealed before You that all my days my ten fingers toiled in Torah, and I did not partake of the earthly world as much as my little finger" (*Kesubos 104a*).

The ethical works consider the human being to be a miraculous creature, one in whom the physical body and the spiritual soul, which are as incompatible as fire and water, peacefully coexist. It is clear, however, that indulging in one detracts from the other. The above quote from *Ethics of the Fathers* indicates that Torah can be acquired only if one subsists on the bare minimum, and does not indulge in unnecessary physical pleasures.

Another characteristic of the desert is that it is a barren place where man's efforts, regardless of how intense they may be, can produce nothing. Survival in the desert was possible only because of direct intervention by G-d through provision of the *manna*. Furthermore, the portions of *manna* were provided daily. There was no accumulating or storing *manna* for a future day. Everyone was directly dependent on the Divine bounty, and there was no concern with providing for tomorrow.

These conditions are requisite for true understanding of Torah. "Grasp of Torah was granted only to those who subsisted on *manna*" (*Mechilta, Beshalach*).

Somehow we seem to have lost sight of this principle. Some people who aspire to Torah scholarship and profess to be dedicated to Torah living also aspire to various luxuries. There is no denying the Talmudic position that this is inconsistent.

The approximation of *Bamidbar* to Shavuos should alert us that today, just as at the time of giving of the Torah, Torah can be acquired only by those who reject partaking of any more of the physical world than is necessary for survival, and only when a person recognizes that he is entirely dependent on G-d, and lives one day at a time, leaving his concerns about the future in the hands of G-d.

Unauthorized Use Constitutes Theft

וְהִתְוַדּוּ אֶת חַטָּאתָם אֲשֶׁר עָשׂוּ וְהֵשִׁיב אֶת אֲשָׁמוֹ — *And they shall confess their sins which they have perpetrated, and he shall make restitution for his sin* (Numbers 5:7)

נשא

Nasso

When rational people behave improperly, it is invariably because of a lack of perception of what life is all about. The Sages say, "A person does not sin unless he is overtaken by a spirit of folly" (*Sotah 3a*). All sin is, as it were, temporary insanity, for which we are nevertheless held accountable.

The Torah philosophy of life is that we are not free to live our lives according to whatever whims we have. Our lives were loaned to us and our souls given to us by G-d for a specific purpose: to do His will. According to *halachah*, if you lend something to someone for a specified purpose, and the borrower puts it to some other use, that is a violation of the terms of the agreement, and unauthorized use is the equivalent of theft.

In today's portion of the Torah we read about the sin of theft, and that in addition to making restitution, the thief must confess his sin. This is one of the few places in Torah where confession is mentioned. Why, of all sins, does the Torah choose to mention confession in regard to theft?

The Rabbi of Gur answered that all our faculties are on loan to us from G-d for specified purposes. Our hands were given to us to do *mitzvos*, our legs to take us where we belong, our eyes to read Torah, our ears to hear the word of G-d, our tongues to pray and speak the praises of G-d, our mouths to eat in order to sustain our lives so that we may fulfill our mission in life.

The Talmud states that before a person is born into the world, the *neshamah* (soul) is given a solemn oath, "Be a *tzaddik* (a just person) and do not be a *rasha*" (a sinful person, *Niddah 30b*). If we use our vision to look at indecent things, our ears to hear gossip, our tongues to slander, our hands to take what is not ours, our legs to go to improper places, and our mouths to eat forbidden foods, we are violating the terms on which we received these faculties. Such unauthorized use of our faculties constitutes theft. All sinful acts are, as it were, theft, and confession is therefore mentioned in relationship to theft, for all sin is a kind of thievery.

Teshuvah, in addition to its usual meaning of repentance, also means "return." A stolen item must be returned to its rightful owner. An object loaned for a specific use that has been put to an unauthorized use must be returned to its proper and rightful use.

Some people who consider themselves to be highly ethical and who would abhor the notion of taking even one cent that does not belong to them may not be, however, as loath to glance at objects of temptation, to speak badly of another person, or to listen to gossip. They fail to realize that such an unauthorized use of our G-d-given or our G-d-loaned faculties is no less theft than committing a burglary, something which they consider repugnant and completely alien to them.

We must remember that our lives do not fully belong to us. They are on loan to us for the extent of our life span. We must be extremely careful not to commit theft by misusing them.

The Centrality of Humility

בהעלתך
Beha'aloscha

וְהָאִישׁ משֶׁה עָנָו מְאֹד מִכֹּל הָאָדָם אֲשֶׁר עַל פְּנֵי הָאֲדָמָה — *The man Moses was humble, more so than any other human being on earth* (Numbers 12:3).

Since Moses had many fine character traits, why does the Torah mention only humility? The answer is simple. Humility is the source of all other commendable traits. True humility invariably leads to character refinement. Conversely, conceit and vanity invariably result in character degeneration.

Humility does not mean that one should be unaware of one's capacities and strengths. To do so would be denying the truth, and there is nothing commendable about falsehood. Moses knew that he was distinct from and greater than all other prophets for all time to come. "I converse with him directly, mouth to mouth, and he perceives the image of G-d" *(12:8)*. But this unique distinction did not cause Moses to be vain. He remained more humble than any other man on earth.

The Torah speaks similarly of Aaron, the High Priest. Although given the most eminent role in the Temple service, the Torah speaks of the praise of Aaron that "He did not change" *(Rashi 5:3)*, which the Rabbi of Pshis'cha interpreted to mean that the honor of the exalted position that Aaron occupied did not affect his true humility.

Some people who might otherwise be humble lose their humility when their achievements or positions bring them wide acclaim and honor.

One of the Chassidic masters related a parable of a king who wanted to have a first-hand look at life in his kingdom. He therefore disguised himself as a foot soldier so that he could mingle with the common folk, and he asked one of his officers to accompany him. Wherever they went, people would acknowledge the officer by standing up for him and saluting him, but they completely ignored the foot soldier. The officer was not at all pleased with this recognition. "If only they knew who it really was that is with me," he thought. "In their ignorance of the presence of the king, they accord honor to me."

Rabbi Menachem Mendel of Lubavitch (the "Tzemach Tzedek") was accompanied on a trip by his young son, Reb Shmuel. The young boy wrote home about the great honor accorded his father by the throngs of followers who greeted him.

On his return home, the Tzemach Tzedek found the letter and reprimanded his son. "My blood was spilling like water, and you took pleasure in this?"

The person who is aware of the constant presence of G-d and the awesome majesty of G-d is not the least affected by honor and claim, except, like the officer who accompanied the king in disguise, to become even more humble.

If we wish to rid ourselves of character defects, the place to begin is with a healthy humility. We should not deny our potential, but with the recognition that whatever we have is a G-d-given gift, there should also be the awareness to whom the honor for our achievements really belongs.

Misguided Humility

שלח
Shelach

וַנְּהִי בְעֵינֵינוּ כַּחֲגָבִים וְכֵן הָיִינוּ בְּעֵינֵיהֶם — *We felt we were like grasshoppers, and that is how we appeared to them* (Numbers 13:33).

In the previous week's portion, the pivotal role of humility in character development was discussed. It is most important to distinguish between true humility, which is a virtue, and the deceptive feeling of low self-worth, which can sometimes masquerade as humility.

A person must know his self-worth. He must not underestimate his capabilities. Particularly, he must not lose sight of his immense value in the eyes of G-d, and that with G-d at his side, there is virtually nothing that is impossible for him to accomplish.

In this week's portion of the Torah we read of the tragic consequences of misguided humility. The saga of the spies sent by Moses to bring back a report of the Promised Land, which eventuated in the Divine decree that the generation of the Exodus must perish during forty years of wandering in the desert, represents both a lack of trust in G-d and a lack of faith in one's self.

The spies reported that Canaan was inhabited by a race of giants. These giants were so tall that, "We felt we were like grasshoppers, and that is how we appeared to them". Here the Torah teaches us an important psychological truth: The way you feel about yourself is the way you think you are perceived by others.

Feelings of unwarranted low self-esteem are always progressive. In addition, they give rise to various types of pathological thinking. This is borne out by Rashi's comment on the above verse. The spies said, "We heard them say about us, 'There are ants crawling about in our vineyards.'" It is unlikely that the spies understood the Canaanite language, yet they were certain they knew what the Canaanites were saying. This is because, given their self-perception, that is what they thought others would say. Furthermore, they quickly shrank in their self-estimation from being perceived as grasshoppers to the more diminutive ants.

How is it that the spies and the people who received their story with anxiety did not believe that the omnipotence of G-d would enable them to triumph, particularly after having seen the many miracles of the Exodus? The answer is that in their low self-esteem, they did not consider themselves to be deserving of Divine favor. This doubt about their deserving Divine help was evident when they questioned, "Is G-d with us or not?" *(Exodus 17:7).* This is why Caleb, one of the minority who contradicted the other spies, said, "If G-d approves of us, He will give us the land . . . G-d is with us, do not fear." The poor self-concept of the Israelites caused them to doubt their own capabilities as well as their meriting fulfillment of the Divine promise.

The yeitzer hara will use any and every technique to prevent us from fulfilling the Divine will. He may come to us under a cloak of piety, pointing out to us how sinful we have been, as though he were urging us to constructive self-examination and teshuvah. If we are not on the alert, we may be taken in by this ruse, under the impression that we are in remorse for our sins, while the true fact is that the yeitzer hara is simply trying to paralyze us with depression.

How can one distinguish between teshuvah and the scheming of the yeitzer hara? It is rather simple. True teshuvah is inevitably followed by joy and an urge toward action. The yeitzer hara-induced depression is followed by lethargy and a feeling of futility.

If one is uncertain as to whether one is experiencing humility and teshuvah, or low self-esteem, the help of a competent spiritual advisor should be sought. We have too much to accomplish to allow ourselves to be disabled by unwarranted feelings of unworthiness.

Deceptive Altruism

קרח
Korach

כִּי כָל הָעֵדָה כֻּלָּם קְדֹשִׁים וּבְתוֹכָם ה' וּמַדּוּעַ תִּתְנַשְּׂאוּ עַל קְהַל ה' — *The entire nation is equally holy and G-d is among them; why do you raise yourselves above G-d's congregation?* (Numbers 16:3).

In the previous two weekly portions of the Torah, we discussed the virtue of humility as distinct from deceptive feelings of unworthiness. We saw how the yeitzer hara may connive to disable a person, coming under the guise of piety, as though he were stimulating one to teshuvah.

Another ruse that the yeitzer hara employs is described in this week's portion of the Torah. This time the yeitzer hara appears as a social reformer, championing the popular cause of egalitarianism. Korach, a brilliant and highly esteemed scholar, leads a rebellion against Moses and Aaron. "We do not need leaders. The entire nation is all equally holy. Everyone heard the voice of G-d speaking directly to him or her. There is no room for elitism." Who can disagree with such a noble argument for equality? However, the Sages of the Talmud disclose Korach's true intentions.

Korach's motivation was not at all pure. Korach was angry and envious because a younger member of his clan had been appointed to a position of leadership to which he had aspired. It was petty envy and not altruism that led Korach to rebel. The tragedy is complicated by the fact that Korach himself was not aware of his true motivation.

Moses suggested a simple test to prove what the Divine Will was, and to demonstrate whether he and Aaron were indeed chosen by G-d to be the leaders of the nation or, as Korach argued, usurped their authority. Korach and his followers were to offer incense on the Altar, a service which if performed without Divine assignment was punishable by death.

Korach was well aware of the lethal consequences of unauthorized participation in the Sanctuary services, yet he exposed himself to this danger. Why? Because he was deluded. Korach sincerely believed that he was championing the cause of the people and that he was doing the will of G-d. Envy, as other self-interests, can blind us from the truth. Korach's envy led to his destruction.

It is not at all unusual to see people acting under the delusion that what they are doing is just and proper, while the true fact is that they are motivated by petty self-interest. How much of the destructive factionalism that has plagued the Jewish nation throughout history was due to people breaking away into splinter groups because some people wished to attain positions of leadership, while they asserted that their defection was due to disagreement in principles, which they could not compromise? How many little *shuls* have been formed ostensibly because a group of people could not comply with the prevailing *nusach* (minor variations in the service), while the truth was that a few people aspired to the position of president or Rabbi, which they could not attain with the parent group?

Korach was deluded, and his mistake was the result of his not accepting Moses' authority. It was his arrogance that precluded his humbling himself before the acknowledged authority. His logic misled him to believe that he was a national hero.

The folly of Korach was costly. Unfortunately, this same mistake has been repeated many times throughout Jewish history, each time with dire consequences. Is it not high time that we learn the lesson?

Absolute Obedience

חקת
Chukas

זֹאת חֻקַּת הַתּוֹרָה . . . וְיִקְחוּ אֵלֶיךָ פָרָה אֲדֻמָּה תְּמִימָה — *This is the law of the Torah . . . you shall take for yourself an entirely red cow* (Numbers 19:2).

The saga of Korach (see above) is followed by the *mitzvah* of the red cow, a *mitzvah* which is cited as the prototype of a Divine decree which is suprarational, totally beyond the grasp of human understanding. A red cow is sacrificed, and its ashes, mixed with spring water, have the potency to remove the state of contamination subsequent to one's contact with a dead body. Yet, a person who is "clean" and who comes in contact with these purifying ashes becomes contaminated! What possible logic can there be to this?

The *mitzvah* of the red cow represents the suspension of logic in deference to the Divine Will. This attitude is not restricted to this *mitzvah*. Scripture introduces the *mitzvah* of the red cow with the words, "This is the law of the *Torah*". Surrendering one's own reasoning and accepting the superior wisdom of G-d is the law of the entire Torah, and it must embrace all of Judaism.

The only human being who was granted insight and understanding into this unique *mitzvah* was Moses. Why?

Rabbi Leibish Harif states that Moses was the only person who was completely untainted by the worship of the golden calf, since he was then at the summit of Sinai during his forty-day communion with G-d. All others were either actively or passively involved in the idolatrous episode.

As we have seen (above, *Lech Lecha*), idolatry goes beyond the worship of graven images. Idolatry is the antithesis of G-d creating man, and man surrendering his own will to the will of G-d. Idolatry is man creating his own god and making that god satisfy man's personal desires. Idolatry is nothing else than self-will running amok. The rebellion of Korach, as was explained, exemplifies man's refusal to surrender to Torah authority, which is invariably due to his desire to pursue his personal interests and gratify his own drives. The rebellion of Korach was thus another manifestation of the principle of idolatry. The *mitzvah* of the red cow, which exemplifies the total surrender of one's reason and one's self to the Divine Will, is thus the antithesis of idolatry.

A complete understanding of the *mitzvah* of the red cow could therefore be achieved only by one who was not even remotely tainted by idolatry, by self-interest. Hence, only Moses was capable of such understanding.

To some people, various aspects of Torah observance may seem illogical. Some people have rejected those observances which they do not understand. The *mitzvah* of the red cow, whose secret was vouchsafed only to Moses, teaches us that our understanding of Torah is directly proportional to our willingness to relinquish our personal drives in deference to the will of G-d. To the extent that we let go of our own will, to that degree we can understand the Divine Will.

Our ancestors at Sinai grasped the truth of this principle when they responded in unison, "*Naaseh venishma*" (We will do and we will understand, *Exodus 24:7*). It is characteristic of Torah that its understanding does not precede its observance, but follows it.

In contrast to what some people may believe, Torah is not beyond our understanding, but we must be willing to make the personal sacrifices that such understanding requires.

Inconsistency

בלק

Balak

תָּמֹת נַפְשִׁי מוֹת יְשָׁרִים וּתְהִי אַחֲרִיתִי כָּמֹהוּ — *May I die a death of the righteous, and may my end be as glorious as theirs* (Numbers 23:10).

One of the strangest phenomena of human psychology is the coexistence of conflicting ideas. There are some people who entertain two-polar opposite concepts, thinking one way and feeling another. This does not refer to hypocrisy, where a person knowingly acts, for ulterior motives, in contrast to what he believes, but rather to the coexistence of two incompatible ideas in the same person.

The conflict often occurs in the intellectual versus the emotional spheres. People can reason rationally and come to a valid conclusion, yet although they are intellectually convinced of the validity of this conclusion, it seems to have no impact on their behavior, because the latter is determined by their emotions rather than by their reasoning.

A prime example of the coexistence of opposites is the character of Balaam, which is described in today's portion of the Torah. Balaam was a prophet, privileged to have direct communication with G-d, but was morally degenerate, evil to the core. Balaam had a degree of prophecy equal in some respects to that of Moses *(Talmud)*. But whereas Moses became a man of G-d, Balaam sank to depths of perversion, as the Midrash relates. Balaam was one who "knows the mind of G-d" *(24:16)*, and who, upon seeing Israel in its entire historical perspective, says, "May I die a death of the righteous, and may my end be as glorious as theirs," yet continued to live as a profligate.

It is important to realize that intellectual concepts do not always influence behavior. There are strong resistances to changes in behavior, especially when the latter provides gratification, or has become ingrained by virtue of habit. Intellectual arguments in favor of change can be counteracted by rationalizations or rational arguments against change. It is only when ideas become feelings that change is likely to occur.

This is what is meant by "G-d desires the commitment of the heart," because it is the emotional component rather than the intellectual knowledge that will lead to behavioral changes.

One might say, "I cannot help it. I cannot control my feelings." This is not quite true. The Midrash states, "The righteous have mastery over their hearts (feelings)" (*Bereishis Rabbah* 34).

How can one gain mastery over one's feelings? Firstly, by doing what one knows to be right even without feeling. One must force oneself to follow intellectual conclusions. Such actions will break down the resistances, and with the latter eliminated, the desired feelings will emerge. Secondly, one must pray sincerely for Divine assistance in achieving the desired feelings.

People who are not hungry can stimulate their appetite with proper appetizers. Prayer is the "appetizer" that can bring about the emotion one wishes to attain.

Life is Spirituality

פינחס

Pinchas

צְרוֹר אֶת הַמִּדְיָנִים וְהִכִּיתָם אוֹתָם — *Harass the Midianites and smite them* (Numbers 25:17).

Some people think of spirituality as an important component of life, along with some other major ingredients. Some may even elevate spirituality to being a very major component of life. The Torah perspective is that spirituality *is* life. It was necessary for the Talmud to find a specific source in the Torah that requires one to transgress a *mitzvah* where there is a danger of death. One would otherwise have thought that martyrdom is required whenever there is a danger of losing one's spirituality by violating the word of G-d. Indeed, when confronted with the three cardinal sins of idolatry, murder, or adultery, which can totally annihilate one's spirit, martyrdom is required. Life without even the potential for spirituality is not worth living.

In today's portion of the Torah, G-d instructed Moses to do battle with Midian because of that nation's nefarious attempt to corrupt the Israelites *(25:17-18)*. On the other hand, in relationship to the Egyptians, the Torah requires that they not be rejected *(Deuteronomy 23:8)*. The Talmud explains that although the Egyptians ruthlessly enslaved the Israelites and cruelly killed their newborn infants, they are not to be totally rejected because their threat was a physical one *(Sifri)*, and painful as it may be, Israel can survive physical dangers. The Midianites did not attack physically, but attempted to corrupt them morally, to destroy their spirituality. This spiritual danger threatens the very essence of Israel, and is far worse than a physical danger.

Do we incorporate this vital principle in our everyday lives? How many precautions do we take for our physical safety? What safeguards would we take if there were a serious threat to our lives or health? On the other hand, how careful are we to avoid things that might diminish our spirituality?

Under the umbrella of freedom of speech and press, the mass media in our society has become replete with both verbal and graphic material that is explicit in violence, vulgarity, and sensuality, which have a greater or lesser impact on our spirituality. Are we as careful to avoid them as we are to avoid physical danger? Do we take as many precautions to protect our children from exposure to these influences as we do to protect them from physical harm?

Various rationalizations are given for permitting children to be exposed to objectionable material. "It is the real world, and they must learn to cope with it. Children cannot be protected in a cocoon." However, communicable diseases are also part of the real world, as are radiation and high-speed traffic. What responsible parent would allow a child to be exposed to a serious contagious disease, or to radiation, or allow him to run out among speeding cars?

How much emphasis we place on spiritual safety versus physical safety indicates just where we stand on valuing the importance of each. The Torah position is clear.

Supremacy of Gratitude

מטות־מסעי

Matos-
Mas'ei

וַיִּשְׁלַח אֹתָם מֹשֶׁה אֶלֶף לַמַּטֶּה לַצָּבָא אֹתָם וְאֶת פִּינְחָס בֶּן אֶלְעָזָר לַצָּבָא
— And Moses sent them — a thousand from each tribe — as an army; (he sent) them with Pinchas ben Elazar to lead them (Numbers 31:6).

In this portion of the Torah we read of an unusual occurrence. G-d instructs Moses to wage battle against Midian to punish them for attempting to corrupt the Israelites. Moses does not carry out the Divine commandment himself, but delegates the task to Pinchas. Why is it that Moses, who was entirely devoted to G-d, does not immediately seize the opportunity to do the Divine will?

The Midrash explains that Moses felt that he should not personally battle against Midian because that nation provided him with asylum when he fled from Pharaoh (Exodus 2:15). He felt a debt of gratitude toward the country that gave him refuge and he reasoned that it could not possibly be G-d's will that he deny his gratitude. The principle of "The ways of the Torah are gentle" (Proverbs 3:17) led him to believe that the Divine intent must be that this assignment be delegated.

Yet Moses' feeling of impropriety was not sufficient to permit deviation from the literal word of G-d. The Midrash states that Moses relied on a precedent. When the plague of converting the Nile to blood was to be implemented, G-d instructed Moses to have Aaron smite the river. Why Aaron rather than him? Because the river had provided a haven for Moses when he was cast upon it as an infant. If gratitude had to be shown even to inanimate objects, how much more so toward people.

This episode teaches us two things: (1) The teachings of Torah provide the highest level of sensitivity and consideration. Gratitude is a trait of supreme importance, and it is unthinkable that G-d would command someone to deny his debt of gratitude; (2) that even with the primacy of gratitude, one cannot rely on his own reasoning to interpret the word of G-d. There must be an authoritative halachic source for interpreting the Divine will.

Moses had to rely on derivation from a precedent in order to interpret the Divine will, because there was no greater authority to whom he could turn.

We have both a comprehensive body of halachah as well as competent Torah authorities to guide us. With recourse to these we can well maintain the principle, "The ways of Torah are gentle."

ספר דברים
Devarim / Deuteronomy

Admonishment with Dignity

אֵלֶּה הַדְּבָרִים אֲשֶׁר דִּבֶּר מֹשֶׁה אֶל כָּל יִשְׂרָאֵל . . . בַּמִּדְבָּר בָּעֲרָבָה מוֹל
סוּף בֵּין פָּארָן וּבֵין תֹּפֶל וְלָבָן וַחֲצֵרֹת וְדִי זָהָב — *These are the words*
which Moses spoke to all Israel . . . in the wilderness, in the
waste, opposite the Suf, between Paran and Tophel, and Lavan, and Chatzeiros,
and Di Zahav (Deuteronomy 1:1).

It is indeed true that when we see another person doing something wrong we
have an obligation to call the errant behavior to his attention. "You shall admonish
your friend," *(Leviticus 19:17)* is a *mitzvah*.

However, pointing out another person's wrongdoings must be done with the
greatest sensitivity and consideration. There is only one reason for admonishing
someone, and that is to help him avoid the improper act and to encourage him to
teshuvah. Any admonishment which is not likely to accomplish these goals is
forbidden *(Yevamos 65b)*.

We know from our own experience that when someone points out a fault to us
we feel deflated. We must understand that chastising another person will have a
similar effect on him. Such deflation can lead to depression and despair, and
rather than stimulate one to corrective action, it can cause a feeling of futility. We
must be careful to couch our criticism in such a fashion that the person feels
encouraged to improve himself.

In today's portion of the Torah we read, "These are the words which Moses
spoke to all Israel . . . in the wilderness, in the waste, opposite the Suf, between
Paran and Tophel, and Lavan, and Chatzeiros, and Di Zahav." Rashi points out
that these apparent names of places are actually abstruse references to various
sins committed by the Israelites during their forty-year sojourn in the desert.
Moses chose this symbolism because he did not wish to list their sins explicitly.

Yet in subsequent chapters of Deuteronomy, Moses goes into great detail about
each of these sins. Why then did he avoid doing so now?

The answer is given by Sifsei Chachamim. When Moses discussed each sin
individually he was not concerned that his chastisement would be counterproduc-
tive. He was able to impress the Israelites that basically they were good people,
descendants of the Patriarchs, the chosen and beloved people of G-d. Yes, they
had made a mistake, but they could correct it.

At the beginning of Deuteronomy, however, Moses wished to list *all* the
major sins of the forty years. Pointing out all the sins explicitly carried too great
a risk of making some people feel that they were degenerate and intrinsically
evil. These people would be discouraged rather than stimulated to *teshuvah*.
Moses therefore worded his admonishment cautiously. Only those people who
felt strong enough to deal with all their mistakes without being crushed would

understand to what he was referring. Those who could not safely absorb the entirety of this message would simply not hear it. They would wait until he dealt individually with each problem.

Moshe Rabbeinu - our great teacher — showed us how we must preserve another person's dignity while providing constructive criticism. If we reprimand someone, we must have exquisite sensitivity and an understanding of the individual's personality.

"Admonish your friend, but do not become responsible for his lack" (*Leviticus 19:17*). If we are thoughtless and inconsiderate in admonishment, we may end up with a sin of our own.

The Delusion of Despair

ואתחנן
Vaeschanan

וּבִקַּשְׁתֶּם מִשָּׁם אֶת ה' אֱלֹקֶיךָ וּמָצָאתָ כִּי תִדְרְשֶׁנּוּ בְּכָל לְבָבְךָ וּבְכָל נַפְשֶׁךָ — *From there you will seek the L-rd your G-d, and you will find Him, for you will seek Him with all your heart and with all your soul* (Deuteronomy 4:29).

Although we generally assume that what we see with our eyes does indeed exist, there are exceptions. We may see something that is so bizarre that we know it cannot possibly exist. We then say, "I must be hallucinating. My eyes are playing tricks on me."

Whereas such incidents are rare, it is not at all infrequent that our *minds* play tricks on us. We may be certain that what we think is absolutely true, and we do not have the slightest doubt of the validity of our convictions, yet sometime later we realize how wrong we were. Solomon cautions us about the certainty of our convictions: "Do you see a man who is wise in his own eyes? There is more hope for a fool than there is for him" (*Proverbs 26:12*). Too often, the realization that we were mistaken comes only in retrospect. If only we could have a correct awareness prospectively, how much misery could be avoided!

There is one area in which such foreknowledge is available. Rabbi Nachman of Breslov says, "Despair does not exist." There is no such thing in reality as hopelessness. If ever we do feel hopeless, we should be aware that our minds are playing tricks on us, and that soon we will discover how wrong we were to have felt hopeless. If we keep this thought in mind, we can avoid the pitfalls resulting from despair, because we will know that regardless of how bleak things may seem, our feeling of hopelessness is nothing but a delusion.

In today's portion of the Torah we are told of the consequences that will follow abandonment of the ways of G-d. "G-d will scatter you among the nations and you will remain few in number . . . And there you will become subservient to gods, the work of men's hands, which neither see, nor hear, nor eat, nor smell.

"From there you will seek the L-rd your G-d, and you will find Him, for you will seek Him with all your heart and with all your soul" (4:27-29).

"From *there* you will seek G-d and you will find Him." From the very depths of oppression and distress will come the search for G-d. You will find Him then because you will seek Him.

At no point may a person say, "I have sunk too low. I cannot possibly establish a relationship with G-d." There is no such entity as despair. "G-d will not let you go and will not let you perish" (4:31). Even if one thinks that he has broken all contact with G-d, let him be aware that a relationship still exists, because G-d has not broken contact with him.

Lest a person become disheartened by his failure to find G-d in his life, the words of the Rabbi of Kotzk are illuminating and refreshing: "You will seek G-d and you will find Him" *(4:29)*. The Rabbi of Kotzk added, "Seeking G-d *is* finding Him." It is not like the search for a treasure, which is all in vain if the treasure is not found. The search for G-d itself, the yearning to come closer to Him, the process of trying to improve oneself in order to become closer to G-d, that *is* the finding Him. Finding G-d is not something external to the search, but is the search itself.

Despair does not exist. We can always search for G-d. All that is required is that we shed our petty self-interests and dedicate ourselves to the search with all our heart and with all our soul. We can always establish a closeness to G-d. The Torah guarantees it.

Maintaining Self-Esteem

עקב

Eikev

וָאֵפֶן וָאֵרֵד מִן הָהָר — *And I turned about and descended from the mountain (Deuteronomy 9:15).*

In every life there are moments when a person feels overwhelmed, when adverse circumstances not only cause distress but so deflate a person that he begins to question his self-worth. These are moments of great spiritual danger, because one becomes vulnerable to the machinations of the *yeitzer hara* (evil inclination), who thrives on confusion, self-doubt, and despair (see above, *Ki Sissa)*. It requires great stamina and fortitude to maintain one's bearing at such times, and to develop the courage to go on with one's mission in life.

Such a moment occurred in the life of Moses, when at the end of the forty days of communion with G-d on Sinai, G-d told him, "Go descend, for your people have corrupted . . . They made for themselves a molten calf" *(Exodus 32:7-8)*. Moses' world was shattered. The people whom he had nurtured in Egypt — whom he had led out of slavery and elevated to such a status of spirituality that they proclaimed *"Naaseh venishma"* (we will do and we will understand) *(Exodus 24:7)* — these people suddenly sank to the depths of depravity and idolatry. At this moment of disillusionment, G-d tells him, "Go descend," which Rashi explains, "Descend from your supreme position. Your greatness was contingent upon the status of the Israelites. Their corruption is your decline."

In today's portion of the Torah, Moses tells us of his conduct. "And I turned about and descended *from the mountain*." Moses is saying, "Although at such a moment of utter shock and bitter disillusionment, when it appeared that all my labors were in vain, when I could have lost my bearings, when I could have descended from my status as G-d said to me, I nevertheless held my own. I descended only *from the mountain*, but not from my status. I was still the leader of Israel with the awesome responsibility of retrieving the errant nation from the quicksand of corruption. I had to face the challenge of pleading before G-d for their survival. I could not afford to relinquish my status."

In a similar vein, the Talmud tells of King Solomon, who was banished from his throne by a demonic usurper, and who roamed the countryside as a common beggar, proclaiming, "I am Solomon," to the jeers of all who considered him a madman. The Talmud says that at first Solomon reigned over the entire world, and later reigned only over his walking cane *(Sanhedrin 20b)*. Rabbi Chaim Shmulevitz points out that despite his precipitous decline from the ultimate heights to the nethermost depths, Solomon never lost his sense of royalty. When all he had that was his own was his walking cane, he considered himself monarch over his cane. His sense of dignity and self-worth never left him even at the worst of times.

Although humility is the greatest of all virtues, we must remember that a healthy self-esteem is essential for the service of G-d. "His heart was lofty in the ways of G-d" *(II Chronicles 17:6)*. When depressing circumstances threaten to cast one into despair, one must gather strength and courage to maintain the dignity and self-respect due to one created in the image of G-d.

Status of Permissibility

ראה
Re'eh

רְאֵה אָנֹכִי נֹתֵן לִפְנֵיכֶם הַיּוֹם בְּרָכָה וּקְלָלָה — *See, I am placing before you this day a blessing and a curse (Deuteronomy 11:26).*

According to *halachah*, if a person hires himself out for a day's work and does not specify in advance that he wishes to have time off for prayer, he must say the abridged *Amidah*, and may not take time off from his work for the full prayer unless it is the accepted practice to do so. This also applies to Grace after Meals. People who have committed themselves to work may not take time off for anything other than meals unless it had been otherwise stipulated.

If we realize that every human being has a commitment to do the Divine Will and that we are essentially servants of G-d who are obligated to do His bidding, it follows that we have no right to spend any time in activities other than those that constitute the Divine service.

Inasmuch as a person must have good physical and mental health to function optimally, anything that enhances good health is essential to the Divine service. For example, eating and sleeping are necessary for human life; exercise is conducive to good health; and judicious rest, relaxation, and diversion are all necessary for optimum function. Hence, these activities can be included as participating in the goal of the Divine service.

Indulging in worldly pleasures beyond those that are necessary for good health, however, is an unauthorized leave from our obligation as Divine servants, and hence is not permissible, even if the activity *per se* is not a prohibited one. Thus, one who indulges in food beyond that which is nutritionally necessary, and does so purely for the pleasure of eating, is being derelict in the service of G-d.

It becomes evident that not everything that is kosher is permissible. Even kosher food is permissible only when it is eaten because good nutrition is necessary for optimum health. When kosher food is eaten solely for pleasure after the nutritional requirements have been satisfied, it is actually not permissible.

The ethical works of *mussar* and *chassidus* stress this point. The verse in Proverbs, "In *all* your ways you shall acknowledge G-d" *(3:6)*, means that Divine service is not restricted to prayer, Torah study , and performance of specific *mitzvos*. G-d is to be acknowledged in all one's ways: in transacting business, in talking with friends, in relating to members of one's family, and in eating, sleeping, and recreating.

Today's portion of the Torah begins with a succinct statement, "See, I am placing before you this day a blessing and a curse." There is no grey area. Just as that which is explicitly prohibited is forbidden, so is that which is not forbidden but does not qualify for being included in any way in the service of G-d.

If this is followed to its logical conclusion, then we have only two categories of behavior: that which is required, and that which is forbidden. In this context, "permissibility" does not exist.

True Righteousness

צֶדֶק צֶדֶק תִּרְדֹּף — *Righteousness, righteousness shall you pursue (Deut. 16:20).*

There is hardly any need to stress the primacy of fulfilling the *mitzvos* of the Torah. There is, however, one essential feature upon which the validity of a *mitzvah* depends. Performance of a *mitzvah* dare not come about via dishonest or improper means, for the latter would constitute a sin rather than a *mitzvah*. The Talmud says that if a person bakes bread with wheat that he stole, gives the *Kohen* the requisite tithe from the bread, and recites a *brachah* (blessing), that would not at all be a welcome *brachah* to G-d, but an act of utter defiance which angers G-d *(Bava Kamma 94a)*.

This theme is repeated many times in Torah writings. Charity given from money that was obtained dishonestly is not a virtue. "I am G-d who loves justice, and I abhor a sacrifice brought from stolen property" *(Isaiah 61:8)*. Many authors who published Torah works took great precaution to see to it that the paper for their books was not manufactured in violation of *Shabbos*.

The Rabbi of Kotzk commented on the verse in Deuteronomy *(4:23)*, "Be cautious lest you forget the covenant with G-d, and make for yourself an idol or a graven image of all that G-d commanded you." The Rabbi noted that the sentence is incomplete, and should read, " . . . of all that G-d commanded you *not* to do." He therefore interpreted the verse as follow: "Be cautious that you do not pervert G-d's commandments into idolatrous practices." It is fully possible that in pursuit of even some worthy goal a person may be oblivious to transgressions committed in its attainment.

This principle applies not only to frank dishonesty, but also to objectionable character traits. Within one's household, one should not scold with anger, even when something wrong was done that requires reprimand *(Gittin 6b)*. Should it ever be necessary to convey the gravity of a misdeed by showing that one has been angered by it, then one may feign anger but not be consumed by anger internally.

There was an incident where a community was faced with making the choice of engaging a Rabbi from among two candidates. Although one was by far more qualified, they leaned toward the other candidate out of respect for his ancestors who were great Torah luminaries. The community leaders consulted a Torah authority for advice, and he was shocked by their thinking. "It would be an absolute insult to these great Torah luminaries that they were the reason for a community bypassing a more qualified person to chose a descendant of theirs. They lived by Torah principles and they taught Torah principles. Torah requires that the position of Rabbi be occupied by the one who is most qualified rather than by someone who can boast of *yichus* (lineage)."

We can understand what the prophet meant when he said, "The ways of G-d are just. The righteous do walk in them, and those who transgress do stumble therein" *(Hoshea 14:10)*. The Torah can be distorted and become a stumbling block, and we must take great caution that we be the just who walk in its ways.

All this is summed up succinctly in today's portion of the Torah. "Righteous-ness, righteousness shall you pursue" upon which Rabbi Bunim of Pshis'cha comments, "You must pursue righteousness *with* righteousness." The end does not justify the means.

Compassion

כִּי תֵצֵא

Ki Seitzei

שַׁלֵּחַ תְּשַׁלַּח אֶת הָאֵם וְאֶת הַבָּנִים תִּקַּח לָךְ לְמַעַן יִיטַב לָךְ וְהַאֲרַכְתָּ יָמִים —
Send the mother away and then you may take the young, so that it shall go well with you and you may prolong life (Deuteronomy 22:7).

One of the most commendable human traits is compassion, which means "feeling along" and empathizing with another person. Compassion is one of the thirteen Divine attributes, and the Talmud says that this is one of the ways we must emulate and identify with G-d. "Just as G-d is compassionate, so must you be compassionate" *(Sifri, Eikev 49)*.

In today's portion of the Torah there is a *mitzvah* that if one wishes to take eggs from a nest, one should not do so in the presence of the mother bird. Ramban says that this *mitzvah* should instill within us sensitivity and compassion.

Compassion must be shown toward animals as well as toward humans. The Talmud says that Rabbi Judah the Prince was punished because he failed to show compassion for a calf that was being led to slaughter, and that his punishment was not revoked until he made amends by an act of kindness towards animals *(Bava Metzia 85a)*.

Indeed, compassion is so fundamental a trait that it is assumed to be a *sine qua non* for Judaism. When the Gibeonites manifested a total lack of compassion, King David rejected their conversion to Judaism *(Yevamos 779a)*.

Yet, there are times when even compassion must be restrained. The ethical work *Orchos Tzaddikim* (*Ways of the Righteous*) states that tolerance of destructive behavior is not at all a virtue, because it gives tacit encouragement to wrongdoing. In such instances, one must overcome feelings of compassion and act with firmness.

In my book, *Caution: Kindness Can Be Dangerous to the Alcoholic*, I pointed out that parents, relatives, and friends, who out of "kindness" for the alcoholic or drug addict will tolerate his abusive behavior, or bail him out of jail, or allow him to have money to finance his habit, are actually his worst enemies rather than his friends. This is true in regard to any self-destructive behavior. True friends do not contribute, actively or passively, to a friend's self-destruction.

Withholding support from one engaged in destructive behavior is not at all a lack of compassion. Quite the contrary, it is being compassionate to prevent the person from harming himself.

However, it may not be easy to distinguish between appropriate versus misguided compassion. Our self-interests may deceive us, and we may act out of hostility or revenge under the guise that we are being constructively firm. This is another example of how we should not rely on our own judgment, but seek the guidance and counseling of competent persons who are not affected by the personal biases that affect our decisions.

In emulating Divine compassion, we should remember, "G-d is compassionate . . . abundant in kindness and *truth*" *(Exodus 34:6)*. Compassion is a virtue only when it is allied with truth.

The "How To" of Gratitude

. . . וְעָנִיתָ וְאָמַרְתָּ לִפְנֵי ה' אֱלֹקֶיךָ אֲרַמִּי אֹבֵד אָבִי וַיֵּרֶד מִצְרַיְמָה — *Then you shall speak up and say before the L-rd your G-d, "An Aramean (Laban) attempted to destroy my father; then he descended to Egypt . . ." (Deuteronomy 26:5).*

The theme of gratitude has appeared repeatedly in these pages, but inasmuch as the Torah and the Sages saw fit to repeatedly emphasize gratitude, we can be certain that we are not remiss if we follow their pattern.

The first fifteen verses of today's portion of the Torah are directed toward the expression of gratitude, and we would do well to read and study them carefully. The Torah instructs us on the *mitzvah* of *bikurim*, bringing the first-ripened fruits of the season to the Sanctuary as an offering of thankfulness.

However, the declaration of gratitude which is recited does not begin with thanks, but with a brief resume of Jewish history. We begin with a narration of how our forefather, the patriarch Jacob, was in servitude to the wicked Laban, how he later went to Egypt where his descendants were brutally enslaved, how we cried out to G-d amidst our affliction, how G-d delivered us from slavery, and finally how G-d gave us the Promised land.

Gratitude must be all-encompassing. We must recall our humble beginnings and the sufferings we underwent. We must recognize that rather than bearing resentments for the suffering we experienced, we must be grateful even for that episode of our history, because it was in the blast furnace of Egypt that we were purified and molded into one people. We include this in our declaration of gratitude to remind us that if we are distressed in the future, we should bear in mind that at a subsequent date we will realize the constructive aspects of our distress.

"And you shall rejoice in *all* the good that G-d has given you" *(26:11).* While we were undergoing the torture in Egypt we were in no position to appreciate the good therein, and we cried out to G-d in pain. But now that is all behind us. Why it had to happen that way is completely beyond our understanding, and we defer to the supreme wisdom of G-d that the ordeal was necessary. And if at the moment we experience pain all we can do is cry out for relief, when it is over we must invoke our trust in the absolute benevolence of G-d, that He does no evil. We are to remember the words of the prophet, "For after I have fallen, I have arisen" *(Michah 7:8),* and the interpretation of the Midrash, "Had I not fallen, I could never have arisen."

So now that we bring the first-ripened fruits to the Sanctuary and thank G-d for His bounty, we declare in our expression of gratitude that we are grateful even for the period of travail, for somehow it, too, was for our betterment. We rejoice with a full heart for the past as well as for the present. Our joy is unrestrained and unencumbered by the painful periods of our history.

The problem with many people is that they seek joy on their own terms. The Torah teaches us how to rejoice. True joy is achieved when one can be grateful for everything.

Equality before G-d

נצבים־וילך

**Nitzavim-
Vayelech**

אַתֶּם נִצָּבִים הַיּוֹם כֻּלְּכֶם לִפְנֵי ה' אֱלֹקֵיכֶם רָאשֵׁיכֶם שִׁבְטֵיכֶם זִקְנֵיכֶם וְשֹׁטְרֵיכֶם כֹּל אִישׁ יִשְׂרָאֵל. טַפְּכֶם נְשֵׁיכֶם וְגֵרְךָ אֲשֶׁר בְּקֶרֶב מַחֲנֶיךָ מֵחֹטֵב עֵצֶיךָ עַד שֹׁאֵב מֵימֶיךָ — *You are standing today, all of you before the L-rd your G-d: the chiefs of your tribes; your elders; and your officers; every man of Israel; your little ones; your wives; and the stranger who is in the midst of your camp; from the hewer of your wood to the drawer of your water* (Deuteronomy 29:9-10).

Nothing has been as destructive to the peace and unity of our people as the bickering and striving for positions of authority, leadership, and prominence. How desperately our great ethicists have cried out about the evils of pride and vanity, of seeking praise and glory. From the very earliest phase of our history with the rebellion of Korach, to this very day when people still bicker and strive for positions of dominance, the character defect of vanity as manifested in this drive has cost us dearly.

We should not confuse the position of leadership with the inherent value of a person. Just as we are not to give *mitzvos* any gradation (*Ethics of the Fathers 2:1*), neither are we to assess the value of human beings. This holds true in spite of the fact that different people have different roles and that the value to society of one person might appear greater than that of another. These differences have no bearing whatever on actual value, which is the worth of the person in the eyes of G-d.

Rabbi Bunim of Pshis'cha said that this is evident in the *halachah* which requires martyrdom in the face of murder. If one is told that he himself will be killed unless he kills another person, he is required to sacrifice his life and not commit the murder, "Because," says the Talmud, "who is to say that your blood is more precious than the other person's blood" (*Pesachim 25b*)? This *halachah* applies even if the demand to kill is made of a prominent leader, scholar, philanthropist, scientist, etc., and the designated victim is the simplest of the simple, who appears to have made no contribution whatever to society. One might argue that of course the life of the former is of greater value than the latter, but that is not the Torah position. Before G-d, the greatest of the great and the lowest of the low are equal.

The Talmud tells of a scholar who fell into a coma, and when he emerged from it, he reported that he had seen a vision of heaven.

"What I saw was a topsy-turvy world," he said. "The great were humbled and the humble were great."

His father corrected him. "No," he said. "What you saw was the just world. It is the world that we see with our human perception that is the topsy-turvy world" (*Bava Basra 10b*).

We should not confuse the dignity and respect we must show to a person commensurate with his position in the social hierarchy with absolute worth. The latter is known only to G-d.

Rabbi Moshe Alschich reads this into the opening verses of today's portion of the Torah. "You are standing today, *all of you before the L-rd your G-d:* the chiefs of your tribes; your elders; and your officers; every man of Israel; your little ones; your wives; and the stranger who is in the midst of your camp; from the hewer of your wood to the drawer of your water."

Before G-d, the most elite of the social hierarchy and the most common stand equally.

We are required to emulate the attributes of G-d. If in relating to another person we are tempted to think that because of our uniqueness, our skills, our knowledge, our wealth, or our social position, we are better than that person and behave condescendingly toward him, we must be reminded that in the eyes of G-d we are equal, and that His is the true assessment of our worth.

Misuse of Our Faculties

צוּר יְלָדְךָ תֶּשִׁי וַתִּשְׁכַּח קֵל מְחֹלְלֶךָ — *The Mighty One created you with forgetfulness but you forgot the G-d who formed you (Deuteronomy 32:18).*

Ha'azinu

The ethical works frequently state that all the faculties with which man was endowed can be used either constructively or destructively. The choice is left to him.

The Baal Shem Tov in particular pointed out that even those traits that appear to be undesirable can have constructive applications. For example, one may be envious of another person's spiritual achievements and be stimulated by this envy to improve himself. One may use hatred to despise evil. One may be vain and proud, and thereby consider improper behavior to be beneath one's dignity.

In today's portion of the Torah, Moses refers to the Israelites as being "obstinate and warped" (32:5), in that they distort their traits and use them in a corrupt manner. As one example he states, "The Mighty One created you with forgetfulness (*teshi* can mean to forget), but you forgot the G-d who formed you."

The Rabbi of Kotzk said that the capacity to forget was given to man so that he could forget the troubles of the past and be able to function without the encumbrance of past distresses. One should also forget unpleasant things that others did to him. Unfortunately, some people retain these memories. They may forget the good things, whether they be the graces of G-d or favors by other people. They misuse their capacity to forget.

The Maggid of Dubno gave the parable of a man who was deeply in debt to many creditors, and could not pay each of them more than a mere fraction of what he owed them. One creditor said to him, "Listen to me. When others come for their money, act as though you were insane. Talk nonsensically and behave in a silly manner. Whatever they ask you, just giggle and say something completely irrelevant. They will conclude that you have gone insane and that there is no purpose in trying to deal with you. They will leave you alone, and then you can pay me what you owe me."

The man did as he was told, and the scheme was most effective. Everybody concluded that he was insane and just wrote off the debts. When the one who had given this advice came for his money, the man responded nonsensically.

"Don't try and pull that stunt on me," the creditor said. "Remember, it was I who gave you this idea. Don't use it against me!"

G-d says, "You go about your daily affairs and you forget about Me and your obligations in the world. But I was the one who gave you the capacity to forget so that you might rid yourself of memories that would inhibit your functioning. Don't use this forgetting capacity against Me!"

Yes, we can be obstinate and warped. Therefore, let us make a list of all the capacities we have, and examine them closely to see whether we are using them all constructively or otherwise.

LIVING EACH DAY / 405

A Man of G-d

וזאת הברכה
Vezos Haberachah

וְזֹאת הַבְּרָכָה אֲשֶׁר בֵּרַךְ מֹשֶׁה אִישׁ הָאֱלֹקִים אֶת בְּנֵי יִשְׂרָאֵל לִפְנֵי מוֹתוֹ — *This is the blessing that Moses the man of G-d blessed the Children of Israel before his death (Deuteronomy 33:1).*

It would seem appropriate that the concluding portion of the Torah be a kind of summation or synopsis, as it were, of what the Torah is all about.

We have already noted that there are *midos* (character traits) that are prerequisites for Torah, and that Torah observance must lead to further refinement and development of *midos*. (*Tanchuma Shemini 12*).

One of the most difficult to attain of the desirable *midos* is to be able to totally overlook a slight or an injury that one has suffered at the hands of another person, and to rid oneself completely of even the minutest trace of resentment. The Talmud cites an incident when Rabbi Eliezer's prayers were not answered, yet Rabbi Akiva's were, because although they were both great *tzaddikim*, Rabbi Akiva had achieved perfection in totally divesting himself of all resentment when offended.

This portion of the Torah describes Moses' final moments. Let us now analyze how Moses might have felt just before his death.

For forty years Moses had guided the Israelites, after delivering them from the bondage of Egypt. They were so cantankerous and obstinate a people that at times he cried to G-d, "Why did you put the burden of this nation upon me?" (*Numbers 11:11*), or "Just a bit more and they will stone me to death" (*Exodus 17:4*). Moses bore their repeated bickering with infinite patience, willing to sacrifice himself to assure their survival, but it appeared to be a thankless task.

Moses had no desires other than to carry out his mission, the Divine will for him. Only one personal desire did Moses have: to set foot on the sacred soil of the Promised Land, the land of the Patriarchs, the land constantly illuminated by the overt presence of G-d. The Midrash states that Moses submitted five hundred and fifty-five supplications to be permitted to enter the Holy Land. He even pleaded that his *neshamah* (soul) be embodied in a bird, so that he might fly over the land and see his people living there. But this one request was denied him. He was only permitted to see the land from afar, but not to enter it. Why? Because one time he had been so provoked by the Israelites' lack of trust in G-d that He would provide water for them that he smote the rock instead of speaking to it (*Numbers 20:10-12*). Moses complained, "G-d became angry with me on your account and said, 'neither shall you enter there' " (*Deuteronomy 1:36*).

Standing at the very shore of the land he so longed to enter, and turning toward the people who had been so unappreciative, had so tormented him, and were responsible for his being denied his only wish in life, what did Moses do? He blessed the Israelites. He blessed them with all his heart. There was not the faintest trace of any bitterness or resentment.

"This is the blessing that Moses, *the man of G-d*, blessed the children of Israel before his death." The first chapter of the Torah begins with G-d Himself infusing into man the form of a *neshamah* (soul), and the Torah closes with the demonstration of how man can indeed become the G-d-like being he was intended to be.